Cross-Cultural Journalism

Built on the hands-on reporting style and curriculum pioneered by the Missouri School of Journalism, this introductory textbook teaches students how to write about and communicate with people of backgrounds that may be different from their own, offering real-world examples of how to practice excellent journalism and strategic communication that take culture into account. Specifically, the book addresses how to:

- engage with and talk across difference;

- identify the ways bias can creep into our communications, and how to mitigate our tendencies toward bias;

- use the concept of fault lines and approach sources and audiences with humility and respect;

- communicate with audiences about the complexity inherent in issues of crime, immigration, sports, health inequalities, among other topics;

- interpret census data categories and work with census data to craft stories or create strategic campaign strategies;

- reconsider common cultural assumptions about race, class, gender, identity, sexual orientation, immigration status, religion, disability, and age, and recognize their evolving and constructed meaning and our role as professional communicators in shaping national discussions of these issues.

In addition to its common sense, practical approach, the book's chapters are written by national experts and leading scholars on the subject. Interviews with award-winning journalists, discussion questions, suggested activities, and additional readings round out this timely and important new textbook. *Cross-Cultural Journalism* offers journalists and other communication professionals the conceptual framework and practical know-how they need to report and communicate effectively about difference.

María E. Len-Ríos is Associate Professor of Public Relations at the Grady College, University of Georgia. Before earning a doctorate in Journalism from the University of Missouri, she worked in advertising/public relations and marketing in Atlanta. She taught the cross-cultural journalism course at Missouri for ten years. In 2014-2015 she served as a board member of the Association for Education in Journalism and Mass Communication.

Earnest L. Perry is Associate Professor of Journalism Studies at the Missouri School of Journalism. Before earning a doctorate in Journalism from the University of Missouri, he worked as a newspaper journalist in Texas, Connecticut and Illinois. He is the lead instructor of the cross-cultural journalism course at Missouri, which began in 1998 and was one of the first required journalism diversity courses in the country.

Cross-Cultural Journalism

Communicating Strategically About Diversity

Edited by
María E. Len-Ríos and
Earnest L. Perry

Routledge
Taylor & Francis Group

NEW YORK AND LONDON

First published 2016
by Routledge
711 Third Avenue, New York, NY 10017

and by Routledge
2 Park Square, Milton Park, Abingdon, Oxon OX14 4RN

Routledge is an imprint of the Taylor & Francis Group, an informa business

© 2016 Taylor & Francis

Library of Congress Cataloging-in-Publication Data
A catalog record for this book has been requested

ISBN: 978-1-138-78488-8 (hbk)
ISBN: 978-1-138-78489-5 (pbk)
ISBN: 978-1-315-76811-3 (ebk)

Typeset in Warnock Pro
by Apex CoVantage, LLC

Publisher: Erica Wetter
Editorial Assistant: Simon Jacobs
Production Editor: Reanna Young
Copyeditor: Liz Barker-Woods
Proof-reader: Dana Richards
Indexer: Birgitte Necessary
Cover concept by Kara Wexler, design by Gareth Toye

Printed in Canada

Brief Contents

Contents

3   Who Is American?   37

Saleem E. Alhabash and Carie Cunningham

PART TWO   Application

4   Making Class Matter: Journalism and Social Class   63

Ryan J. Thomas and Marina A. Hendricks

5   Gender and the Media: Envisioning Equality   85

Yong Volz and María E. Len-Ríos

6   Mass Media and the LGBT Community   119

Gary R. Hicks

7   Missing in Action: Religion in Mass Media Markets and News   137

Debra L. Mason

8 Reporting and Strategic Communication Across Borders   157

Beverly Horvit and Yulia Medvedeva

11 The Complexity of Disability   227

Chad Painter

12 Rx for Communicating About Health Inequalities   249

Amanda Hinnant and María E. Len-Ríos

13 Talkin' 'bout My Generation: Understanding Generational Differences   273

Teri Finneman

14 Race and Gender in Sports   297

Cynthia M. Frisby

Acknowledgments

This book would not be possible without the hard, dedicated work of 15 chapter authors who provided their expertise to this endeavor. A great many of them taught the Cross-Cultural Journalism course at the Missouri School of Journalism or served as regular guest lecturers throughout the years. Everyone should know that it is extremely rare that any one individual be expert across the spectrum of issues we address in this book. Without the chapter authors we could not offer the breadth of material with the depth that this book provides. We would also like to thank the media industry professionals who shared their individual stories or provided expert advice that adds the "here's how it's done" perspective to this book. We would also like to acknowledge the many dedicated journalists and strategic communicators who "get it" and produce exceptional work that inspires our commitment to the teaching of this topic.

We would be remiss if we did not thank the thousands of students who have played a major role in the formation not only of this book, but the continuing goal of educating future journalists and strategic communicators. The written, verbal and even non-verbal responses you provided were invaluable. We have tried to address your feedback in this book. We also owe a great debt to the many Mizzou master's and doctoral students who poured their time and skill into teaching this material to the thousands of students who have taken the course in the last decade. Guiding students through the course material is not for the faint of heart and, if we were in any part successful, it was because our teaching assistants made it happen. Yes, some of you worked so many hours together, you decided to get married. Others of you decided that you loved the topic so much you wanted to study it more through another advanced degree. Still others of you went into industry at weeklies, magazines, PR firms, ad agencies, TV and radio stations and online news organizations, and are the future leaders of the industry (watch out world!). You were always impressive. There are too many of you to name individually, but you special ones—you know who you are! And to the professionals who visited our classrooms from around the state, country and the world—regulars like Jacqui Banaszynski, Lewis Duiguid, Debra L. Mason, Beverly Horvit, Larry Powell, Robert M. Baum, Peter Morello, Greeley Kyle, Renee Thomas-Woods and Suzanne Burgoyne and her interactive theater group—thank you! And to the communities in and around mid-Missouri that allowed our students "in" to develop their final projects—thank you for helping them achieve a great learning experience.

Throughout this book are references to professionals and scholars who believe in the importance of inclusion and presenting stories and images from people's lived experiences. It would be unfair for us not to acknowledge their efforts in moving our profession forward. We would also like to thank Erica Wetter at Routledge, who believed in this book, and Simon Jacobs at the New York editorial offices for his encouragement and guidance.

We would also like to thank the faculty and staff of the University of Missouri School of Journalism who supported the course and continued to encourage students to use concepts we introduced in our classes in their upper-level reporting and projects. The "Missouri Method" of practical, hands-on training backed by extensive research is a guiding principle of this book. We would also like to thank the Henry W. Grady College of Journalism and Mass Communication at the University of Georgia, which also supported the work of this book.

And finally, a huge thank you to our families, friends and colleagues, who provided encouragement, listened to us complain and, more importantly, challenged us on some of our assumptions.

María Len-Ríos here—I would like to express my gratitude to my co-editor and dear friend Earnest L. Perry. Earnest's frequent "reality checks" offered me perspective when I experienced common frustrations or tried something that didn't work out as I'd planned. "You have to remember—they're young"; "Journalists, like others, are sometimes prone to be lazy"; "You have to remember you're not going to reach everybody"; "Tell them—it's not all about you!"; and, my favorite, "What surprises you about that?" Of course, behind that brusque exterior is a kind-hearted, good-humored mentor—not just to students, but also to me and numerous others. Thank you, "Dr. P," as the kids would say.

I'd like to thank my husband John for his consistent wise advice and for understanding just how much it takes to teach courses on diversity (i.e., evenings, weekends, vacations—cross-cultural issues, and grading, are everywhere). And to my children, Andrew and Francesca, both who stayed a little later at Pre-K, listened to all these lectures in the womb and slept in the car carrier or played under the J-school library tables during weekly teaching assistant meetings. To my mother Janet, the most gifted writer I know. She taught me that women can become strong leaders. To my father Felipe, who taught me the importance of education. My family teaches me every day that (1) there is always something new to learn and (2) I can do anything.

Earnest L. Perry here—I'm grateful to have Maria Len-Rios as my co-editor, teaching partner and close friend. We not only shared the joys and struggles of teaching Cross-Cultural Journalism, but the trials and tribulations of work and family life. Although we are at separate universities now, we still find time to stay connected. Maria led the effort on this project and kept it on track when our teaching, research and service responsibilities threatened to send it off the rails. Even through the disruption of starting a new job hundreds of miles away, she kept me and the contributors on schedule. Thanks for everything.

I'd also like to thank Dean Mills whose vision and ongoing support for this class never wavered. I'd also like to thank Brian Brooks and Lynda Kraxberger. As associate deans for undergraduate studies they fielded the complaints and ran interference from those who were unable or unwilling to see the importance of what we are doing.

Thanks to my wife Debra, a master teacher, who put up with my rants and streams of consciousness that I'm sure at times made no sense. And to my daughters, Danielle and Alexandra, without your love and support this would not have been possible.

Preface

Earnest L. Perry and María E. Len-Ríos

In 1997, Missouri School of Journalism Dean R. Dean Mills formed a committee of faculty and staff. They were charged with creating a course that would help journalism and strategic communication students learn how to reach diverse audiences. Cross-Cultural Journalism became one of the first required journalism diversity courses in the country when the first class began in 1998.

In 2004, we began a major restructuring of the course. Our goal, which continues today, is to teach students concepts and techniques that will start them on the road to producing journalism that is representative of people's lived experiences, not the stereotypes that permeate much of today's media. We have used several books over the years, including *Journalism Across Cultures, The Authentic Voice, How Race is Lived in America, Class Acts* and *Overcoming Bias*. Each of them helped us in one way or another, but there was not one book that dealt with the theoretical and practical aspect of inclusive journalism and strategic communication. That is what led to the creation of this book.

Many of the concepts, examples and exercises contained in this book were developed for use in the class and have been shared with other instructors around the country. The core principles were based on work done in Teaching Diversity Across the Curriculum seminars at the Poynter Institute, a journalism think tank. We must also pay homage to the Maynard Institute for Journalism Education for providing valuable resources to those of us striving for more inclusion in media coverage.

The chapter authors are educators and practitioners who have practiced and/or conducted research on the most effective ways to communicate with people of various cultures and ethnicities. The chapters start with clear learning objectives and provide examples, exercises and additional readings.

The first three chapters provide conceptual grounding. Chapters 1 and 2 discuss why it is important for journalists and strategic communicators to communicate with people of cultures that may be different from their own. The core concepts of cross-cultural journalism—excellent journalism, talking across difference, fault lines, etc.—are introduced. These principles make up the foundation of the curriculum and can be seen throughout the book. Chapter 3 takes a look at stereotypes and the role they play, both positive and negative, in telling stories. We also introduce the use of U.S. census data to help students better understand the demographic changes taking place throughout the country.

The remainder of the book looks at how the concepts are applied. Chapter 4 provides an overview of social class in the United States, looks at the problems of defining social class, and discusses class mobility and income inequality. Chapter 5 focuses on gender, how the selection and presentation of sources, images and words portray women and men in news and advertising content. Chapter 6 discusses the LGBT community and provides tips on how journalists and strategic communicators can more authentically represent this audience.

Chapter 7 addresses the problems communicators face in accurately presenting religion and its role in culture and society. Chapter 8 looks at the complexity of practicing journalism and strategic communication outside the U.S. and in presenting those stories and images authentically. Chapter 9 focuses on the immigration issue in the United States. This chapter provides the skills, insights and tools needed to report and write about the nation's newest Americans. Chapter 10 deals with crime coverage and how disparities in the criminal justice system can lead to bias in reporting and long-term mistrust of the media in communities of color.

Chapter 11 explores the term disability to understand better the complexity of the lived experiences of these individuals. The way media frame disability can have a major influence on public understanding. Chapter 12 looks at health inequities and the complex health system, both in the present and historically, that rob individuals of their quality of life and also cost communities in many ways. Chapter 13 discusses generational differences and how your age and experiences growing up play an important role in how you perceive the world. Chapter 14 addresses the role of race and gender in sports and how journalists and strategic communicators can think critically about how women and people of color are presented in stories and images.

Chapter 15 looks at what comes next. We point out that cross-cultural journalism is more than just a class. It is the beginning of a lifelong learning process in which journalists and strategic communicators practice their craft from the lived experiences of others and not the perceived, stereotypical, ill-informed ways of the past.

The concepts and practical information we provide in this book are just the beginnings of practicing excellent journalism. Over the years many of our students, who we believed did not get the lessons we tried to teach, reached out to us later for guidance and advice based on what we discussed in class. Those post-course interactions are why we teach the class and why we wrote this book.

PART ONE
Conceptual Grounding

1

Conceptual Understanding

Earnest L. Perry and María E. Len-Ríos

What we've learned over the years is that students studying for careers in communication, journalism and strategic communication want to get out there and "do." Give us the skills classes, you clamor. How do I shoot pictures at night? Do aggressive online sports updates? Write HTML code for interstitial ads? Write copy for cellphone texting campaigns? Design infographics explaining the 2016 electorate in Iowa? Use Photoshop® software to create my Oreo® ad? How do I write my news release in AP Style? And, while we agree those are good things to know—even essential things to know—they aren't the skills at the core of good storytelling or salesmanship. It's hard to tell a good story if you haven't lived or observed life. One of us has a child in elementary school who learned editing marks in second grade. We know teenagers who can create YouTube videos with several clicks of a button.

We argue throughout this book that to be communication professionals, you need to know how to evaluate information and find the right research, as well as how to interact, learn from and communicate with and understand other people—many of whom may have different beliefs, opinions, life experiences and attitudes than you may have. In

LEARNING OBJECTIVES

By the end of this chapter, you should be able to:

- understand the concept of excellent journalism.

- recognize when fault lines are important to the story.

- identify privilege and how it may limit your perspective and viewpoints.

- appreciate how knowing about excellent journalism, fault lines and privilege can lead to communicating strategically about issues of diversity.

journalism, we rely on sources, readers, advertisers and news audiences. In public relations, we have many publics (i.e., consumers, employees, regulators, journalists, politicians, etc.). And advertisers and marketers have target audiences (i.e., soccer moms between 25 and 44 who work outside the home). Across all our professions, we create messages for specific audiences. We're only in our jobs if people feel that what we produce is useful, valuable or entertaining. While we can teach a class of 8th or 10th graders to use Photoshop® or code HTML, a majority probably aren't at the sophistication level or have the maturity to fully understand the concepts that we will discuss here. It is the ability to think critically, process information and understand how best to communicate with others that will set you apart. You produce something great by generating story ideas and campaign strategies that resonate with the lived experiences of your audiences.

In your heart, you may be eager to grab a camera and start filming your documentary on what it's like to live with bipolar disorder. Or, perhaps, you are dying to travel to the Hawaiian Islands and write stories about the endangered humpback whale. Or maybe even more appealing to you—you want to create ads and promotions for Jay-Z's new music distribution service to air during the next Super Bowl. We're going to ask you to slow down and reflect on life for a while. Some students take a year off before they come to college—a gap year—think of this class as a "gap year," where you take time to think about the world and your place in it. (Don't worry, we do not propose an exercise where you hold hands and sing together—however; we cannot guarantee your professor won't have you do it.) What follows is the conceptual grounding for this course: excellent journalism, fault lines and privilege. We will start with excellent journalism.

▶ THE CONCEPT OF EXCELLENCE AND EXCELLENT JOURNALISM

Fairness. Crucial to democracy. Clear writing. Consistency. Information we need to be free and self-governing. Verification of truth. Flow. Style. Accuracy. Creativity and storytelling. Providing a service. Grammar. Something that provokes thought. Unbiased voice. Being ethical. Checks on government. Independence. These are all terms that our students have used to describe what they think when we ask them to define excellent journalism. While these elements do characterize the purpose and reasons for the creation of journalism, we have narrowed it to five words. (Read on!)

According to Keith Woods (author of Chapter 2), the concept of *excellent journalism* was originally derived from conversations with more than 20 journalists that informed the development of the textbook he and Arlene Notoro Morgan and Alice Irene Pifer edited in 2006, *The Authentic Voice: The Best Reporting on Race and Ethnicity*.[1] We (Dr. Len-Ríos and Dr. Perry) were introduced to the concept in workshops on diversity that Keith Woods led while he was dean of faculty at the Poynter Institute, a center providing professional training to journalists. Over the years, we have adapted the concepts based on the final projects students have completed in our courses and through the many, many questions we have received from students. Still, we believe these concepts are true to those developed by Mr. Woods and his colleagues.

The idea of excellence is that it comprises several essential components that lead to the best kind of reporting. These concepts include *context, complexity, voices* and *authenticity*. Over the years, we added a fifth concept to the equation, which is *proportionality*. So, derived from the work of many, the equation we have adapted, employed and taught in the classroom for achieving excellent journalism is:

EXCELLENCE = context + complexity + voices + authenticity + proportionality

Let's unpack what each of these components means.

At this point in the chapter, we're inviting you to take a drive or bike ride to the country and find a nice spot to sit under an old (but safe) tree, or visit your local community library (not the campus library), or sit outside of Town Hall or simply find a cozy spot in a local restaurant. Why? We want you to take a break, get out of your comfort zone, to read an excellent piece of journalism that we will use in the following discussion. Remember this is a gap-year class. To find the article, go to the New York Magazine website (nymag.com) and read "Paper Tigers"[2] by Wesley Yang. We'll wait here—probably a good hour or two—until you have a chance to read all 8,500+ words of it . . .

> **TIP:** You can also most likely find a full-text copy of the article via Lexis-Nexis® Academic through your university's library website.

Welcome back! We hope you are refreshed. We also hope you observed what was going on around you in someplace new. And, well, of course, read the article. So, let's discuss the components of excellent journalism: *context, complexity, voices, authenticity* and *proportionality*.

Context

A colleague of ours, Dr. Suzanne Burgoyne, has a great exercise she has used to describe context to our students. She has two volunteers come down to the front of the classroom and "freeze" while shaking hands. Next, she asks one of the volunteers to sit down and the other stays "frozen" in the pose. Then she asks the class what it looks like the person is doing. She gets various responses and laughs from the class: "Holding the door open," "Milking a cow," "Knocking on the door," "Asking for a handout," "Disco dancing," "Bowing." You get the point. Without the other person there, there is no context. Good writing provides context so people understand what is happening and where the story fits into the larger world or bigger issue. It helps people understand why protesters in Venezuela in 2015 are unhappy with the government. (See, don't you want more context?)

Let's turn to the article "Paper Tigers." The context for this story is 2011. At this time, Dr. Amy Chua's book *Battle Hymn of the Tiger Mother* (we recommend it) has received much press coverage—conversations are swirling about whether an "Asian approach" to education is better than that of other American parents. Yang's story is specifically set at a point in time: when young Asian men, who have excelled in high school and college, face the work world and realize that the skills that had made them academically successful were not the same skills essential for success in the business world. As Yang writes, "It is a part of the bitter undercurrent of Asian-American life that meritocracy comes to an abrupt end after graduation." It's a story of U.S. white protestant culture that clashes with numerous Asian cultures that share similarities. It's about straddling those cultures.

> **Context** is the time, place, history, social setting, environment and culture necessary to give meaning to the story.

Yang provides context for understanding how well Asians do academically at the top schools in the country. He also tells us how poorly they are represented at the tops of companies. He writes that "The top 3.7 percent of all New York City students . . . are accepted," an elite public high school in New York, and that while Asian-Americans make up 12.6 percent of residents in the city, they are 72 percent of the students at Stuyvesant. This piece of information helps us understand exactly how well Asian-American students in New York City do on these high school admission exams. He also tells us that "Asian-Americans represent roughly 5 percent of the population but only 0.3 percent of corporate officers, less than 1 percent of corporate board members and about 2 percent of college presidents." Yes, it would be good to include the name of the source of the study. However, the point is that these are the kinds of details that help us understand the story. This should be the type of information that you, as a storyteller, get by doing essential background research. Background research is critical to telling an excellent story.

Complexity

Truth. TRUTH. truth. TrUth. THE Truth. Need we say more? There are many versions of truth. Whose truth? You may hear one version of facts on MSNBC, another on Fox News, and still yet another on the Sina.com, the BBC or Al Jazeera. What is the truth? Which facts are valid? Who says so? Can it be that the truth is squishy? Stories may have many actors. In "Paper Tigers," Yang talks about all the reasons why Asian men with excellent educations do not seem to do as well as white men when it comes to attaining leadership positions in corporate America: Asian men are cultural outsiders, Asian men are too meek, their cultural upbringing taught them not to show off; they are stereotyped, discriminated against and misunderstood by whites. There is no *one* reason to explain the issue of inequality that Yang raises. He also points out that even though the young men with whom he speaks may feel they have "failed," others are striving, and still others have succeeded—he cites as an example zappos.com CEO Tony Hsieh.

So, for those of you who are looking for a definition, we define complexity as elements added to a story that show there are gray truths. That doesn't mean that the stories should be confusing, hard to understand or use language that no one can comprehend. It means that a story has more than "two sides," there is more nuance to the truth than painting everything in black or white. People aren't all good or all bad. And . . . hold on to your hats . . . we're going to use the "O-word," complexity fosters—wait for it—objectivity. Objectivity is achieved when you look for the bigger, fuller picture of the story that includes different viewpoints, look at the gradations of truth and challenge one-sided comments with other voices or opinions. #Iheartcomplexity. (It's OK to tweet it.)

> **Complexity** is providing assessments of facts through a 360-degree look at the issue or story. It entails background research, multiple views and perspectives, and avoids stereotypes and simplistic thinking.

Voices

"I mean like, he's so cute." "Yeah, he is so, so cute." It's just another day among tweens who are watching a YouTube video of the Brit boy band One Direction. Ask Mom, oh, she has a different perception. While Yang's article "Paper Tigers" puts the author at the center of the article, he also includes the voices of other men who have had their challenges with making it socially and professionally in a culture that they feel does not embrace them. When he talks to J. T. Tran, who leads training sessions for Asian-American men who have trouble dating, he quotes Tran saying, "Creepy can be fixed . . . Many guys just don't realize how to project themselves." Tran presents another perspective that the other men do not.

Bringing voices to stories means delivering the people's voices to the audience and letting them tell their part of the story. This conveys humanity and demonstrates the writer's humility. Humility in that you as the journalist or communicator realize that you are, in part, gathering information for your audience through information that other people possess. The people who trust you with their stories expect you will accurately communicate what they said without distorting, truncating or twisting what they said. In incorporating voices, your job is to make sure that the quotes you use are purposeful and reveal their perspectives.

Some students will ask now, well, Yang's story does not include many voices from Asian-American women. And it talks about Asian-American men wanting to date blond, white women. Yes, it does. It largely omits a woman's perspective. Yes. So can it really be excellent? Let's reflect. What is the point and thesis of the story? Any storyteller knows you can't make a story about everything because then it will be a story about nothing. In its context, Yang brings in a lot of voices. And, he does it quite well.

Authenticity

When we first started teaching about excellence, we used to say that context + complexity + voices = authenticity. And that is probably pretty true. However, our thinking has evolved over time. Originally, authenticity referred to whether the other components were done well. At least, that is how we explained it. If you look at strategic communication companies and how they sell their services today, somewhere in their definition it refers to communicating in an *authentic* way. What does this mean?

If you look up the definition in the online version of *Webster's New World College Dictionary*, which is used by the *AP Stylebook*, it has five definitions. First, it talks about the trustworthiness and reliability of information. Second it says what is authentic is "genuine" or "real." The third definition is legal. The fourth concerns whether something is "true to its type." The last definition is simply "authoritative."

So, what does that mean for us? It means that as a communicator you engage in genuine, trusted conversations with your sources so that they will tell you their lived experiences and not simply provide superficial answers. This requires the communicator (you) to be respectful and humble and not exploitative—otherwise you will ruin your relationship with your sources or partners. You also may burn a bridge with that source. Sources and people who have felt "burned" by journalists figuratively put up walls and refuse to participate in news stories again.

Let's go back to Wesley Yang's article. From the start, he tells us what he thinks, "Here is what I sometimes suspect my face signifies to other Americans: an invisible person, barely distinguishable from a mass of faces that resemble it." He is raw and honest. He later interviews Sach Takayasu and shows how she evolved from thinking she was not raised as "Asian" to concluding that she was, after all, remembering that her parents would tell her, "Don't create problems. Don't trouble other people." Yang's article is far from shallow. It includes candid voices.

> **Authenticity** is the unvarnished truth of the physical reality that you observe and experience and includes the lived experiences of people and sources who have lent you their voices to tell the story.

Proportionality

We added this concept to the equation as we were influenced by the work of Bill Kovach and Tom Rosenstiel in their 2007 book, *The Elements of Journalism: What Newspeople Should Know and the Public Should Expect*. In it, the authors write:

> If we think of journalism as social cartography, the map should include news of all our communities, not just those with attractive demographics or strong appeal to advertisers. To do otherwise is to create maps with whole areas missing.[3]

Kovach and Rosenstiel map concept can be applied nationally, regionally and locally. It can also be applied to the news coverage of any particular outlet, e.g., does X story deserve front page/home page coverage? What is a more representative problem in our community? You can also apply this concept to an individual story, e.g., how well do the voices in the story represent the issue? Am I giving someone's opinion too much emphasis? You can even drill this down to any particular interview, e.g., how does the quote I'm using from Georgia Gov. Nathan Deal represent the totality of what he said, or am I just picking up the most controversial thing I think will garner click-thrus? Clearly there is some judgment here, and it presumes that you know what the entire map looks like—and you may not. But it does encourage you to chart out the territory and to survey the landscape and see how well you do. And if you do have a precise map of your community, you should ask yourself whether your portrait of it is accurate. Not to do so is irresponsible.

There are other points in the process where we can consider proportionality. For instance, when you are taking notes at a news conference. What are you writing down? Are you getting a full picture of what is being said? Or are you selecting bits and pieces? And are the bits and pieces you're choosing the essential landmarks that will help your reader navigate through the story without getting lost or missing important things? Similarly, if we are advertisers, public relations people or marketers, we deal with data all the time. Whether it's information that characterizes our target audiences or internal information about our products or services, what will we choose to examine? What information will we choose to include in our client report? In our speech? Proportionality can be applied to many things.

Let's again apply this concept to Wesley Yang's "Paper Tigers" article. Let's look at the national news landscape. How often do we have stories told from and about the perspectives of 20-something/30-something bicultural, highly educated Asian-American men? All right. Yes, you're correct; Mr. Yang has a February 2015 article about Eddie Huang in *The New York Times Magazine* about selling his story for

> **Proportionality** is responsibly representing the story, issue or audience based on well-researched observations of the lay of the land.

the ABC comedy *Fresh Off the Boat*. But other than that, how many stories do you remember addressing the lives of Asian-Americans in the United States? Proportionality. How well are we doing? (We're seeing a master's thesis idea develop here.)

▶ FAULT LINES

Along with excellent journalism, *fault lines* are another crucial component to improving your journalism. You will find that consideration of "fault lines" is a critical concept that will appear throughout this book. Fault lines are social categories that shape lives, experiences and social tensions.[4]

In other words, they are the main categories of diversity. The primary fault lines are race/ethnicity, gender, generation, class and geography,[5] but other social categories like religion (see Chapter 7) and ability/disability (see Chapter 11) can also be considered fault lines. Researchers believe that your particular fault lines influence your view of the world. Your fault lines will influence what story ideas or campaigns you pitch, what interview questions you ask, how you frame stories or advertisements and what word choices you use.

To help you understand fault lines better, take a minute to think what your fault lines are. Write down your race/ethnicity, your gender, your generation (or your age, if you aren't sure), your family's social class status (i.e., low income, middle class, wealthy), and your geography (i.e., what country or part of the United States you're from). Look at what you wrote down and think about how your fault lines influence your beliefs, views and experiences. Recognizing your fault lines will help you determine whether it is influencing your journalism.

Worldview and life experiences differ greatly. Yet too many communicators do not consider fault lines, which can lead to biased and stereotypical journalism. For example, have you heard before that people who use wheelchairs are slow, confined and/or helpless? Where did you hear that? Is it true? How do you know?

Acclaimed journalist Robert C. Maynard developed the concept of fault lines while working as the first African-American editor of a big city newspaper, the *Oakland Tribune*. He came up with the idea after considering the frequent earthquakes in California. Maynard believed the chasms that occur during quakes are similar to the separation we see in society. Our journalism can exacerbate that and cause further tension.

When approaching a story or campaign, you generally take into consideration who, what, when, where, why and how. Maynard's fault lines help provide the next step: *context*. Fault lines can inform your journalism in several ways.

First, you can use fault lines to assess your perspective and what assumptions you are bringing to a story or strategic communication campaign. Acknowledging the perspective that you bring to the creation of content is important. So, if you are writing a story about "free-range parenting," your experience with the topic may be limited if you have not "parented." Acknowledging your experience, recognizing what you know and don't know is important to deciding what you *need to know*. You'll probably find it necessary to talk to several moms informally to see what issues should guide how you go about your reporting—where to explore.

Second, you can consider what perspectives—across fault lines—are important to include in your story or campaign. So, this is where you think of story sources or consumer research that you need to inform your work. The sources and consumer research should be used to provide context and voices critical to your project. So, let's go back to your story assignment to write about "free-range parenting." You may consider the sourcing and photos you include in your story. If you only include opinions of suburban moms who have one child, you are probably missing perspectives of parents with multiple children, parents who live in rural areas or those who live in the city. Younger moms and dads may also have different perspectives than older moms and dads or grandparents. In addition, this may only be an issue or concern in certain socioeconomic groups or it may apply across all social classes—that is what you need to find out. Clearly, you cannot include all perspectives—most campaigns focus on limited issues and many stories will have word or time limits. However, within the parameters of your story or campaign, have your represented context and complexity?

Third, fault lines can be used in thinking about your *potential audiences.* How might audience characteristics influence how you deliver your message? Considering your audience means providing multiple perspectives and giving the audience what it needs to understand and care about the piece of journalism or campaign.[6] Again, think about your story on free-range parenting. Will the story go in *Time* magazine? How is that audience different from the *Atlantic*? *Mother Jones* magazine? *Good Housekeeping* magazine? *Parenting* magazine? Is it a broadcast piece for *NBC Nightly News*? Slate.com? *Fox & Friends*? The demographic characteristics of the audience will guide how you will create your story. You will want to choose context that makes the story relevant to the experiences of your audience members.

Not all fault lines are present in every story or advertisement you create. If a fault line is not relevant, don't include it. However, you should be aware of the fault lines as you determine how you are going to put together your story, campaign or advertisement. Journalists too often go back to the same sources over and over rather than seeking out points of view from fresh perspectives. Adding diversity to your work adds more fairness, factuality and balance, which can increase objectivity and credibility. In addition, you are giving a voice to populations who too often are voiceless.

The Five Fault Lines—Maynard Institute

Race/Ethnicity: Black, Asian, Hispanic/Latino, Native American, mixed-race, white
Gender: Male, female, gay, lesbian, transgender
Generation: Youth (0–19), 20s, 30s, 40s, 50s, 60s+; baby boomer (born
    1946–1964), Generation X (born 1965–1976), Generation Y or millennials
    (born 1977–2002). While age can alter a point of view, that same point of
    view often is defined by generational experiences. For instance, Generation
    X didn't watch Richard Nixon resign as president. The baby boomers did not
    live through the Great Depression.
Class: Rich, upper-middle-class/wealthy, middle class, working class, poor
Geography: Urban, suburban, rural; plus region

Fault Lines Perspectives—Yours and Your Sources'
Race/Ethnicity: Your race or your ethnicity influences your view of events.
Gender: Your gender or sexual orientation affects your view of events.
Generation: When you grew up affects your view of events.
Class: Financial circumstances influence perspectives.
Geography: Where you're from can shape how you see events.

Fault lines can be used in the reporting of simple stories such as buying back-to-school supplies for children or major events that can impact an entire community. Purchasing back-to-school supplies cuts across race, class, gender. And today, with grandparents, same-sex couples and blended families raising children, the relevance of fault lines for a particular community story should be considered. When major snowstorms occurred in the northeast United States in 2015, it affected residents across the fault-line spectrum. For instance, take class and geography as fault lines. Some families had alternative places to go or lived in areas that got energy back first. In both stories, it is important that reporters go through the fault lines to make sure there is representation that reflects the entire community affected.

▶ PRIVILEGE

Assessing fault lines when you are preparing your work requires some self-reflection. That is also the case with embracing the concept of privilege. *Webster's II New College Dictionary* defines privilege as "special advantage, immunity, permission, right, or benefit granted to or enjoyed by an individual, class or caste." It goes on to state that privilege can be due to "one's status or rank, and exercised to the exclusion or detriment of others." While privilege is a term that has been around a long time, we follow the definition as presented by Peggy McIntosh, of Wellesley College, who wrote about it in 1988. In her working paper *White Privilege and Male Privilege: A Personal Account of Coming to See Correspondences Through Work in Women's Studies,*[7] McIntosh reflected on how privilege shaped her life and experiences. She defines privilege this way:

> I have come to see white privilege as an invisible package of unearned assets which I can count on cashing in each day, but about which I was "meant" to remain oblivious. White privilege is like an invisible weightless knapsack of special provisions, assurances, tools, maps, guides, codebooks, passports, visas, clothes, compass, emergency gear and blank checks.

While privilege may offer benefits, it also is a disadvantage, according to McIntosh, because it often shields those with privilege from seeing the reality that others without privilege face. As a result, the privileged miss out on important life lessons and enjoyment. However, being in a privileged group often lets a person go unnoticed—and that can be very good. For instance, if police do not expect the clean-cut high school student from a tiny suburban neighborhood of illegally dealing the most Adderall° at the school, she is less likely to get busted. McIntosh illustrates many instances where privilege may be a bonus—here are two:

> I can criticize our government and talk about how much I fear its policies and behavior without being seen as a cultural outsider.[8]

> I can choose blemish cover or bandages in "flesh" color and have them more or less match my skin.[9]

Of course, things have changed since 1988. Even so, many of the issues she addresses still hold true. Here are a couple of additional statements we've added:

> When I apply for an internship, scholarship or a job, I am pretty sure people won't question that I got it "just because" of my race or gender.

> I am pretty sure that if I had to interact with a police officer that I would be treated justly.

The concept of privilege is controversial in today's polarized society, especially as it relates to race, gender and class. Why? People want to feel as if they are treated equitably. Privilege, in and of itself, raises the issue of: what is fair? You remember when your mom or dad was serving cake—one piece for you and one piece for your brother or sister. Both you and your sister were convinced that you each had gotten the smallest piece. Privilege is perceived as a competition for rights and finite resources, and that is why it's touchy. Imagine the fights you had with your siblings about who got to ride in the front seat. Whose turn it was to use the car? Who had "control" over the middle section in the back seat? No one wants to feel "one-down." But you had to share. Your parents made you share because it was the right thing to do. When it comes to privilege, sorting out what the "right thing to do" is something we should know to do, but it is not something that we "want" to do. Especially if we already have the advantage—how do we make sure we share advantage? We may have advantage and feel like we don't need to share.

Context is important in considering privilege. Discussing white privilege and male privilege puts white men in the spotlight, which can be uncomfortable. (Our students have told us this many times!) We're used to talking about the *other*. We talk about *gender* (meaning women), *sexual orientation* (meaning non-straight people), *race/ethnicity* (meaning non-whites), but "male studies" and "white studies" often go unexamined. Some argue it's unexamined because we don't examine those who represent what is *normal*. Think of this—if it is okay to talk about what it means to be a woman today, or gay today, what makes it wrong or troublesome to talk about what it means to be white today? (We'll discuss Talking Across Difference in the next chapter). What we have to guard against is that the conversation doesn't degenerate to discussing "us" versus "them." We must talk *with* each other instead of at each other.

Some whites claim that the term is used to make them feel guilty about perceived advantages they may have for being white. Others claim that *white privilege* does not take into account class. Some whites living in poverty have a hard time seeing how their race gives them an advantage over a person of color or someone from another country. Others believe that they should not be made to feel guilty because the hard work and sacrifice of their ancestors helped them have a higher standard of living. What is imperative to know is that privilege comes in many forms, and you may have privilege in some situations and not others.

Understanding privilege is not about assigning fault or defending an advantage one may have. It is about recognizing it exists and being knowledgeable about its impact on the lived experiences of those around you. To be an effective communicator you have to acknowledge your own privilege and recognize the impact it has on your life, both positive and negative. In her piece, "Explaining Privilege to a Broke White Person," Gina Crosley-Corcoran discusses her initial frustration with middle-class, educated white people who talked about how their "whiteness" provided advantages that others did not have. Her white skin did little to help her escape the poverty of her childhood. Crosley-Corcoran states that it was not until she attended college that she began to see the complexity of privilege.

She learned there are many types of privilege. It can come from simply being born in one country as opposed to another. You can be born into a financially stable family that provides a high-level of health care, safety and future opportunities. If you were born straight, there are laws that protect and grant you privileges that non-straight people do not have, case in point the ongoing battle for inclusion of sexual orientation in non-discrimination laws in various states. Able-bodied people have privileges that those with physical disabilities do not have when it comes to accessing certain venues and services. The list of the kinds of privileges is broad and can change, but the important thing to remember is that you must be self-aware and recognize when your privilege could impact your ability to produce excellent storytelling.[10]

▶ CHAPTER SUMMARY

Context (there's that word again) is very important in conversations about fault lines and privilege. What are the circumstances surrounding the conversations? Who is privileged and why? Is it important to the story? Are you taking into account your own privilege? Is it informing your story or reinforcing a stereotype? You also need to consider fault lines, those that are present and those that are missing. For example, a journalist reporting on the gentrification of a poor neighborhood needs to consider the fault lines present in the story and how privilege and/or non-privilege played a role in the lives of those involved in the changes taking place. From a strategic communication perspective, you need to understand if you are doing marketing that your perspective may shape what you think is right or feasible. Nestlé and Bristol-Myers' introduction of powdered-milk baby formula to mothers in underdeveloped countries was seen as exploitation, but also a result of privilege.[11] Babies in underdeveloped areas of Africa, South America and Asia were getting sick or dying because mothers sometimes did not use clean water to mix the powered formula, could not sterilize the bottles, were poorly educated in its use or tried to *stretch* the formula, altering its nutritional benefits, leaving the children with insufficient nutrition. Breast milk is less expensive (well, free, if mothers can produce it!) and has fewer health risks to babies from lower socio-economic classes, yet the companies avidly marketed the product to mothers when it wasn't in their best interest or that of their children.[12] Privilege played a role in the business and marketing decisions of the senior management and it raised many ethical issues in business marketing practices. Similar parallels to today could be to look at some companies in the mortgage industry or others in the banking industry for which the practice of redlining, denying loans based on race, is documented.

The excellence equation works equally well when considering privilege:

EXCELLENCE = context + complexity + voices + authenticity + proportionality.

▶ SUGGESTED ACTIVITIES

1. Find a news story in the media that interests you. Identify whether it meets the five criteria of excellence. Explain: why or why not?

2. Imagine that you are marketing the National Hockey League to a larger audience. Your boss says the league needs more diverse fans. Use research about the fault lines to determine who will be your main target market. What should you consider?

3. Make up your own privilege checklist based on any other personal characteristic (e.g., religion, appearance, etc.). What items can you come up with? How are these advantages apparent in our society? What is your evidence (i.e., facts)?

▶ NOTES

1 Arlene Notoro Morgan, Alice Irene Pifer and Keith Woods, *The Authentic Voice: The Best Reporting on Race and Ethnicity* (New York: Columbia University Press, 2006).

2 Wesley Yang, "Paper Tigers: What Happens to all the Asian-American Overachievers when the Test-Taking Ends?" *New York*, May 16, 2011, http://nymag.com/news/features/asian-americans-2011–5/.

3 Bill Kovach and Tom Rosenstiel, *The Elements of Journalism: What Newspeople Should Know and the Public Should Expect* (New York: Three Rivers Press, 2007), 209.

4 Sue Ellen Christian, *Overcoming Bias: A Journalist's Guide to Culture and Context* (Scottsdale, AZ: Holcomb Hathaway, 2012), 11.

5 Ibid.

6 "Chapter 5: Beyond the Five w's and the h," Maynard Institute, http://mije.org/chapters-v-and-vi

7 Peggy McIntosh, "White Privilege and Male Privilege: A Personal Account of Coming to See Correspondences through Work in Women's Studies" (Working Paper 189, 1–20, Wellesley College, Center for Research on Women, Wellesley, MA, 1988), 1–2.

8 Ibid., 7.

9 Ibid., 9.

10 Gina Crosley-Corcoran, "Explaining White Privilege to a Broke White Person," *Huffington Post* (blog), September 3, 2014, http://www.huffingtonpost.com/gina-crosleycorcoran/explaining-white-privilege-to-a-broke-white-person_b_5269255.html.

11 Allen H. Center and Patrick Jackson, *Public Relations Practices: Managerial Case Studies and Problems*, 4th ed. (Englewood Cliffs, NJ: Prentice-Hall, 1990).

12 Ibid.

▶ **ADDITIONAL READINGS**

http://theauthenticvoice.org/

Hull, Anne. "Part I: In the Bible Belt, Acceptance Is Hard Won." *Washington Post*, September 26, 2004, A1.

Kwok, Jean. *Girl in Translation*. New York: Riverhead Books, 2011.

Mirta, Ojito. "Best of Friends, Worlds Apart." In *How Race is Lived in America: Pulling Together, Pulling Apart*. New York: Times Books, 2001.

Rothman, Joshua. "Origins of 'Privilege.'" Page-Turner, *New Yorker*, May 12, 2014. http://www.newyorker.com/books/page-turner/the-origins-of-privilege.

McIntosh, Peggy. "White Privilege and Male Privilege: A Personal Account." In *Race, Class and Gender: An Anthology*, ed. M. Anderson and H. Collins, 70–81. Belmont, CA: Wadsworth, 1992.

Steinbeck, John. *The Grapes of Wrath*. New York: Viking Press, 1939.

2

Talking Across Difference

Keith M. Woods

In the spring of 2014, I was invited to lead a public discussion about race relations in Madison, Wisconsin. A few months earlier, a statewide nonprofit organization had released a scorching report outlining striking disparities in the ways black people and white people lived in Wisconsin. There emerged in the ensuing weeks a groundswell of debate about poverty, education, business, and a black incarceration rate that was the highest in the nation.

The conversation I was invited to lead would have an edge to it—that was for sure. It would also provide an example of how the craft of journalism can clarify—or confuse—discourse in this increasingly pluralistic country. I'd led hundreds of these conversations over the previous 20 years, most of them with journalists, professors and students of journalism and mass communication. I'd come to the view early in my time training professionals at the Poynter Institute for Media Studies that this thing called *talking across difference* was an essential skill.

LEARNING OBJECTIVES

By the end of this chapter, you should be able to:

- become more aware of the dynamics at work when people communicate across a significant difference.

- develop an understanding of how these dynamics impact the pursuit of excellence in journalism and strategic communications.

- discover ways of applying this new understanding to reporting, writing and editing, regardless of platform or profession.

Do it well, and deeper, more meaningful and—most importantly—more accurate storytelling results. Like any skill, though, it's developed over time through learning and practice.

These conversations, whether interviews with sources, strategy discussions or creative meetings, can be fraught with fear and misunderstanding, enough so that many people opt out. When that happens, critical questions go unasked; important angles go unexplored, and some of journalism's immutable values—accuracy, fairness and clarity, to name three—are threatened.

Done well, though, a conversation across difference can help professionals steer clear of mistakes and yield insights that add truth, context and depth to storytelling, whether the subject is race/ethnicity, class, ideology, sexual orientation, age, faith, gender or any of the other demographic characteristics that unite and divide communities across the United States and around the world. Quality conversations across difference can help illuminate issues in a community and deliver on one of journalism's most ambitious promises: To "provide people with information they need to understand the world."[1]

The issue in Madison was that distrust fueled by class and racial estrangement was keeping political, civic and religious leaders from talking honestly about big problems, problems that everyone had an interest in solving. When the *Capital Times*, an online newspaper with a point of view, began stoking a conversation about race relations through essays and reporting, the stage was set for the public discourse.

More than 500 people crammed into the First Unitarian Society church near the University of Wisconsin. Before them sat an eight-person panel of community leaders: black and white; men and women; religious and lay people; key players in the civic, business and nonprofit quarters of Madison. If there was change or growth or problem solving happening in the community, these were some of the central figures in those efforts.

One of the panelists was the Rev. Everett Mitchell, director of community relations at the university. His answer to the first question of the night drew a gasp from the audience and guaranteed that this conversation would not linger on the superficial surface.

> I'll be honest, I think sometimes what gets in my way is my own fear . . .
> that I don't trust white people. I don't trust . . . white women. And actually
> I'm afraid. I was telling one of my friends the other day that I notice how . . .
> I won't even allow myself to be in the same office with a white woman
> without the door open, or a window, so somebody can see.
>
> My greatest fear sometimes is to be seen as something . . . that I'm not
> at all . . . that I'm a brutal, black, rapist, out of control, angry; that if I'm
> passionate, then I'm angry; that if I raise my voice, then I'm about to hurt
> you; that if I . . . sit up with my body you gotta call security because you don't
> know what's about to happen in the room. That gets in my way.[2]

If you're a journalist covering the event, you're less than 15 minutes into a 90-minute conversation and you already know that this moment will be in your story. If it's your job to handle strategic communications for the Rev. Mitchell or any of the other key participants in the conversation, you know you have a delicate task ahead of you. The town hall meeting was called "Together Apart: Talking Across the Social Divide," and it would provide a good case study on what it means to talk across difference. It would also challenge journalists to report on an issue in a way that employed the skills necessary to successfully have such a conversation in the first place.

▶ FRAMES FOR THE CONVERSATION

What happens to information when it passes through the filters of a journalist, marketing director or public relations specialist, who crafts it into one storytelling form or another, then sends it out to be consumed and interpreted by an extraordinarily diverse public? It's a wonder most days, given all the variables at play, that we ever communicate successfully. Professionals can gain some great insights into what goes on when people discuss tough topics by deepening their knowledge about *cognitive dissonance theory*, confirmation bias, and the study of listening. What they all point out is that there is a part of human nature that can lead people to distort information they receive, no matter how objectively it's presented. We'll look at three overlapping frames for explaining this dynamic in journalism and strategic communications:

Frame 1: Meanings can change, depending upon speaker, listener or context.

Frame 2: *Attribution* is bigger than the story.

Frame 3: *Talking across difference* is a skill you can master.

The first thought, the idea that what we say can mean something different depending upon who says it, who hears it and when, can be a destabilizing one for people in the business of communicating. But it happens all the time, this shifting meaning, especially across any of the significant differences that complicate our world.

If comedian Jerry Seinfeld tells a Jewish joke in his standup act, listeners are likely to know that he is Jewish, and they probably won't think he's being anti-Semitic. Change the *speaker* to someone raised Catholic; change the *context* from a comedy club to a local bar, or change the listener from fan to stranger, and the *meaning* of that same joke can shift dramatically.

This has real significance for professional communicators. During the 2012 political campaign season, *Politico* reporter Jonathan Martin caused a small stir when he offered

MSNBC host Chuck Todd this characterization of the Florida electorate: "a lot of those counties in the Panhandle, in North Florida, the cracker counties, if you will, more resemble Georgia and Alabama than they do Florida." [3]

Several media watchers took umbrage at Martin's use of *cracker*, a word that is widely regarded as a racial slur aimed at white people. While it is unmistakably a slur to many, its meaning can change dramatically depending upon who says it, who hears it, and in what context it's used. In this case, a white reporter was talking about white voters in a part of the country where *cracker* is used by some as an ironic term of endearment, much the way comedian Jeff Foxworthy has used *redneck*. Martin made that point in an interview with one of his critics, Noel Sheppard of *NewsBusters*, in February 2012.

> So, it's simply not a controversial term in Florida politics and in Florida culture, and that is the context that I was using it . . . So people should take a few seconds or even minutes to figure out the context I was using it before they jump to conclusions.[4]

There are at least two *talking across difference* lessons here:

1. Because the meaning of some words can change with small variations in context—often charged by history with the destructive power of a subway's third rail—communication professionals should think carefully about language choices. For the people familiar with the way some Floridians refer to the northern counties, Martin's phrase might not raise an eyebrow. But what of the many others across the country who hear *cracker* and think "low class" or, perhaps, "racist?" Without an explanation of what the reporter meant, what were they to think of Martin or MSNBC host Chuck Todd, or MSNBC itself?

2. When someone's choice of words becomes the story, journalists and others need the skills to report down to the root of the controversy and help the public understand not just what was said or what the fallout might be, but why there was a problem in the first place. Journalists who are skittish or who otherwise fail to do this basic but critical reporting fall short of the mission to help foster an informed public.

This idea of shifting meaning is especially important for those in strategic communications. How well professionals anticipate problems or how expertly they respond can be the difference between disaster and triumph. Two cases bring that point home.

During the 2007 Super Bowl, a Snickers® ad featured two male auto mechanics who found the need to do "something manly" after their lips accidentally met as they ate a candy bar from each end. The gag, ending with the men ripping out their chest hair to prove their masculinity, brought an immediate roar of condemnation from those who felt the company was anti-gay, implying that it's unmanly for two men to kiss. An alternate ending offered on the candy maker's website had the two men pummeling one another instead, compounding what many saw as tacit endorsement of violence against gay men. Mars Inc.'s subsidiary, Masterfoods USA, quickly apologized and immediately shelved the campaign, which cost more than $2 million to make.[5]

Here is how the company responded in a story from *The New York Times*: "As with all of our Snickers advertising, our goal was to capture the attention of our core Snickers consumer, primarily 18-to-24-year-old adult males," said a spokeswoman for Masterfoods, Alice Nathanson:

> Feedback from our target consumers has been positive, and many media and Web site commentators on this year's Super Bowl lineup ranked the commercial among this year's best. . . . We know that humor is highly subjective and we understand that some consumers have found the commercial offensive. . . . Clearly that was not our intent. We do not plan to continue the ad on television or on our Web site.[6]

The message of the first ad framed the way viewers would receive two subsequent ads. In 2008, an ad starring former *A Team* actor Mr. T—an ad that was also later pulled—was labeled homophobic. This time, the ad implied that speed walking is unmanly because athletes walk with a pronounced swing in their hips. In the ad the super-macho Mr. T fires Snickers bars at a speed walker from a pickup-mounted machine gun.

Then in a 2014 ad, rookie NFL quarterback Johnny Manziel played an aerobics instructor who wasn't quite himself until he bit into a Snickers bar. AMERICAblog writer John Aravosis was among some commentators who, already suspicious of the candy-bar maker's view of gay men, saw a pattern. "Whoever does Snicker's [sic] PR should really be fired at this point," wrote Aravosis, who said he saw the ad six months after it first aired:

> There's a latent homophobia in the company's advertising — advertising that finds gay-bashing funny. And considering that this has happened before, repeatedly, it's likely not a fluke. It's by intent. There's someone high up in Snicker's marketing department who thinks that in 2015 bashing gays is funny.

> In the commercial in question, Cleveland Browns quarterback Johnny Manziel plays a seriously effeminate aerobics instructor who is clearly intended to be flamingly and effeminately gay. He swishes around the room, and his voice is kinda gay too.

But once he eats a Snickers bar he turns back in to a real man. His voice even deepens (like a "real" man).

Lovely.[7]

Sometimes, history is the context. The Manziel ad might not have raised an eyebrow in 2007. But by 2014, things had changed. Whatever the true intent of the ads, the speaker, listener and context were now influencing the meaning of the message.

It was a very different story for General Mills, maker of Cheerios® cereal. In the spring of 2013, the company rolled out an ad from Saatchi & Saatchi in New York that depicted a family with a white mother and black father. The ad, a cute cut on the company's claim that Cheerios is good for the heart, introduced the country to "Gracie," the precocious, curly haired daughter who sprinkles cereal on her sleeping father's chest. The ad "generated vituperative comments online" from people troubled by interracial relationships, *The New York Times* reported.[8] It also generated a lot of good will.

General Mills stood behind the commercial, then doubled down in early 2014 with another ad featuring the fictional family. This time, "Gracie" negotiates for a puppy when her father tells her they're expecting another baby. The ad itself may have kept to the simple theme of "love" that the agency employed the first time around, but given the context of recent history, it was ennobled further by fans who saw greater meaning. "It's hard to imagine Cheerios handling a sequel any more deftly than this," wrote Tim Nudd of *Adweek*:

It obliquely references the earlier controversy, but by embracing a simpler story that has nothing to do with it, it suggests the controversy was dumb to begin with—that this is just America now, and families like this are just like everyone else, with better things to worry about.

Plus, of course, the very decision to devote an expensive buy on the Super Bowl to this spot—it's Cheerios' first appearance ever on the game, and only General Mills' second, following a Wheaties ad in 1996—is a nice rebuke to any detractors, and a proud moment for everyone else.[9]

No speaker can fully control how a listener receives a message. Nor is it possible to anticipate every context into which a message may fall. What professional communicators can do, however, is understand how the speaker–listener–context dynamic has influenced cases like these and apply some of the tools we'll discuss later in the chapter.

▶ FRAMES FOR THE CONVERSATION: ATTRIBUTION THEORY

In his comments to *NewsBusters*, MSNBC reporter Jonathan Martin hit on a particularly important part of *talking across difference* that can serve journalists well: Take a few seconds "or even minutes," he said, to think about what someone means before you react to their words. Many of those who study communication theory say that for people to do that, they have to battle human nature. Fortunately, journalism provides some excellent tools for drilling down to deeper understanding and greater truths.

Here, then, is the second frame for *talking across difference*: *attribution theory*, the process of drawing inferences from behavior. My thinking on this subject has been most influenced by the foundational work of psychologist Fritz Heider, who outlined the pathway for how people reach judgments, with a twist that is especially applicable to the tougher conversations across difference.

Those who have interpreted Heider through the years, people like Emory Griffin, author of *A First Look at Communication Theory*, hold that in our daily encounters, people are constantly categorizing the actions of others and routinely attributing those actions to motives they can only guess to be true.[10] Attribution, Griffin writes, works quickly, and it works this way:

First, we *perceive*. It's as close to objectivity as we get in the process, observing and registering what's happened. Someone has said or done something that has come to our attention.

Second, we *judge*. We ask ourselves a simple question: How does it feel? Fun? Offensive? In that judgment, what psychologists call the Fundamental Attribution Error, we tend to be more forgiving of ourselves than of others, which Griffin explains this way: "When things turn out badly for others, we assume it's their fault; but for our own failures, we tend to blame circumstances or other people. We see others as causal agents, but we give ourselves an excuse."[11]

Next, we *attribute*. Human nature, Heider theorized, leads us to do a sort of mind reading, often basing judgments on motives we attribute to people with little or no information to back us up. So in our attributions, we say things like, "It's because she's homophobic," or "it's because he's sexist."

Often, people then act on the attribution. They say or do something based largely, if not exclusively, on scant information and judgments. In our everyday lives, that march to judgment can lead to misunderstanding and conflict. For Snickers maker Masterfoods USA, it taints—fairly or unfairly—the way many people will see its ads. In journalism, it can harm people unnecessarily.

This disconnect would become a problem for the Rev. Mitchell after the Madison town hall meeting. His comments about not trusting white people and being particularly cautious around white women came at the very start of the conversation. He would go on to elaborate on his ideas of tolerance, to offer suggestions for how people might better learn about one another across the lines of race, ethnicity and sexual orientation, and even to talk about how he is learning new ways to get past some of those self-imposed barriers. But when the story appeared that night on the website of the *Wisconsin State Journal*, only a snippet of what the Rev. Mitchell said made it:

> Everett Mitchell, pastor of Christ the Solid Rock Baptist Church and a former Dane County assistant district attorney, went further, saying that he doesn't trust white people.

> There was a time, he said, when he would not allow himself to be in a closed room with a white woman. His greatest fear is to be seen as something he is not, Mitchell said: 'brutal, black rapist, out of control, angry . . . That if I raise my voice I'm going to hurt you.'[12]

People complain all the time to journalists that their comments were taken out of context, and it wouldn't be hard to make that argument here. Throw in what we know about attribution and the volatile nature of the subject matter, though, and the consequences of a story lacking such context become all the more pronounced. That's how Bill Kovach and Tom Rosenstiel saw it when they wrote about the essentials of the craft in *The Elements of Journalism: What Newspeople Should Know and the Public Should Expect*:

> Those who have worked in news, or worked in public life, say much the same thing: Getting news that comes closer to a complete version of the truth has real consequences.

> In the first hours of an event, when being accurate is most difficult, it is perhaps most important. It is during this time that public attitudes are formed, sometimes stubbornly, by the context within which the information is presented.[13]

In these tough conversations, where the stakes are high and the possibility of misunderstanding is heightened, professionals can use critical tools of the journalism trade—simple questions—to produce better results:

1. *What did they say?* Report as fully as possible all comments and context so that the whole thought is represented.

2. *What did they mean?* Suspect your assumptions, no matter how obvious you think the meaning might be. Then ask the question anyway. How might the

stories have been different if reporters had approached *Politico's* Jonathan Martin or Madison's the Rev. Mitchell and asked that question?

3. *Why does it matter?* Bring the necessary context to bear on the issue. A little context to understand how a region came to be called "Cracker Counties" or why a black man in America might want to avoid being alone with white women, could take either of those stories into a deeper place—or, at least, head off the confusion that followed.

▶ FRAMES FOR THE CONVERSATION: TALKING ACROSS DIFFERENCE

Ask yourself this question: If you wanted to have a constructive conversation with someone across a significant difference, what would you need from the other person?

I've asked the question of journalists from across the country and around the world; journalists from Indonesia and Denmark, England and Zimbabwe, the Middle East and Middle America. I've asked rooms filled with lawyers, business leaders, college students and everyday people like the crowd in Madison. We're all different enough that the answers run a wide gamut of possibilities. But some answers almost always arise. Most people say they want others to do five things:

- Be honest.

- Seek clarification before judging.

- Challenge with passion, not poison.

- Be open to change.

- Stay in the room.

Consider those five bullet points to be journalistic tools and they'll serve you well in any conversation, especially those across meaningful difference. Look deeply into the words and phrases and there are lessons in reporting and writing. Notice all the ways they translate into stronger journalism and more successful strategic communication.

Be Honest

People in the U.S. tend to use the word honesty as a synonym for candor, fearing that others will hold back and not say what they really mean. They worry about the euphemisms that can accompany these conversations when someone is uncomfortable getting to the point.

Pastor Michael Schuler, whose church hosted the Madison town hall, was one of the panelists there. He spoke of another way that that discomfort plays out—a fear that sometimes also stops us from going deep in conversations across difference. "When I try to engage in a conversation like this I'm deathly afraid of saying something that is culturally inappropriate out of ignorance," Schuler said that night.

> I think I've probably read more than the average person about race relations in the United States and about white privilege, and about a lot of these topics, but I exist in a fairly homogeneous environment and these conversations do not happen on a regular basis, so I always have some significant trepidation about entering into the conversation. . . . So that fear is inhibiting.[14]

I have heard this lament often from journalists, journalism professors and strategic communications students as they've reflected on their own fears over the past two decades. In the essay *The Woods Theorem: A New Formula for Diversity in American News Organizations*, I looked at how easily that fear plays out in everyday journalism. "Whenever race comes up in my newsroom," a TV reporter in Virginia said at a Columbia University workshop in the summer of 2000, "fear comes after." The reporter continued:

> Considering all the things that can go wrong and the great personal stake people think they wager on the conversation, avoidance seems like a reasonable human response.

> The problem, of course, is that it's not a particularly good journalistic response. Ignorance unchallenged perpetuates itself and fuels fear. Fear leaves doors unopened, questions unasked, claims uncontested. Stories never get fully discussed or adequately critiqued. Coverage decisions go unexamined. In the end, that leaves people uninformed or underinformed, and that falls well short of journalistic excellence.[15]

Journalists should acknowledge the fear in conversations and overcome it in storytelling. Use clear, concise language in your reporting and writing. If you mean "poor Latinos," for example, don't say "inner city youth." Excellent journalism calls for precision, not obfuscation. On a more practical level, dodging candor in the name of sensitivity or the result of discomfort can undermine the trust you're trying to develop with peers, superiors and sources.

This definition of honesty is often complicated across culture and nationality. Any study of communication across these differences—the bluntness of Dutch culture, for example, or the deferential indirectness you might find in Japan—underscores how important it is to factor in the cultural when *talking across difference*.

Seek Clarification

Most of us don't want to be judged harshly, whether or not we deserve it. We want to know that the other person will ask a few questions before judging something we've said or done, that they'll seek clarification before reaching a conclusion. That takes work, if you consider what Heider and others describe in attribution theory.

When it comes to talking with journalists, people are wary of the "gotcha!" They fear that moment when they've said something they can't take back; when they're pilloried before they can explain themselves; when the journalist doesn't seek clarification.

It's not the job of journalists to protect people from themselves. But at the core of ethical journalism is the notion that we owe to the public simple acts of fairness that carry profound weight. At the least, it means asking, *"What do you mean?"* whenever possible. Imagine the power of that question in the creative discussions of an advertising agency or the wrangling over words at a public relations firm. For many journalists, the question sometimes seems unnecessary, so clear is the transgression.

As long as journalists believe that the only stakeholder due our consideration is the person at the center of the controversy, it's easy to dismiss the question, "What do you mean?" as an exploration of the obvious. Here is another way to look at it: Many people harbor variations of the ideas, beliefs or ideological positions that sound a lot like the controversial things others have said. When journalists delve into the question, "What do you mean?" they allow the public to distinguish between their own ideas and those uttered by the newsmaker. The act of fairness—suspending judgment long enough to understand better what the source meant—extends, then, to a larger public.

Challenge with Passion, not Poison

In the hundreds of times I've heard this expressed, it most often comes out as a request for respect. What do people mean by "respect?" That depends. Most often, though, it comes down to "don'ts." In conversation, don't shout. Don't discount what someone is saying or talk while they're talking. Don't dismiss another's concerns without first hearing them out.

For professional communicators, especially journalists, it means holding back on labels. It may ultimately be accurate to declare someone racist, or sexist or homophobic, or to label their actions with any of the words ending in "ist" or "ism." But if you favor informing over inflaming, those words are best left to direct quotes and sound bytes. Better for journalists to describe what happened and leave the labeling to others.

When University of Missouri football player Michael Sam announced that he was gay prior to the 2014 National Football League draft, TV analyst and former coach Tony Dungy was asked if he would have drafted Sam were Dungy still an NFL coach. Dungy said no, given "the distractions" that would accompany the man who would be the league's first openly gay player. Here is what the former coach first told the Tampa Tribune's Ira Kaufman: "I wouldn't have taken him. Not because I don't believe Michael Sam should have a chance to play, but I wouldn't want to deal with all of it. It's not going to be totally smooth . . . things will happen."[16]

A firestorm ensued. *Slate* magazine labeled Dungy's remarks "homophobic" in a piece headlined, "Tony Dungy Brings Some Late-Breaking Homophobia to Michael Sam." *Slate* blogger Tyler Lopez ended his post by declaring: "Only homophobia can explain why Dungy would not extend that same kind of opportunity to Michael Sam."[17]

Dungy then elaborated on his comments with a statement released to several media outlets, complicating the story:

> On Monday afternoon while on vacation with my family, I was quite surprised to read excerpts from an interview I gave several weeks ago related to this year's NFL Draft, and I feel compelled to clarify those remarks.
>
> I was asked whether I would have drafted Michael Sam and I answered that I would not have drafted him. I gave my honest answer, which is that I felt drafting him would bring much distraction to the team. At the time of my interview, the Oprah Winfrey reality show that was going to chronicle Michael's first season had been announced.
>
> I was not asked whether or not Michael Sam deserves an opportunity to play in the NFL. He absolutely does.
>
> I was not asked whether his sexual orientation should play a part in the evaluation process. It should not.
>
> I was not asked whether I would have a problem having Michael Sam on my team. I would not.
>
> I have been asked all of those questions several times in the last three months and have always answered them the same way—by saying that playing in the NFL is, and should be, about merit.
>
> The best players make the team, and everyone should get the opportunity to prove whether they're good enough to play. That's my opinion as a coach. But those were not the questions I was asked.
>
> What I was asked about was my philosophy of drafting, a philosophy that was developed over the years, which was to minimize distractions for my teams.

I do not believe Michael's sexual orientation will be a distraction to his teammates or his organization.

I do, however, believe that the media attention that comes with it will be a distraction. Unfortunately we are all seeing this play out now, and I feel badly that my remarks played a role in the distraction.

I wish Michael Sam nothing but the best in his quest to become a star in the NFL and I am confident he will get the opportunity to show what he can do on the field.

My sincere hope is that we will be able to focus on his play and not on his sexual orientation.[18]

Be Open to Change

Who wants to start a conversation with someone who's already decided how it's going to end? The journalists, professors, students and ordinary citizens I've talked to tell me that they're not asking for guarantees that someone will change their point of view. They just want to know it's possible. That open-mindedness is important at every step of the journalistic process, including meetings about stories and interviews with sources.

Veteran journalist Ted Koppel proved the value of that openness when he and his team at ABC's *Nightline* took on tough issues of difference in the series *America in Black and White,* one of the network's most heralded news franchises ever. In one of the most poignant stories in the series, which ran in the late 1990s, Koppel told the story of Cynthia Wiggins, a young, working class black woman from Buffalo, New York, who was struck and killed by a truck on her way to work. What the reporting exposed was the systemic biases that prompted executives from the shopping mall where Wiggins worked to arrange things in such a way that the bus she took to work from one of the poorest neighborhoods in Buffalo would not be allowed onto the mall property. That decision created the dangerous commute that ultimately cost Wiggins her life.

When producer Eric Wray first pitched the story to Koppel, the award-winning correspondent saw nothing there but "a traffic accident for which no one was particularly responsible," Koppel told me in an interview in 2004. "I've known Eric for a long time. I trust him," Koppel said. "He was adamant. He said this is a story about racism, and I didn't get it."

It was "skin color," Koppel said, that stopped him from seeing the story at the outset. Koppel is white, Wray is black. "I saw what was obvious," Koppel said. "Eric saw what was implied and knew instinctively that there was more to it."

Koppel kept an open mind and Wray did more digging, producing enough compelling reporting that it got the *Nightline* team on a plane for Buffalo. Once there, tough conversations across difference delivered the award-winning story.

Koppel said it was "an accretion of things" that convinced him there was a story to be told:

> It wasn't any one thing. It was going into the neighborhoods and seeing that there was no work; that in order to find a job, it was necessary to move outside of the neighborhood; it was necessary to get from this part of town to that part of town. It was walking that particular stretch of highway; it was seeing how difficult it is in a Buffalo winter. Just getting across the street can be a Herculean effort.
>
> What we ended up doing in effect was consolidating in half an hour what it had taken people several hours to teach me.[19]

Stay in the Room

One of the central paradoxes of *talking across difference* is this: People ask for honesty, but they're not always willing to hang around after they get it. So when they answer the "What would you need . . ." question I posed earlier, they often say they want to know that the other person will stay with the conversation when it gets tough; that they will "stay in the room." That's the path to stronger strategic communication. That's the bargain an ethical journalist strikes with sources: Give candid, honest answers, and you'll get fair, complete coverage. It's the expectation the Rev. Everett Mitchell had when he began his remarks at the Madison town hall with the words, "I'll be honest . . ."

After the *Wisconsin State Journal* published its story about the Rev. Mitchell's remarks, he wrote to me and to Paul Fanlund, editor of *The Capital Times*, the *Journal's* sister paper and one of the town hall co-sponsors along with Wisconsin Public Radio.

> Even though I thought there were more extensive narratives that explained and discussed other perspectives, those were the ones the paper highlighted. I often think the media has a way of taking statements [of] all people, but particularly men of color, out of context. When this happens it makes the opportunities for transparency and dialogue almost impossible. It would seem that I have fallen victim to the vulnerable comment, taken out of context, that is now being used to distort my character and intention regarding building relationships across cultural and gender lines.
>
> It will make honest participation difficult if my, or others, transparent statements are not given context as we attempt to discuss 'what gets in the way of productive conversations about race relations?'

The Rev. Mitchell "stayed in the room," and so did Fanlund. The editor brought Mitchell together with another of the town hall panelists, Leslie Howard, who was CEO of the United Way of Dane County and "not incidentally," Fanlund later wrote, "a white woman." He asked them to talk about reactions to the stories. In that way, they found a way to continue the conversation across difference that could easily have ended at the First Unitarian church.[20] "Mitchell says he received positive feedback from those who heard all of what he had to say, but often a negative one from those who did not," Fanlund wrote, describing their conversation in a subsequent column.

> From those in attendance, the reaction "has been somewhat positive, in that they were able to feel and respect the level of transparency that I was offering to the conversation. And they understood the risk that I was taking by opening up that gate too, because I don't think the majority of people would enter into a conversation that says, you know, as a black man, I'm afraid, that I have fears, and what that fear looks like and how you struggle with trust when you're trying to build relationships," Mitchell says.

> Conversely, he says, those who read brief excerpts of what he said seem to see him differently: "They walked away with impressions . . . that I walk around all day mistrusting white people, and that I don't want to be around white women, and I don't want to be in the same place with white women.

> "And so, some people would call me on the phone saying, 'Well, how is it that you work at the university with a chancellor who's a woman? Don't you respect her?'"[21]

▶ TALKING ACROSS DIFFERENCE: THE OTHER SIDE OF THE CONVERSATION

If there are core elements that people universally want from others in the conversation across difference, there are also things you can do to cross those divides and get to deeper storytelling and clearer messaging. Like the five ideas discussed earlier, these strategies come from countless encounters with people who live this challenge every day:

- *Acknowledge the Fear*—The conversation across difference is fraught with fear. Straight people worry about using the wrong words when talking about people who are lesbian, gay, bisexual and transgender. Men fear getting tongue-tied when talking gender with women. People like the Rev. Michael Schuler worry that their ignorance will be revealed and people like the Rev. Everett Mitchell worry they'll be misjudged. Start the tough conversations by naming the fears that might otherwise stifle candor.

- *Sharpen your language*—Listen to yourself and correct for muddled phrases, clichés, euphemisms, generalizations, innuendo and other forms of indirect communication. Clarity is a two-way street. Make sure you understand, but work on improving your chances of being understood.

- *Become a Student*—Read, watch and listen more about the vast arenas of difference. The choices are myriad. You just have to start. Join online conversations through Facebook groups, blogs, Twitter, anywhere people are discussing difference. Join a book club. Start a book club. Do something.

FOR DISCUSSION

1. How do you think changes in the national conversation on sexual orientation affected the way people talked about the Michael Sam and Snickers cases? How would it change the way you would do your job in either case?

2. Read TV football analyst Tony Dungy's full statement. How might the Tampa Tribune's Ira Kaufman have challenged Dungy when he made the first comment? Does Dungy's subsequent statement change your point of view?

3. What, if anything, would you change about the way the *Wisconsin State Journal* reported the Rev. Everett Mitchell's remarks?

4. How does the comment section on online stories or the unbridled conversations on social media hinder or help *talking across difference*?

▶ SUGGESTED ACTIVITIES

1. Research 10 words in common usage whose meanings have either changed substantially over time or change significantly depending upon who hears them, who says them, or in what context they're used.

2. Interview 10 people and ask them the question we posed in the chapter: If you wanted to have a constructive conversation with someone across a significant difference, what would you need from the other person? Write an analysis of what you learn.

3. Write a case study of the speaker–listener–context dynamic discussed in this chapter using a recent example in your area of specialization. Include advice for how someone in your profession could improve the communication in this case.

▶ NOTES

1 Bill Kovach and Tom Rosenstiel, *The Elements of Journalism: What Newspeople Should Know and the Public Should Expect* (New York: Crown, 2001), 149.

2 First Unitarian Society. "Together-Apart: Talking Across the Racial Divide," last modified April 30, 2014, https://www.youtube.com/watch?v=Q30XmKHyFog&sns=em.

3 Real Clear Politics. "Politico's Martin Calls Panhandle Florida Voters 'Cracker Counties,'" last modified January 31, 2012. http://www.realclearpolitics.com/video/2012/01/31/politicos_jonathan_martin_calls_conservative_florida_voters_cracker_counties.html.

4 mrcNewsBusters. "Newsbusters Discusses 'Cracker Counties' with Politico's Jonathan Marti," last modified February 3, 2012. http://newsbusters.org/blogs/noel-sheppard/2012/02/02/martin.

5 Paul Farhi, "Mars Scraps Snickers Ad After Complaints," *Washington Post*, February 7, 2007, http://www.washingtonpost.com/wp-dyn/content/article/2007/02/06/AR2007020601871.html.

6 Stuart Elliott, "Thanks to the Web, the Scorekeeping on the Super Bowl has Just Begun," *The New York Times*, February 6, 2007, http://www.nytimes.com/2007/02/06/business/media/06adco.html?pagewanted=1&.&_r=3.

7 John Aravosis "Yet Another Supremely Homophobic TV Commercial from Snickers," Americablog, January 14, 2015, http://americablog.com/2015/01/yet-another-supremely-homophobic-tv-commercial-snickers.html.

8 Stuart Elliott, "Vitriol Online for Cheerios Ad With Interracial Family," *The New York Times*, May 31, 2013, http://www.nytimes.com/2013/06/01/business/media/cheerios-ad-with-interracial-family-brings-out-internet-hate.html?_r=0

9 Tim Nudd, "Ad of the Day: Cheerios Brings Back Its Famous Interracial Family for the Super Bowl," *Adweek*, January 29, 2014, http://www.adweek.com/news/advertising-branding/ad-day-cheerios-brings-back-its-famous-interracial-family-super-bowl-155302.

10 Emory Griffin, *A First Look At Communication Theory*, 2nd ed. (McGraw-Hill: New York, 1994), 137–146, http://www.afirstlook.com/docs/attribut.pdf.

11 Ibid., 141.

12 "Race Forum: Blacks Need to be Seen as 'Totally Human' before Conversation can Take Place," http://host.madison.com/news/local/race-forum-blacks-need-to-be-seen-as-fully-human/article_2ab93fc9–1ca1–5c1b-872f-c35d4cd729ca.html.

13 Kovach and Rosenstiel, *The Elements of Journalism: What Newspeople Should Know and the Public Should Expect*, 45.

14 https://www.youtube.com/watch?v=Q30XmKHyFog&sns=em

15 Keith Woods, "The Woods Theorem: A New Formula for Diversity in American News Orga-
    nizations," in *The Values and Craft of American Journalism: Essays from the Poynter Institute*
    (Gainesville, FL: The University Press of Florida, 2002), 108.

16 Ira Kaufman, ""NFL Holding Players to Higher Standard," *Tampa Tribune*, July 20, 2014,
    http://tbo.com/sports/bucs/nfl-holding-players-to-higher-standard-20140720/.

17 Tyler Lopez. "Tony Dungy Brings Some Late-Breaking Homophobia to Michael Sam," Slate.
    com, July 22, 2014, http://www.slate.com/blogs/outward/2014/07/22/tony_dungy_makes_
    homophobic_statement_about_michael_sam.html.

18 Mike Florio. "Dungy's statement regarding his Michael Sam comments," NBC Sports, July 22,
    2014, http://profootballtalk.nbcsports.com/2014/07/22/tony-dungys-statement-regarding-
    his-michael-sam-comments/.

19 Arlene N. Morgan, Alice I. Pifer, and Keith Woods, *The Authentic Voice: The Best Reporting on
    Race and Ethnicity* (New York: Columbia University Press, 2006).

20 Paul Fanlund. "Paul Fanlund: When race is the topic, honesty can sometimes backfire,"
    The Capital Times, Madison.com, May 27, 2014, http://host.madison.com/news/local/
    writers/paul_fanlund/paul-fanlund-when-race-is-the-topic-honesty-can-sometimes/
    article_cd92512b-d2ea-53e9-bab2–6422928f6359.html#ixzz3RG4TduNY\.

21 Ibid.

▶ ADDITIONAL READINGS

Barry, Dan. "Going Public, N.B.A. Figure Sheds Shadow Life." *The New York Times*, May 16, 2011.

Chideya, Farai. "Fair Share: How Can We Improve American Media's Coverage of Race, Class,
    and Social Mobility?" *Columbia Journalism Review*, March/April (2013): 20–28.

Dines, Gail and Jean Mcmahon Humez. *Gender, Race, and Class in the Media: A Text Reader*.
    Thousand Oaks, CA: Sage, 2003.

Diuguid, Lewis W. *Discovering the Real America: Toward a More Perfect Union*. Boca Raton, FL:
    BrownWalter Press, 2007.

Greenhouse, Linda. "Challenging 'He Said, She Said' Journalism." *Nieman Reports* Summer
    (2012): 21–24.

Lind, Rebecca Ann. *Race/Gender/Media: Considering Diversity Across Audiences, Content and
    Producers*. Boston: Allyn & Bacon, 2010.

Wilson II, Clint C., Félix Gutiérrez and Lena M. Chao. *Racism, Sexism, and the Media: Multicul-
    tural Issues in the New Communication Landscape*. Thousand Oaks, CA: Sage, 2013.

3

Who Is American?

Saleem E. Alhabash and Carie Cunningham

In *The Hunger Games*, when characters Katniss Everdeen and Peeta Mellark are the last two players alive, they must each decide whether they will go through with killing the other, or create another way. They ultimately choose another way, but in doing so, they each have to assess the other and make quick judgments. As humans, it takes us just milliseconds to evaluate someone else. We do it so quickly that our brain barely registers how fast we mentally process and categorize others as friends or foes.

The United States has long been described as a *melting pot*, referring to how immigrants of different ethnic and religious backgrounds have been transformed "into Americans sharing a common culture—developing common attitudes, values, and lifestyles."[1] While the melting pot metaphor often indicated people who came to the U.S. integrated to form a homogenous country, others took more novel approaches, leaning toward perceiving the U.S. more as a *tossed salad*; thus, hinting at a unified existence, yet acknowledging the heterogeneity within American society.[2] What constitutes U.S. citizenship, nationality and culture is of great importance as journalists and

LEARNING OBJECTIVES

By the end of this chapter, you should be able to:

- understand cognitive mechanisms affecting how we make judgments about others.

- understand the complexity of drawing a comprehensive racial/ethnic map of the United States.

- differentiate between race and ethnicity.

- understand the ramifications of using 'minority' and 'majority' as labels.

- apply racial and ethnic categorizations to various contexts.

strategic communicators embark on finding ways to reflect differences and similarities in American culture.

During the U.S. Summer Olympics, citizens of each competing country cheer their athletes on to victory. In that moment, when athletes are about to cross the finish line, we are unified in a common aspiration. However, the question of *who is American?* goes beyond legal status, citizenship and nationality. While this question might be easier answered outside the borders of the United States, the defining characteristics of who is American within the United States remains an issue of controversy meddled with preconceived notions about social, cultural, racial, socioeconomic and other group categorizations, thus transforming this question from *who is* American to *how* American is a person. The process through which we judge a person's belongingness to a certain group over another is called *social categorization*, which all humans use to define their social world in terms of similarities and differences.[3] Unfortunately, distinguishing your group from another group often comes with affective evaluations, often referred to as stereotypes. The objective of this chapter is to understand the defining characteristics of who is American. However, in order to do that, we are taking a step back and looking at the micro level, in a way digging through people's brains, to understand how we make these evaluative categorizations; how we learn (or maybe unlearn) that a certain group of people are defined by specific characteristics that distinguish them from other groups.

It is worth noting that not all stereotypes are negative. Some are positive. What you'll discover in the following section is that sometimes, based on multiple factors, including our own personal experiences, where we grew up, with whom we surround ourselves and at times the way our brains are wired, these evaluations, especially the negative ones, tend to be the gateway for prejudice, discrimination and unfair treatment. As journalists and strategic communicators, failing to understand these intricacies is a moral and ethical violation of the profound standards of these professions. As you prepare yourself to be the next Pulitzer Prize–winner or an award-winning advertiser, this might be a good time to stop and think about these issues. We cannot promise that it will be easy to think through these controversial issues, yet with an open mind, you might be able to enhance your moral and ethical standards. OK, maybe the best thing to do is to play a game. That's exactly what we're doing next. Play on!

▶ UNDERSTANDING STEREOTYPES

Take a Moment to Think!

For each individual, guess. . .

- what they do for a living
- their religion/faith

- their sexual orientation
- what they do for fun.

Be as fast as you can. Record your answers.

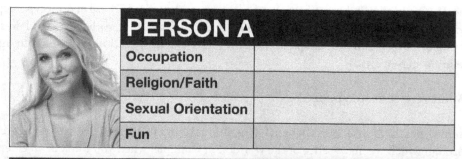

PERSON A	
Occupation	
Religion/Faith	
Sexual Orientation	
Fun	

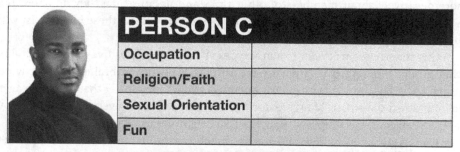

PERSON B	
Occupation	
Religion/Faith	
Sexual Orientation	
Fun	

PERSON C	
Occupation	
Religion/Faith	
Sexual Orientation	
Fun	

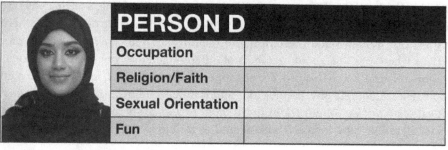

PERSON D	
Occupation	
Religion/Faith	
Sexual Orientation	
Fun	

FIGURE 3.1 The guessing game.
Images courtesy of iStock; © GlobalStock, © coloroftime, © PickStock, and
© PeopleImages.

Inevitably, when you saw these individuals, certain characteristics popped in your head, some of which you were uncomfortable to put on paper. We've carried out this activity in previous classes. Students often guess that Person A is a fashion model, Person B is gay, Person C likes to play basketball and finally thinking Person D is a stay-at-home mother. Students also come up with other descriptions, yet more often than not, there's consistency in how these four characters are described. These common perceptions are stereotypic evaluations of these individuals based on how they look and dress, the color of their skin, the shape of their eyes, etc. The next section goes in-depth into defining stereotypes.

What Are Stereotypes?

Stereotypes comprise our thoughts (cognitions) and feelings (affective structures) through which we make sense of the world.[4] For example, when you think of an elderly person, you tend to think of someone with grey hair, glasses, wrinkled skin, who walks slower than a 20-year-old person. These ideas used to describe an elderly person are stereotypes that we use to organize and categorize individuals into groups in our social and cultural worlds. This process of categorization happens automatically without our conscious thinking, and, at times, these evaluations are well thought out and the product of controlled mechanisms.[5] *Automatic evaluations* happen with little cognitive effort (thinking) and outside of our consciousness, while *controlled evaluations* are the product of our thinking and require more effort. Generally, individuals think and feel more negatively about members of other races and nations than they do about their own group.[6] Although such biases are rarely overtly expressed, these biases exist without our awareness and are sometimes expressed symbolically.[7]

In this chapter, we will refer to stereotypes as negative or positive perceptions about other groups of people that are activated automatically in our brains. In other words, we can't help but think that an elderly person is going to be slower than the 20-year-old walking down the street. Now, we don't necessarily act upon every single thought we have. Oftentimes, we suppress thoughts that might get us in trouble. Let's say one of your friends got a new haircut and you absolutely hate it. In most cases, you'll probably think that the haircut is hideous, yet prefer not to hurt your friend's feeling and instead "lie" and say it looks good. This process is where cognitive control kicks in, where we suppress our thoughts and don't verbalize them or act upon them. The same process happens when we think about members of different genders, racial groups, sexual orientation, religions, etc. This process of suppressing stereotypes, unlike thinking about people in a stereotypic way, is conscious and is influenced by intrinsic and/or extrinsic motivations.[8] *Intrinsic motivations to withhold prejudice* are internal mechanisms that restrict stereotypic/prejudiced thinking and expressions, while *external motivation to withhold prejudice* are mechanisms found in one's environment that restrict prejudiced thinking and expression. For example, one suppresses stereotypic thinking because of his/her internal egalitarian (equality) values, whereas another inhibits stereotypic expressions due to external factors: e.g., to sound "politically correct," to appease others, or avoid negative consequences.

Let's look at another example. John grew up in a predominantly white town. He rarely (if ever) interacts with people from other races. In his hometown, people are not very fond of blacks and Asians. They often make insensitive jokes about people from the two racial groups, and by default think that whites are superior to blacks and Asians. In this environment, John has no intrinsic or extrinsic motivations to withhold prejudice and refrain from partaking in these—what some might refer to as—*racist* conversations. John graduates from high school, and gets accepted to the state's top university. He comes to the new town, and all of sudden, he is interacting with blacks, Asians, Arabs and Hispanics . . . you name it. He also takes a course on cross-cultural journalism and communication and learns that it's—for the lack of a better word—wrong to describe blacks and Asians in a negative way. His roommate at the dormitory also happens to be Asian, and they become friends. In this new environment, John is receiving cues that it's not acceptable to joke about blacks and Asians. This is an example of extrinsic motivations to withhold prejudice. Additionally, the more he interacts with people of different races and the more he reads about issues related to stereotypes, his values change. He becomes a champion for civil rights and believes that it's wrong to negatively stereotype individuals from other racial groups, and by default refrains from doing so himself. This, then, becomes an example of intrinsic motivation to withhold prejudice. Even though he's learned a lot, unconsciously, he still attributes negative descriptions to blacks and Asians, yet he is now motivated to control these unconscious thoughts by not expressing them out loud and through his behaviors to not discriminate against members of these racial groups.

Stereotypes can be sporadic at times. However, within the course of history, we can easily see how stereotypes have been attributed to certain groups and not others. These negative and/or positive thoughts become markers of how, in our thinking, we organize society and the world around us into groups. This process refers to social categorization, which is described in the following section.

Social Categorization

Echosmith's song "Cool Kids" reminds us that we're quite familiar with putting ourselves in groups—whether we see ourselves as athletes, artists, Christians, vegetarians or cool kids—we put ourselves in groups just like others put us in groups based on what they see of us. Marketers do this as well through branding—are you an Abercrombie®

customer? Are you the type of person who wears Dockers® or Calvin Klein® or Prada®? Social categorization deals with how our minds make sense of the world around us by categorizing individuals into social groups or categories. Categorizing people primarily deals with realizing commonalties and differences between others and ourselves. From an evolutionary standpoint, we are predisposed to recognize differences as a way of defining who we are, even at an early age.[9] We are hardwired to make sense of our social world by differentiating those who are and aren't like *us*. Social categorization is expressed in three ways:

- *in-group favoritism* deals with identifying with one's own group (i.e., in-group) and expressing affection and appreciation for being in that group as opposed to other groups.

- *out-group prejudice* deals with instances when we recognize that our in-group (i.e., us) is different from other out-groups (i.e., them), and by default out-groups are negatively evaluated.

- *intergroup conflict* deals with instances where in-group/out-group differentiation is taken as basis for discrimination; where one group believes it is morally, physically and intellectually superior to other groups.

So, the cool kids demonstrate in-group favoritism and may express out-group prejudice. Let's explain this with another example. You're enrolled in a course with multiple sections, each taught by a different instructor. Your specific section is the in-group and all other sections are out-groups. In-groups are generally evaluated positively (in-group favoritism) as opposed to out-groups that are evaluated negatively (out-group prejudice).

Let's say, hypothetically, all sections are competing for an award from the instructor. This can cause tension between different sections that can at times be so pervasive that members of your own in-group start feeling and expressing superiority toward members of the other sections. This is called intergroup conflict.

Humans naturally develop social categories, without objective biological basis for regarding one group superior to another. While some social categories reflect subtle biological differences (e.g., race, gender), the meaning and placement on the hierarchy of a particular group is socially constructed. Take for example Jane Elliott's experiment with her classroom after the assassination of Dr. Martin Luther King Jr. in 1968. Elliot grouped her third-graders into blue-eyed and brown-eyed groups. On the first day, blue-eyed students were told they were superior in terms of who they were (e.g., they were smarter) and because of that, they deserved special privileges (e.g., longer recess). On that day, blue-eyed students acted aggressively against brown-eyed students and performed better at educational tasks. The next day, Elliott switched the categorization; brown-eyed students were now superior to blue-eyed students. Not surprisingly, brown-eyed students performed better and acted more aggressively than blue-eyed students.[10]

Elliot's experiment is an excellent example of how social categories are manufactured by humans. On both days, kids assigned to the superior group (blue-eyed on the first day; brown-eyed on the second) did not only think they were better than the other group members, but also members of the inferior group (brown-eyed on the first; blue-eyed on the second) started feeling as though they were not worthy, and actually performed worse on in-class exercises. This is an example of what psychologists call *stereotype threat*, where even individuals in the stereotyped group start feeling and behaving in ways that are aligned with the stereotypes. Research has shown that in cases when people are reminded of their racial group and the stereotypes attached to it, they end up performing worse on intellectual and educational tests (e.g., IQ, GRE, etc.) than when they're not reminded of their racial category.[11]

Studies investigating stereotypes and stereotype threat give an idea of what it means to belong to a group that is negatively portrayed and perceived by others, including by the media. Research tells us how harmful stereotypes can be to the development and empowerment of different racial groups, which in turn harms the society at large. If a racial group is generally considered lazy, violent and uneducated, how can group members fight these negative portrayals and excel in school or work? And if they don't perform well, then how does this burden the country in general? More importantly, how would this define the country as a whole, with its different colors and variations? What makes an individual more or less a member of that country?

In the United States, how do stereotypes of racial groups intertwine with descriptions of American-ness? What are the characteristics of an American? Who decides these characteristics? Finally, as a journalist and a strategic communicator, when is it appropriate to reference someone's race and make it part of the story or the ad campaign? Even before getting to this stage, how can you describe people from other races and ethnicities? Chapter 1 explained fault lines, which were first introduced by Robert C. Maynard (1937–1993). Maynard said: "This country cannot be the country we want it to be if the story is told by only one group of citizens . . . Our goal is to give all Americans front-door access to the truth." Fault lines (race/ethnicity, class, gender, generation, geographic) are "the most enduring forces that have shaped social tensions since the founding of the United States."[12] Recognizing the major fault lines in the U.S. helps journalists and strategic communicators to better represent and more effectively reach consumers with good information and products. While we often recognize differences related to fault lines—without conscious awareness—some questions remain unanswered: how do these differences contribute to Americans' understanding of who is American? And how do other nations view Americans and define who is and who is not American? Next, we focus on race and ethnicity within the broader context of the U.S. census.

▶ THE U.S. CENSUS BUREAU: DEFINING *WHO IS AMERICAN*

The context in which we make evaluations of others matters. When a student participates in a study-abroad program, regardless of her ethnic and racial background, when faced with other out-groups, the category that might be most salient is that she is American and can identify with her fellow American peers. When she returns home, she will notice that the larger group of Americans is broken down into smaller groups and sub-groups with limitless divisibility. Laurance J. Splitter argues that citizenship is vastly different from identity and identification with a group.[13] An individual is called a citizen of country X if he/she holds a passport from that country and has legal rights to live in it. For example, a U.S. citizen is any individual who has been born in the United States or certain U.S. territories or outlying possessions; one whose parent or parents were U.S. citizens at birth, or an individual who applies to become a U.S. citizen either derived/acquired through U.S. parents or through naturalization.[14] Citizenship, over time, can translate into national identity or nationalism.

Mead defines nationalism as a

> type of social consciousness or movement, sometimes associated with an ideology but always with ethnic interests, and it should be noted that we do not have interests, but are possessed by them, identified with them, or "constituted out of" them.[15]

While the boundaries between citizenship and national identity or nationalism can be blurred at times, these concepts are not synonymous. A U.S. citizen might not feel *American*, as much as a citizen of Nicaragua can feel *American*. The notion of national identity has also been intertwined with intergroup conflict in the United States as it relates to race, gender and class, among others. Some might view a black Muslim American as less American than a blonde-and-blue-eyed white American. Amongst these complex relationships, another layer of complexity emerges in trying to distinguish race from ethnicity. Race and ethnicity are often used interchangeably and the distinction has (and will continue to) become blurrier. In all cases, let's define each concept:

- *Race* refers to social group membership based on physical commonalities among group members (e.g., skin color/pigmentation, eye shape, nose, hair, etc.). While the basis of these defining characteristic can be physical, the meaning a racial group gains is a result of social and cultural norms.[16]

- *Ethnicity* refers to social group membership based on cultural characteristics, such as, but not limited to, historical origins, language and customs.[17]

Some might argue that race is easier to define than ethnicity, yet the social construction surrounding both concepts makes it hard to visually distinguish whether individuals belong to a certain racial group and even harder to infer their ethnicity. As you might have guessed, setting up the census while taking into consideration all of the intricate definitions and descriptions of racial and ethnic groups is not an easy task. Before discussing the racial and ethnic make-up of the United States, it's time for a discussion of the U.S. census.

The U.S. Census: A Historical Overview

Since 1790, the United States Government has commissioned a nationwide census of all individuals living in the United States of America and its territories. The survey asks each U.S. citizen questions about his/her living situation, first and last names, age, gender and race/ethnicity. It is administered at the household level, and each member of the household is asked to record his/her answers.[18] In this chapter, we are mostly concerned with race-related questions on the U.S. census. Sharon M. Lee argues "census categories represent political, legal, and professional authority to the public, even when the process by which such categories emerged may be tainted by political struggles and ideological biases."[19] Lee documented the different categories used to organize individuals into racial groups since 1890 to 1990. Table 3.1 summarizes these categories and extends the timeline to include two other census surveys in 2000 and the most recent one in 2010. It's not hard to see the diversification in the list from 1890 to 2010. The list in each of the decades is a reflection of the social, cultural and political climate in the United States. Despite the diversification of the list, some groups still don't identify with these large groups and decide to self-report their own idea of their racial grouping (see Table 1).

Recent Census Findings and Future Projections

In the last few decades, social and migration movements have reshaped our racial and ethnic makeup. The U.S. Census Bureau estimates that as of 2013, 316,138,839 people makeup the U.S. population. In just three short years (April 1, 2010- July 1, 2013), the U.S. Census Bureau estimates the population has swelled by 2.4 percent. These increases, along with a changing racial makeup of the population have continued to push changes in the way race is measured. Between the two census measures of 1990 and 2000, several changes were made to the race category.[21] One major change for race considerations was making the survey measure inclusive of mixed raced individuals.[22] Traditionally, race

TABLE 3.1 This chart is adapted from Sharon M. Lee's work and shows the U.S. census racial categories from 1890 to 2010.[20]

1890	1900	1910	1920	1930	1940	1950	1960	1970	1980	1990	2000	2010
White	White	White	White	White	White	White	White	White	White	White	White	White
Black	Black	Black	Black	Negro	Negro	Negro	Negro	Negro or Black	Black or Negro	Black or Negro	Black, African Am. or Negro	Black, African Am. or Negro
Mulatto		Mulatto	Mulatto	Mexican	Indian	American Indian	American Indian	Indian (Amer.)	Japanese	Indian (Amer.)	American Indian or Alaska Native	American Indian or Alaska Native
Quadroon				Indian	Chinese	Japanese	Japanese	Japanese	Chinese	Eskimo	Asian-Indian	Asian-Indian
Octoroon				Chinese	Japanese	Chinese	Chinese	Chinese	Filipino	Aleut	Chinese	Chinese
Chinese	Chinese	Chinese	Chinese	Japanese	Filipino	Filipino	Filipino	Filipino	Korean	Asian or Pacific Islander (API)	Filipino	Filipino
Japanese	Japanese	Japanese	Japanese	Filipino	Hindu	Other	Hawaiian	Hawaiian	Vietnamese	Chinese	Japanese	Other Asian
Indian	Indian	Indian	Indian	Hindu	Korean		Part Hawaiian	Korean	Indian (Amer.)	Filipino	Korean	Japanese
		Other	Other	Korean	Other		Aleut	Other	Asian-Indian	Hawaiian	Vietnamese	Korean
				Other			Eskimo		Hawaiian	Korean	Other Asian	Vietnamese
							Other, etc.		Guamanian	Vietnamese	Native Hawaiian	Native Hawaiian
									Samoan	Japanese	Guamanian or Chamorro	Guamanian or Chamorro
									Eskimo	Asian-Indian	Samoan	Samoan
									Aleut	Samoan	Other Pacific Islander	Other Pacific Islander
									Other	Guamanian	Some Other Race	Some Other Race
										Other		

had been a single selection, but in the 2000 U.S. census, respondents could select multiple categories. Furthermore, this updated census allowed for additional write-in space under more than one category. This space is known as self-reporting another race.[23] It is important to know that when you interpret census information, it is self-reported. That means, your race or ethnicity is recorded based on what you check off or write in. If you fill in Hawaiian, that is what is recorded—correct or not.

United States Census 2010

Use a blue or black pen.

Start here

The Census must count every person living in the United States on April 1, 2010.

Before you answer Question 1, count the people living in this house, apartment, or mobile home using our guidelines.

- Count all people, including babies, who live and sleep here most of the time.

The Census Bureau also conducts counts in institutions and other places, so:

- Do not count anyone living away either at college or in the Armed Forces.
- Do not count anyone in a nursing home, jail, prison, detention facility, etc., on April 1, 2010.
- Leave these people off your form, even if they will return to live here after they leave college, the nursing home, the military, jail, etc. Otherwise, they may be counted twice.

The Census must also include people without a permanent place to stay, so:

- If someone who has no permanent place to stay is staying here on April 1, 2010, count that person. Otherwise, he or she may be missed in the census.

1. How many people were living or staying in this house, apartment, or mobile home on April 1, 2010?

Number of people =

2. Were there any additional people staying here April 1, 2010 that you did not include in Question 1? Mark X all that apply.

- Children, such as newborn babies or foster children
- Relatives, such as adult children, cousins, or in-laws
- Nonrelatives, such as roommates or live-in baby sitters
- People staying here temporarily
- No additional people

3. Is this house, apartment, or mobile home — Mark X ONE box.

- Owned by you or someone in this household with a mortgage or loan? Include home equity loans.
- Owned by you or someone in this household free and clear (without a mortgage or loan)?
- Rented?
- Occupied without payment of rent?

4. What is your telephone number? We may call if we don't understand an answer.

Area Code + Number

OMB No. 0607-0919-C: Approval Expires 12/31/2011.

Form **D-61** (1-15-2009)

5. Please provide information for each person living here. Start with a person living here who owns or rents this house, apartment, or mobile home. If the owner or renter lives somewhere else, start with any adult living here. This will be Person 1.
What is Person 1's name? Print name below.

Last Name

First Name   MI

6. What is Person 1's sex? Mark X ONE box.
- Male   - Female

7. What is Person 1's age and what is Person 1's date of birth? Please report babies as age 0 when the child is less than 1 year old. Print numbers in boxes.

Age on April 1, 2010   Month   Day   Year of birth

➜ NOTE: Please answer BOTH Question 8 about Hispanic origin and Question 9 about race. For this census, Hispanic origins are not races.

8. Is Person 1 of Hispanic, Latino, or Spanish origin?
- No, not of Hispanic, Latino, or Spanish origin
- Yes, Mexican, Mexican Am., Chicano
- Yes, Puerto Rican
- Yes, Cuban
- Yes, another Hispanic, Latino, or Spanish origin — Print origin, for example, Argentinean, Colombian, Dominican, Nicaraguan, Salvadoran, Spaniard, and so on.

9. What is Person 1's race? Mark X one or more boxes.
- White
- Black, African Am., or Negro
- American Indian or Alaska Native — Print name of enrolled or principal tribe.

- Asian Indian   - Japanese   - Native Hawaiian
- Chinese   - Korean   - Guamanian or Chamorro
- Filipino   - Vietnamese   - Samoan
- Other Asian — Print race, for example, Hmong, Laotian, Thai, Pakistani, Cambodian, and so on.   - Other Pacific Islander — Print race, for example, Fijian, Tongan, and so on.

- Some other race — Print race.

10. Does Person 1 sometimes live or stay somewhere else?
- No   - Yes — Mark X all that apply.
  - In college housing   - For child custody
  - In the military   - In jail or prison
  - At a seasonal or second residence   - In a nursing home
  - For another reason

➜ If more people were counted in Question 1, continue with Person 2.

USCENSUSBUREAU

FIGURE 3.2 The first page of the 2010 US census questionnaire.

The U.S. Census Bureau estimates that as of 2013, the racial and ethnic makeup of the United States had diversified to: white (not Hispanic/Latino) 62.6 percent, black or African-American alone 13.2 percent, Native American and Alaska Native alone 1.2 percent, Asian alone 5.3 percent, Native Hawaiian and other Pacific Islander alone 0.2 percent, two or more races 2.4 percent and Hispanic or Latino, 17.1 percent.[24]

Racial categories in the United States census have evolved throughout the years. In the 2010 census, U.S. Office of Management and Budget race categories[25] were: white, black or African-American, American Indian or Alaskan Native, Asian, and Native Hawaiian or Pacific Islander.[26] These categories proved to not be an accurate measure for measuring the 50,477,594 individuals who make up the Hispanic population in America, evidenced by 13 percent of Latinos who did not respond to the race question and 30.5 percent who selected another race.[27] This calls for the need to make changes to the accuracy of measuring racial information among Latinos.

According to the U.S. Census Bureau,[28] by 2060 it is estimated that the Hispanic population will double to 128.8 million (one-third of U.S. residents), the Asian population will double to 34.4 million (8.2 percent) and the black population will rise slightly to 14.7 percent, leaving an only 0.3 percent gain for the remaining race groups. Additionally, the number of people identifying with two or more races is expected to jump to 26.7 million people. These groups that have been often described as minority groups will soon comprise, altogether, 57 percent of the United States. Often times, reporters and marketers refer to groups as minorities based on their race, gender and sexuality. Is it accurate to describe nonwhites as a minority and whites as a majority in the United States, especially within the future projections of population growth among the different "minority" groups? As a reporter, you may find yourself responsible for documenting and responding to the demographic changes in your community. You will need to evolve your writing to fit your audience and key demographics, and most importantly, accurately represent the people in your stories. Since we talked about the majority/minority conundrum, why don't we take a deeper look at these terms?

Minority vs. Majority vs. Plurality

The U.S. census projections give an idea of the evolution of race in the United States. Even with the current racial makeup of the United States, one should question whether *whites* are the majority. *The New York Times* created a project by which Internet users can see the racial makeup of the United States using an interactive map[29], "state by state, county by county." Check the link and hover over different parts of the United States, and check whether *whites* are the 'majority' in every single corner of the country.

There are multiple ways of defining what a majority is. For argument's sake, let's assume that a *majority* is defined as comprising 50 percent or more of the population in a certain geographic area. Following the same logic, a *minority* is a group that comprises fewer than 50 percent of the population in a certain geographic area.

Taking a full snapshot of the United States, one could argue that *whites* are the *majority*, since they comprise the single largest group sharing a common racial background in the Unites States. However, four U.S. states (California, Hawaii, New Mexico and Texas) as well as the District of Columbia all have below 50 percent of non-Hispanic whites.[30] In these four states, as whites are not the majority, Latinos are considered the plurality, where *plurality* is defined as the instance in which a racial or ethnic group (Latinos in this case) "are not more than half but they comprise the largest percentage of any group."[31] In Arizona, Florida and Nevada, non-Hispanic whites are approaching the non-majority status with a little over half of the population there.[32]

In 2012, half of U.S. residents under the age of five belonged to one or more 'minority' racial group (groups other than non-Hispanic whites).[33] Hope Yen reports "About 353 of the nation's 3,143 counties, 11 percent, are now 'majority-minority,' " where non-Hispanic whites are no longer the majority. While there are four U.S. states in addition to the District of Columbia where whites are not the majority, the number of U.S. states where children under 5 years old are "majority-minority" increased from 5 to 13 states in 2012,[34] thus indicating a major shift in U.S. racial make-up, as well as projecting even greater changes within the next few decades. These changes are not only fueled by immigration. Interracial relationships and marriage contribute to this growing phenomenon (or better yet, we should call it "reality").

Demographic changes in the United States tell a story of a different reality than what we live in. References to a group as a *majority* or *minority* often have ramifications for how a group sees and evaluates itself as well as how it is seen and evaluated by others. The term "majority," from a linguistic standpoint, points to something of greater importance or stronger presence and effect. Think about when a patient goes to the doctor and the doctor tells him that he has to undergo an operation. The levels of anxiety and stress are different in situations when the operation is described as major or minor. Continuing to use these terms, when in fact, the United States is moving exponentially to a plurality-based society begs the question of how the terms affect race relations, developments within racial groups and opportunities offered to individuals who, not by choice but rather by birth, happen to be of a different race. In other words, it justifies privileges given or taken by one group and also implies a subtle acceptance of discrimination against other groups.

Interracial Relationships: The Future?

Over the past few years, the United States has witnessed an increase in interracial relationships, dating and marriage. Between 1980 and 2012, the percentage of marriages in the United States between individuals of different races more than doubled from 6.7 percent to 15 percent, as well as the acceptance of interracial relationships and marriage, which doubled from 33 percent to 63 percent in the same time period.[35] This further explains the future projections of the racial make-up in the United States discussed earlier in the chapter. However, despite these *big strides* in acceptance and the prevalence of interracial relationships, racial stereotypes are still evident in everyday life. While we think that the way a person looks is the only way to categorize him or her in a racial group, research shows that these indicators are widespread in our realm of cognition. In other words, there are multiple ways in which we can identify a person as white, or black, or Asian, etc.

Studies conducted on computer-mediated communication (CMC) and the Internet have shown that there are racial differences in communication patterns that transcend the effect of visual identification.[36] For example, Grasmuck et al. and Knadler, found that compared to their white counterparts, blacks tended to focus on religious, spiritual, and racial justice themes in online communities.[37] It goes beyond this. The use of certain words or phrases can certainly elevate our sense of identification of the communicator's race, especially when we cannot visually identify and categorize that individual.

In a series of studies conducted within the context of online dating, Alhabash, Hales, Bake, and Oh[38] showed that the activation of stereotypes happens even in situations where the online dater was visually anonymous (e.g., no picture or name). In the first study, they used online-dating profiles from popular dating websites to write profiles that were either black-stereotypic or white-stereotypic. Without having to see who the person is and how he/she looks, college students (the majority of whom were whites) rated the individual as more attractive when he/she had a white-stereotypic rather than a black-stereotypic profile. In their second study, they took the same black- and white-stereotypic profiles and included pictures of black and white individuals and names. So, in this case, they had four experimental conditions: a black person with a black-sounding profile; a black person with a white-sounding profile; a white person with a white-sounding profile; and a white person with a black-sounding profile. What is so interesting about this study is that participants (all of whom were white) consistently rated the white online daters as more attractive and expressed greater intentions to date them compared to the black online daters. It did not matter what the individual's characteristics were, race that was visually identified by looking at the picture of the online dater was sufficient to activate evaluations of a larger group and led participants to evaluate individuals differently.

Put in a larger context, this says a lot about how individuals' preconceived notions and their automatic evaluations might override any other considerations that would otherwise be important in evaluating an individual.

▶ CHAPTER SUMMARY: RESPONSIBILITIES OR OBLIGATIONS

The complex dynamics (or dynamic complexities) of race in the United States are the center of journalistic reporting and strategic communication, whether practitioners agree or not—whether they like it or not. Representing the different racial groups and ethnicities in the United States is no longer an act of kindness, but rather a necessity and an obligation. Whether you're a journalism, advertising or public relations practitioner, understanding these complex dynamics is important for enhancing the quality of one's work, and in doing so, the outcome of respectful, transparent and unequivocal representation of racial and ethnic groups in professional communication leads to greater reach, circulation, purchase and loyalty, among other positive outcomes. From a business perspective, representing a group as close to how its members expect to be represented would bring about more successful business and generate brand loyalty (not just for commercial products, but also for ideas, news organizations and services). So often, we tend to attribute these responsibilities at a greater importance level for journalists as opposed to strategic communicators. It is plausible that we do so because we often attribute characteristics of justice, equality and the public good with journalistic practices. These same principles should be extended to the field of strategic communication, especially with the current new media environment where little can be hidden, and any mishap could be easily blown out in social media and can have dire effects on the brand as well as the agency. Misrepresenting a racial group in an advertisement or through a public relations effort will be hard to contain once it appears in social media.

To boil this down, companies, advertisers, marketers, PR practitioners and journalists both have a responsibility and an obligation to discuss these issues. Financial gain is a big part of the equation. However, the motivation should be socially oriented, in that each company and news organization has an ethical obligation to represent different groups in ways with which they are comfortable. This is not an easy task. This takes hard work and, quite frankly, better quality work to achieve such goals. Without a doubt, it is hard to please every single individual belonging to a racial/ethnic group. This hardship should not become an unsurmountable hurdle preventing professional communicators from attempting to do a better job.

BOX 3.1   From the Field: Jorge Rodas, Reporter, WIFR TV, Rockford, IL

Jorge Rodas

It's hard determining when it's appropriate to report on racial issues because no matter how we run the story, people on both sides are going to be upset with the other.

That said, we cannot ignore a racial conflict when there is one. However, we are very careful that we're not just adding to a racial conflict or reporting that angle if it's not legitimate.

Race is relevant, in our mind, when it's obvious race played or may have played a role in the story.

I meet people from different ethnic backgrounds all the time who try to pull the race card when they shouldn't, and in those occasions, as a reporter, I simply try to keep that out of the story. It's irresponsible otherwise.

As a reporter I never have a problem when asking about someone's racial background. It's just like asking where they're from, or where they were born. I was born and raised in a very diverse part of my hometown, so that really isn't a difficult thing to do.

BOX 3.2   From the Field: Matt Tiedgen, Vice President, Lead Marketing Agency

Matt Tiedgen

We reference census data at times to provide a snapshot of household and demographic information, specifically to areas on local market levels, including city/township and county, as they relate to individual clients and their target audience segments. Simply put, our team sees census data, as it is presented today, as a good reference tool for deeper research, but recognizes that it is not accurate and timely for purposes of sole plan development influence. Interestingly, in many markets, the amount of media catered to a

(Continued)

BOX 3.2 Continued

specific demographic is not representative of that market's population, especially when it comes to race.

I learned from day one in this business that my personal makeup, opinions, beliefs, etc. has no bearing on those of the intended target(s). In this day and age it's easy to gauge audience makeup and message acceptance with digital reporting, surveying, social media monitoring, among other tools. That doesn't mean a client may not mandate specific messaging or delivery tactics, based on his/her opinions, beliefs, background, company values, and so forth, that could be biased at times. As an agent, it is my job to research and give the most informed, unbiased, relevant, opportunity-focused recommendations to my clients and let them decide on approving the direction.

BOX 3.3   Tips for Journalists

Reporting Tips

- While race and ethnicity are important, they should not be the focus of every single story. Evaluate whether talking about race is important and/ or necessary to the story.

- In cases when race is important/necessary to the story, make sure to portray individuals in ways that would represent who they are and not your own thoughts about who they are.

- Don't make assumptions that people are going to be OK with what you write/produce.

- Be critical of your own coverage.

- Don't succumb to the deadline pressure as a way of justifying errors.

- Go beyond the terminology of minority vs. majority. Find other terms that better represent different groups.

- Percentages should not be the guiding criteria for editorial decisions. Compelling stories that serve the public good should overrule any preset quota in the coverage in general, and within the story itself.

(Continued)

BOX 3.3 Continued

- As a journalist, you have the responsibility to dig deeper and go beyond the fault lines.

- If you have a little doubt that something you've written would make a group unhappy because it is stereotypical, then it probably will make a group unhappy. Take this as an opportunity to rewrite, expand and make the coverage better.

Interviewing Tips

- Never guess someone's racial group membership. Always ask, despite how uncomfortable that may seem.

- Be aware of your own biases while interviewing individuals from different racial/ethnic groups. We all have biases that we cannot control. If you don't recognize these biases, your interviewing will yield biased results. Bias can affect the types of questions you ask, the way you ask them and how you address your interview subjects. Train your cognitive system to recognize and correct bias.

- Prepare your interview questions in advance and ensure they are comparable for all your interviewees.

- During the interview, be professional and don't try to simulate what you think are appropriate modes of behavior of that racial/ethnic group just to fit it. In most cases, you'll end up being offensive.

- While we often prepare for our verbal communication during an interview (e.g., preparing questions), in most cases we ignore preparing for our non-verbal communication. Prior to the interview, make sure that you rehearse the ways you communicate and your body language to make your interview subject feel comfortable and respected.

- Give your interview subject the opportunity to review their profile descriptions and make sure you understand what they said in what you quote. Adjust as much as you can in accordance with your newsroom policy.

BOX 3.4   Tips for Strategic Communicators

Tips for Advertisers

- Use multiple research methods to investigate your target audience, not only in terms of what they like and their lifestyle, but also in terms of how they view themselves and how they'd like to be portrayed in ads. In other words, go beyond demographic and psychographic segmentation.

- At all costs, avoid the use of derogatory stereotypes in any ad, including the use of stereotypes that may seem humorous to you, but haven't been tested on a diverse or representative audience group.

- When designing ads, make sure that they adequately reflect the target audience in ways that are not reductionist. In other words, don't portray a certain racial group in a way that you think applies to all members of that group. Instead, look for alternative views and means of portraying that group.

- Don't rely on superficial research to test your messages and tactics. A major challenge in advertising and market research is reliance on biased samples to evaluate ads and tactics. Focus groups do not necessarily represent a larger public. Even though it might be more time-consuming, test ads and tactics with individuals representing diverse groups.

- Refrain from using the standardized approach to advertising to diverse populations. Instead, tailor ads and tactics (as well as strategies) to fit the specificities of the target group.

Tips for Public Relations Practitioners

- Be inclusive in organizing PR events and efforts.

- Know your target audiences and stakeholders before communicating with them.

(Continued)

BOX 3.4 Continued

- Be honest about your goals and objectives. Avoid deceiving people at all cost.

- Develop a strategy for race-related crises with buy-ins from management and the legal counsel.

- Understand the culture and sub-culture of the group with which you're communicating prior to initiating contact.

- If a race-related crisis emerges, act fast and act strategically. Don't resort to tactics like denial that would tarnish your reputation more than mend it.

FOR DISCUSSION

1. America, as a continent, refers to North America, Central America and South America. Why is the term "American" mostly associated with those who reside in or are from the United States? Do you perceive a Canadian, Mexican, Peruvian, Argentinian, Chilean, etc., as an American?

2. Can a person have white skin color and be of African origin? What does this mean in terms of differentiating individuals based on race and ethnicity?

3. Can you visually and accurately guess the race of an individual? What is the problem of guessing race rather than asking about it?

4. When is it relevant and/or important, as journalists and strategic communicators, to ask someone about his/her race?

▶ SUGGESTED ACTIVITIES

1. Find a news story from any news source, including public relations, marketing and advertising trade magazines, that includes racial categories from census data. Evaluate the story. Does the story provide context for the categories of people described in the story? How are groups compared to one another, if at all? What information is conveyed through the use of the data? How is the information useful? What could be improved?

2. Identify a group to which you belong. It can be a club, organization or one you were born into. List all the characteristics of what membership in that group means and what being a member entails (e.g., activities, rules). For instance, if you belong to 4-H, the school swim team, a band, are a Baptist, etc., what characterizes your group membership and what's important to that membership? After you have your list, get in a group with your classmates that have also made up their own list. Start with one person and see what the other members know about the group each person belongs to. What are the things the group member knows that other classmates who aren't members don't know? What do the responses you hear from others about your group tell you about stereotypes?

3. Some people will argue that all stereotypes are bad. Are stereotypes all bad? What are some positive stereotypes? Do stereotypes have to be good or bad?

4. The June 2015 story about Rachel Dolezal, a Spokane, Washington, leader in the NAACP, began a national conversation about how people present their identities. In the same month, the Pew Research Center released a report on being multiracial in America. How is identity, across one's lifespan, fluid? Can your identity, across fault lines, change over the course of your lifetime? What does that say about who we are? How does learning about this change your approach to journalism or strategic communication?

▶ ADDITIONAL READINGS

El Nasser, Haya. "Census Rethinks Hispanic on Questionnaire." *USA Today*. Last modified January 4, 2013. http://www.usatoday.com/story/news/nation/2013/01/03/hispanics-may-be-added-to-census-race-category/1808087/.

Elliott, Stuart. "An American Family Returns to the Table." *New York Times*. Last modified January 28, 2014. http://www.nytimes.com/2014/01/29/business/media/an-american-family-returns-to-the-table.html?ref=business&_r=2.

Fazio, Russell H., Joni R. Jackson, Bridget C. Dunton and Carol J. Williams. "Variability in Automatic Activation as an Unobtrusive Measure of Racial Attitudes: A Bona Fide Pipeline?" *Journal of Personality and Social Psychology* 69, no. 6 (1995): 1013.

Macrae, C. Neil, Alan B. Milne and Galen V. Bodenhausen. "Stereotypes as Energy-Saving Devices: A Peek Inside the Cognitive Toolbox." *Journal of Personality and Social Psychology* 66, no. 1 (1994): 37.

Macrae, C. Neil, Miles Hewstone and Riana J. Griffiths. "Processing Load and Memory for Stereotype-Based Information." *European Journal of Social Psychology* 23, no. 1 (1993): 77–87.

Mead, George Herbert. *Mind, Self, and Society*. Chicago: At the University Press, 1955 [1934].

"Multiracial in America: Proud, Diverse and Growing in Numbers," Pew Research Center, Washington, DC: June 2015. http://www.pewsocialtrends.org/2015/06/11/multiracial-in-america/.

Payne, B. Keith, Clara Michelle Cheng, Olesya Govorun and Brandon D. Stewart. "An Inkblot for Attitudes: Affect Misattribution as Implicit Measurement." *Journal of Personality and Social Psychology* 89, no. 3 (2005): 277.

Powers, Rod. "US Military Enlistment Standards." *About Careers*. Last modified 2014. http://usmilitary.about.com/od/joiningthemilitary/a/enlcitizen.html.

▶ NOTES

1 Alberto Bisin and Thierry Verdier, " 'Beyond the Melting Pot': Cultural Transmission, Marriage, and the Evolution of Ethnic and Religious Traits," *Quarterly Journal of Economics* (2000): 955.

2 Leana B. Gloor, "From the Melting Pot to the Tossed Salad Metaphor: Why Coercive Assimilation Lacks the Flavors that Americans Crave," *HoHoNu: The Journal of Academic Writing for UK Hilo and Hawaii Community College* 4.1 (2006). Web. 25. Jan. 2012. https://spelee07.wordpress.com/2011/07/30/a-melting-pot-or-a-tossed-salad/.

3 Henri Tajfel, Michael G. Billig, Robert P. Bundy and Claude Flament, "Social Categorization and Intergroup Behaviour," *European Journal of Social Psychology* 1, no. 2 (1971): 149–178.

4 Marilynn B. Brewer, "The Social Psychology of Intergroup Relations: Social Categorization, In-group Bias, and Out-group Prejudice," in *Social Psychology: Handbook of Basic Principles*, ed. Arie Kruglanski and E. Tory Higgins (New York: Guilford, 2007) 695–715.

5 Ibid.; James L. Hilton and William Von Hippel, "Stereotypes," *Annual Review of Psychology* 47, no. 1 (1996): 237–271; C. Neil Macrae and Galen V. Bodenhausen, "Social Cognition: Categorical Person Perception," *British Journal of Psychology* 92, no. 1 (2001): 239–255.

6 Gordon W. Allport, *The Nature of Prejudice*, (Cambridge, MA: Addison-Wesley, 1954).

7 John F. Dovidio, Nancy Evans and Richard B. Tyler, "Racial Stereotypes: The Contents of their Cognitive Representations," *Journal of Experimental Social Psychology* 22, no. 1 (1986): 22–37.

8 John A. Bargh and Tanya L. Chartrand, "The Unbearable Automaticity of Being," *American Psychologist* 54, no. 7 (1999): 462; Galen Bodenhausen and Neil Macrae, "Stereotype Activation and Inhibition," in *Stereotype Activation and Inhibition: Advances in Social Cognition*, ed. Robert S. Wyer Jr. (Mahwah, NJ: Erlbaum, 1998) 1–52; Patricia G. Devine, "Stereotypes and Prejudice: Their Automatic and Controlled Components," *Journal of Personality and Social Psychology* 56, no. 1 (1989): 5; Patricia G. Devine and Andrew J. Elliot, "Are Racial Stereotypes Really Fading? The Princeton Trilogy Revisited," *Personality and Social Psychology Bulletin* 21 (1995): 1139–1150; Stephanie Madon, Max Guyll, Kathy Aboufadel, Eulices Montiel, Alison Smith, Polly Palumbo and Lee Jussim, "Ethnic and National Stereotypes: The Princeton Trilogy Revisited and Revised," *Personality and Social Psychology Bulletin* 27, no. 8 (2001): 996–1010.

9 Allport, *The Nature of Prejudice*.

10 *PBS*, http://www.pbs.org/wgbh/pages/frontline/shows/divided/

11 Steve Stroessner and Catherine Good, "Stereotype Threat: An Overview. Excerpts And Adaptations From Reducing Stereotype Threat.Org," last modified 2011, http://diversity.arizona.edu/sites/diversity/files/stereotype_threat_overview.pdf.

12 "Robert C. Maynard: Life and Legacy," *Maynard Institute*, last modified 2014, http://mije.org/robertmaynard.

13 Laurance J. Splitter, "Questioning the Citizenship Industry," *Journal of Social Science Education* 10, no. 1 (2011).

14 "U.S. Citizenship," U.S. Citizenship and Immigration Services, last modified 2013, http://www.uscis.gov/us-citizenship.

15 Mead, George Herbert. 1955 [1934]. *Mind, Self, and Society*. Chicago: At the University Press; Slobodan Drakulic, "Whence Nationalism?" *Nations and Nationalism* 14, no. 2 (2008): 386.

16 Augie Fleras and Jean Leonard Elliott, *Unequal Relations: An Introduction to Race, Ethnic and Aboriginal Dynamics in Canada* (Prentice Hall, Canada, 1999); Isik Urla Zeitinoglu and Jacinta Khasiala Muteshi, "Gender, Race and Class Dimensions of Nonstandard Work," *Relations Industrielles/Industrial Relations* (2000): 133–167; Sharon M. Lee, "Racial Classifications in the US Census: 1890–1990," *Ethnic and Racial Studies* 16, no. 1 (1993): 75–94; Pierre L. van den Berghe, *Race and Ethnicity: Essays in Comparative Sociology* (New York: Basic Books, 1970).

17 Richard D. Alba, "The Twilight of Ethnicity among Americans of European Ancestry: The Case of Italians," *Ethnic and Racial Studies* 8, no. 1 (1985): 134–158; Richard D. Alba, *Ethnic Identity: The Transformation of White America* (New Haven, CT: Yale University Press, 1990); Olga I. Davis, Thomas K. Nakayama and Judith N. Martin, "Current and Future Directions in Ethnicity and Methodology," *International Journal of Intercultural Relations* 24, no. 5 (2000): 525–539; George Dearborn Spindler and Louise S. Spindler, *The American Cultural Dialogue and its Transmission* (The Falmer Press: Bristol, PA, 1990).

18 U.S. Census Bureau, last modified 2014, www.census.gov.

19 Lee, "Racial Classifications in the US Census: 1890–1990," 76.

20 Ibid.

21 "State & County QuickFacts," U.S. Census Bureau, last modified 2014, http://quickfacts.census.gov/qfd/states/00000.html.

22 "Major Differences in Subject-Matter Content Between the 1990 and 2000 Census Questionnaires," *U.S. Census Bureau: Population*, last modified 2010, http://www.census.gov/population/www/cen2000/90vs00/.

23 Merarys Ríos, Fabián Romero and Roberto Ramírez, "Race Reporting Among Hispanics: 2010," U.S. Census Bureau, last modified 2014, https://www.census.gov/population/www/documentation/twps0102/twps0102.pdf.

24 U.S. Census Bureau, "State & County QuickFacts."

25 Rios et al., "Race Reporting Among Hispanics: 2010."

26 Ibid.

27 Ibid.

28 "U.S. Census Bureau Projections Show a Slower Growing, Older, More Diverse Nation a Half Century from Now," Newsroom, U.S. Census Bureau, last modified 2012, https://www.census.gov/newsroom/releases/archives/population/cb12–243.html.

29 http://projects.nytimes.com/census/2010/explorer?ref=censusbureau.

30 Mark Hugo Lopez, "In 2014, Latinos Will Surpass Whites as Largest Racial/Ethnic group in California," Pew Research Center, last modified January 24, 2014, http://www.pewresearch.

org/fact-tank/2014/01/24/in-2014-latinos-will-surpass-whites-as-largest-racialethnic-group-in-california/.

31 Ibid.

32 Ibid.

33 Hope Yen, "Census: White Majority in U.S. Gone by 2043," *NBC News*, last modified June 13, 2013, http://usnews.nbcnews.com/_news/2013/06/13/18934111-census-white-majority-in-us-gone-by-2043?lite.

34 Yen, 2013

35 Paul Taylor, Wendy Wang, Kim Parker, Jeffrey S. Passel, Eileen Patten and Seth Motel, "The Rise of Intermarriage: Rates, Characteristics Vary by Race and Gender," Pew Research Center, Last modified February 16, 2012, http://www.pewsocialtrends.org/files/2012/02/SDT-Intermarriage-II.pdf.

36 Sherri Grasmuck, Jason Martin and Shanyang Zhao, "Ethno-Racial Identity Displays on Facebook," *Journal of Computer-Mediated Communication* 15, no. 1 (2009): 158–188; Stephen Knadler, "e-Racing Difference in e-Space: Black Female Subjectivity and the Web-Based Portfolio," *Computers and Composition* 18, no. 3 (2001): 235–255; S. Kretchmer and Rod Carveth, "The Color of the Net: African Americans, Race, and Cyberspace," *Computers and Society* 31, no. 3 (2001): 9–14; Heidi McKee, " 'Your Views Showed True Ignorance!!!':(Mis)Communication in an Online Interracial Discussion Forum," *Computers and Composition* 19, no. 4 (2002): 411–434.

37 Grasmuck et al., "Ethno-Racial Identity Displays on Facebook"; Knadler, "e-Racing Difference in e-Space: Black Female Subjectivity and the Web-Based Portfolio."

38 Saleem Alhabash, Kayla Hales, Jong-hwan Baek and Hyun Jung Oh, "Effects of Race, Visual Anonymity, and Social Category Salience on Online Dating Outcomes," *Computers in Human Behavior* 35 (2014): 22–32.

PART TWO
Application

4

Making Class Matter: Journalism and Social Class

Ryan J. Thomas and Marina A. Hendricks

"She is a class act."

"He has no class."

"Those guys are working-class heroes."

From where we sit on airplanes to the people we choose as friends, class consciously or subconsciously plays an integral role in our lives. Every U.S. election cycle, we hear candidates for public office constantly invoke the fabled American "middle class" as they vie for votes from the widest possible segment of the population. It is no wonder, then, that "class has a pervasive influence on the way we live, work, and think."[1]

When you think about social class, what comes to mind? Income? Wealth? Power? Status? Material goods? This is a matter that has perplexed economists and sociologists for decades. But the questions don't stop there. What are the classes, and how many are there? How do people move between classes?

This chapter begins with an overview of social class in the United States, exploring the reasons why Americans are uncomfortable talking about it as well as how class mobility is embedded in the national identity. We examine the problems in defining class, and trace the evolution of the U.S. class system. From there,

LEARNING OBJECTIVES

By the end of this chapter, you should be able to:

- understand social class and how it has evolved in the United States over time.

- acknowledge the many influences of social class on your community.

- recognize how perceptions of social class influence news coverage.

- apply your awareness of social class to your communication career.

we look at why class matters in the United States and how it touches upon every aspect of our lives—jobs, homes, health, education, safety, community and much more.

This overview leads to a frank assessment of journalism's role in shaping perceptions of social class: portraying the elite as "just like us"; neglecting coverage of poverty; focusing on personal (not collective) responsibility for welfare and other issues; and overlooking worker perspectives in reporting on labor issues. We conclude with a call for realistic coverage of social class, and how journalists can accomplish that.

▶ SOCIAL CLASS AND THE AMERICAN DREAM

Social class in the United States has been described as "the most unmentionable of topics"[2] and "one of America's best-kept secrets."[3] Why is social class so *difficult* to talk about?

Part of the problem may lay in the mythos surrounding the United States itself and the promise it holds. The "American dream," a term coined by the historian James Truslow Adams,[4] has fueled for generations the belief in upward mobility—the ability to move from one social class to another. The American dream pivots on the belief that anyone, regardless of background, origin or obstacle, can "make it" and achieve success in the United States, with the right combination of hard work and perseverance. The American dream is the promise of equal and unlimited opportunities for those bold enough to grasp them. Such rewards are typically thought to include "financial security, home ownership, family, higher educational levels (leading to upward mobility), greater opportunities and rewards for the next generation (compared with the present generation), a successful career, freedom, happiness, and a comfortable retirement."[5]

How accurate is this? A cynic might agree with the late comedian George Carlin, who once said, "That's why they call it the American dream; you have to be asleep to believe it." Let's look at the history to try to make sense of this.

If we look at the history of social class in the United States, we start to see some patterns emerge. Mass industrialization after the Civil War propelled a shift from rural to urban life, a move into occupational specialization and an immigration wave to meet the labor demands of emerging corporations.[6] Until then, upper classes were defined by economic drivers particular to areas of the country—for example, shipbuilding in New England, plantation farming in the South and mining in the West. As the United States industrialized, a working class emerged—much of it made up of immigrants—employed in manufacturing, mining, utilities and transportation, as well as a white-collar middle class of salaried professionals, salespeople and office workers.[7]

Until approximately 1945, class structure in the United States was a locked system, where—generally speaking—the class you were born into was the class you remained in until you died. The Great Depression deepened the gap between those on the top and those on the bottom ends of the class structure. This changed after the World War II, as America's middle class expanded, wages trended upward and working-class individuals were afforded access to higher education and thus access to more traditionally prestigious jobs.[8] This period, lasting until roughly the end of the 1970s, bolstered the strength of the American dream "as a cultural ideal among members of virtually all social classes."[9]

Since then, however, upward mobility has been much more limited. Between 1977 and 2007, the income of families at the 99th percentile increased by 90 percent. By contrast, the income of those at the bottom 20th percentile increased by 7 percent.[10] U.S. Census Bureau data reveals that incomes have not kept pace with economic growth; while the median household income in the United States rose from $47,000 in 1980 to $51,000 in 2012, the median income of the top 0.1 percent shot up from $730,000 to $1.9 million over the same period, holding constant for inflation.[11] Data from the Demos think tank reveal that the top 10 percent of white families own an astonishing 65 percent of all wealth in the United States.[12] These are not natural phenomena, by the way, but the result of choices made by those with power. (See Figure 4.1.)

Yet the American dream endures. In part, this is because of its seductive, alluring nature. Who *wouldn't* want to live in a society where there is equal opportunity for all? Think of the references you see and hear to a "self-made man," a person who has "pulled himself up by his bootstraps" or embodies a "Protestant work ethic." This is the American dream in action. However, the currency of journalism is not dreams but *facts*. Journalism has a mission to explain the *realities* of lived experience and do so in a thorough, accurate and informative manner.

 BOX 4.1   From the Field: Class Conflict

When news reports about a young black man shot dead by a white police officer first began filtering out from Ferguson, Missouri, in the summer of 2014, Todd C. Frankel (writer, *The Washington Post*) had recently moved from St. Louis to the nation's capital to report on politics and policy for *The Washington Post*.

Frankel, who had just concluded a lengthy stint as a reporter for the *St. Louis Post-Dispatch*, quickly wrote a piece for *The Washington Post* to provide context for the outraged response to the shooting of 18-year-old Michael Brown.

Todd C. Frankel   (Continued)

Box 4.1 Continued

"What I knew from having been there for a decade was that these suburbs out-side of St. Louis don't identify as much with the term 'Ferguson' as they identify with the term 'St. Louis.' So a lot of the people who were upset and protesting and angry and getting quoted were not from Ferguson," he said. "The anger and upset was much wider than that town. It was representative of a challenge that the region faces."

It's not only a regional challenge, Frankel said, but also a national one—and it ultimately comes down to class.

"We like to believe that America is classless and all, but it's to me the dominant issue right now," Frankel said. "What happened in Ferguson was a class issue, right? Most of the stories at some point seem to play up through a class prism. . . . We're hesitant to talk about that. The right talks about 'class warfare.' We're shut-ting down that debate. And no one wants to think that they're a member of a cer-tain class. But we are, and it's important to acknowledge that."

Yet rather than cover the full spectrum of class, journalists typically are drawn to the margins.

"We tend to focus on the very rich and the very poor—the extremes," Frankel said. "And so you hear a lot of talk about the middle class, but you don't have quite as much coverage of the middle class. And it's also a very nebulous term, right? What is middle class?"

Contrast that with the struggles of the poor, which are easier to identify.

"The most obvious class, quite frankly, is the poor people, the people who are struggling," Frankel said. "The conflict there is attractive [for reporters], whereas the conflict of this day-to-day survival when you're doing OK but you're not hurt-ing horribly, like the middle class, is tougher to see."

In an era of "explainer journalism" that demands broad, easy explanations, he said coverage of class requires going beyond the surface.

"Things are shades of gray, right? The world's actually more complicated, not less. There's no good answer. You try and get to some sort of truth, try to be cog-nizant of these different things playing out, these class issues.

"It's complicated," he repeated, with emphasis.

▶ CLASS IN THE UNITED STATES

We can see there are distinctions between and among people of different classes—we know this from where they live, how they live, what they wear and what they own. Where this becomes much trickier, however, is outlining the dividing lines between classes—where one class "ends" and another "begins." There is no single answer to the question of how many classes there are in American society (or any other society) and different scholars have different perspectives on the issue.

This problem is compounded by our perception of ourselves. By definition, a class structure is hierarchical, indicating that some have more than others have. We may perceive there to be a stigma or shame with being on the lower end of the class structure. Perhaps this is why we say "working class" instead of "lower class"! A quote often attributed to the author John Steinbeck talks of how, in the United States, "the poor see themselves not as an exploited proletariat but as temporarily embarrassed millionaires." Public polling reveals that most Americans consider themselves to be middle class.[13] However, if the middle class extends from John, who is making $100,000 a year and considering buying a second car, to Jane, who is working two jobs but still struggling to make payments on her first, we are clearly dealing with some definitional issues.

Let's talk specifics. We use here a model by the sociologists Earl Wysong, Robert Perrucci and David Wright.[14] Their model comprises two classes: a *privileged class* comprising of roughly 20 percent of the population, and a *"new working class"* comprising roughly 80 percent of the population. They developed their model to address the changes in the class structure since the late 1970s, when class mobility started to stagnate. Their model is broken down further as follows:

 BOX 4.2   Class Strata

PRIVILEGED CLASS (20 PERCENT)

Super class (1–2 percent)

Owners, employers and senior executives. Income from investments, business ownership and senior management in large firms; incomes from upper seven- to nine-figure levels; exceptional consumption and investment capital.

Credentialed class; Managers (9–11 percent)

CEOs and mid- and upper-level managers of mid-size corporations and public organizations. Incomes from top seven-figure range among CEOs and upper-level managers in six figures.

Credentialed class; Professionals (12–14 percent)

(Continued)

Box 4.2 Continued

> *Possess credentialed skill in form of college and professional degrees. Use of social capital and organizational ties to advance interests. Incomes from $200K to upper-six figures.*

NEW WORKING CLASS (80 PERCENT)

Comfort class (14–16 percent)

> *Nurses, teachers, civil servants, owners of very small businesses and skilled/ unionized workers such as machinists or electricians. Incomes in the $40K–80K range but little investment capital.*

Contingent class; Wage earners (44–46 percent)

> *Work for wages in clerical and sales jobs, personal services and transportation as truck drivers, clerks and machine operators. Members of this group are often college graduates. Incomes at $40K and lower.*

Contingent class; Self-employed (3–4 percent)

> *Usually self-employed with no employees, or family workers. Very modest incomes with high potential for failure.*

Excluded class (10–15 percent)

> *In and out of the labor force in a variety of unskilled, temporary and low-wage jobs. Incomes at $15K–20K.*

As you can see, the majority of people in this model fall into the contingent, wage-earning class. However, you will continually meet people from every level of the model, which is why it's essential to be mindful of how the contemporary class structure plays out in your community—and whose stories might receive only cursory attention or be overlooked entirely. For journalists, the challenge lies in digging deep for the stories that reflect and represent all members of a community.

Economic data indicate that it remains very difficult to transcend the gap between classes.[15] The developers of the model used here suggest that current trends indicate a return to a society where your background at birth is the "primary determinant of class rank for life."[16] They note the "disappearing middle class" as a key feature of the current class structure.[17]

Data released by the U.S. Census Bureau in the fall of 2013 illustrated a striking gap between the uppermost class and those below it. It found that incomes had stagnated for the majority of Americans for over a decade (Figure 4.1).

> The census report found that median household income, adjusted for inflation, was $51,017 in 2012, down about 9 percent from an inflation-adjusted peak of $56,080 in 1999, mostly as a result of the longest and most damaging recession since the Depression. Most people have had no gains since the economy hit bottom in 2009. The government's authoritative annual report on incomes, poverty and health insurance . . . underscores that the economic recovery has largely failed to reach the poor and the middle class, even as the unemployment rate continues to sink and growth has returned.[18]

Furthermore, it might surprise you to learn that more than 46 million people in the United States were living in poverty in 2012—15 percent of the population.[19]

So, that's where we stand in terms of structure. Things could change, but they might not. That's an issue for politicians, not journalists. What should journalists do? Let's talk first about why class matters.

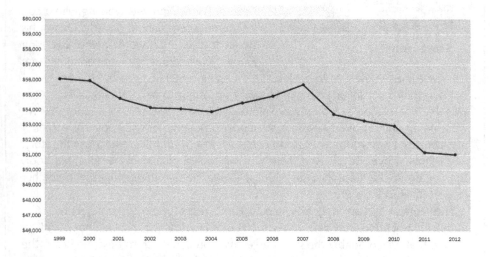

FIGURE 4.1 U.S. Median Household Income, 1999-2012
Data source: U.S. Census Bureau, Current Population Survey, Annual Social and Economic Supplements, www.census.gov/hhes/www/income/data/historical/household; Graphic by Amanda Knowles

FOR DISCUSSION

1. How does the contemporary class structure play out in your community? Can you provide examples of people who fit each level? Where do you and your classmates fit into the picture?

2. What are the realities of the American dream in your community? As a journalist, how would you report on them?

3. Have you used food stamps or encountered someone doing so? With your classmates, talk about how that made you feel.

 BOX 4.3   From the Field: Words Matter

Scott Finn

Scott Finn, executive director and CEO of West Virginia Public Broadcasting, still remembers a source's negative reaction to a story he wrote early in his career.

Then a reporter with *The Charleston Gazette* (WV), Finn was working with a colleague on a series about poverty. One of his stories focused on a woman who was using a newly created bus route to commute from her home in a remote area to her job at a shopping center in a nearby county.

"Two things conspired to make this very upsetting to her," Finn recalled. "One was that I had failed to properly explain that this story was part of a series that we were doing about poverty—about solutions to poverty, but still poverty. I think it was because I was young, I was kind of embarrassed, I didn't want to lose the story, and I glossed over it. . . . And then two, we took a picture of her kids, barefoot, running down the road, that ran with the story. The two things together made her infuriated—just so angry."

The woman also strongly objected to Finn's use of a particular adjective. "She said, 'I am not poor. How dare you use that word to describe me. I am not poor.' . . . To her, that was probably the worst adjective you could use to describe her in the universe. She would have accepted anything else but that."

(Continued)

BOX 4.3 Continued

Finn learned something from the experience that has stayed with him through his transition from reporter to news director to head of the Mountain State's public radio and television operation.

"It was a lesson in how nobody considers themselves poor—nobody," said Finn, who also worked at WUSF in Tampa, Florida. "And that is almost a more powerful pejorative than anything else you can think of to call somebody. And also, [it's] just the realization that how difficult it is to cover these things honestly, to cover this issue honestly."

He likened the woman's frustration in not having power over how she was portrayed to the frustration that West Virginians feel when stories in national media outlets do not accurately represent them.

"It's the people who are in power who get to choose how everyone else is portrayed," Finn said. "And that lack of feeling the ability to tell your own story in the way that you want it told; that's where the anger comes from. . . . I think there are lots of opportunities to give low-income people the resources to tell part of the story themselves. It doesn't mean that you totally abdicate all responsibility for telling the story. Truth be told, sometimes you might have to say things that the people you're covering don't like to hear, but it's true, or necessary.

"There is the need for us to face up to unpleasant things—all of us. But what I'm saying is that I think the power is way too much in the hands of the powerful, and we could all do a better job . . . of trying to empower the people to tell their own stories."

The bottom line? What you write—and the way you write it—matters, Finn said. "Every once in a while, before [you] push send, just look at it twice and think about it."

▶ WHY CLASS MATTERS

Class matters because it is so pervasive; it impacts everything we do, and everything we are *able* to do. To quote one scholar, "saying that class is about money is the same as saying that ethnicity is about skin color."[20] Class is about much more than just money. Practically from birth, our perceptions about social class are shaped first by family and friends, and then by teachers and co-workers. These perceptions are further influenced by the neighborhoods in which we live, the schools we attend, the jobs we hold and the activities we pursue in our spare time. Down to the clothes we wear and the mode of transportation we use, class matters. One of the reasons why class is considered one of the major fault lines is because it surrounds us and informs everything we do (and are able to do).

Empirical research indicates that income inequality correlates with an array of quality-of-life indices, including physical health, mental health, drug abuse, education, imprisonment, obesity, social mobility, violence, teenage pregnancies and child wellbeing.[21] Journalists deal with such topics on a regular basis. Authentic, proportional and accurate coverage of these and other vital community issues illustrates why class matters.

Journalists can help bridge the gap between the classes by shedding light on the societal and economic forces that combine to alienate communities. A better understanding of why class matters benefits all citizens, regardless of where—and how—they live.

FOR DISCUSSION

1. How do your perceptions of social class differ from those of your peers?

2. Think of the ways that social class affects the opportunities you have (and do not have). As a group, share and reflect on ways that social class has influenced your life.

 BOX 4.4   From the Field: "It's Important to be Respectful"

Rebecca Catalanello

When you think about it, class can permeate most of the issues we cover as journalists, whether we acknowledge it or not: crime, education, health, religion and the environment. By tuning into the impact of financial and social circumstance on a person's mindset, perspective and experience, you can find yourself asking better questions and looking for larger context that can inform a story.

A rate hike in the federally funded free and reduced-price lunch program in schools may seem insignificant on its surface. But talk to a parent whose children qualify and you may find that another 25 cents per meal per student is a significant challenge, especially when put in the context of what the family already earns and where they must spend their money. All it takes is finding and speaking with someone who is affected.

(Continued)

BOX 4.4 Continued

A man challenges police to "Shoot me!" in a confrontation following a store robbery. After he is shot, his family and community express outrage. To some, the reaction lacks understanding. But ask more about his history of police encounters and you learn that not only he but also members of his family and community have had numerous interactions with police that they feel were antagonistic and unfair. Talk to them, get those stories and share that context.

One thing that's hard, but so worth the effort, is finding the voices of people outside your own personal social sphere. It can be a lot easier to listen to people in power or the people who are more like you—they're the ones with the jobs and, usually, the ones holding the microphones.

I found a story while trying to learn more about the state of mental health services in New Orleans. In the process of asking local activists about the issue, one of them invited me to a new home for indigent mental health patients with no other place to go. It wasn't until I was in that place and talking to those patients and residents that I began to feel I had a clearer understanding of the complexities facing people who are mentally ill, especially when their illness exiles them from jobs and family, leaving them destitute, hopeless and incredibly vulnerable.

We got a tip about a visiting college student who was tossed out of a Subway in the French Quarter after offering to buy a homeless man a sandwich. We couldn't find the homeless man, but we confirmed the incident happened.

The story could easily have been ignored. But I tuned into it and pursued it because I felt it was an important story about the intersection of the complications of being a business owner in the French Quarter coupled with tourism, idealism and the realities of homelessness in New Orleans. Though a small moment, I felt it was important to discuss—and it touched off enough of a nerve that it generated lots of online discussion and inspired us to hold an online chat with an advocate for people who are homeless.

When covering matters in which differences in social class clearly play a role, it's important to be respectful. People are people. No matter where they come from, what they do, how they live, no one person's experience is more or less valid than another's. The Golden Rule is incredibly useful in your work as a journalist: Treat others as you want to be treated, whether they're making six figures or three.

Rebecca Catalanello is now assistant director of publications and communications at the University of New Orleans. Previously, she reported on health care for two years for NOLA.com and The Times-Picayune in New Orleans. She also spent nine years covering education and crime for the *Tampa Bay Times* (FL), and also has worked at *The Lens* in New Orleans, the *Charleston Daily Mail* (WV) and the *Press-Register* in Mobile, Alabama.

▶ JOURNALISM AND SOCIAL CLASS

Let's recall the foundations of excellent journalism discussed in Chapter 1 of this text-book: context, complexity, voices, proportionality and authenticity. How does this pertain to coverage of class?

Context

Excellent journalism puts social issues into context with respect to the local community. It provides audiences with the necessary historical, economic, cultural and political know-how for them to understand an event better. Events do not occur in isolation but are shaped by prior events and impact subsequent events in turn. Acknowledging this can enrich our journalism. Context provides the audience with the knowledge they need to make an informed opinion.

Consider the "5 W's" of journalism: Who, What, When, Where, and Why? Answering each of these questions about an event you are reporting on is among the first things you are likely to do as you try to make sense of what it is you are covering. But notice that each of them lends itself to what education researchers call "higher-order thinking." If we consider the 5 W's together rather than in isolation, we can start to see what we mean about context, as we connect events to other events, subjects to other subjects, issues to other issues.

It is sometimes said that "journalism is the first draft of history," and there's some truth to that. When you think of what historians do, they don't simply report what has happened. They give that event meaningfulness so the audience knows the full history and can place that event into a broader narrative. This means that the journalists need to know the topic they are covering intimately, which can be done through significant research and conversations with community members.

Complexity

Excellent journalism comes from a mindset that realizes that there are no simple answers in a massively complex world. It comes from recognizing how class intersects with issues of race and gender, and understanding the deeply complex history of inequality in the United States. We shouldn't shy away from complexity, even when the facts are uncomfortable. In fact, we ought to *embrace* uncomfortable facts because that is the essence of the learning process. This means we shouldn't see journalism as simply a set of skills but a commitment to broadening our intellectual horizons so that we can craft journalism informed by a richer understanding of history, economics and public policy, for example.

Nobody is saying this is easy, by the way! Kevin Fagan of the *San Francisco Chronicle* invokes the word "messy" when talking about reporting on tough issues. "The trouble with reporting about poverty for most news outlets is that it is messy. It always has been," writes Fagan. "Poverty reporting comes automatically freighted with left-and-right wing arguments that paint the economic landscape in black and white terms and sling contrasting statistics and anecdote-driven contentions to prove their points," Fagan notes. "You have to give them all attention, sorting through the mountains of official and unofficial accounts to get to some bedrock facts."[22]

Scholars have argued that all too often, news coverage provides "little guidance in reconciling the conflicting emotions toward poverty embedded within American culture, with its simultaneously sympathetic and impatient assumption that America offers the promise of escape from poverty to all who work hard."[23] Journalists tend to report on issues involving poverty and inequality in a manner that stresses individual problems and individual solutions.[24] This means that more systemic issues go under-reported and the public tend to "blame the victim" rather than look to structural solutions.

This is not to say that journalism is consistently terrible at dealing with these issues—far from it! A more than yearlong investigation by *The New York Times* led to *Class Matters*, a comprehensive look at the economic, education, employment, social status, lifestyle, family dynamics and other issues at work in the nation's class structure. The series, researched and written by a team of reporters, was first published in the newspaper (accessible online at http://www.nytimes.com/national/class/) in the spring of 2005 and later compiled into a book. "In a country where the overwhelming majority of people identify themselves in polls as 'middle class,' there seemed to be no consensus as to what class meant, let along whether it mattered," Bill Keller writes in the introduction to the book.[25]

During the year the series was in production, Keller notes that he talked regularly in speeches and interviews "about what seemed to me a worrying decline in the credibility of the news media."[26] Reasons for this decline include media scandals, public skepticism and political partisanship. However, underneath it all lies "the way we have retreated from the hard labor of journalism under grinding commercial pressure, the steady downsizing and dumbing down, the pandering, the substitution of dueling blowhards and celebrity gossip for actual reporting."[27] He offers a solution: "more ambitious journalism." Specifically, that means, "launching the best reporters at the hardest subjects, and holding their reporting and thinking to the highest standards."[28] So, embracing complexity means going beyond two-dimensional storytelling and getting at the multi-faceted nature of the world we live in.

Voices

Excellent journalism brings to light the lived experience of those affected by a given issue. Journalism, at its most basic level, is a series of choices, including choices about whose voices to include and exclude. Such choices are part of the process of doing journalism, and shouldn't be feared. But we should aim to ensure that the voices we include add something important to our reporting; in other words, we should have good journalistic reasons for who is included and excluded.

We want to ensure as many voices as possible are included in our journalism. "One-and-done" coverage of a societal concern results in audience perception being framed by the limited perspectives of the journalist telling the story and the person or group chosen to illustrate it. By relying on the voice of one rather than the voices of many, journalists run the risk of putting biased and incomplete information out there for public consumption. "When the media frame stories in such a way as to emphasize the shortcomings of the poor or homeless," Diana Kendall maintains, "those who are better off may conclude that these less fortunate individuals have created their own problems."[29]

Ensuring that we have a range of voices in our journalism is a way of ensuring that we are accurately representing the communities we serve.

Proportionality

Excellent journalism is proportional. This means in coverage terms we don't "over-egg" something by covering it more than it needs to be covered (this is the fast track to sensationalism), but it also means we don't ignore something that needs to be covered. This is a tricky balancing act and there is no exact formula to resolve it. The solution comes in knowing your community, your audience, and the values of excellent journalism, and developing solid journalism accordingly.

Proportionality also means that we don't draw false equivalencies that ignore or gloss over differences in life opportunities. A story from the *Reuters* news service featured the headline "Recession, bear markets hit the rich, too" and the lead "Turns out the rich may not be so different from you and me: They too are falling behind on their mortgages."[30] Published two years after the 2008 economic crisis, the article looked at trends in foreclosures of homes worth $5 million or more. The story noted how "growing numbers of well-heeled Americans, their portfolios hammered by depressed markets, have stopped repaying loans or even walked away from mortgages." Is this proportional to the actual reality? How might such a story be viewed by less affluent readers who are spending their modest savings or cashing in their retirement plans in order to keep their homes after losing their jobs? What are the consequences to society when the rich walk away from their mortgages?

Authenticity

Excellent journalism must be an authentic representation of life. Journalism is a bridge that connects members of a community to one another, helping audience members on one side of town know what's occurring on the other side of the tracks. Journalism can only be that bridge if it is built on a bedrock of authenticity. "Journalism's first obligation is to the truth," veteran journalists Bill Kovach and Tom Rosenstiel write in *The Elements of Journalism: What Newspeople Should Know and the Public Should Expect*. Ultimately, journalism "attempts to get at the truth in a confused world by first stripping information of any attached misinformation, disinformation, or self-promoting bias and then letting the community react . . . The search for truth becomes a conversation."[31]

In *Nickel and Dimed: On Not Getting By in America*, Barbara Ehrenreich recounted the results of her field experiment in living on minimum-wage earnings. Ehrenreich, a columnist and author with a Ph.D. in cell biology, put her life and career on hold to wait tables, clean houses and motel rooms, feed nursing-home patients and stock women's clothing at Wal-Mart.[32] Diana Kendall identifies growing poverty of the working class as a theme looked at by journalists and academics alike "through the lens of people who are employed full-time but cannot make ends meet."[33] She cites *Nickel and Dimed* and other books as sparking stories in this vein: "The attention the media gave these books through reviews, reprints of excerpts, author interviews, and other commentaries turned the subject of the working poor, at least temporarily, into a hot topic."[34] Without such books, Kendall maintains, there would be less coverage of the working poor and less knowledge of the issues they face. "Through media framing of stories about this group and the increasing problem of long-term unemployment, journalists provide media audiences with information and explode myths that have perpetuated and exacerbated economic and social inequalities in this country for many years."[35]

Kendall singles out Ehrenreich and *Nickel and Dimed* for raising awareness of causes other than personal responsibility, noting that the book "provides more anecdotal evidence, based on her personal journey as a low-wage worker, to suggest that corporate greed and other societal factors, rather than the behavior of the working poor, should be blamed for their economic condition."[36] In addition, Kendall mentions the contention of Ehrenreich and others that people can be "too poor to make the news."[37]

Putting This Together

Context, complexity, voices, proportionality and authenticity are essential ingredients to excellent journalism. Don't think of them as separate things; they relate to one another and support one another. In order to have context, you certainly need voices. When you are considering voices, you definitely need to take proportionality into account. Avoid simplistic "check the box" thinking and make your journalism the best possible journalism it can be.

There are many examples of journalism that achieves this. The Journalism Center on Children and Families (www.journalismcenter.org) offered an annual awards program, the Casey Medals for Meritorious Journalism, from 1994 to 2013. Each year's list of winners featured journalists from media outlets of all sizes. Among the 2013 winners was photojournalist April Saul of the *Philadelphia Enquirer*, whose work focused on Camden, New Jersey. "The judges praised her tenacity and grace in capturing the tragic consequences of living in persistent poverty, but also the hope and joy found in the community."[38] David Sarasohn of *The Oregonian* won for a series of columns on child hunger that "put a human face on a shocking statistic and illustrated the real social cost of hunger."[39] Katie Falkenberg and Mary Vignoles of the *Los Angeles Times* were honored for a long-form video on families struggling to recover from the economic downturn. Their "stunningly beautiful, intimate look at the impact of the recession . . . reveals the strain on relationships of rapid downward mobility and snowballing personal debt."[40] The *Milwaukee Journal Sentinel* was lauded for a yearlong investigation into infant mortality in neighborhoods "where babies born in Botswana stand a better chance of survival."[41] The judges praised reporters for "eloquent writing and enormous skill and compassion in interviews with bereaved young families and for integrating science, public health, economics [and] sociology in their reporting."[42]

These exemplify the best ideals of journalistic excellence as applied to issues of social class. Remember that as a journalist you bear a lot of power, which comes with a lot of responsibility.

FOR DISCUSSION

1. Find a class-related story in a local news outlet. Does it include the foundations of excellent journalism (context, complexity, voices, proportionality, authenticity)? Why or why not?

2. As a journalist, what could you do to bridge the gap between classes? Are there specific stories you could tell? With a few of your classmates, choose a story and talk about how you could tell it from multiple perspectives and across platforms (print, broadcast, Web, social media, etc.).

3. What do you think about Barbara Ehrenreich's "field experiment" method of learning about the working poor? What are some other effective ways to learn about segments of your community? Share your thoughts with your classmates.

4. Consider the *Class Matters* series by *The New York Times.* If you could undertake a similar project, what would it look like? With two or three of your classmates, brainstorm a plan for a series about class in your community.

 BOX 4.5   From the Field: Summary Advice from the Pros

SCOTT FINN, EXECUTIVE DIRECTOR AND CEO, WEST VIRGINIA PUBLIC BROADCASTING

"I don't think it's something you can just dip your toe in every once in awhile and say you're done. If you're serious about trying to really cover issues of poverty and people who are struggling to make ends meet, I think it has to be something you commit to for the long term, and that you know you're going to be working on as an ongoing project as part of your reporting career. You can't do it in a story or even in a series. It has to be an ongoing commitment. Otherwise, you can do a lot more damage if you just try to dip in and then don't spend the energy and time on it. . . . If you feel like, 'Well, I can't really afford to become an expert in this and to really work at it over time,' just stay away from it and don't touch it, because you could do a lot of harm."

TODD C. FRANKEL, *THE WASHINGTON POST*

"There is this tendency to draw with the broad stripe of class stereotype—everyone in the Midwest is wholesome and middle class and loves America, and everyone in Appalachia is a backwards hick. But the best stories, the ones that resonate, are the ones that show the more complicated aspects of that. You don't have to be from a place to understand it, but it's good to have some sort of context for what's really going on, that not everyone there is illiterate. It's just harder to see things beyond the stereotypes. It takes work . . . and getting entrenched in communities that you cover and understanding and really paying attention to the idea that you don't just want to be writing about poor people. Look at the data and really understand who these people are."

Christopher R. Martin

(Continued)

BOX 4.5 Continued

"As journalists, we're always attracted to the extreme—the very highs and the very lows. Really, the greatest stories often are right there in the middle. You just have to work harder and be more sensitive to paying attention to that. In the middle is where a lot of the great stories reside."

CHRISTOPHER R. MARTIN, PROFESSOR AT THE DEPARTMENT OF COMMUNICATION STUDIES, UNIVERSITY OF NORTHERN IOWA, CEDAR FALLS, IOWA

"It's not likely that any editor is going to be in favor of starting up a labor beat, for both ideological and newsroom resource reasons. But to fully cover the topic of 'work' and all of the great stories it would entail—health care, safety, pensions, immigration (including work visas for high-tech workers), the minimum wage movement (especially in fast food across the U.S.), increasing inequality, the Occupy Movement, the outsourcing of jobs, the difficulty of part-timers to get their schedules in advance, race and gender discrimination, unemployment, the increasing problem of classifying workers as 'independent contractors' and more—is a much easier sell. These are all issues that connect with the news audience, so why ignore them? Citizens want to hear 'their' story in the news."

▶ CONCLUSION

Orienting yourself toward excellence is the first step in addressing some of the barriers to excellent journalistic coverage of matters of social class. Whether you are reporting on poverty in your community, a labor strike or the effects of the latest economic downturn, we hope you are sufficiently equipped to address these issues with confidence and competence.

▶ CHAPTER SUMMARY

- Social class has a complex history in the United States and it is a subject a lot of people find difficult to talk about.

- While the "American dream" was once obtainable for many people, since the late 1970s onward there has been a significant gulf between the richest and poorest in American society, brought about by transformations in the American economy.

- Class surrounds us and impacts the choices we make, and those we are able to make.

- Journalism can play a key role in helping audiences understand social class by embracing the qualities of excellent journalism—context, complexity, voices, proportionality and authenticity.

▶ SUGGESTED ACTIVITIES

1. Investigate the U.S. census data for your community. Determine how income, education, jobs and other factors shape your community's class structure. Create an infographic to reflect your findings and/or use the data to brainstorm on story ideas.

2. Find out the poverty-level monthly income for your community. Draw up a budget and figure out how you would live on that amount, accounting for rent, utilities, food, transportation and other necessary expenses. If you come up short, consider what you would do to make up the difference: Take on an extra job? Apply for food stamps or other public assistance?

3. Shadow a social worker for a day to learn more about the needs of lower-income residents of your community.

4. What is it like to live on food stamps? Determine the weekly food-stamp allowance for residents in your area, and see if you can feed yourself on that amount for a week.

▶ ADDITIONAL READINGS

Cooke-Jackson, Angela and Elizabeth K. Hansen. "Appalachian Culture and Reality TV: The Ethical Dilemma of Stereotyping Others." *Journal of Mass Media Ethics* 23, no. 3 (2008): 183–200. doi:10.1080/08900520802221946.

Coy, Peter. "Staggering Drunks and Fiscal Cliffs: Why Journalists Need to Be Masters of Metaphor." *Nieman Reports*, Spring 2013, 14–15.

Ingraham, Christopher. "Child Poverty in the U.S. Is Among the Worst in the Developed World." *The Washington Post*, October 29, 2014. http://www.washingtonpost.com/blogs/wonkblog/wp/2014/10/29/child-poverty-in-the-u-s-is-among-the-worst-in-the-developed-world/.

Keller, Bill. *Class Matters*. New York: Times Books, 2005.

Kim, Sei-Hill, John P. Carvalho and Andrew G. Davis. "Talking About Poverty: News Framing of Who Is Responsible for Causing and Fixing the Problem." *Journalism & Mass Communication Quarterly* 87, no. 3/4 (2010): 563–81.

Kroll, Andrew. "Home Wreckers." *Mother Jones*, November/December 2010, 52–57.

Morin, Rich and Seth Motel. "A Third of Americans Now Say They Are in the Lower Class." Pew Social & Demographic Trends, September 10, 2012. http://www.pewsocialtrends.org/2012/09/10/a-third-of-americans-now-say-they-are-in-the-lower-classes/.

Rosin, Hanna. "Who Wears the Pants in This Economy?" *New York Times Magazine*, September, 2012, 22–9, 38.

Shafer, Jack. "Lost in the Flood: Why No Mention of Race or Class in TV's Katrina Coverage?" Slate.com, August 31, 2005. http://www.slate.com/articles/news_and_politics/press_box/2005/08/lost_in_the_flood.html.

▶ NOTES

1 Michael Zweig, The Working Class Majority: America's Best Kept Secret (Ithaca, NY: ILR Press, 2012), 2.

2 Susan J. Douglas, "Class Consciousness Is Back," *In These Times*, 2011, http://inthesetimes.com/article/12413/class_consciousness_is_back.

3 Zweig, *The Working Class Majority*, 3.

4 James Truslow Adams, The Epic of America (Boston, MA: Little, Brown, 1933).

5 Earl Wysong, Robert Perrucci and David Wright, *The New Class Society*, 4th ed. (Lanham, MD: Rowman & Littlefield, 2014), 4.

6 Dennis Gilbert, *The American Class Structure in an Age of Growing Inequality*, 7th ed. (Los Angeles, CA: Pine Forge Press, 2008).

7 Ibid.

8 Wysong, Perrucci and Wright, *The New Class Society*.

9 Ibid., 5.

10 Greg J. Duncan and Richard J. Murnane, *Whither Opportunity?* (New York: Russell Sage Foundation, 2011).

11 Carmen DeNavas-Walt, Bernadette D. Proctor and Jessica C. Smith, "Income, Poverty, and Health Insurance Coverage in the United States: 2012," U.S. Census Bureau, 2013, http://www.census.gov/prod/2013pubs/p60–245.pdf.

12 Matt Bruenig, "The Top 10% of White Families Own Almost Everything," *Demos*, 2014, http://www.demos.org/blog/9/5/14/top-10-white-families-own-almost-everything.

13 "Inside the Middle Class: Bad Times Hit the Good Life," Pew Research Center, 2009, http://www.pewsocialtrends.org/files/2010/10/MC-Middle-class-report1.pdf.

14 Wysong, Perrucci, and Wright, *The New Class Society*.

15 Ibid.

16 Ibid., 99.

17 Ibid., 103.

18 Annie Lowrey, "Household Incomes Remain Flat despite Improving Economy," *The New York Times*, September 17, 2013, http://www.nytimes.com/2013/09/18/us/median-income-and-poverty-rate-hold-steady-census-bureau-finds.html?pagewanted=all&_r=0.

19 "Poverty: Current Population Survey (CPS), 2013 Annual Social and Economic Supplement (ASEC)," U.S. Census Bureau, http://www.census.gov/hhes/www/poverty/about/overview/index.html.

20 Will Barratt, *Social Class on Campus: Theories and Manifestations*, (Sterling, VA: Stylus, 2011), 1.

21　Kate Pickett and Richard Wilkinson, *The Spirit Level: Why Greater Equality Makes Societies Stronger* (New York: Bloomsbury Press, 2011).

22　Kevin Fagan, "Missing from the Media: News about Poverty," *Spotlight on Poverty and Opportunity*, 2011, http://www.spotlightonpoverty.org/ExclusiveCommentary.aspx?id=2689b2bd-274f-48c3-bcb4-cac7580a4b2f.

23　Robert M. Entman and Andrew Rojecki, *The Black Image in the White Mind: Media and Race in America* (Chicago, IL: University of Chicago Press, 2001), 94.

24　Shanto Iyengar, *Is Anyone Responsible? How Television Frames Political Issues* (Chicago, IL: University of Chicago Press, 1991).

25　Bill Keller, "Introduction," in *Class Matters*, ed. *New York Times*, ix–xviii (New York: Times Books, 2011), ix.

26　Ibid., xviii.

27　Ibid., xviii.

28　Ibid., xviii.

29　Diana Kendall, *Framing Class: Media Representations of Wealth and Poverty in America*, 2nd ed. (Lanham, MD: Rowman & Littlefield, 2011), 117.

30　Joseph A. Giannone, "Recession, Bear Markets Hit the Rich, Too," *Reuters*, 2010, http://www.reuters.com/article/2010/06/25/us-privatebanks-credit-idUSTRE65O47Y20100625, quoted in Kendall, *Framing Class*.

31　Bill Kovach and Tom Rosenstiel, *The Elements of Journalism: What Newspeople Should Know and the Public Should Expect*, rev. ed. (New York: Three Rivers Press, 2007), 44.

32　Barbara Ehrenreich, *Nickel and Dimed: On (Not) Getting By In America* (New York: Metropolitan Books, 2001).

33　Kendall, *Framing Class*, 157.

34　Ibid., 158.

35　Ibid., 159.

36　Ibid., 158.

37　Ibid., 214.

38　"2013 Casey Medals for Meritorious Journalism," The Journalism Center on Children & Families, 2013, http://www.journalismcenter.org/content/press-release-13.

39　Ibid.

40　Ibid.

41　Ibid.

42　Ibid.

5

Gender and the Media: Envisioning Equality

Yong Volz and María E. Len-Ríos

We've learned in Chapter 3 that we all hold inherent biases toward people we see as different from us. Some group distinctions though—such as gender—are often considered a natural result of our biology. The fault line of gender is a naturally assumed cause of difference. As with most stereotypes, some gender stereotypes are rooted in real differences. However, others are based on assumptions that feed our biases.

Consider the mental images you have of people working in these jobs: president, leader, chief executive officer, nurse, teacher, nanny, chef, scientist, car salesman, accountant, soldier, construction worker and musician. Did your mind come up with a picture of a man or a woman? Most people can conjure mental images quickly. How do we develop our ideas about gendered work roles? Certainly we learn about gender through our culture, and part of that culture is reinforced through news and entertainment media.

Researchers studying film and prime-time TV characters from 2006–2011 found that family films rarely show women as C-suite executives, high-level politicians or editors-in-chief at news organizations. The researchers' report notes that in real life, 25.5 percent of chief executives in 2010 were women—that is one in four. Furthermore,

> **LEARNING OBJECTIVES**
>
> By the end of this chapter, you should be able to:
>
> - recognize the potential for media bias in the selection of sources, images and words.
>
> - implement strategies to improve the excellence of the portrayals of women and men in news and advertising content.
>
> - understand why gender equality makes for good business.

the study's[1] authors point out that of the 4.5 percent of females who were high-level politicians, none were central characters. Women featured in prominent roles are even fewer when we consider older women and women of color. While society has greatly changed, media generally show that men are firmly in charge.

There is voluminous research on news content in the U.S.[2] and other countries[3] demonstrating that journalists portray women and men differently in news content. Scholars have also analyzed how women and men are displayed in advertising and entertainment media, and their analyses suggest that media offer men and women limited and exaggerated visions of what it means to be men or women in society.

You, as a future journalist or media professional, will choose how to represent women and men in the content you produce. Media content creates societal expectations about gender—whether it's the next Ikea® furniture ad or a story about the candidates in the upcoming U.S. presidential election. The media content you produce matters because what you choose to show and tell people can influence what audiences come to expect as *normal*. The boundaries of media representations can limit or expand our thinking about what "can be," or maybe what "should be." Limited representations of gender restrict our expectations of what is possible—for women and men alike.

> Over the years, we have had students ask, "Why should we make a conscious effort to consider the gender of our news sources? Shouldn't we just pick the best sources?" Our response: How are you defining best sources?

As we begin the discussion of gender bias in the media, it is important to note that biological sex—whether a person's physical anatomy is male, female or intersex—is often defined as separate from gender.[4] Gender is often broken down into *gender identity*, an individual's psychological sense of self as a man or a woman,[5] and a person's *gender expression*, which refers to how someone chooses to dress and communicate their sense of self to others. Gender expression is frequently described as ranging from masculine to androgynous to feminine. Sexual orientation is different from gender identity or gender expression because it relates to one's sexual response.

In this chapter when we talk about gender bias, we are referring to how men and women, defined by their presumed biological sex, are depicted in media. When we refer to gender roles, we are referring to how men or women are portrayed as characters or persons in various professional, domestic, romantic and leadership functions.

▶ IDENTIFYING GENDER BIAS IN NEWS

News media play a central role in informing the public of current events, social situations and policy issues. Yet in the process of selecting certain news stories while excluding others, highlighting certain issues while downplaying others, privileging certain people while disadvantaging others, media can also create bias and shape misconceptions about social groups. Gender bias is one of the most subtle and pernicious biases that pervade U.S. news media. It is important, therefore, to identify gender bias in its various forms that are currently present in media, to improve media. As future journalists, you can be, and should aspire to be, a force in promoting gender equality by providing your audiences with fair and accurate representations.

Lack of Women's Voices

One major form of gender bias can be found in the imbalance of sources used in news stories, resulting in a notable lack of women's voices. Numerous studies show that women have been far less visible as newsmakers, and that reporters rely on women less often as professional experts and spokespersons. Studies of major network evening news in the late 1980s found that males made up 88 percent of the sources—far greater than did women (12 percent). When quoted, male sources appeared as experts while women more often represented the voice of *ordinary citizens*.[6] This gender discrepancy continued into the 2000s and 2010s, especially in political news (the public sphere that represents the greatest power in our society aside from business). A study of TV network news (ABC, CBS and NBC) coverage of the 2000 presidential campaign shows that female non-candidate sources appeared in only 26 percent of news stories.[7] Ten years later, in 2012 election coverage, men's voices still dominated general election topics, averaging 81 percent of the quotes on the 11 top TV news shows. Overall, women were 14 percent of sources journalists interviewed and 29 percent of Sunday morning talk show guests. On the 2011, Hillary Clinton, then Secretary of the State, was the only female guest to appear in the top 10 of most frequent Sunday talk-show guests.

Studies of print media and online media show similar trends. A study of *The New York Times* during the first two months of 2013 revealed its journalists quoted male sources 3.4 times more often than women sources in front-page news stories. Not surprisingly, international and political news stories had the fewest women. In 2011, the Global Media Monitoring Project found women comprised only 23 percent of newsmakers on the 84 news websites it monitored.[8] Women from racial minority groups, the working class, and older generations receive even less attention.

Even media coverage of women's issues, such as abortion and birth control, lacks women's voices. Researchers studying the 2012 election found that in stories about abortion in 35 U.S. national print media, female sources comprised only 12 percent of all the quotes, while men provided 81 percent of the quotes (organizations supplied the rest). Coverage often emphasized the choices faced by male politicians on the abortion debate, while seldom quoting teenage girls and young women who had the most at stake. Similarly, in stories about women's rights topics, journalists used women's quotes (31 percent) less than they did men's quotes (52 percent).[9]

Such sourcing practices undermine media credibility and public trust. It also creates a distorted social reality that contributes to audience misperceptions of women's roles in society. Media critics particularly caution that the underrepresentation of women as news sources, especially as experts, may heighten young audience's expectations that men rule the professional world while women's stories are less relevant and their perspectives less valuable.

So how do we solve the problem? There have been some serious efforts among news organizations and journalists to decrease the gender gap in news source selection. MSNBC's Christopher Hayes, for example, instituted a diversity quota on his weekend morning show to ensure that out of four panelists on every show "at least two are women." In an interview, Hayes said that having a quota system could help force journalists to be more resourceful and avoid defaulting to the "usual suspects," the same small pool of experts that is dominated by men. By having female guests, Hayes believed that "the show can highlight a range of voices and opinions."[10]

Diversity quotas, however, are not common practice, and many media professionals question whether such a solution is truly suitable or practical on a daily or weekly basis, especially when journalists are on deadline. But there are a number of other ways that the situation can be improved. One important step is for journalists to examine their own sourcing practices and to consciously recruit and cultivate female sources. Along with building your own rolodex, here are several resources for identifying and connecting with female experts in different areas.

- The POWER Sources Project (http://www.wimnonline.com/psp/) was founded in 2001 as "the first national network of diverse female sources developed specifically to help journalists increase the quantity and diversity of women's voices appearing in print, broadcast and online media."

- Women's Media Center's SheSource (http://www.shesource.org) provides a database of leading female experts for journalists and producers seeking "expert perspective or a source on the leading issues of the day." The project was founded in 2005 to "positively and significantly impact the visibility of women in media," "increase the inclusion of women's voices on key issues in the national dialogue" and "fight media sexism and bias in coverage."

- The OpEd Project (http://www.theopedproject.org) was founded in 2008 to vet and channel female experts to news media to "increase the number of women thought leaders contributing to key commentary forums."

- In addition, many women's organizations also provide ready lists of female experts on various topics. Some to explore are National Women's Law Center, National Organization of Women, Journalism and Women Symposium and the National Foundation for Women Business Owners.

Differing Framing of Gender and Gender Roles

Along with the underrepresentation of female sources in news stories, media are also criticized for stereotypical portrayals of both women and men. Media stereotypes reproduce and reinforce traditional gender roles in society. According to a 2000 study by the Global Media Monitor Project, women were three times more likely than men to be reported in the news as victims (of violence, war, natural disaster, poverty, scandal, etc.). Women were also often portrayed as homemakers or caretakers and were identified according to family status. Only a small percentage of stories featured women's achievements and addressed women's issues and status in the political arena.

Women and Political News

Moreover, media tend to apply differing frames and double standards when covering women and men working in the same professional field. The most telling example is media's gendered coverage of politicians. Studies have consistently found that when covering female candidates, media habitually focus more on their appearance, personality traits and personal life and less on their issue stances and professional accomplishments. When media do report on female candidates' professional achievements, studies show that media often emphasize stereotypically "feminine" issues, such as health care, education and social welfare. Such gendered coverage may undermine voters' perception of the capacity and credibility of female candidates in handling national security and foreign policy, thus putting female candidates at a disadvantage.[11] A study of the 2008 campaign coverage of Hillary Clinton and Sarah Palin found that news media collectively framed the two female candidates as "sex object," "mothers" and "iron maiden," images that may have affected voter confidence in the candidates' political abilities.[12] Similarly, in covering Elizabeth Warren's bid for the Massachusetts Senate in 2012, journalists and pundits who described her appearance said she was "off-putting," "shrieking" and a "granny." Imagine former Florida Gov. Jeb Bush or New Jersey Gov. Chris Christie depicted as "shrieking" or as looking like "gramps" by journalists. The ongoing bias in news that presents female candidates as less viable than their male opponents may deter women from seeking public office, and it makes it harder for women to win elections.

Masculinity and the Making of Men

Gender bias can often cut both ways when not just women, but men are subjected to gender stigmas exhibited and reinforced by media. Australian sociologist Raewyn Connell created the concept of "hegemonic masculinity" to describe how masculinity is socially constructed, maintained and reproduced in a given society. Media scholars use the concept to study how mass media reinforce normative cultural ideals of manhood that expect men to be professional, assertive, independent, invulnerable, active, tough and risk-taking. These masculine norms are highly present in sports coverage, where body-contact sports, such as American football and wrestling, are promoted as symbols of masculinity. Men's fashion and lifestyle magazines are also criticized for endorsing narrow masculine ideals that tell men they should engage in bodywork to attain the lifestyle they want.[13] (This is particularly true if men do not have money or superior intellect.) A study of windsurfing magazines shows the sport as a predominantly male preserve, and that male surfers possess traits such as sporting prowess, heterosexuality, willingness to take physical risks and the financial ability to pursue this leisure lifestyle.[14] The problem of hegemonic masculinity as represented in media is that it leaves little room for alternative forms of masculinity. Media ascribe traditional gender roles and social expectations to men. Male domestic roles, therefore, are often dismissed, and men working in traditionally female fields (e.g., primary education, nursing, social work) are demeaned.

Gender and LGBT Coverage

News media are especially challenged when covering the LGBT community (See also Chapter 6). Ten years ago, few newspapers reported same-sex commitment ceremonies, and group members were frequently framed as villains or victims. Although media portrayals of LGBT people have, overall, become more positive, studies even now find that pride parades are still covered mainly as drag shows or social riots, and LGBT people are still associated with risky behavior and flawed character. For instance, *Grantland's* January 2014 feature on "Dr. V" and a game-changing golf putter she invented shed light on mistakes journalists can make when reporting on members of the transgender community. In the article, reporter Caleb Hannan described his discovery of the putter and his desire to learn about its inventor. In the course of the piece, Hannan revealed a variety of deceptions on the part of Dr. V and identified her as a transgender woman. As Poynter reported,

> In describing Dr. V's gender identity with her résumé-related deceptions, *Grantland* made the mistake of equating something intrinsic about a human

being (gender identity) with a character flaw (con artist). In outing Dr. V to her investors and ultimately the entire world, *Grantland* invaded her privacy and took away her dignity.[15]

Gender: Yesterday, Today and Tomorrow

In the last two decades, activist groups, journalism educators and professional organizations have made concerted efforts to raise awareness of gender bias in news reporting and of media stereotypes. Many senior journalists have done this by sharing their experiences of fighting gender inequality, discussing the importance of equity in media stories and providing helpful advice on how to cover issues with proper awareness and accuracy (see Box 5.1).[16]

 BOX 5.1   Advice from Senior Women Journalists (Excerpts from the JAWS Oral History Project, http://herstory.rjionline.org)

Mary Kay Blakely (Contributing editor to *Ms. Magazine* since 1981; "Hers" columnist for *The New York Times*; associate professor emerita at the Missouri School of Journalism)

I've been writing all my life about women and equality . . . and talking about why it's so important for women to not only have as many bylines and front page assignments as men, but also as many promotions and managerial positions. That's true in nearly every profession—but most importantly, it's true in journalism. Why is it so critical that journalism reflect the gender and diversity of the culture it's covering? Because newspapers, magazines, radio, television, photography and documentaries provide pictures and stories about the society being examined, planting indelible ideas and images in the minds of its citizens. Until the craving for "herstory" identified a new way to understand history, the books and courses mainly studied wars, governments, laws and businesses conducted by men. Although women and children were living and learning and working alongside them, their existence was a footnote, if they were mentioned at all.

It's astonishing that most university and college journalism programs have had female enrollments higher than 50 percent for some time—70 percent is more common today—women are still "disappeared" from the profession after they

(Continued)

BOX 5.1 Continued

graduate. For decades, I've been counting the number of women's names that appear on the front pages and mastheads of newspapers and magazines, but almost never reach 50 percent. You don't have to be a feminist to find this depressing. Silencing women's voices and perceptions is harmful to the whole society.

I'm hugely empathetic with how difficult it is to raise a family and simultaneously meet demanding deadlines, but also know how punishing it is for women not to enter *any* profession until after their children are grown, how dismal the salary gap still is for anyone without "experience." I once worked for a secondary school that credited veterans with experience for every year spent in the military, but credited mothers who spent half their lives teaching children with no experience. *Really?* It's not the exclusive responsibility of young women to change family structures, professional institutions, social attitudes and salary structures. It's everyone's responsibility. In the meantime, it's vitally important to hear and see and know what female journalists think.

> **Tad Bartimus** (Columnist for the *United Features Syndicate*; Associated Press reporter for 25 years, including being war correspondent in Vietnam and covering international assignments in Europe)

I think a successful career is recognizing your shortcomings as a journalist. Finding an editor or a writing partner or a team that fills those gaps and to which you can contribute. So that you make this magical, make journalism happen that's magical. Whether it's investigative, whether it's a feature, or whatever it is. To be a person who relies on their instincts, who's able to grow in the profession, who's self-motivated, who likes the creativity of working as a team, who's not looking to be the star, who likes collaborative, and who takes on stories that are a real challenge. And that you take on a story and it's leading somewhere and you don't know where it's going. And you keep following it.

I can tell you that I steered my own course. I think most successful women do that. I had mentors. Most successful women have mentors. I think it should be what the woman chooses to be. Institutionally, I think it's wonderful that so many of these women are being encouraged and promoted and given equal pay, if not more pay, who are getting there on the basis of their abilities. It's that the portals have opened for it to happen. And should they lean in? Yeah.

I think you have to have a good general education still. If you have an idea of what you're good at, you should specialize in that. And I think you should pick

(Continued)

BOX 5.1 Continued

something that you're willing, that you're willing to go to the mat for and sacrifice for because it's that important to you. I don't know if that's management. I don't know if that's street reporting. I don't know if it's being a backpacking journalist. I don't know if it's being a freelance. Whatever that is. I had a passion. And I always try to probe young people to say, but what is your passion? What really makes you happy? Not what your parents want or your professors say you're good at. What do you love? I think you have to love something to work that hard at it to be successful.

Kathy Kiely (Managing editor for the Sunlight Foundation; political reporter for *USA Today*; Washington bureau chief for the Houston Post)

You know, being a journalist requires you to put yourself in somebody else's shoes and try to understand their story. I think the most important thing is when you're a journalist, your notions of power are very different. I mean, you're skeptical of power.

The idea that just because people are different doesn't mean that's wrong. And I think that women bring—we all bring something unique to the table. And so having more of that is a good thing. I think certainly, I know men who are in professions who feel trapped by a set of expectations that doesn't allow them to spend time with their family or do other things that are important to them. And I think if you had more women who have been socialized to accept responsibility for some of these things in decision-making positions, you then make space for that. You make space for alternative work styles, alternative lifestyles, which I think in the global economy that we're living in are necessary.

I think you have to be diplomatic but persistent and aggressive, which are actually all great journalism tools. But I would say, you know, treat your colleagues and your superiors like you would your sources, which is to say, don't assume. And don't assume that people are going to give you what you want. You have to actually actively go after it and insist that you're being taken seriously. But I would say that when you do that, you have to use common sense and calibrate things. Not everything is a federal case. You know, not everything is a let's-take-it-to-the-judge sex discrimination suit. So, like the cliché, you have to know when to hold them and when to fold them. I think there are different ways to deal with these situations, but you have to basically put yourself in a situation where you demand to be taken seriously.

(Continued)

BOX 5.1 Continued

Jacqui Banaszynski (Pulitzer Prize–winner in feature writing for the *St. Paul Pioneer Press* in 1988; associate managing editor at the *Seattle Times*; Knight Chair in Editing at the Missouri School of Journalism)

My best advice to young journalists is don't quit until you get good. And it takes a while to get good. Find the best mentors that you can. Maybe they're in your newsroom or in your immediate orbit, but maybe they're not. So reach out and seek mentors, and take advantage of them. Look around for the opportunities that grow you and challenge you so you play a little bit scared and you have to learn something every day. That could be moving up to a bigger newsroom. It could be figuring out how to latch onto a little web startup where you have to figure out how to make something work. And understand that, again, you have to keep working at it, and watching and learning from other people, until you get good enough to then say, "Okay. Now I can take this somewhere." And it doesn't happen overnight.

Glenda Holste (An editor for 30 years with *The St. Paul Pioneer Press* before working as a public affairs editor for a state-wide educators union)

I think one of the answers to the big question is, "know your own heart." Know what your passion is, where you want to go and where you want to take this career. Why are you doing this? And for whom? And what do you hope your work can accomplish that makes the world better? Do something for another woman every day. It's just like putting it on your to-do list. Consciously do something every day.

[A good leader is] one who builds honest relationships with both sources and colleagues, who can listen as well as dictate. And this is sometimes very hard in the newsroom, because you're on a fast pace. You need to get from point A to point B. But take time to understand the person. Knowing how to do that in a constructive way. Not being afraid you're going to hurt someone's feelings.

Diana Henriques (Financial journalist for 22 years at *The New York Times*; author of four business history books, including *The Wizard of Lies*, on the Bernie Madoff scandal)

One of the best pieces of advice that I got when I arrived at *The New York Times* was from Sarah Bartlett, who is now the new dean of the graduate school of journalism at

(Continued)

BOX 5.1 Continued

CUNY in New York . . . When I arrived at the *Times*, she and I had coffee. And she said, "You know, the best way to manage here at the *Times* is to think of yourself as an independent contractor. Think of yourself as a free-floating freelancer who can work among the different desks, who can find the editor that you want to work for and pitch stories to them." And it was a revelation to me. Because I always sort of thought that when you arrived in a newsroom, you sat in your spot in the hierarchy and you tried to manage within that sphere. And she helped me see that within a great big place like the *Times*, no one was going to manage my career for me. I needed to do that myself.

Media professionals have developed numerous toolkits for self-assessment and reflection of gender coverage.[17] There are three basic questions that journalists can ask of themselves: (1) *What are my underlying assumptions and suppositions about women, men and LGBT people and their place in both the public and the private domains?* (2) *Do I use double standards when I write about women versus men, especially in profiling their professional skills and professional performance?* For instance, in 2006, when the *Washington Post*'s media critic wrote about Katie Couric's debut as the first solo female network TV anchor, among the numerous things he wrote, he noted that Couric "wore a white blazer over a black top and skirt, the blazer buttoned in such a way as to make her look chubby, bursting at the button, which we know she isn't."[18] Would we critique a male anchor's performance by mentioning his weight? 3) *Are your language and/or images loaded with gendered terms that may carry inaccurate impressions of men, women and the LGBT community?* (e.g., he was firm; she was shrill; he was effeminate.)

There are also numerous excellent news stories that break gender stereotypes and present a different kind of narrative about women, men and transgender people. The *New Yorker*, for example, published a profile of long-distance swimmer Diana Nyad, a woman in her 60s reviving her long-held dream to swim from Cuba to Florida. The story, recognized by *Slate* magazine as one of the best stories about women in 2014, exemplifies strength, endurance and the power of women athletes—an image that is quite different from the sexualized portrayal of former tennis player Anna Kournikova. *Washington Post*'s 2013 profile on U.S. Sen. Dianne Feinstein, on the other hand, was praised by the Women's Media Center as an excellent example of news coverage of a political woman that refrains from mentioning her skin, makeup, hair color, clothing and purse, despite the story appearing in the newspaper's Style section. Instead, the story features the oldest member of the Senate as a hardworking role model and the ideal senator. A third example is *Dateline NBC*'s "Josei's Story." Nominated for a 2013

Emmy Award for Outstanding Feature in a News Magazine, this story profiles a 9-year-old transgender female child considering gender reassignment hormones and surgery. Breaking the social stigma, the story provides an intimate and empathetic portrait of transgender children and their families who try to find their own rightful place. More examples of news stories covering gender issues can be found in Box 5.4.

▶ GENDER DISPARITY IN THE NEWSROOM

In addition to the lack of female sources in news stories and the stereotypical representation of women in media, another major concern is the low level of involvement and influence of women in the news profession. Indeed, many attribute the pervasive gender bias in news coverage to gender disparity in the newsroom. There has been a constant call to recruit more women to the field because it is widely believed that when women are on news staffs and are commonly represented in leadership positions, that media coverage of women could be improved. Of course, not all female journalists are gender sensitive, or deliberate in presenting women's perspectives, and some studies have found that female journalists tend to adopt male-dominated newsroom values in the selection and presentation of news in order to advance their careers.[19] Even so, a large body of studies have shown that women reporters, compared with their male counterparts, are more likely to use female sources and to reflect women's concerns and perspectives.[20] It is also argued that the presence of female journalists in print, radio, television and new media can serve as role models for young women, to have a voice and exert influence in the public sphere, and to improve women's status in society, as well as to attract and expand the female audience base for the media.

So what is the status of women in the news media in the U.S.? How wide is the gender gap in the field? Despite progress in the last few decades, women have remained a minority in the field.[21] For daily newspapers, the 2013 American Society of News Editors (ASNE) newsroom census showed that women accounted for only 36 percent of newsroom staff, a figure that has remained largely unchanged since the 1980s. Women had an even smaller tally—24.9 percent—of photographers, graphic artists and videographers. The Gawker.com 2013 survey also showed that male editorial writers outnumber women almost 4 to 1 in three top newspapers, including *The New York Times*, *Washington Post* and *Wall Street Journal*, and in large newspaper syndicates such as Creators Syndicate, Universal Press, King Features and Tribune Media. The troubling gender inequality also exists in television and radio. According to the Women's Media Center report, women currently make up 34.2 percent of radio staff, but talk radio and sports talk radio hosts are even more dominantly male. Women made up only 11.1 percent of the 117 general news talk show hosts, and there were two lone women among the 183 sports talk show hosts on the 2013 "Heavy Hundred" list from *Talkers* magazine. Women managed to make more inroads at local television stations where they made up

40.3 percent of the workforce, but were not as successful in finding positions as anchors and correspondents for ABC, CBS, FOX and NBC news programs, where on average they made up only 35.6 percent of the total. (But don't despair—you can be the change!)

The gender gap is even wider at the leadership level. According to the University of Denver's Benchmarking Women's Leadership report, only 23.3 percent of the leadership ranks in journalism and related media in 2012 were women. Female leaders were least visible in radio news stations with only 7.5 percent of national leadership roles, including top radio hosts and behind-the-scenes leadership. Women seemed to be better represented in leadership roles in other media sectors, averaging 19.2 percent in newspapers, 21.6 percent in television news and 43.2 percent in the magazine industry.

 BOX 5.2   News Leadership

TABLE 5.1 Top Leadership Positions in the 10 Largest U.S. Daily Newspapers, 2014

Rank	Newspaper	Circulation (in million)	Leadership
1	Wall Street Journal	2.1	Gerard Baker (editor)
2	USA Today	1.8	Larry Kramer (editor), David Callaway (editor-in-chief)
3	The New York Times	1.6	Arthur Ochs Sulzberger Jr. (publisher), Dean Baquet (editor)
4	Los Angeles Times	0.62	Austin Beutner (publisher), Davan Maharaj (editor)
5	New York Daily News	0.58	Mortimer Zuckerman (publisher), Colin Myler (editor)
6	San Jose Mercury News	0.58	David J. Butler (editor)
7	New York Post	0.55	Jesse Angelo (publisher), Col Allan (editor)
8	Washington Post	0.51	**Katharine Weymouth** (publisher), Martin Baron (editor)
9	Chicago Sun-Times	0.42	Tim Knight (publisher), Jim Kirk (editor)
10	Chicago Tribune	0.42	Tony W. Hunter (publisher), Gerould W. Kern (editor)

Source: http://www.easymedialist.com/usa/top100news.html (female leaders in **bold**)

(Continued)

BOX 5.2 Continued

TABLE 5.2 Top Leadership Positions in the 10 Largest U.S. Magazines, 2014

Rank	Magazine	Circulation (in million)	Leadership
1	AARP Magazine	22.3	**Nancy Perry Graham** (editor-in-chief)
2	AARP Bulletin	22.2	Jim Toedtman (editor)
3	Game Informer Magazine	7.6	Andy McNamara (editor-in-chief)
4	Better Homes and Gardens	7.6	**Gayle Butler** (editor-in-chief)
5	Good Housekeeping	4.3	**Jane Francisco** (editor-in-chief)
6	Reader's Digest	4.3	**Liz Vaccariello** (editor-in-chief)
7	Family Circle	4.1	**Linda Fears** (editor-in-chief)
8	National Geographic	4.0	**Susan Goldberg** (editor)
9	People	3.5	Jess Cagle (editor)
10	Woman's Day	3.3	**Susan Spencer** (editor-in-chief)

Source: Alliance for Audited Media, http://auditedmedia.com/news/blog/2014/february/us-snapshot.aspx (female editors in **bold**)

TABLE 5.3 Percentage of Women in Local Television Stations and Radio, 2014

	Female News Directors	Female News Staff
All Television	30.8	41.2
Network Affiliates	29.7	41.4
Independents	29.2	38.8
All Radio	23.1	31.3
Major Market	26.7	42.1
Large Market	32.0	39.4
Medium Market	24.1	25.2
Small Market	17.7	16.9

Source: Bob Papper, "Women, minorities make newsroom gain," see http://www.rtdna.org/article/women_minorities_make_newsroom_gains#.VMxGs2jF_ng

(Continued)

BOX 5.2 Continued

TABLE 5.4 Top 10 Most Visible Reporters on Network News in 2013

Rank	Reporter	Network	Assignment	Minutes
1	Tom Costello	NBC	DC bureau	303
2	David Muir	ABC	Domestic	296
3	**Andrea Mitchell**	NBC	State Department	275
4	**Nancy Snyderman**	NBC	Medicine	226
5	Jonathan Karl	ABC	White House	224
6	Pete Williams	NBC	Justice	216
7	**Nancy Cordes**	CBS	Capitol Hill	201
8	Chuck Todd	CBS	White House	180
9	**Elaine Quijano**	CBS	Domestic	180
10	**Anne Thompson**	NBC	Environment/Vatican	176

Source: "Top 20 most used reporters" at http://tyndallreport.com/yearinreview2013/ (women in **bold**; this list includes only reporters, not anchors)

The presence of women begins to thin out even more in the highest leadership tiers (see Box 5.2). In 2014, among the top 10 media companies, only 15.3 percent of the board members were women, with only one female CEO, Gannett Company's Gracia Martore. Similarly, for the top 10 largest daily newspapers, Katharine Weymouth is the only female publisher, and none of those dailies has a female editor-in-chief. In network evening news, NBC's White House correspondent, Nancy Cordes, was the only woman on the top 10 list of the most visible network reporters in 2012. The situation, however, was significantly improved in 2013, with four more women on the top 10 list, including CBS' Elaine Quijano, NBC's Andrea Mitchell, and Anne Thompson. Comparatively, women were more visible at the top leadership in the magazine industry, with 70 percent of editors-in-chief being women at the 10 largest circulated magazines in 2014.

The challenges faced by a woman trying to carve out a niche in the male-dominated field of journalism do not end when she finds a job. Reports continue to show that women journalists earn less than men do,[22] and find it harder to advance their careers and get professional recognition in the field. Among Pulitzer Prize–winners, for example, only 13.9 percent were women from the period of 1917 to 2010. Women were almost completely excluded from the award in its first decades with only two women winning awards before 1951. Even after 1991, only 26.9 percent of all the winners were women, a percentage much lower than that of females in American newsrooms.[23] Of the 12 Pulitzer Prize–winners in 2014, one sole woman was included, a record low representation compared with the previous few years (see Table 5.5).

In addition, there is still an inherent gender bias against women, who, despite the odds, make significant achievements. Indeed, it is argued that there is a greater degree of sexism against women in power who have a much higher public visibility. When Jill Abrahamson was fired from the executive editor position at *The New York Times* in June of 2014, it spurred a range of media coverage speculating about the factors leading to the decision. Articles portrayed Abrahamson as brusque, pushy and polarizing, with many referencing her tough management style as a key element of her dismissal. Again, imagine a description of a male editor as having a tough management style—does that sound like a flaw or a skill?

Though the picture of gender bias painted here may seem quite bleak, the percentage of women in leadership in media has been increasing, as has coverage of gender-related issues. There is an even greater number of young women studying to become journalists. Perhaps most importantly, there is a much greater awareness of gender bias, the harm it can cause, and the benefits of having greater balance.

TABLE 5.5 Pulitzer Prize–Winners in Journalism, 2014

Category	Name(s)	Publication
Investigative Reporting	Chris Hamby	The Center for Public Integrity
Explanatory Reporting	Eli Saslow	*Washington Post*
Local Reporting	Will Hobson; Michael LaForgia	*Tampa Bay Times*
National Reporting	David Phillips	*The Gazette* (Colorado Springs)
International Reporting	Jason Szep; Andrew Marshall	Reuters
Commentary	Stephen Henderson	Detroit Free Press
Criticism	**Inga Saffron**	*The Philadelphia Inquirer*
Editorial Cartooning	Kevin Siers	*The Charlotte Observer*
Breaking News Photography	Tyler Hicks	*The New York Times*
Feature Photography	Josh Haner	*The New York Times*
Total # of awards: 10	Total # of winners: 12 Percentage of women: **8.3 percent**	

Source: http://www.pulitzer.org/awards/2014 (female winners in **bold;** this list includes only individuals, not the public-service newspapers)

▶ BIAS IN REPRESENTATION OF GENDER IN STRATEGIC COMMUNICATION

The discussion about gender bias in marketing and advertising, specifically, and public relations generally, are fraught with conflict. Why? Professionals and students alike argue that while they may personally value and believe in gender equality, sexy sells, and that's the job. Let's take a look.

In contrast to news representations of gender, the argument is that advertisers and strategic communicators are not as accountable to the public because their profession is not one that is supposed to "serve" or "reflect" society. In a free market society, many argue, advertisers are just responsible for selling their products and answer primarily to the company's stockholders. If sales go up because messages make girls and women unhappy and insecure about themselves and their looks, so be it. Consumers exercise their personal freedom and individual autonomy. If they buy it, it must be good, right?

In elementary school, we can perhaps remember the saying "Sticks and stones may break my bones, but words will never hurt me." We know that's not true. If a kid grows up and is always told, "You're not good enough just as you are," nine times out of 10, the child is going to have self-esteem issues. Research by the Always® brand feminine pads surveyed girls, and 9 out of 10 said words hurt.[24] So, what makes that different for advertising messages and images?

Aspirational Advertising

Unilever's Dove brand set out to improve the messages it sends to women based on recommendations from Ogilvy & Mather, the advertising agency created by the legendary David Ogilvy. The result? Its "Campaign for Real Beauty" in 2004.[25] The campaign was shaped by the results of a 10-country survey of 3,200 women that showed nearly one quarter of women felt they had no sway over how their own beauty was defined, and only 2 percent said they thought they were beautiful.[26] Instead of using fashion models, Dove included regular, everyday women in its advertising. Dove reported that sales of products featured in the campaign rose 600 percent just in the first two months.[27] The company reported that Dove's sales have nearly doubled from $2.5 billion over the 10 years of the campaign, to greater than $4 billion.[28] Sales suggest women like Dove's products *and* its affirming message. Ogilvy had teams in the U.S., the U.K., Canada, Germany and Brazil develop the messaging—in fact, its "Evolution" video was created in its Toronto offices and the "Sketches" video was created in Sao Paulo. The message is—in every language—"You are beautiful." From a public relations perspective, Dove also established its Dove Self-Esteem fund in 2002, focused on raising adolescent self-esteem.

Unilever's Dove brand is not the only brand to take this approach. Others have cited the "Big Butts, Thunder Thighs and Tomboy Knees" campaign by Nike as one that empowers women to achieve athletic feats—rather than just "be happy with how you look."[29] Recently, the "Like A Girl" campaign by Leo Burnett for Proctor & Gamble's Always® brand sanitary napkins (see figure 5.1) reached 114.4 million people during Super Bowl XLIX.

The idea behind the campaign was to take the negative stereotype of what it means to do things "like a girl" and raise awareness that stigmatizing our girls is limiting them. In an interview with *The New York Times*, Fama Francisco, vice president, Global Always said

> We feel so strongly about this, that we're now taking this message to a
> bigger stage, the Super Bowl, so even more people can join us to champion
> girls' confidence and change the meaning of 'like a girl' from an insult into
> something positive and amazing.

FIGURE 5.1 The Always® advertising campaign featuring young women attempts to reclaim the phrase "Like A Girl" to mean strong and positive.
Photo courtesy of Always® and Always' public relations firm MSL Group.

Although the campaign spawned a #LikeABoy backlash on Twitter, advocates for the campaign point out that supporting girls doesn't have to come at a cost to boys. We can value boys and girls. (Great parents demonstrate this all the time!)

So why can't more advertising take this approach? Some industry professionals say it's because women comprise few creative director positions in advertising agencies. Kat Gordon, an advertising creative and agency owner, questioned why women make up just 3 percent of creative directors at ad agencies, while women make 80 percent of purchase decisions. In 2012, Gordon began The 3% Conference for industry professionals and advocates interested in cultivating female leaders in the creative departments of advertising agencies. The rationale: It is good for business. You don't think it's good for business? Walmart, the largest retailer in the U.S., believes empowering women is vital to improving the economic conditions of people worldwide [see Box 5.3 and read about Walmart's Women's Economic Empowerment initiative].

 BOX 5.3 From the Field: Q&A with Beth Keck

Q: What is Walmart's global initiative for women's economic empowerment (WEE)?

A: Our initiative supports our philosophy of investing in areas that align with our core business. WEE focuses on sourcing from women-owned businesses, the diversity and inclusion of suppliers and professional service providers to Walmart, and training women. The training initiative includes training female farmers in agricultural practices; providing female factory workers and women in retail technical, communications and leadership skills for job readiness and advancement; and providing skills and leadership training to low-income U.S. women so they can advance to higher paying jobs.

Beth Keck, senior director, Women's Economic Empowerment, Walmart

Q: Why is it important for a company like Walmart to support global initiatives to invest in women?

A: Women are incredibly important to our business, as they make up the largest percentage of both our shoppers and employees. We depend on

(Continued)

BOX 5.3 Continued

women, so it only makes strategic sense to align our initiatives with our interests. As the largest grocer in the world, the issues of food insecurity, the supply of goods from agricultural suppliers and factories, and the ability to excel in the retail market are significant for us. Our commitment to women's progress—to increase female suppliers, to support the number of women who move into higher paying jobs and managerial roles, and to better serve our customers—ultimately serves us as well. It's good business.

Q: *In the U.S. and globally, what has been the biggest barrier to women's advancement economically?*

A: Access. Across the board, when we talk to and survey women, we find that they want education and training leading to their advancement, but they need it to be convenient—when they can be available—which can mean making sure it's at specific times of day and in locations convenient to their homes. Here in the U.S. and around the world, women are often caregivers of small children, so providing childcare can be critical.

Q: *If you were advising a journalist, what stories should journalists be following about women's economic empowerment in the U.S.? Globally?*

A: Journalists should look for where women are included or excluded from business and economic opportunity. Countries and companies are waking up to the fact that women matter. For instance, look at a country like Japan. The government there realized that it was missing out on the knowledge and expertise of a large proportion of its potential workforce. Look at the U.K. where the government has made a concerted effort to focus on women's success because it grows the country's economy. Countries that do not include women are not seeing the same economic growth as countries that do.

Q: *If you were advising a PR or advertising person, what messages are consumers and stockholders looking to hear from corporate social responsibility efforts with women?*

A: You must look at your business and come up with programs aligned with your business goals. Look at the comprehensiveness of your program and make sure your efforts or initiatives are sustainable. At Walmart, we are proud that our program encompasses sourcing, training and diversity and inclusion. We ask merchandise and professional service suppliers to report the gender and diversity representation of their Walmart and Sam's Club teams using an online tool.

What responsibilities do advertising, marketing and strategic communications professionals have in creating a better society for all? The fundamental concern is that so much focus on gender ideals tied to outward appearance harms children and other vulnerable populations. This leads us to ask: *Do advertising, public relations and strategic communication images and campaigns represent gender in a way that is beneficial to our children and society?* Drumroll . . . just like your momma will tell you: You must decide for yourself. (It's OK to groan and roll your eyeballs.) How do the messages you create measure up to creating excellence in my profession?

What follows is an examination of the research that raises concerns for society about how gender is, has been and will be depicted by strategic communicators.

▶ GENDER ISSUES IN ADVERTISING AND STRATEGIC COMMUNICATION

During the 72nd Golden Globe Award show, comedian Tina Fey said, "Steve Carell's 'Foxcatcher' took two hours to put on, including his hair styling and makeup. Just for comparison, it took me three hours today to prepare for my role as human woman." Fey was poking fun at U.S. beauty standards for women. Many cultural critics believe advertisers, marketers and entertainment media set U.S. beauty standards in ways that fuel our need to buy more products. We are all familiar with the young, beautiful people that inhabit the world of TV and advertising. They little resemble most people that you encounter shopping at your local grocery store. (Next time you're shopping, look around—do the people you see in real life largely reflect the people you see on TV?)

Dehumanizing Women through Images

One of the most enduring and studied concepts is that of the *male gaze*. This was introduced to media studies by Laura Mulvey in her 1975 work "Visual Pleasure and Narrative Cinema" appearing in the journal *Screen*.[30] The term, applied to advertising, refers to how women are shown through the power of the camera lens—as if men were looking at them. In a 2011 interview, Mulvey describes the male gaze as depicting, "gender roles along active/male narrative control and female/eroticized spectacle."[31] She further notes that the male gaze is about power relationships and the role of sexuality in those relationships. She notes that the female body and who had control of it was central to early feminists. She comments, "Thus, if the female body was a site of oppression, questions of representation could not be ignored, so it was impossible to conceive of liberating the female body without analyzing oppressive representations of the female body."[32] The scholar who interviewed Mulvey brought up the point that in Italian advertising, transgender models are included in pictures and asked whether that changes what it means for the male gaze. Mulvey responded noting that gender is on a range from masculinity and femininity and the male gaze concept is still relevant, as it has a lot to do with who has power.

Although a comedian, and not a journalist, Jon Stewart has used his sharp wit to address contemporary cultural issues and how media cover them. In a segment on his June 2, 2015, show, he addressed the media coverage of Caitlyn Jenner's cover shot on *Vanity Fair* magazine, by analyzing TV news coverage through the lens of the male gaze. (See Figure 5.3) In his assessment of media coverage, Stewart said, "You see, Caitlyn, when you were a man, we could talk about your athleticism and business acumen, but now you're a woman, which means, your looks are the only thing we care about. . ." He went on to point out the irony that TV personalities and journalists started comparing her attractiveness to other female celebrities, and then went on to ponder how much airbrushing was done and finally complimented her—that she "looks good for her age. "Stewart was pointing out that when Jenner was previously in the media as a former decorated Olympian, his looks weren't the main story.

While Mulvey studied film, representations of the male gaze abound in advertising. For instance, models are presented in a way that shows them as figures on display for the opposite sex. In addition, the women viewing these types of ads over time are conditioned to see themselves similarly as objects to be viewed by other men or other

FIGURE 5.3 Former host of *The Daily Show*, Jon Stewart, illustrates how media talk about women by showing how media reacted to Caitlyn Jenner's photo on the July 2015 cover of Vanity Fair magazine.
Credit: Comedy Central, The Daily Show with Jon Stewart, June 2, 2015, http://www.cc.com/video-clips/oekklq/the-daily-show-with-jon-stewart-brave-new-girl

women. For example, we look in the mirror to see how others will see us. The idea is that the photographs of women in advertisements lead women to strive to be objects of beauty and to be concerned about how we look when others look at us.

Try this: Next time you enter a public or campus restroom, try to go in and out without looking at yourself in the mirror. Can you do it? Do we want to see what others will see when they look at us?

We are often asked, "What's wrong with advertising that shows off a woman's body? I like people looking at me when I look good." Well, the consequence of the ubiquity of this type of advertising is that we start to view our bodies as objects of display, as "things," that are disembodied from actual real people who think, feel, are smart and have hopes and dreams. It desensitizes us to think of people, of women, as having intrinsic spiritual value. In this way, the value that we begin to place on women (and men too, but to a lesser extent) focuses on the outside—our physical being—and not on the inside—our spirit, our essence, our values, beliefs, our hearts and intelligence. Maybe that is why marketers are searching for authenticity—it has been lost along the way. Not only do ads emphasize to society that a women's value is the "way she looks," and you get what you pay for, but it also leads some women to internalize this beauty standard. Some psychologists and media scholars believe that this internationalization is perhaps why the percentage of women that are happy with their bodies can be as low 2 percent, as identified by Unilever's Dove campaign research. The argument is that we need more of a balance of portrayals, and to see girls and women in ways that value the core of who we are, not just for our outside "shells," which will naturally wear and tear as we age.

Erving Goffman, famous sociologist, studied the portrayal of women in advertising and identified ways in which advertisers showed women and their bodies that put women in less powerful roles. A sister concept to the male gaze is Goffman's concept of *licensed withdrawal*. This refers to models' blank, vacant stares—models who avert their eyes from directly looking into the camera.[33] This absence of personality, human expression or emotion reinforces the idea that there is nothing else important to who the woman is aside from her looks, the clothes and accessories she is wearing or the products she is using. While advertising is intended to sell products, we also know that people like to buy products from people they can identify with—real people. That's, of course, why celebrity endorsers are popular. Again, the idea is that we need more of a variety of portrayals of gender in advertising.

Other visual portrayals of women that present women as less powerful identified with Goffman's work include emphasizing qualities associated with *femininity*, showing adult women as *childlike*—sucking their fingers or lollipops; portraying women as *subordinate* to men—physically in the photo shoot or as serving men; and portraying women as *victims of violence.*

▶ WOMEN'S BODIES: CONSEQUENCES AND DEBATES

Advertising and Violence

Yes, you read that right—women are portrayed in advertising as victims of violence. Dolce & Gabbana, the Italian high-end fashion house, in 2007 ran an ad in *Esquire* magazine. The ad depicted a beautiful women lying down with her pelvis raised being held down by a man leaning over her, and four other men in the background standing around. Even though she was clothed, the fashion ad seemed to depict the model as the victim of a potential gang rape. In an Adfreak column in *Adweek*, writer Todd Nunn reported that Stefano Gabbana in a *Newsweek* interview said that "we have always declared our love, as the feminine market represents 60 percent of our worldwide sales." Gabbana, as reported in *Adweek*, interpreted the ad as "an erotic dream, sexual game." This type of advertising, meant to be edgy and provocative, can fall flat and cause public relations problems for companies, as women account for about 80 percent of consumer purchases.

If we use the excellence concept to examine advertising that portrays "fantasy" violence toward women, we must ask ourselves whether this is authentic, proportional and contextual. How are women treated in society and is this OK? A Centers for Disease Control survey of 8,000 women in 2000 indicated that nearly 1 in 5 of the women they surveyed said they had been victims of a completed or attempted rape, and more than half reported they were under the age of 18 when it happened.[34] One in five women is too many. Do media help perpetuate a culture that makes it acceptable to inflict violence on women (and men)? Do depictions of violence toward women perpetuate this?

Public Relations and the Politics of Women's Bodies

Controversies surrounding women's bodies and who controls them have been a debate probably as far back as we have good records. Recently, public relations professionals working for politicians also have had to consider the implications of what their employers say about women's bodies. In 2012, a number of communication blunders contributed to candidates losing their political races. Famously, during a 2012 debate in Indiana for the state's U.S. Senate seat, candidate Richard Mourdock, Indiana's state treasurer, discussed abortion and said, "Even when life begins in that horrible situation of rape, that is something that God intended to happen."[35] Some felt it offensive that the candidate seemed to suggest God would intend a woman to be raped. The candidate apologized for his unfortunate language choice yet reaffirmed his belief in the value of all life. Even though he apologized, the comment was considered offensive and many believe it damaged his campaign, especially among female voters.[36]

The Indiana U.S. Senate race was often compared with the Missouri U.S. Senate campaign that year. In Missouri, Senate candidate Rep. Todd Akin, in an interview with St. Louis' Fox affiliate KTVI, also discussed his position on abortion saying, "First of all, from what I understand from doctors, (pregnancy) is really rare (in rape cases). If it's a legitimate rape, the female body has ways to try to shut that whole thing down."[37] The uproar that resulted after his comments were broadcast led Akin to apologize and say, "I believe deeply in the protection of all life, and I do not believe that harming another innocent victim is the right course of action."[38] While both Mourdock and Akin did what most public relations practitioners would suggest—apologize—the candidates' statements damaged their reputations in the eyes of many. Rep. Todd Akin lost the support of his political party, which pulled its endorsement of him and its money, providing U.S. Sen. Claire McCaskill the chance to retain her seat, which was not expected to happen.[39] What was worrying to many was that men who would take leadership positions in which they would make decisions that would affect half our population—women—expressed such thoughts. In her tenure, U.S. Sen. Claire McCaskill has led bipartisan efforts to reduce sexual assault on college campuses and in the military.

Senate candidates were not the only ones to make missteps. Presidential candidate and former Massacheusetts Gov. Mitt Romney created a meme sensation during the second presidential debate with President Barack Obama. While discussing his position on equal pay and employment for women, he attempted to provide a heartwarming story from his days as Massachusetts governor. In describing his efforts to find qualified women, he recounted that he had approached several women's groups asking, "Can you help us find folks? And they brought us whole binders full of women." (If you get a chance, search the Web for "Binders Full of Women" and see if you find images the meme spawned on Tumblr.) Gov. Romney had led Obama with women voters up until that unfortunate gaffe. In addition, a fact check of his story by the publication *Phoenix*, indicated some inaccuracies in what he said.[40]

Truly, 2012 was the year for voters to hold politicians accountable for their misstatements about gender. To public relations practitioners for the opponents of these candidates, these expressions of their views of women were a godsend. For the PR practitioners working for the candidates who insulted voters, this was a nightmare. How do you come back from statements that appear to suggest women must bear the consequences for barbarous acts committed by others?

In politics, it is clear that decisions affecting women have immediate consequences in the form of laws and policies. However, politics is not the only arena where gender issues concern public relations practitioners. However, politics may be the most consequential, as politicians command the power to enact laws that govern society and societal institutions as well as distribute our country's resources.

▶ CHAPTER SUMMARY

There are entire courses devoted to the issues of gender inequality, gender and the media, and gender and work. We have briefly touched on issues of gender and raised issues for you to think about as future communicators. Because gender roles change by culture, by society and over time, it may seem impossible to practice excellence when thinking about how gender might instantiate itself in your journalism, advertising or communication. From the day your parents had your baby shower (pink or blue), to the toys we grow up with (regular Legos® or girl Legos®), to what classes we were encouraged to take (engineering or teaching), and whether we're ready for a promotion (he's a strong leader; she's aggressive), gender colors our lived experiences. Many times we act automatically and without thinking and will make assumptions about gender or not even think about inclusion. In fact, in writing this chapter, you will notice that our sources are overwhelmingly female. You don't know if this was intentional, if we just thought the best people to talk with on this topic were female or whether men didn't want to talk with us about gender. Maybe men told us they thought a chapter about gender was the "fluff" section of the book (they didn't). The truth is, we wanted to share the voices of experience from women journalists and communicators.

In reality, while representation matters, and it does, bias is much more insidious. It works in ways that devalue women and women's experiences, makes it seem like women's opinions matter less and suggests that women should "look pretty," but "keep quiet." But, you can do it differently. Think about it in this way: How do you want the women you care most about to be treated? What about the men in your life whom you love? So, let's strive for excellence to avoid the simple gender stereotypes and remember how gender also intersects with all of the fault lines—and that the way we treat people—men or women—matters.

 BOX 5.4   Examples Of Good Reporting on Gender-Related Issues

1. *NEW YORKER* DIANA NYAD PROFILE:

This profile of 64-year-old long-distance swimmer Diana Nyad was recognized by *Slate*'s Amanda Hess as one of the top stories about women written in 2014.

Media Links:

- http://www.newyorker.com/magazine/2014/02/10/breaking-the-waves-2

(Continued)

BOX 5.4 Continued

- http://www.newyorker.com/culture/culture-desk/out-loud-ariel-levys-powerful-women
- http://www.slate.com/blogs/xx_factor/2014/12/30/_2014_in_review_the_best_things_written_about_women_this_year.html

2. *NEW YORK TIMES* ARTICLE ON A STARBUCKS BARISTA:

This feature offered insight into the daily life of a 22-year-old Starbucks barista and single mother to address the impact of new work-scheduling technologies on low-income workers, particularly those with children.

Media link:

- http://www.nytimes.com/interactive/2014/08/13/us/starbucks-workers-scheduling-hours.html

3. *WASHINGTON POST* PROFILE OF DIANNE FEINSTEIN:

The Women's Media Center recognized this June 2013 profile of the U.S. senator as an example of news coverage of a female politician that refrains from mentioning her skin, makeup or clothing, despite appearing in the newspaper's Style section.

Media links:

- http://www.nameitchangeit.org/blog/entry/a-profile-of-a-powerful-woman-that-doesnt-suck
- http://www.washingtonpost.com/lifestyle/style/feinstein-nsas-top-congressional-defender-has-built-respect-over-decades-of-service/2013/06/25/69a5ec4e-dd17–11e2–9218-bc2ac7cd44e2_story.html

4. *TEXAS MONTHLY* WOMEN'S HEALTH ISSUE:

Mimi Swartz's feature on the status of women's health issues in Texas following the 2011 legislative session, "Mothers, Daughters, Sisters, Wives," won a National Magazine Award in 2013.

Media link:

- http://www.texasmonthly.com/story/mothers-sisters-daughters-wives

(Continued)

BOX 5.4 Continued

5. *THE STRANGER* FEATURE ON A WOMAN'S SURVIVAL OF AN ATTACK:

Eli Sanders, of Seattle's *The Stranger*, won the 2012 Pulitzer Prize for feature writing for "The Bravest Woman in Seattle," his account of a woman who survived an attack that killed her partner. According to the Pulitzer citation, the article used "the woman's brave courtroom testimony and the details of the crime to construct a moving narrative."

Media links:

- http://www.pulitzer.org/citation/2012-Feature-Writing
- http://www.thestranger.com/seattle/the-bravest-woman-in-seattle/ Content?&oid=8640991

6. THE *HONOLULU ADVERTISER* SERIES ON FEMALE DOMESTIC VIOLENCE SURVIVORS:

This seven-part investigative series, which chronicled the experiences of native Hawaiian women who experienced domestic violence, won a 2009 Dart Award for coverage of trauma.

Media links:

- http://dartcenter.org/content/crossing-line-abuse-in-hawai%E2%80%99i-homes#.VNjUOWTF8qY
- http://dartcenter.org/content/dayshas-diary#.VNjUdGTF8qY

7. PBS DOCUMENTARY "THE INVISIBLE WAR":

This 2012 documentary, which addresses the problem of rape and sexual assault within the U.S. military, prompted New York Sen. Kirsten Gillibrand to present a bill addressing the issue of sexual assault in the military. It received Emmy and Peabody awards and was nominated for an Academy Award. The film features interviews with veterans from various military branches recounting their assaults.

(Continued)

BOX 5.4 Continued

Media links:

- http://invisiblewarmovie.com/
- http://www.pbs.org/independentlens/invisible-war/

8. CURRENT TV INVESTIGATION "RAPE ON THE RESERVATION":

This Livingston Award–winner for National Reporting investigated rapes committed by male members on young women of the Rosebud Indian reservation in South Dakota. According to the award citation, "The report brought to light the violent epidemic and the disturbing acceptance of this behavior by perpetrators who saw these crimes as part of normal behavior."

Media links:

- http://www.livawards.org/winners/past_winners.php?y=2011
- http://vimeo.com/54786283

9. DATELINE NBC'S "JOSIE'S STORY":

This Dateline NBC profile of a 9-year-old transgender female child considering gender reassignment hormones and surgery was nominated for a 2013 Emmy Award for Outstanding Feature in a News Magazine.

Media link:

- http://www.nbcnews.com/video/dateline/50696582#50696582

▶ **SUGGESTED ACTIVITIES**

1. Choose a national or local newspaper and examine a day's front-page stories. First, count and compare the total number of male sources versus female sources quoted in all those stories. Next, compare the backgrounds and identities (e.g., experts, non-experts, victim) of female sources versus male sources quoted in the stories. Are there gender discrepancies in the news sources? If so, in what ways? Come up with specific strategies for how more diverse sources could have been found for reporting the stories.

2. Choose a news magazine and examine the news photographs appearing in a recent issue. What kinds of men are featured (age, profession, ethnicity, etc.)? How are they portrayed visually? What messages do those photos convey about the specific gender roles and social expectations of men? Identify any gender stereotypes you may find in those photos.

3. Find any advertisement that portrays a woman in *licensed withdrawal* and redo the ad to show a women who is empowered using the product. What symbolizes women's empowerment in your ad? Show the original ad and your reconstructed ad to several female friends. What are their reactions? Do you think you were successful in showing an empowered woman? Why or why not?

4. Some would argue that the use of steroids in sports has resulted from pressures on men to be masculine, bigger and better. Look at ads featuring men in the 1950s and compare them to how men are portrayed in ads for similar products today (*and if you want to have a cultural experience—check out the microfiche/microfilm section of the library*). Do men look different today, compared to the 1950s? Do you see any other changes in how men are shown? What do you think that means about expectations placed on men? If there are also women in the ads, how are their portrayals different?

5. Interview a young professional in journalism. Do they think about gender representation in their work? Do they engage in any strategies to improve the inclusion of women or men? Do their bosses tell them that inclusion of diverse sources in their stories is important? What does the gender representation look like in their newsroom? In their newsroom's management? (Remember, you should agree with your source about what in your conversation may be confidential.)

▶ NOTES

1 Stacy Smith, Marc Choueiti, Ashley Prescott and Katherine Pieper, "Gender Roles & Occupations: A Look at Character Attributes and Job-Related Aspirations in Film and Television," 5 (Los Angeles: Geena Davis Institute on Gender in Media, 2012).
2 Cory Armstrong, "The Influence of Reporter Gender on Source Selection in Newspaper Stories." *Journalism & Mass Communication Quarterly* 81, no. 1 (2004): 139–54; Dustin Harp, Ingrid Bachmann and Jaime Loke, "Where Are the Women? The Presence of Female Columnists in U.S. Opinion Pages," *Journalism & Mass Communication Quarterly* 91, no. 2 (2014):

289–307; Geri Zeldes, Frederick Fico and Arvind Diddi, "Race and Gender: An Analysis of Sources and Reporters in Local Television Coverage of the Michigan Gubernatorial Campaign," *Mass Communication & Society* 10, no. 3 (2007): 345–63.

3   Wolfram Peiser, "Setting the Journalist Agenda: Influences from Journalists' Individual Characteristics and from Media Factors," *Journalism & Mass Communication Quarterly* 77 (2000): 243–57; Karen Ross, "The Journalist, the Housewife, the Citizen and the Press: Women and Men as Sources in Local News Narratives," *Journalism* 8, no. 4 (2007): 449–73.

4   David Newman, *Identities & Inequalities* (New York: McGraw-Hill, 2007), 53.

5   Ibid.

6   Dhyana Ziegler and Alisa White, "Women and Minorities No Network Television News: An Examination of Correspondents and Newsmakers," *Journal of Broadcasting and Electronic Media* 34 (1990): 215–23; Carol Liebler and Susan Smith, "Tracking Gender Differences: A Comparative Analysis of Network Correspondents and Their Sources," *Journal of Broadcasting and Electronic Media* 41 (1997): 58–68.

7   Geri Zeldes and Frederick Fico, "Race and Gender: An Analysis of Sources and Reporters in the Networks' Coverage of the 2000 Presidential Campaign," *Mass Communication and Society* 8 (2009): 373–85.

8   "The Status of Women in the U.S. Media 2014," Women's Media Center, http://wmc.3cdn. net/6dd3de8ca65852dbd4_fjm6yck9o.pdf.

9   "Silenced: Gender Gap in 2012 Election Coverage," Fourth Estate, http://www.4thestate.net/ female-voices-in-media-infographic/.

10   Mallary Tenore, "Chris Hayes On Why 'Diversity . . . Benefits the Project,'" *Poynter*, March 28, 2013, http://www.poynter.org/news/mediawire/208755/chris-hayes-on-why-diversity-benefits-the-product/.

11   Karen O'Connor, Sarah Brewer and Michael Fisher, *Gendering American Politics: Perspectives from the Literature* (New York: Person Longman, 1994).

12   Diana Carlin and Kelly Winfrey, "Have You Come a Long Way, Baby? Hillary Clinton, Sarah Palin, and Sexism in 2008 Campaign Coverage," *Communication Studies* 4 (2009): 326–43.

13   Rosemary Ricciardelli, Kimberley Clow and Philiip White, "Investigating Hegemonic Masculinity: Portrayals of Masculinity in Men's Lifestyle Magazines," *Sex Roles* 63 (2012): 64–78.

14   Belinda Wheaton, "Lifestyle Sport Magazines and the Discourses of Sporting Masculinity," *The Sociological Review* 51, no. S1(May 2003): 192-221, http;//, doi:10.1111/j.1467–954X.2003. tb03612.x.

15   Lauren Klinger and Kelly McBride, "Lessons learned from Grantland's tragic story on Dr. V, Poynter," Jan 22, 2014, http://www.poynter.org/news/mediawire/236657/lessons-learned-from-grantlands-tragic-story-on-dr-v/.

16   The authors would like to thank Joy Jenkins and Youn-Joo Park for helping prepare boxes 5.1, 5.2 and 5.4.

17   For example, Global Media Monitoring Project (2005), *Mission Possible: A Gender and Media Advocacy Toolkit*; International Federation of Journalists (2009), *Getting the Balance Right: Gender Equality in Journalism*; UNESCO (2012), *Gender-Sensitive Indicator for Media: Framework of Indicators to Gauge Gender Sensitivity in Media Operations and Content*;

UNESCO (2014), *Women Make the News 2014*; IAMCR, AIECS, AIERI (2014), *Media and Gender: A Scholarly Agenda for the Global Alliance on Media and Gender*.

18 Tom Shales, "No News Not the Best News for Katie Couric's Debut," *Washington Post*, September 6, 2006, C01.

19 Margaret Gallagher, *Unequal Opportunities—The Case of Women and the Media* (Paris: UNESCO, 1981); Anthony Delano, "Women Journalists: What's the Difference?" *Journalism Studies* 4 (Summer 2003): 273–86; Pamela Creedon, *Women in Mass Communication: Challenging Gender Values* (Newbury Park, CA: Sage, 1993); Marjan de Bruin and Karen Ross, *Gender and Newsroom Cultures: Identities at Work* (Cresskill, NJ: Hampton Press, 2004).

20 Geri Zeldes and Frederick Fico, "Race and Gender: An Analysis of Sources and Reporters in the Networks' Coverage of the 2000 Presidential Campaign," *Mass Communication and Society* 8 (2009): 373–85; "The Status of Women in the U.S. Media 2014," Women's Media Center, 2014, http://www.womensmediacenter.com/pages/2014-statistics.

21 Maurine Beasley and Sheila Gibbons, *Taking Their Place: A Documentary History of Women and Journalism* (Washington, DC: American University Press, 2003).

22 The 2001 median income for a female journalist was $37,713, significantly lower than that of a male journalist at $46,780. See David Weaver et al., *The American Journalist in the 21st Century* (Mahwah, NJ: Lawrence Erlbaum, 2007).

23 Yong Volz and Francis Lee, "What Does it Take for Women Journalists to Gain Professional Recognition? Gender Disparities among Pulitzer Prize Winners, 1917–2010," *Journalism and Mass Communication Quarterly* 90 (2013): 248–66.

24 Natalie Zmuda and Ann-Christine Diaz, "Marketers Go Soft on Feminism," *Advertising Age* 85 (2014): 16.

25 "Top Ad Campaigns of the 21st Century: Dove Campaign for Real Beauty," *Advertising Age* 86 (January 12, 2015): 16.

26 "Top Ad Campaigns. . ."; Diann Daniel, "Real Beauty = Real Sales?" *CMO Magazine*, (January 30, 2006), http://www.cmomagazine.com/read/current/real_beauty.html; Michelle Jeffers, "Behind Dove's 'Real Beauty,'" *Adweek*, (September 12, 2005,), http://www.adweek.com/news/advertising/behind-doves-real-beauty-81469.

27 Diann Daniel, "Real Beauty = Real Sales?"

28 "Top ad campaigns. . ."

29 Diann Daniel, "Real Beauty = Real Sales?"

30 Roberta Sassatelli, "Interview with Laura Mulvey: Gender, Gaze and Technology in Film Culture." *Theory, Culture & Society* 28 (2011): 123–43.

31 Ibid., 130.

32 Ibid., 131.

33 Anthony Cortese, *Provacateur: Images of Women and Minorities in Advertising*, 2nd ed. (Oxford, UK: Rowman & Littlefield, 2004).

34 Patricia Tjaden and Nancy Thoennes, *Full Report of the Prevalence, Incidence and Consequences of Violence Against Women: Findings from the National Violence Against Women Survey*, November 2000, https://www.ncjrs.gov/pdffiles1/nij/183781.pdf.

35 Judy Keen, "Rape Remark Churns Indiana Race," *USA Today*, November 2, 2012.

36 Ibid.

37 Kevin McDermott, "Senator Pounced on 'Legitimate Rape' Remark to Rebound," *St. Louis Post-Dispatch*, November 7, 2012, A1.

38 John Eligon and Michael Schwirtz, "In Rapes, Candidate Says, Body Can Block Pregnancy," *The New York Times*, August 20, 2012.

39 Ibid.

40 Josh Hicks, "Romney's Anecdote During Debate Prompts a Closer Look Inside His Binder," *Washington Post*, October 18, 2012.

▶ ADDITIONAL READINGS

Armstrong, Cory. "The Influence of Reporter Gender on Source Selection in Newspaper Stories." *Journalism & Mass Communication Quarterly* 81, no. 1 (2004): 139–54.

Blakely, Mary Kay. *American Mom: Motherhood, Politics, and Humble Pie*. Chapel Hill, NC: Algonquin Books of Chapel Hill, 1994.

Correa, Teresa and Dustin Harp. "Women Matter in Newsrooms: How Power and Critical Mass Relate to the Coverage of the HPV Vaccine." *Journalism & Mass Communication Quarterly* 88, no. 2 (2011): 301–19.

D'oro, Rachel. "Shock-Jocks Suspended over Slur against Alaska Native Women." *Seattle Times*, April 16, 2008.

Frisby, Cynthia M. and Jennifer Stevens Aubrey. "Race and Genre in the Use of Sexual Objectification in Female Artists' Music Videos." *Howard Journal of Communications* 23, no. 1 (2012): 66–87. doi:10.1080/10646175.2012.641880.

Katz, Jackson. The Macho Paradox: Why Some Men Hurt Women and How All Men Can Help. Naperville, IL: Sourcebooks Inc., 2006.

Katz, Jackson. "Advertising and the Construction of Violent White Masculinity: From Eminem to Clinique for Men." In *Gender, Race and Class in the Media: A Text Reader*, ed. Gail Dines and Jean M. Humez, 349–58. Thousand Oaks, CA: Sage, 2003.

Kay, Katty and Claire Shipman. *The Confidence Code: The Science and Art of Self-Assurance—What Women Should Know*. New York: HarperCollins, 2014.

Kilbourne, Jean. "The More You Subtract, the More You Add: Cutting Girls Down to Size." In *Gender, Race and Class in the Media: A Text Reader*, ed. Gail Dines and Jean M. Humez, 258–67. Thousand Oaks, CA: Sage, 2003.

Knobloch-Westerwick, Silvia and Joshua P. Romero. "Body Ideals in the Media: Perceived Attainability and Social Comparison Choices." *Media Psychology* 14, no. 1 (2011): 27–48. doi:10.1080/15213269.2010.547833.

Len-Ríos, María E., Shelly Rodgers, Esther Thorson and Doyle Yoon. "Representation of Women in News and Photos: Comparing Content to Perceptions." *Journal of Communication* 55, no. 1 (2005): 152–68.

Ross, Karen and Margie Comrie. "The Rules of the (Leadership) Game: Gender, Politics and News." Journalism Theory, Practice and Criticism 13, no. 8 (November 2012). 969-84. doi:10.1177/1464884911433255.

Sandberg, Sheryl. *Lean In: Women, Work, and the Will to Lead*. New York: Alfred A. Knopf, 2013.

Stern, Susannah R. "All I Really Needed to Know (About Beauty) I Learned by Kindergarten, a Cultivation Analysis." In *Race/Gender/Media: Considering Diversity Across Audiences, Content and Producers*, ed. Rebecca Ann Lind, 22–6. Boston, MA: Pearson, 2004.

Tan, Yue, Ping Shaw, Hong Cheng and Kwangmi Kim. "The Construction of Masculinity: A Cross-Cultural Analysis of Men's Lifestyle Magazine Advertisements." *Sex Roles* 69, no. 5/6 (2013): 237–49. doi:10.1007/s11199–013–0300–5.

Van Zoonen, L. "One of the Girls?: The Changing Gender of Journalism." In *News, Gender and Power*, ed. Cynthia Carter, Gill Branston and Stuart Allan, 33–46. London: Routledge, 1998.

Zayer, Linda Tuncay and Catherine A. Coleman. "Advertising Professionals' Perceptions of the Impact of Gender Portrayals on Men and Women: A Question of Ethics?" *Journal of Advertising* 44, no. 3 (2015): 1–12. doi:10.1080/00913367.2014.975878.

Zernike, Kate. "Postfeminism and Other Fairy Tales." *New York Times*, March 16, 2008.

6

Mass Media and the LGBT Community

Gary R. Hicks

Homosexuality shears across the spectrum of American life—the professions, the arts, business and labor. It always has. But today, especially in big cities, homosexuals are discarding their furtive ways and openly admitting, even flaunting, their deviation. Homosexuals have their own drinking places, their special assignation streets, even their own organizations. And for every obvious homosexual, there are probably nine nearly impossible to detect. This social disorder, which society tries to suppress, has forced itself into the public eye because it does present a problem—and parents especially are concerned. The myth and misconception with which homosexuality has so long been clothed must be cleared away, not to condone it but to cope with it.[1]

The above passage is from a 1964 *Life* magazine feature story titled "Homosexuality in America," and was accompanied by a two-page photo of men at a San Francisco gay bar

LEARNING OBJECTIVES

By the end of this chapter, you should be able to:

- understand how homosexuality has historically been treated by the mainstream media in both news coverage and advertising.

- realize the power of the media to marginalize groups and individuals.

- recognize how major societal and cultural events have impacted media coverage of LGBT people.

- apply non-stigmatizing principles and practices to your own work in the media industries.

called the Tool Box. Historians have pointed to this photo as being the first picture of the inside of a real gay bar ever to run in a mainstream publication in the United States. And it was this type of image—the homosexual as deviant, sick and constantly in trouble with the law—that persisted well beyond the first stirring of the gay rights movement. It was, in fact, the 1969 riots at the Stonewall Inn in New York City that marked the first time that gays stood up to police during a raid. At the time, it was illegal in most parts of the country for gays to openly congregate. Newspapers often-times ran photos of—mostly men—being paraded out of bars and into paddy wagons. Despite now being called the beginning of gay rights in America, the riots at the time garnered little media interest. Papers that did cover the riots (note how even labeling them "riots" framed the protesters as dangerous lawbreakers) did so in the most ste-reotypical and condescending manner. "Homo Nest Raided, Queen Bees Are Stinging Mad," read the headline of the story about the raid in the *New York Daily News*.[2] The reporter's lead read:

> She sat there with her legs crossed, the lashes of her mascara-coated eyes beating like the wings of a hummingbird. She was angry. She was so upset she hadn't bothered to shave. A day old stubble was beginning to push through the pancake makeup. She was a he. A queen of Christopher Street.

The story went on to refer to the patrons of the Stonewall as "the homosexual element," as "girls," and quoted a police officer saying that the rioters were "throw-ing more than lace hankies." While this reporting seems outlandish to contempo-rary readers, it represents the first way that mainstream audiences learned about the gay community. For all accounts, gay people had been invisible in the nation's press. According to one study of *Time* and *Newsweek* magazines, only two sto-ries concerning gays and lesbians appeared in the entire 1940s, and only 21 in the 1950s.[3]

The Stonewall riots are widely recognized as the catalyst for the LGBT rights move-ment. The event also forced journalists to cover the community, theretofore largely invisible outside of the police beat. The press had previously covered gays in much the same ways they were seen by society—as deviants and criminals. And they cov-ered them with alarm. "Growth of Overt Homosexuality in City Provokes Wide Con-cern," headlined a story about the New York State Liquor Authority's attempts to deny licenses to bars and restaurants frequented by gay clientele.[4] With the exception of Illi-nois, all states had sodomy laws on their books, and began enforcing them with greater intensity in relation to the growing gay rights movement. And it was not until 1973 that the American Psychiatric Association removed homosexuality as a mental illness from its official list of mental disorders.

▶ MARGINALIZATION BY MEDIA

So why focus on the media? What are their roles in contributing to public perceptions of LGBT people, or for that matter their perception of themselves? People, of course, define themselves in relation to their environment. Today, this environment is mediated. In a mediated world, this environment is shaped by words and images.

> Radio, television, film and other products of media culture provide materials out of which we forge our very identities, our sense of selfhood; our notion of what it means to be male or female; our sense of . . . sexuality; of 'us' and 'them.'[5]

Media organizations organize and "make sense of" stories through well-defined patterns of behavior.[6] What does this mean? It means that how a news organization or advertising agency represents people, through words, images or even the processes they use, creates a sense of "reality" and common understanding. Along with our gender, our race, our religion and ethnicity, few markers of our humanity are as central to who we are as is our sexuality. In today's mediated world, that sexuality is described, defined and either accepted or rejected by how we are depicted in the mass media. And the impact extends far beyond news and advertising. Studies have shown that positive portrayals of lesbian and gay characters in movies and television shows "serve as sources of pride, inspiration, and comfort" to lesbian and gay youth during the coming out process and in terms of self-realization.[7]

▶ ALPHABET SOUP OF INCLUSION: NOT ALL LETTERS ARE EQUAL

In an attempt to be as inclusive as possible, Wesleyan University in Connecticut came up with a 14-letter acronym to attach to its "safe space" center that encourages understanding of sexual diversity. The letters stand for "lesbian, gay, bisexual, transgender, transsexual, queer, questioning, flexural, asexual, genderf—k, polyamorous, bondage/discipline, dominance/submission and sadism/masochism." It's easy to see how such identification can perplex the general public and create a linguistic nightmare for the reporter or editor trying to cover these communities.

While this chapter uses the acronym LGBT for lesbian, gay, bisexual and transgender people, it is important to understand that many other identifications used by sexual minorities are important to consider, and that not all have experienced the same levels of public support or media coverage. Most of the social progress made over the past decades has been for lesbians and gay men. According to surveys attempting to determine the size of the LGBT population in the United States, approximately nine million Americans, or 3.5 percent of the entire population, identify as LGBT. Interestingly, more—1.8 percent—identify as bisexual than those who identify as lesbian or gay—1.7 percent.[8] Yet, there is very little coverage of bisexuals in media. According to a 2013 study by GLAAD, an organization dedicated to improving the mediated image of LGBT people, gay men represent the majority of LGBT characters on cable television, at 53 percent. Lesbians come in second at 24 percent. And only six percent of characters are portrayed as bisexual men and 15 percent as bisexual women.[9] Oftentimes, the female bisexuals are presented in highly sexualized ways to appeal to a straight male audience and play into its perceived fantasies. In these situations, even the word bisexual is rarely used.

Just as with bisexuals, transgender individuals have—until very recently—had to look hard to find any representation of themselves in media. Amazon's comedy-drama "Transparent," which debuted in 2014, deals with a family's coming to terms with their father's new transgender identity. Most news accounts of the transgender community have focused on whether or not sex reassignment surgery should be covered by insurance and Medicare, children not being allowed to attend school dressed in biological gender "non-conforming" clothes, and which restroom a transgender person should be allowed to use. Journalists sometimes can't resist an attempt to be clever, often at the expense of the transgender person. "The last time Rachel Pepe was at school, she was known to her teachers and classmates as Brian."[10] Even the venerable *New York Times* ran a 1998 feature on a prominent pianist who was transitioning from male to female. The lead described him as he did spring cleaning on his Upper West Side apartment, piling tailored Italian suits, ties and cashmere sweaters together to donate to the Salvation Army to make room for "a summery frilled blouse, a plum chiffon dress, a black Chanel gown and dozens of off-the-rack dresses."[11]

FOR DISCUSSION

1. Can you think of groups of people who are still today being marginalized by the media? Try to come up with specific examples of media products

or practices that you believe lead to this marginalization. What can be done to counter this marginalization?

2. Have you ever been marginalized, or made to feel like an outsider, by something that you have read, watched or heard in the media? Have you ever seen anything in the media that reaffirmed your identity?

3. Is it necessary to lump sometimes very different people under an acronym like LGBT or even longer? Does this labeling make the journalist's job easier or harder?

▶ ALTERNATIVE COVERAGE

It took decades after Stonewall for the tone of news coverage of homosexuality to get past the clichéd language and oftentimes dehumanizing characterizations. In the meantime, lesbians and gay men looked to the community-produced alternative press to connect with each other and to provide a space for community-positive news. This alternative journalism can, among other things, serve to "construct realities that oppose the conventions and representations of the mainstream media."[12]

The first widely distributed, relatively speaking, alternative publication for the gay and lesbian reader dates back to 1952 and the creation of *One Magazine*, primarily for gay men, and *The Ladder*, a magazine for lesbians that debuted the following year. While containing stories, essays and editorials by openly gay and lesbian writers, these publications almost uniformly extolled the goal of assimilation, "explicitly opting for a '50s-style conformism as they argued for gay inclusion in the postwar dream world."[13] What would become the *Advocate*, today's largest circulation magazine for the gay and lesbian market, began in 1967, and was closely followed by a number of city-focused gay publications, such as the *Washington Blade*, *NewsWest* in Los Angeles and Chicago's *GayLife*. Unlike the ones from the 1950s, these publications were highly political and stressed resistance, social change and gay rights.[14]

As the 1970s progressed, so did the alternative gay press. Mainstream media also began paying greater attention to the lesbian and gay community, though not always in a positive way. Buoyed by the strides made in the civil rights movement and the nascent second wave of the women's rights movement, the gay community pushed for more visibility in society—which meant the need for greater exposure in the mainstream media. But while newspapers and television began carrying more stories about lesbian and gay people, some of it amounted to what scholars refer to as a "backlash" against the community. One 1970 article in *Harper's* magazine referred to gays and lesbians as being "cursed."[15] Major news organizations, including *The New York Times*, refused to use the word "gay" (the name of choice by many in the gay rights movement) in their coverage, instead requiring the more clinical, some might say more stigmatizing, "homosexual." With issues such as voter referendums on whether to provide some degree of legal protection to gays and lesbians in employment and housing occurring in many locations in the nation in the 1970s, the community saw significant growth in media attention. It was also the decade when lesbian and gay journalists at major mainstream news outlets began to come out at work. Some lost jobs, while others became marginalized in a different way, by becoming their organizations' go-to people for any story related to gays and lesbians. Some walked the fine line between journalist and community activist.[16] While not always—or usually—positive in tone, the gay-and-lesbian community's size and its presence in many aspects of American society became visible to the nation through the mass media. Much of this visibility came at a price. Mainstream media became more willing to discuss the undeniable presence of gays and lesbians in society—though usually on its terms. A groundbreaking 1990 cover of *Newsweek* magazine highlighted a story called "The Future of Gay America."[17] It showed two male clasped hands with the words "testing the limits of tolerance" superimposed over their hands. What message was this cover sending? Not only does it distort the reality of the gay experience in America as belonging only to men (and white men for that matter), but frames gays and lesbians as needing to be tolerated by their heterosexual fellow citizens.[18] Did this magazine cover really paint lesbians and gays as fellow citizens or still as highly marginalized people?

The alternative press served a vital role in the gay rights movement, providing much-needed paths for communication and visibility. Today, there are still thriving media outlets that serve the LGBT community. The *Advocate*, which bills itself as the world's leading source of LGBT news, has a circulation nearing 200,000 for its print edition. Its online edition has more than a quarter million Facebook followers.[19] Other magazines include *Curve*, marketed to lesbians, *Out*, a fashion and lifestyle magazine, as well as regional publications and those targeting niche groups within the LGBT community, such as gay travel enthusiasts, gay sports fans and those living with HIV/AIDS.

FOR DISCUSSION

1. What strengths do you believe alternative media sources have in changing social awareness that mainstream media outlets do not have? Why?

2. How do you view the saying, "visibility at any cost"? Are there times when negative attention is necessary for a community?

3. Is there a problem with having gay reporters covering the gay community? Is it the same for Hispanic or African-American reporters to be assigned to cover news of those communities?

4. Do you believe that the LGBT alternative media today play a different role than the early papers like *The Ladder* and *One*? If so, what is its role? How do you see the role changing in the future?

▶ CULTURE SHIFT AMID CRISIS

Whatever gains the lesbian and gay community had made in the 1970s in public visibility and tolerance seemed to recede in the wake of the first reported case in 1981 of what would become known as AIDS. "Rare Cancer Seen in Gay Men" was the headline of a July 3, 1981, story about an illness impacting the gay community, one that didn't even have a name yet.[20] AIDS activist Larry Kramer wrote a decade into the epidemic that "no modern catastrophe has been more consistently badly reported throughout the length and breadth of the Anglo-American mass media than HIV/AIDS."[21] With HIV/AIDS being so closely associated with gay men and at such an early stage by the nation's media, stigma related to homosexuality resurfaced with a vengeance. And it has continued. Polling as recent as 2006 showed that half of Americans believe HIV/AIDS continues to add to anti-gay stigma.[22] When more was learned about how the virus is transmitted, accompanied by news reports of large-scale HIV infections among heterosexuals in Africa, a *Life* magazine cover proclaimed with a sense of panic, "Now No One Is Safe From AIDS."

▶ JOURNALISTIC FALLOUT FROM AIDS

Outing, the unauthorized disclosure of a person's sexual orientation, emerged in the late 1980s with the creation of magazines such as *OutWeek*, whose main goal was to "out" closeted celebrities and politicians, particularly those deemed hypocritical. Fueled by the AIDS crisis and the resulting stall in LGBT progress, activists created their own media and used it to stop what they called the "conspiracy of the closet"—a perceived plot by the political elite and the media to keep homosexuals hidden in society.[23] Business tycoon Malcolm Forbes was one of first to be outed with his photo on the cover and the caption, "The Secret Gay Life of Malcolm Forbes."[24] Major news organizations were not above outing, either. The *Wall Street Journal* picked up a London tabloid's story about *Rolling Stone* magazine founder Jann Wenner's being gay and included it in a front-page story.[25] It was actually the major newsweeklies that came up with the term "outing" to describe—and criticize—the work of *OutWeek*.

Even in a tell-all culture, outing was considered by many to be unethical. Many in the gay community see it as a personal decision and a process to be done at one's own initiation. Some gay activists and AIDS activists saw outing as counter-productive. Their argument was, what kind of role model would someone be who had to be pulled from the closet in this manner?

FOR DISCUSSION

1. Do crises ever alter the "rules" of news coverage? If so, how?
2. Is disclosing someone's sexual orientation still an ethical issue today? Is ethical behavior dictated by cultural and societal change?

▶ LGBT SOCIAL PROGRESS AND THE ROLE OF REPORTERS: COURIERS OF INFORMATION OR AGENTS OF CHANGE?

What is the difference between being a gay journalist and a journalist who happens to be gay? It seems like an easy question, but is one that has worried generations of gay journalists concerned about either being fired for being gay or, as mentioned above, being relegated to what some have called the "gay ghetto" of the newsroom. They are called upon to cover all stories dealing with LGBT issues. The last few decades have seen a seismic shift in public opinion on the gay community and its relationship with the rest of society. From the establishment—and later repeal—of "Don't Ask, Don't Tell" as a tool for keeping lesbians and gays hidden in the military, through state and municipal battles over job protection for gay employees and into the debate over gay marriage, there has been no dearth of important stories relating to LGBT people. While the early days of the AIDS epidemic kept some lesbian and gay reporters in the closet, these more recent developments in LGBT social progress have been accompanied by more and more mainstream media professionals self-identifying as LGBT. In 2014 the *Advocate* published a story on the 50 most influential LGBT people in media. Included were Rachel Maddow of MSNBC, Don Lemon of CNN, Ari Shapiro, a reporter for National Public Radio (NPR) and Josh Barrow of *The New York Times*. Independent and online media professionals were also on the list, including freelance journalist Jose Antonio Vargas and Gawker Media founder Nick Denton.[26] Transgender woman, Eden Lane, has been the on-air talk show host at a Denver PBS affiliate since 2009.

▶ ADVERTISING AND THE USE OF "GAY VAGUE"

If the gay community was caricatured by the news media, it was ignored completely by advertisers. Not that imagery that closely resembles today's advertisements targeting gay men—muscle-bound bodies, buddies playing sports—didn't exist, it was just cloaked in heteronormative deniability. Enter gay vague, the "wink" to the gay viewer to translate and decode the advertisement in ways that can be read by gay people as representing them and their lives. "The imperative that gay people stay in the closet during most of the 20th century necessitated a shared, private language."[27] Not until the

1990s did advertisers directly market to gay consumers in advertisements for products such as home furniture, automobiles and—especially—alcohol. While a few advertisements have appeared in mainstream media, most continue to be relegated to publications for the gay audience, such as the *Advocate* magazine. Most are targeted to gay men. Anheuser-Busch ran a series of print ads in the 1990s and early 2000s that, while not mentioning sexuality specifically, much less homosexuality, left little doubt about its target audience. "Another one coming out," was the tagline on an image of a six-pack of Bud Light being removed by a male hand from a refrigerator. Another more explicit ad—again only to those in the know—showed the bottom of a glass coffee table with bottles of Bud Light and caps strewn about. The tagline was "Tops and Bottles," alluding to the sexual roles sometimes applied by and towards gay men.

Why target advertising to the gay consumer? Why engage in masking practices like gay vague? The answer to the first question is simple—money. A 2013 analysis of the buying power of the LGBT population found that their disposable personal income (what's left over after taxes) was at an all-time high of $830 billion.[28] There is no question that money is to be made by targeting the gay community. Doing so, however, is a fairly new phenomenon.

"As a specific targeted group, gays have long been ignored by corporate interests. Seen as either too invisible (how do you market to the closet?), too despised, or too dispersed within the general population, gays have largely escaped the *direct* onslaught of advertising."[29] As public opinion of gays and lesbians has become more positive in recent years, so too has the corporate world's willingness to openly court the gay dollar. Examples of what are considered positive ads that focus on the LGBT community, along with suggestions for best practices can be found at www.adrespect.org.

▶ GAY VAGUE GOES BEYOND ADVERTISING

The use of gay vague imagery and language is not limited to advertising. One example is a *Wall Street Journal* article about then Supreme Court–nominee Elena Kagan. It was accompanied by a 17-year-old photo of Kagan playing softball with the caption "Court Nominee Comes to the Plate."[30] Many in the gay and lesbian community objected to what they saw as the use of the clichéd idea that lesbians play softball to imply that Kagan was lesbian.[31]

FOR DISCUSSION

1. How would you compare the power of advertising to the power of journalism to define a community?

2. Are there different standards for journalists than there are for advertising professionals when dealing with a marginalized community? If so, why?

3. Does the use of gay vague pose any ethical issues? If so, are there ways advertising professionals can address them short of not using gay vague images and text?

▶ A COMMUNITY'S OWN STYLE

At the heart of what we do as journalists and advertisers is the story. We learn to be great storytellers first and foremost, and then worry about having the skills to deliver those stories to audiences on a multitude of different platforms. Storytelling involves the use of language and image. And in the fast-paced media world, it helps to have certain guidelines that help us tell our stories fairly and in ways that benefit our society and lessen the chance that our words will hurt, stigmatize or marginalize people. Just consider the difference between writing that someone "admits" being gay—as papers used to do routinely—and that someone "identifies" as gay. The Associated Press Stylebook and others like it are used by news organizations around the world to ensure continuity and maintain standards in the use of language. When it comes to sexual minorities, both the *AP* and *The New York Times* style guides restrict the use of the term homosexual to clinical uses and sexual activity, not as a descriptor of individuals. To address more broad concerns of how media should cover the LGBT community, the National Lesbian and Gay Journalists Association (NLGJA) developed its own supplement to be used when reporting on LGBT issues or people. It covers issues ranging from using "transgendered people" instead of "transgendered," when describing individuals to how to appropriately report that someone is "straight." The full stylebook can be found at http://nlgja.org/stylebook.full.

In addition to the stylebook, NLGJA also provides a "Journalist's Toolbox" http://www.nlgja.org/Toolbox, and "tip sheets" on how to provide accurate and innovative ways to cover the community: http://www.nlgja.org/resources/tips.

▶ TIPS FOR COVERING THE COMMUNITY

- Remember that a person's sexual orientation is not always germane to a story. Include it only if it is essential to making the story complete.

- If a person's sexuality is necessary to telling the story, be upfront in asking your source about it. Don't make assumptions based on stereotypes because you feel uneasy asking someone to talk about sexuality.

- Remember that LGBT people "identify" as such. They never "admit" and rarely "acknowledge." Use people-positive attributions.

- Include the LGBT voice in stories that are not necessarily about LGBT issues. Remember that in stories about taxes, insurance and government benefits, for example, LGBT people do not necessarily receive the same treatment as heterosexuals.

- In designing advertising campaigns, do not assume what an LGBT audience looks like. While the alphabet soup of letters is joined to infer a single identity, the truth is that people are all individuals.

- Sexuality isn't always about sex. Respect that people are multi-dimensional.

 BOX 6.1   Bearing Witness to the Fuller Story

Jacqui Banaszynski
Knight Chair Professor ~ Missouri School of Journalism
1988 Pulitzer Prize in feature writing

On a mild evening in May 1987, I rode an elevator up to an apartment in Minneapolis and asked a man if I could watch him die. Dick Hanson was 37 years old, a son, brother and uncle, a farmer, political activist and singer in his Lutheran church choir. He also was gay and dying of AIDS.

The story of Hanson and his partner, Bert Henningson Jr., was told in "AIDS in the Heartland," published in four chapters between June 1987 and April 1988 in the *St. Paul (Minnesota) Pioneer Press*. At heart, the story was a timeless tale about two people who pledged unconditional love in the face of all that would defy it. Think "Romeo and Juliet."

But it also was a controversial and time-sensitive story: Hanson and Henningson embodied the AIDS crisis at a fever-pitch time in America.

They contracted, suffered and died from a mysterious disease—cancer-like symptoms, skin lesions, pneumonia, wasting bodies, wasting minds. There was, as yet, no known treatment. Death usually came within two years of diagnosis. Even when science determined that the underlying virus was transmitted through intimate contact with blood or semen, those findings were trumped by fear: What about doorknobs? Public toilets? Saliva?

(Continued)

BOX 6.1 Continued

As extreme as the disease itself was, so was the public reaction to it. The vast majority of early HIV cases in the U.S. were gay men. So the terror of AIDS deepened a societal revulsion against homosexuality and fueled more widespread discrimination just as the gay rights movement was gaining traction. From the Stonewall Riots of 1969 through the activism of the 1970s, gay rights was on a trajectory similar to other social justice movements, including civil rights and the women's movement. Across the country, gays were demanding equal rights to jobs, housing and privacy.

But when AIDS ripped through the population, it became a justification for pushing back against that movement. The Religious Right considered homosexuality a perversion; some celebrated AIDS as a punishment for sin. Terrified parents didn't want gay men teaching their children or serving their food. There was even talk of putting people with HIV in quarantine—locking them away from the general public.

AIDS also tore deep rifts in the gay community itself. Partisan groups raged over whether to shut down the bathhouses, where men who denied their sexuality in public indulged in frequent, anonymous and unprotected sex with strangers. Should closeted gays be allowed their privacy or be "outed" as a sign of solidarity with the larger community?

Stepping into that morass as a journalist was like parachuting into a foreign land. I had been covering issues related to AIDS and gay rights for three years by then. But writing about policy debates and transmission rates is not the same as immersing yourself in another culture—a culture steeped in secrets and boiling in a complicated stew of judgment, shame and defiance. The challenges of gaining access to that world were exacerbated by harsh criticism from readers, who decried any stories that hinted of empathy towards AIDS patients or support for gay rights. Many readers simply didn't want to know.

Then Rock Hudson died. His fans were stunned when the Hollywood star, a hunky romantic lead and the antithesis of the stereotyped effeminate gay, announced in July 1985 that he had AIDS; he died three months later. Headlines exploded and the broader American public had to rethink notions of what it meant to be gay. That heightened interest provided a window of opportunity to make AIDS and gay rights a coverage priority for the mainstream press.

"AIDS in the Heartland" was just one story of dozens we tackled at the *Pioneer Press* in an attempt to cover all facets of the AIDS crisis—political, legal, moral, societal, economic and medical. And to understand how all that played out from a

(Continued)

BOX 6.1 Continued

personal, rather than policy, perspective, we set out to find someone who would let us inside his life as he dealt with the physical and social ravages of AIDS.

It took almost another year to find Dick Hanson. Despite all that was now being written about AIDS, many of those with the disease remained closeted. Photographer Jean Pieri and I talked to people who were afraid of losing their jobs or insurance, of being shunned by family or unknowing friends. Even in the bigger markets on the East and West coasts, where AIDS was taking horrendous tolls, personal stories of AIDS sufferers usually were published without real names, or posthumously.

We took a different tack, believing that journalism has the greatest credence when story subjects are portrayed honestly and fully. If we were to do a diagnosis-to-death AIDS narrative, we wanted to follow someone who would give us unconditional access and whose experience reflected the entirety of the disease, including all its ugliness. Perhaps most important we wanted someone with whom many readers could somehow relate, even if they didn't approve. We sought a central character who had more in common than not with most of our readers—someone who did daily chores, had difficult relationships with his family, tended a garden, loved baseball and worried about money.

Hanson and Henningson granted us that, and more. The courage and generosity they showed in giving up the last year of their lives to exposure, criticism and even death threats cannot be overstated.

"AIDS in the Heartland" played out almost 30 years ago. But the journalistic lessons it offers are as timeless as the story. Those lessons come not from academic research, but from experience that has proved solid over time. Key among them:

- *Language has power*, and is wielded as a weapon in battles of politics, perception and personal values. Consider "terrorist" vs "freedom fighter," "pro-choice activist" vs "abortion rights advocate." In the earliest days of the AIDS crisis, the disease was dubbed "gay cancer" or, by some, "the gay plague." The first medical term was GRID —gay-related immune deficiency. Those labels forever linked a dreaded disease with a disenfranchised sub-culture. Which means, in the U.S., AIDS became synonymous with homosexuality. At the time, few news organizations in the U.S. used the term "gay"; the sanctioned term—homosexual— put the spotlight on men's sexual activity and undervaluing their fuller lives. As journalists, we had to navigate that semantic territory and find a way to be respectful to both the story subjects and the readers.

(Continued)

BOX 6.1 Continued

- Walk-in-someone's-shoes journalism requires getting as close as possible to the center of the story. The *boundaries of "objectivity"* that guide more traditional reporting become problematic and, perhaps, dishonest. You can't ask people to trust you with their most intimate, human moments unless you give some humanity in return. Jean Pieri and I came to care about the two men; we shared meals with them, hugged them when we said hello or good-bye, changed their bedpans if needed, wept after their funerals. But we never forgot our obligation as professional journalists. Nothing was off the record. Any conditions were negotiated with transparency and honesty was paramount. The most painful of questions had to be asked. Examples: Who likely brought the virus into the relationship? Did the men continue to have sex outside their relationship? It is tempting to romanticize intimate story subjects as oppressed victims or defiant heroes; it is essential that, instead, they are presented as who they are—full, wonderful and flawed human beings.

- It is imperative to include all relevant perspectives. That doesn't mean bowing to *false equivalency* where every voice is given equal volume. But it does mean probing the shades and layers in any story, and giving all their due. "AIDS in the Heartland" was reported from the point of view of the two men who shared a love for each other and, as a result, a fatal disease. But it included the authentic pain felt by family members, fellow churchgoers, confused neighbors. One of the most important interviews I had was with three of Dick Hanson's brothers who were repulsed by his lifestyle and, even more, by the attention he garnered. They represented more of my readers than Hanson did. Journalism that gives "voice to the voiceless" won't be heard unless it respects the counter-voices. The goal is not to sway opinion, but to expand awareness and understanding.

- Stories live in the *context of the times*. The journalist's job is to understand that context but not be a slave to it. The *Pioneer Press* served a readership that was largely blue-collar, Catholic, traditional; and yet we told a story that challenged much of that. At the same time, we made decisions respecting those readers: we ran a photo of Hanson being helped off the toilet and cleaned by Henningson and a nurse's aide; we did not run a photo of a chaste kiss between the two men. Thirty years

(Continued)

BOX 6.1 Continued

later, with gay marriage front-page news, that photo would not be an issue; at the time, it was.

- Stories are not confined to a certain time. They simmer for years in the background, then suddenly boil over into the news. That may be especially true of stories involving social justice movements. Gays, blacks, women, the disabled—name your sub-culture—were either non-existent or labeled in the mainstream media until something erupted that couldn't be ignored. Journalists covering those uncovered communities need to delve into the past and *imagine the future*. They need to heed the lessons of past social justice movements to cover those that emerge now—struggles for the rights of immigrants, the poor and unemployed, Muslims. And they need to understand that *truth is elusive*, and often claimed by those who have the loudest voice. Which means the journalism needs to be both empathetic and independent.

A few final points that, in my experience, extend to all immersion journalism:

Meet the story where it is. Park your own presumptions, and the *pressures of public perception*. Everyone who has a stake in litmus issues like this also has an agenda. The journalist's job is to understand all of those agendas but not to bow to any one of them.

Don't assume you know what you think you know. That means you need to ask the sensitive question, the hard question, the offensive question, the seemingly stupid question. You need not to know, but to learn.

Respect the story subject but *serve the reader*. One of the hardest moments in our work on "AIDS in the Heartland" came when Hanson raged over the first chapter, and felt it painted too negative a picture. He wanted a positive story about support and community; I wrote a story about that, but also about impending death. I had to convince myself, and then him, that the honest story was the better story.

Believe the work matters. In journalism, we can't draw a straight line between effort and outcome. The "first draft of history" is not the full or final draft. But without it, only those in power—those with a sanctioned voice—are heard, and only they get to shape the narrative that determines perception and policy. Journalists need to *bear witness* to the fuller story of life.

▶ CHAPTER SUMMARY

- News coverage of lesbians and gay men has historically been negative and has resorted to stereotypes and clichés.

- Mass media play an important role in helping us to understand about different people, as well as understand about ourselves.

- LGBT—like heterosexuality—is a constructed reality. And it's media workers who do a lot of the building.

- In the early days of the gay rights movement, the alternative press provided a necessary space for more positive portrayals of the community.

- Crises, such as the AIDS epidemic, can lead to a backlash in the tone of media coverage of the gay community.

- In order to appeal to a gay market, while not "offending" the straight viewer, advertisers sometimes use a gay vague approach. News media can also use gay vague to infer an idea that they don't want to come out and say.

- Learning how to cover a community appropriately takes time, research and asking questions. If you are not LGBT yourself, don't think that you can't cover LGBT people or issues. There are many resources available.

▶ SUGGESTED ACTIVITIES

- Find a major story related to the LGBT community that has been covered both in the mainstream media, as well as by gay-targeted media such as the *Advocate*. Compare the coverage. Is the tone different? Do their main sources of information differ?

- Look through major fashion or lifestyle magazines. Can you spot any that appear to use gay vague appeals? If so, describe what elements of the ad made you feel that way. Do you believe that the ad resorts to clichés and stereotypes?

- Interview members of the LGBT community. Ask how media depictions influenced their own self-awareness. Did the media images make it easier or harder to come out?

▶ **NOTES**

1 Paul Welch, "Homosexuality in America." *Life* 56 June 26 (1964): 66.

2 Jerry Lisker, "Homo Nest Raided, Queen Bees Are Stinging Mad," *New York Daily News*, July 6, 1969, B1.

3 Lisa Bennett, "Fifty Years of Prejudice in the Media," *Gay & Lesbian Review Worldwide* 7, no. 2 (2000): 30–34.

4 Robert C. Doty, "Growth of Overt Homosexuality in City Provokes Wide Concern," *New York Times*, December 17, 1963, 1.

5 Rhonda Hammer and Douglas Kellner, *Media/Cultural Studies: Critical Approaches* (New York: Peter Lang, 2000), 5.

6 Pamela J. Shoemaker and Stephen D. Reese, *Mediating the message: Theories of influences on mass media content* (White Plains, NY: Longman, 1991).

7 Sarah C. Gomillion and Traci A. Giuliano, "The Influence of Media Role Models on Gay, Lesbian, and Bisexual Identity," *Journal of Homosexuality* 58, no. 3 (2011): 330, http://dx.doi.org /10.1080/00918369.2011.546729.

8 Gary J. Gates, "How Many People are Lesbian, Gay, Bisexual, or Transgender?" April 2011, http://williamsinstitute.law.ucla.edu/wp-content/uploads/Gates-How-Many-People-LGBT-Apr-2011.pdf.

9 "Where We Are on TV," GLAAD, 2013, http://www.glaad.org/files/2013WWATV.pdf.

10 Carol G. Williams, "Transgender Teen Told She Can't Come to School as Girl," *USA Today*, August 16, 2014, http://www.usatoday.com/story/news/nation/2014/08/15/transgendered-teen-told-she-cant-come-to-school-as-girl-14151795/.

11 Andrew Jacobs, "His Debut as a Woman," *New York Times*, September 13, 1998, 333.

12 Chris Atton and J. Hamilton, *Alternative Journalism* (Thousand Oaks, CA: Sage, 2008), 124.

13 Suzanna D. Walters, *All the Rage: The Story of Gay Visibility in America* (Chicago, IL: University of Chicago, 2001), 50.

14 Edward Alwood, *Straight News* (New York: Columbia University, 1996), 79.

15 Ibid., 104.

16 Ibid., 120.

17 *Newsweek*, March 12, 1990.

18 Margaret Cruikshank, *The Gay and Lesbian Liberation Movement* (New York: Routledge, 1992), 23.

19 Cision, June 6, 2012, http://www.cision.com/us/2012/06/top-10-gayand-lesbian-magazines/.

20 Lawrence K. Altman, "Rare Cancer Seen in 41 Homosexuals," *New York Times*, July 3, 1981, A20.

21 Larry Kramar, *Reports from the Holocaust: The Story of an Aids Activist* (New York: St. Martin's Press, 1994), xxviii.

22 Ethel Klein, "U.S. Public Opinion Toward HIV/AIDS; Perceptions of Risk, Bias, and Government Spending," Gay Men's Health Crisis, 2009, http://www.gmhc.org/files/editor/file/per ceptions_klein3.pdf.

23 Michelangelo Signorile, *Queer in America: Sex, the Media, and the Closets of Power* (Madison, WI: University of Wisconsin Press, 1993).

24 Michelangelo Signorile, "The Other Side of Malcolm," *Outweek* 38, March 18, 1990, http://www.outweek.net/pdfs/ow_38.pdf.

25 Patrick Reilly, "A Rolling Stone," *Wall Street Journal*, March 3, 1995, A1, http://www.lexisnexis.com/hottopics/lnacademic/.

26 "The 50 Most Influential LGBT People in Media," *Advocate*, September 16, 2014, http://www.advocate.com/politics/media/2014/09/16/50-most-influential-lgbt-people-media.

27 Robert Klara, "Gay Advertising's Long March Out of the Closet," *AdWeek*, June 16, 2013, http://www.adweek.com/news/advertising-branding/gay-advertising-s-long-march-out-closet-150235.

28 "America's LGBT Buying Power Estimated at $830 Billion," Witeck Communications, November 18, 2013, http://www.witeck.com/pressreleases/lgbt-2013-buying-power/.

29 Suzanna Danuta Walters, *All the Rage: The Story of Gay Visibility in America* (Chicago: University of Chicago Press, 2001).

30 Trish LaMonte, "Gay rights activist upset over Wall Street Journal's use of Elena Kagan softball photo" *The Post-Standard*, (May 12, 2010) Accessed Date. http://www.syracuse.com/news/index.ssf/2010/05/gay_rights_activists_upset_ove.html.

31 Stephen Hicks, *Lesbian, Gay and Queer Parenting: Families, Intimacies, Genealogies* (Basingstoke, UK: Palgrave, 2011)

▶ ADDITIONAL READINGS

Alwood, Edward. *Straight News.* New York: Columbia University Press, 1996.

Burgess, Susan. *The New York Times on Lesbian and Gay Issues.* Thousand Oaks, CA: CQ Press, 2011.

Gross, Larry. *Up from Invisibility: Lesbians, Gay Men, and the Media in America.* New York: Columbia University Press, 2001.

Gross, Larry and James D. Woods. *The Columbia Reader on Lesbians and Gay Men in Media, Society, and Politics.* New York: Columbia University Press, 1999.

Hicks, Gary. "The Use of 'Gay Vague' as a Tool for Outing: The Case of Elena Kagan and the *Wall Street Journal* Photo." *International Journal of the Image* 1, no. 1 (2011): 223–230.

Johnson, Gail and Michael C. Keith. *Queer Airwaves: The Story of Lesbian and Gay Broadcasting.* New York: Taylor Francis, 2001.

San Fillipo, Maria. *The B Word: Bisexuality in Contemporary Film and Television.* Bloomington, IN: Indiana University Press, 2013.

Shoemaker, Pamela J. and Stephen D. Reese. *Mediating the Message: Theories of Influences on Mass Media Content.* London: Longman, 1995.

7

Missing in Action: Religion in Mass Media Markets and News

Debra L. Mason

It was summertime in 2013, and Iranian-American writer Resa Aslan was promoting his book, titled *Zealot: The Life and Times of Jesus of Nazareth*, a historical account of Jesus Christ. When Aslan appeared as a guest on Fox News Network's online program, *Spirited Debate*, he was asked over and over how a Muslim could write a legitimate, scholarly book about Jesus. Many viewers interpreted this to mean the interviewer was suggesting that someone who practices Islam could not write a book about the historical figure Christians revere as a savior. Aslan, who earned a doctorate in the sociology of religion and a master's degree from Harvard in history of religion, pushed the point that it was his scholarship—his research and interpretations on the topic—that qualified him as an expert, not his personal faith. The interview went viral, with more than five million views on *BuzzFeed.com* and follow-up publicity for Aslan on Comedy Central's *The Daily Show*, among others. The book became number one on *The New York Times*' Best Seller list nearly as soon as it was released.

LEARNING OBJECTIVES

After reading this chapter, you should be able to:

- explain why religion is an important component of mass communication.

- compare how religion or faith relates to fault lines in news coverage.

- discuss the history and past failures of communicating about religion.

- list the challenges and problems for the media regarding religion today.

- explain how journalists and strategic communicators can do a better job with religion by including context, complexity and authenticity.

- describe the five-point test for avoiding destructive hate speech.

- find resources to improve inclusion of religion in accurate and meaningful ways.

For the public, the interview conformed to popular assumptions that Fox News' national news programming promotes a conservative, Christian-right and anti-Muslim agenda. For Aslan, the interview surely helped him sell thousands of books. It's rare to find as blatant of an example of a mainstream journalist exhibiting clear anti-Muslim sentiment on the air. Yet misrepresentations, omissions and stereotypes about religion are common in journalism and strategic communication. At a time when the publication of offensive religious cartoons in the French satirical magazine *Charlie Hebdo* can lead to a mass slaughter of journalists, journalists and strategic communicators need to do a better job of understanding the fault line of religion and when it risks becoming dangerously offensive.

▶ WHY RELIGION IS AN IMPORTANT COMPONENT OF MASS COMMUNICATION

Few topics are as complicated as religion. Across the globe, nearly 80 percent of the world's population is estimated to adhere to some faith. Religion is, and always has been, at the root of many of the world's biggest conflicts. It influences the schools children attend, where we volunteer, who we socialize with and how we vote. Religion is routinely the biggest category of philanthropic giving in the United States. Religion is the basis for the judicial, legal and banking systems in some countries.

Blasphemy laws, which prohibit the defamation of religious views or deities, are growing as a restriction to free speech across the globe.[1] In some countries, denouncing your religion can lead to death. Religion provides the framework for key values, morals and ideals. Even for people who do not belong to a specific religious institution or who are avowed atheists, beliefs of some type frame their worldviews.

▶ WHAT DO WE MEAN BY RELIGION AND BELIEF?

For our purposes, religion is any organized system of beliefs, ceremonies and rules used to worship a god, group of gods or the supernatural. Included in this definition is everything from the world's largest single religious institution—the 1.2 billion–member Roman Catholic Church—to something as small as one person meditating on Buddhist teachings at home. (See Figure 7.1 for a snapshot of the world's major religions.) "Beliefs" includes the morals, values and ethics people use to navigate the world, and they may not always believe in a god. Increasingly, religion encompasses people dubbed the "spiritual but not religious." These are people who reject institutionalized religion as the only path toward spiritual growth. Among these people are the "nones" who recent public opinion surveys talk about—people who do not feel they fit neatly into any religious organization.[2] Furthermore, increasingly atheists and other non-believer groups

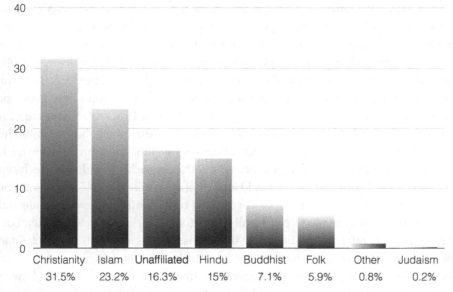

FIGURE 7.1 Major religions in the world
Data from Pew Research Center's Forum on Religion & Public Life Global Religious Landscape, released December 2012. Based on estimated world population of 6.9 billion. "Other" includes Bahai's, Jains, Sikhs, Shintoists, Taoists, Wiccans and others. "Folk" includes followers of African traditional religions, Chinese folk religions, Native American religions and Australian aboriginal religions. Percentages may not add up to 100 due to rounding. Graphic by Debra L. Mason. ©2015, used by permission.

such as free thought and humanist groups, which embrace non-religious ethical values, are organizing socially and politically in ways akin to religious denominations. For example, several universities including Harvard and Columbia have humanist chaplains and a federal court in 2014 ruled that humanism was an established belief system prisoners may claim. So broadly speaking, the term religion as used here encompasses formal and informal religion, faith, belief, spirituality and values—whether a deity or institutional edifice is involved or not.

▶ FAITH AS A FAULT LINE

In the U.S., when neighbors, families or coworkers get together over the holidays or on special occasions, people joke it's best to avoid talk of politics and religion—the two topics of conversation most likely to spark acrimony. Politics and religion are tied to deep-seated worldviews and opinion. Often, belief (or nonbelief) is something we learn and are taught as children and teenagers. For some, religion is impossible to separate from our physical identity. Religion can determine how or when we dress, style our hair, wear a beard, interact with the opposite gender, participate in worship services, consume alcohol or caffeine, eat meat or shellfish, use technology, schedule work, travel, create music and a host of other physical or sensory aspects of our lives. For other people, there is no obvious physical clue to a person's religious identity. Whether visible or not, faith may have an enormous impact on one's views about race, class, geography, gender and generation. Religion is not one of the Maynard Institute's core fault lines used to help journalists include diverse perspectives in the media, but we argue here that it is in fact a significant fault line that influences the public and our media in critical and often problematic ways. Religion interacts with every other fault line and is inseparable from them. "You can't understand Hobby Lobby's successful U.S. Supreme Court case challenging the health care law's coverage of birth control unless you understand the evangelical beliefs of the Green Family," says former Religion News Service Editor Kevin Eckstrom[3], referring to the family that owns the arts and crafts store chain and which ardently opposes some forms of birth control as abortion.

In another example of how religion interacts with other fault lines, consider how religion intersects with race in the United States. Certain racial and ethnic groups can be associated culturally with specific religions, although caution should always be used in making generalizations. For example, the vast majority of Hindus in the U.S. are from India or its neighbors, and it's impossible to separate Hinduism from Indian folk tales, music, art and dance. Although Islam is associated with many Arab-Americans, they are far from synonyms, as any Egyptian, Lebanese or Palestinian Christian will tell you. In fact, nearly 60 percent of United States African-Americans belong to historically black protestant denominations—the African Methodist Episcopal Church (AME), Church of God of Christ (COGOC) or National Baptist Convention churches, for example—some of which played important roles in civil rights battles. Although a much smaller number of African-Americans are Muslims, they comprise about one third of the entire U.S. Muslim population and include the minority of African-Americans belonging to the U.S.-founded Nation of Islam.

Religion and geography are related because strong religious identities are associated with particular regions, both in the U.S. and abroad. It would surprise no one that Utah has more Mormons than any other U.S. state. But did you know that China has more actual people practicing Islam than Saudi Arabia? Southern states such as Texas, Oklahoma, Arkansas, Mississippi, Alabama, Georgia, Tennessee and South Carolina comprise the "Bible Belt" for a reason. These states have a much higher percentage of people who believe the Bible is the literal word of God—one of several core beliefs often used to classify people as evangelical Christians—than states in the Pacific northwest, for example. Such context is vital. "Almost every survey story I have ever written tracks the cross tabs of religion, race and gender," said long-time *USA Today* Religion

Reporter Cathy Grossman, who now writes for *ReligionNews.com*. She recalled several 2014 stories about Pew Research Center's poll about end-of-life care. Although a main story had the overall data, in a sidebar, she "went much more deeply into how religion coupled with race is particularly influential in end-of-life decisions among minorities," Grossman said.

When the fault line of gender is considered, it's useful to know that research shows women are typically more "religiously adherent" than men in Western countries. Yet, just as very few women lead U.S. corporate boardrooms, women are in the minority in leading religious institutions. Several religions, including Roman Catholicism, Orthodox Judaism, most of Islam, Mormons and some evangelical Protestant groups, do not allow women or openly gay and lesbian people to be ordained as priests, pastors, rabbis or imams. Women journalists sometimes face similar challenges with these groups, as their gender can prohibit them from certain meetings or gatherings important to information gathering.

Religion plays a role in class distinctions, too, which can affect stereotypes about religions. One stereotype about religion is that all evangelicals are mostly poor or uneducated. But numerous studies and reports show that evangelical Christians have owned and managed some of the country's largest corporations, such as Hobby Lobby, Best Buy and Coca-Cola.[4]

When considering the fault line of generation, religion is one of the most significant differences between the young and old. Ever since sociologists have been able to measure religious participation in reliable ways, they have found that as people age and move closer to death, they also become more devoted to a religious belief or institution. This is partially a reflection of the human life cycle; every religion responds in some way to mortality and the closer one gets to death, the more people adopt beliefs about life beyond death. Although the number of people in the U.S. and Western Europe who say they have no religious identification has grown in the past two decades, according to surveys from Pew Research Center the trend toward secularity is most striking among millennials—people born roughly between the years 1982 and 2000.

▶ HISTORY AND KNOWN ISSUES: A LEGACY OF PAST FAILURES

Journalists and strategic communicators have had difficulty communicating about religion to mass audiences for centuries. In the U.S. and Western Europe, faith groups have had well-organized public relations offices since the early 1900s, when reporting and writing about religion in the mainstream media became professionalized. A professional association of public relations and other communications professionals today called the Religious Communicators Council was born in the 1920s, a time in which radio was fast growing as the latest mass communication technology. In this time period, anti-Semitic and anti-Catholic speech was mainstream, sometimes finding its way into popular radio broadcasts. To combat religion-based hate speech, the Inter-faith Council of Christians and Jews founded an independent Religion News Service in 1934. The news service, which still operates today, was intended to provide high quality, diverse and fair reporting on religion, at a time when the perception was that little such balanced news about religion existed. The Religion Newswriters Association was formed in 1949 to encourage excellence among journalists and today the group has nearly 500 members and associates.

Religious groups have historically been proactive in calling out the media's mis-takes but religious institutions also attack the news professions, even when the media report serious problems within religious institutions. The Anti-Defamation League was founded in 1913 as a watchdog against defamatory communication directed at Jews, including remarks carried by news agencies. Catholics, Mormons, evangelical Chris-tians and Muslims all have similar groups speaking out today against instances of perceived bias or their definition of misreporting in the media and corporate commu-nications. Several of these groups have credibility among the mass media but others, such as the Catholic League, have been criticized for intentionally distorting the media's reporting of problems within the Catholic Church.

Today, a number of associations provide guidelines, best practices, training and con-tests to encourage excellence in how religion is covered both within religious organi-zations and by independent news media. In addition to the Religion Communicators Council and Religion Newswriters Association, these organizations include the Jew-ish Press Association, Catholic Press Association, National Religious Broadcasters, National Religious Booksellers, Catholic Marketing Network, National Communicators Network for Religious Women, World Association of Christian Communicators, World Catholic Association for Communication and several religion and media units within large scholarly associations. Although such groups exist, most of them are small and support professionals who are highly specialized. As the existence of these groups might indicate, there are times in which communications professionals employed by religious groups and professionals employed by independent media companies have antagonistic relationships.

Of course, errors about religion in the news exist. In contrast, the vast majority of news coverage of religion is posted, written, edited, photographed or broadcast by peo-ple who are not trained religion specialists. Nearly all reporting about religion is done by general assignment journalists or communicators who have little advanced knowl-edge or experience with diverse religious institutions, beliefs and practices. Every day, media large and small include examples of errors about religion that hurt our credibility as a profession and reputations as truth-tellers. Some groups publicize such errors as evidence that the mainstream media have a blind spot for religion, but such complaints often have their own political or religious agendas, particularly promoting the percep-tion that mainstream media are anti-religious. A number of anti-media sites had a good time with this 2013 *New York Times* correction to a story about Pope Francis' first Easter Mass at the Vatican: "An earlier version of this article mischaracterized the Christian holiday of Easter. It is the celebration of Jesus's resurrection from the dead, not his resurrection into heaven."[5]

Even without such glaring gaffes or armies of media watchdogs, reporting on religion is hard. "It took me a few years on this beat to stop the dreaded 'deference' approach, where I talked too formally and respectfully about organized religion," says Michelle Boorstein of the *Washington Post*. "You need to approach the topic seriously but curiously, like sports or sex or health; it's simply part of life. You will be criticized by a tiny number of people no matter what you do. It can't be avoided."

▶ CHALLENGES AND PROBLEMS FOR THE MEDIA REGARDING RELIGION OMISSION AS BIAS

The challenges of getting religion right in mass communication should not be an excuse to avoid the topic, as too often it is. For journalists assigned to write stories rich with context and complexity, one of the biggest obstacles to achieving excellence is failing to include the religion angle. This is understandable, given surveys show that about one-third of all U.S. journalists claim no religious belief—about twice that of the general population, according to scholars.[6] Having one-third of the news media claiming no religious preference is important because it means journalists might fail to understand the deeply personal ways in which religion influences many of the "publics" they serve. Omitting the religious context of a story is a form of bias. Religion is often neglected when it is, in fact, an important motivation behind a person's actions or values. This is especially true in reporting about government elections and social policy issues. Understanding a person's religion gives journalists insight into how a politician or public official might view issues such as abortion, marriage of same-sex couples, charter schools, the role of women and many other cultural conflicts. One-time *Newark Star-Ledger* religion reporter Jeff Diamant recalled covering the 2004 presidential election campaign. He found an angle others had ignored about how then-president George Bush's opposition to same-sex marriage could increase support from African-Americans. "At the time, African-Americans tended to be less likely to support same-sex marriage than the American population as a whole," says Diamant, who teaches journalism ethics at Rutgers University. The unique religious traditions of African-Americans is among the reasons. Diamant adds, "In a country as diverse as the United States, the religious components of stories are increasingly linked to, and often inseparable from, coexisting narratives of race, ethnicity, and gender."

The omission of religion is not just an issue for news coverage. Religion is often omitted in the planning of media campaigns. Yet faith impacts consumerism and consumption in notable ways, in everything from banking to diet to dress. Nike, one of the most successful brands in the world, wound up having to destroy some 800,000 shoes by being tone-deaf to religion. In 1997, Nike introduced a line of summer basketball products emblazoned with a logo intended to suggest flames, but which also resembled the script for "Allah" in Arabic. After strong public outcry accusing the company of using the Muslim word for God inappropriately, Nike's then vice president of Europe, Martin Coles, issued this apology: "While we never intended to offend, we did; we have done everything possible to communicate our sincere apologies and to address issues related to the distribution of any products offensive to the Muslim community."[7] Although the shoe giant didn't plan to offend thousands of Muslims, an absence of thorough product testing using diverse groups led to public embarrassment and untold wasted time and money. The strategic communication field learned from the mistake, however. Today, a specialized field of marketing aimed at Muslims is an emerging field of research and practice.[8]

▶ CENSORSHIP AND FREE SPEECH

Although careless omissions are one form of bias, intentional omission is another. Even in countries that embrace democracy and a free press, the most common type of religious censorship is self-censorship—stemming from a fear of offending or inciting violence. But in countries with neither a free media nor freedom of religion, censorship occurs at institutional and governmental levels, especially with state-owned media that prohibit coverage of minority religious groups. For strategic communicators, advertisements in countries such as the UAE may require formal approval by government censors to assure enforcement of modesty standards in dress and sexuality.[9] Government censorship of the news media can have obvious effects on what the public sees and hears about religious controversies, too. In 2013 and 2014, the government in Myanmar, a predominantly Buddhist country also known as Burma, began restricting foreign journalists' visas because they were trying to report on suspected massacres of ethnic Rohingya Muslims living in the country's Rakhine region. At a 2014 international conference on free speech, government officials and Burmese journalists at state-owned media refused to discuss publicly the restrictions to coverage and humanitarian aid of the country's Muslim Rohingya population, especially when the audience included the government's minister of information.

▶ RELIGIOUS PREJUDICE AND STEREOTYPES

Another way that religion coverage can fail to reach excellence is when journalists knowingly or unknowingly insert prejudice and bias in their reporting. A 2010 Gallup poll found that more than 40 percent of U.S. citizens admitted to at least "a little" prejudice toward Muslims. Only about 18 percent felt the same prejudice about Christians,

15 percent about Jews and 14 percent about Buddhists. Bias against Islam and its followers is not the only religious prejudice common in the 21st Century.[10] In early 2015, reports noted rising anti-Semitism in Europe, fueled by the ability for hate groups to organize and inflame emotions via the Internet and social media. Stereotypes can be just as harmful as blatant bigotry, and the media are guilty of repeating stereotypes about certain religious groups.

For example, about one fourth of the U.S. identifies as evangelical Christians, which includes people affiliated with hundreds of different religious groups.

Although no one standard definition of an evangelical Christian exists, evangelicals generally are Christians who believe the Bible is the authoritative word of God for all aspects of their life, that they have been saved from eternal damnation by Jesus Christ's death and resurrection and that they are compelled to actively convert others. The most common stereotype of evangelicals is that they are all politically conservative, all vote Republican and that televangelists such as Pat Robinson represent most evangelicals; yet younger evangelical leaders are trying to expand the image of evangelicals in the public eye. The media have not done a good job of showing the diversity within the evangelical community or the ways African-American and Hispanic evangelicals differ from white evangelicals.

> Some journalists mistakenly use the often pejorative word "fundamentalist" as synonymous with "evangelical," which is wrong. ("Fundamentalist" should only be used when it's part of a group's official name. This rule applies to its use in all religious contexts, including Islam, Judaism, Buddhism and Hinduism.)

Others who have faced stereotypes are Mormons, as members of the Church of Jesus Christ of Latter-day Saints (LDS) are called. They have been both a fascination in U.S. culture but also subject to religious stereotyping. When the public was asked in a 2007 study to give one word describing Mormons, two of the most common words mentioned was "polygamy" and "cult."[11] Mormon leaders officially ended polygamy about 125 years ago. But sects rejected by the LDS church—including the Fundamentalist Church of Jesus Christ of Latter-day Saints" (FLDS)—still practice polygamy and have become visible in popular culture via the television show "Sister Wives." The HBO fictional series "Big Love" was similarly based on a real polygamous family and *National Geographic* featured the large extended family of a FLDS bishop on its cover. Furthermore, in 2011 a religious musical comedy opened on Broadway called "The Book of Mormon." This Tony Award–winning musical satire is written by the creators of the animated television comedy South Park and mocks the faith.

Faced with the media's focus on the sensationalistic aspects of splinter groups that the public confused as being part of the mainstream Mormon church, and prominent Mormon politician Mitt Romney running for the 2012 presidential election, the

LDS church in 2011 adopted a sophisticated strategic plan to counter public stereotypes of Mormons. Strategic communicators within the LDS church created a series of videos, a billboard campaign, subway signs, search engine optimization techniques and an online advertising campaign to counter Mormon stereotypes. These included a YouTube campaign called "I am a Mormon," which featured diverse ethnicities, family structures and occupations among U.S. Mormons. "Our church is known for our efforts to share our message," LDS missionary head Richard G. Hinckley told a CNN reporter. "This is one way to get to know us—through the lives of members of the Church of Jesus Christ of Latter-day Saints."[12] The public relations and advertising strategies worked in the U.S.: By 2012, surveys showed Americans held a somewhat more favorable attitude toward Mormons compared to just five years earlier, especially among evangelical Christians, some of whom previously called Mormonism a cult. Although Mitt Romney lost the 2012 election, the church gained tremendously from its smart media campaigns.

> Blindness toward belief's complex role in society, overt censorship, stereotypes and bias are indeed challenging problems in the media's efforts to be truth-tellers where religion is concerned. But understanding religion's complexity, adding context, and adopting careful ethical values can help journalists incorporate religion in ways that are insightful, accurate and fair.

▶ USING CONTEXT, PROPORTIONALITY AND DETAIL TO AVOID OVERSIMPLIFICATION

Few things are as complicated as religion. Religion is lived in individual and collective ways that are constantly adapting to the times. Avoiding oversimplification is one of the most commonsense ways to improve religion coverage in mass media. Journalists and strategic communicators in the United States have the benefit of robust scholarship and polling that provides us with detailed data on religious trends about belief. This makes adding detail and context easier than in the past. Relying on this data and religious studies experts is vital for journalists to use, as religious diversity grows. Most people writing about religion regularly know the demographics of the major world religions and their prevalence regionally.

For example, about 70 percent of U.S. citizens consider themselves Christian, but that number has dropped considerably since the 1980s. Although most people in the United States identify with Christianity in some way, the specific theology, interpretations of the Bible, rituals and other aspects of the faith have thousands of variations in the United States alone. Scholars have identified more than 63 official Baptist denominations alone, in addition to literally thousands of independent Baptist congregations. Journalists must take the time to understand these differences and not assume that just because someone is a Baptist that they all believe and worship the same.

One continuing story demonstrating the importance of context and detail in religion stories involves a small, controversial church called Westboro Baptist Church in Topeka, Kansas. Westboro Baptist, which is an independent Baptist church not affiliated with any larger Baptist group, is famous for its hate-fueled pickets of military funerals, college campuses, sporting events and other venues. The group runs the website God-HatesFags.com, which condemns homosexuality, among other things. Westboro is also listed as a hate group by the Anti-Defamation League, which calls it, "a small virulently homophobic, anti-Semitic hate group that regularly stages protests around the country, often several times a week."[13] Of course, Westboro Baptist's use of "Baptist" in its name created a public relations problem for other Baptist groups, and one to which strategic communicators involved in shaping church image had to respond. The American Baptist Church, one of several national Baptist denominations, issued a strong statement in 2012 that said in part:

> We have received questions about Westboro Baptist Church in light of increased media attention related to the recent shooting in Connecticut. American Baptists want to be clear that we denounce their message and tactics of hate. It grieves us that in bearing the Baptist name they destroy the reputation of thousands of Baptists who daily give themselves in selfless acts of love as followers of Jesus.[14]

Although Westboro Baptist is extreme, it's an excellent example of how a name alone is not sufficient to understand anything about a religious group's beliefs or identity. The diversity of viewpoints that exist within Christianity is similarly present in every major world faith, whether Islam, Buddhism, Hinduism, Judaism, Sikhism, Paganism and Atheism.

The most important guidance to including context and avoiding the problem of oversimplification in religion is to conduct detailed research in advance and to know the prevalence or proportionality of a group's followers. Nearly all major religions have online sites that carry details about a religion's core beliefs, practices, leadership, organizational structure and rituals. Naturally, the actions of groups that have large numbers of followers carry more weight than an independent and small group like Westboro Baptist. If a group seems to be an outlier in its beliefs compared to the mainstream of thought within a faith, ask an expert in religious studies or similarly independent scholar to clarify this for you. Be sure to communicate such distinctions to audiences, so they can judge the import of a religious group and understand it in relationship to others within that faith.

Similar considerations surround the debates about ISIS, or Islamic State, the extremist terrorist group known for videotaping public beheadings. Some argue that the word "Islamic" in the group's name hijacks its meaning and unfairly links their terrorism to the world's more than 1 billion Muslims. President Barack Obama tried to address this problem in a February 2015 speech, when he was criticized for noting bloody conquests in the name of Christianity during the Crusades.[15] Similarly, Manya Brachear, a reporter for the *Chicago Tribune*, recalled a 2015 story about charges of sexual abuse against an imam in Chicago.

> This imam was a revered scholar in the orthodox South Asian Chicago Muslim community. Not the Arab Muslim community. Not the Progressive Muslim community. And I honestly don't think he was a national figure, just a local leader. Orthodox, South Asian, Chicago, which I think is important context to add when religious traditions are so often painted with broad brushstrokes.

For strategic communicators, simply including some religious context can even improve a campaign's effectiveness. Scholars have found that advertisements reflecting cultural values can be more persuasive than those ignoring cultural values. But conversely, a 2004 study of 1,400 consumers found that some religiously devoted survey respondents found advertisements of sex-related, health care and addictive products more offensive than those who described themselves as less religious. Without sufficient context, a religious reference can quickly turn offensive, as was the case of American Eagle's Ganesh flip flops, or lingerie maker Victoria Secret's Buddha bikini.[16]

▶ BEING ETHICAL AND AUTHENTIC

Most journalists have plenty of practice reporting about people they disagree with. Religion introduces a new intensity to that challenge. It's one thing to be a political reporter who votes Democrat and interviews Republicans. It can be an even more challenging problem when a journalist's sacred beliefs are ridiculed by a person who's likely to be a client or the lead of a story. You might be asked to report, analyze, create media plans or produce media for organizations or people whose beliefs you disagree with. Ethical journalists learn to assess their ability to be fair to people who believe differently from themselves. Because there are many reported biases against various religions, it is especially important that journalists be aware of their own biases at the outset, understanding their biases' origins, and acknowledging when you can't put them aside. One test is to write a lead before you do all your reporting; if your lead is unchanged once you have researched a topic, you may have only used sources who confirm your own views. Long-time religion reporter Jeffery Sheler, formerly of *U.S. News & World Report*, is a practicing Christian who reminds journalists that being true to your own religion doesn't require being false to someone else's.

Another issue that will arise is the question of your own beliefs by sources or clients. If you are reporting on religion or working for a religious media company or product, you will likely be asked about your own personal beliefs. In terms of revealing your own personal faith, it's important that you do what you feel comfortable with. Until the late 1990s, it was rare for reporters to reveal their religious views to a source or group they were covering. However, as the public has demanded greater transparency for journalists and social networks make it harder to keep religious views private, some journalists find it does no harm to be honest about personal belief and that it builds trust. Others prefer to give a general response, such as "I'm Jewish." Even if you are not comfortable sharing your beliefs—or lack of them—you can assure whoever is asking that regardless of your personal views, you will be fair (if you're reporting) or that you will work on their behalf, regardless of your beliefs (if you're a strategic communicator or working for a religious media outlet).

> The most authentic presentation of a faith is going to be from the people who practice it—and people who are not practitioners of a particular faith may have a bias or viewpoint they are trying to influence.

Journalists also have an obligation to capture all sides of an issue authentically. If you are trying to describe a group's faith, rely primarily on people who are practitioners of that religion as well as scholars of religion.

But also be sure to include in your reporting people who break down assumptions and preconceptions. As has already been discussed, faith and belief is highly individualistic. There are, however, authoritative viewpoints of what is and isn't an "approved" belief within organized religions. Stories about excommunications from an organized religion center on being able to distinguish between what individuals may believe are true expressions of their faith and what the official "keepers" of a faith's authentic tenets say is permissible.

For journalists working in news media there are a few additional words of caution. These include not covering your own specific house of worship, not promoting your faith tradition above others, and not reporting on issues for which you advocate on behalf of a faith group. Journalists should also decline to report on social or moral issues such as abortion and homosexuality, for which they have strong opinions—often grounded in faith or values. Likewise, strategic communicators need to be honest with clients about how their personal beliefs could affect their ability to work effectively for a client. Because this can be challenging, a number of faith-specific public relations firms have emerged in the last 20 years, such as the prominent A. Larry Ross

Communications firm in suburban Dallas, and the Atlanta-based The DeMoss Group (DeMoss.com), which promotes movies, political candidates, books and issues from a Christian perspective similar to those of their clients.

▶ THE SPECIAL CASE OF HATE SPEECH

Hate speech is a problem that is growing in part because of the ease of creating and spreading vitriol via social and online media. Religiously and otherwise offensive content has always existed in the mass media. It's been the subject of key court cases testing the limits of the United States' embrace of free speech. But the killing in January 2015 of 10 journalists who worked for the Paris-based satirical magazine *Charlie Hebdo*, and other examples of the media distributing what others considered religiously offensive speech, mandates that journalists understand the line between acceptable and unacceptable speech about religion.

The Europe-based Ethical Journalists Network (EJN) has issued a five-point test for helping to determine if something is dangerous hate speech. As an EJN 2014 report asks,

> While most journalists understand that they have a duty to tell the truth and to report on what is being said and who is saying it, they often fail to balance that responsibility against another widely recognized cardinal principle of journalism, which is to minimize harm.

EJN suggests this five-point test should be used "in the gathering, preparation and dissemination of news" and says it "helps place what is said and who is saying it in an ethical context":

1. Status of the speaker. How might their position influence their motives? Should they even be listened to or just ignored?

2. Reach of the speech. How far is the speech traveling? Is there a pattern of behavior?

3. Goals of the speech. How does it benefit the speaker and their interests? Is it deliberately intended to cause harm to others?

4. The content itself. Is the speech dangerous? Could it incite violence towards others?

5. Surrounding climate: social, economic, political. Who might be negatively affected? Is there a history of conflict or discrimination?[17]

As this chapter shows, religion is a vital, yet often problematic topic in journalism. The many examples of these problems in the news media and strategic communications are important lessons in what can happen when an issue's religious context is excluded or poorly informed. To do better, journalists must be wary not to oversimplify or repeat prevalent religious stereotypes and bias. They can learn by doing advance research and preparation, relying on neutral scholars or other experts and by keeping context and proportionality in mind. Finally, in an era in which dissemination of religious hate speech can get you killed, it's important to be mindful of the ethical values that help assure journalism is supporting democracy and the public good, rather than divisiveness and violence.

▶ RESOURCES AND TOOLS ON RELIGION FOR JOURNALISTS

Pew Research Center (http://www.PewResearch.org) has the most comprehensive data and research on religion in the U.S. and across the globe. It's known for using high caliber methodologies, resulting in the most accurate demographic data on religion available.

Religion Communicators Council (http://www.religioncommunicators.org/) is the professional organization for public relations officers at religious organizations.

ReligionLink.com (http://www.religionlink.com) is a free source guide and primer on covering religion created by journalists, for journalists. Its content is keyed toward major religion stories and issues in the media.

Religion Newswriters Association (http://www.RNA.org) is a professional, global journalism organization for journalists who write about religion in the mainstream media.

ReligionStylebook.com (http://www.ReligionStylebook.com) is a free, mobile-enabled stylebook of hundreds of terms and recommended usage, based on the AP Stylebook but expanded to include additional terms.

FOR DISCUSSION

1. If you are assigned to cover a demonstration by a religious group, where would you start to gather information about the group? How would you check the proportionality or size of the demonstrating group, when compared to groups with similar names or identities?

2. A gunman shoots a dozen Amish schoolchildren in rural Pennsylvania. As photo editor for the local newspaper, you are expected to come up with

appropriate photographs. But the Amish consider it against their religion to have photographs or pictures showing the faces of adult Amish men and women. How will you handle this challenge?

3. You're asked to help a group of Atheists publicize a new campaign to get famous people to come "out of the closet" and admit they are atheists. What issues or concerns should your media campaign address?

▶ SUGGESTED ACTIVITIES

1. Visit a worship service for a faith tradition you know nothing about. Some good options include a mosque, a synagogue or a Buddhist or Hindu temple. Describe the interior and how the faith community uses it. Write a 500-word paper describing what you learned about that religion from attending the service, and how the visit will help you as a journalist. (When doing this, be sure to abide by any rules regarding special entrances or seating for men and women. Ask in advance before taking photos or video.)

2. Create an 8-by-11-inch (horizontal or vertical) magazine advertisement for any famous women's clothing line and target the ad to an audience of predominantly Muslim women living in the U.S. or Western Europe. Write a 400–500 word rationale explaining the choices you made in creating the ad and how it employs the themes in this chapter.

3. Select a religion survey report from among those at www.PewForum.org. Write a 500-word paper answering these questions: What is the most surprising finding? What is the least surprising finding? Did this confirm or break some religious stereotypes for you?

4. Write a 500-word paper describing your own personal beliefs and how you think they might help or hurt your ability to be an ethical and professional member of the news media, advertising, public relations or media strategy professions.

▶ KEY TERMS

Belief   Trust, faith or confidence in someone or something, often a deity, but increasingly used to encompass humanists or those who do not believe in a god. It is common in Europe, for example, to use the phrase, "freedom of religion or belief."

Evangelicals	Christians from many denominations and independent churches who share similar views on the Bible, on the mandate to evangelize and on salvation, among other things.
Fundamentalist	A term often used to refer to someone who adheres to a strict and literalist interpretation of sacred scripture, often in a pejorative way. It is most often applied to Christians but it has been used in relationship to other faiths, too. It can be used when it is part of a formal name of a religious organization, but otherwise, should be avoided.
Jihad	This Arabic word is among several terms pertinent to Islam that are often misunderstood and used inaccurately. It is most often used properly to refer to a personal, internal struggle or striving for self-control and adherence to the faith.
Hate Speech	Spoken, written, audio, video or graphic expressions that serve primarily to insult or threaten a group based on religion, ethnicity, race, sexual orientation, disability, ethnicity or other characteristics.
Humanist	Humanism is among the philosophies growing in North America and Western Europe that emphasize the ability to use rationalism and empiricism over belief in a god or religion. Often it is paired with the word "secular," but not always.
Nones	The term given people who say they have no religious preference, encompassing everything from true atheists to people who are "spiritual but not religious."
Religion	Any organized system of beliefs, ceremonies and rules used to worship a god, group of gods or the supernatural.
Secular	Attitudes and activities that have no religious basis. Often paired with the word "humanist."

▶ NOTES

1 Angelina Theodorou, "Which Countries Still Outlaw Apostasy and Blasphemy," Pew Research Center, May 28, 2014, http://www.pewresearch.org/fact-tank/2014/05/28/which-countries-still-outlaw-apostasy-and-blasphemy/.

2 "'Nones' on the Rise," PewForum.org, October 9, 2012, http://www.pewforum.org/2012/10/09/nones-on-the-rise/.

3 Quotes from Diamant, Brachear, Boorstein, Eckstrom, and Grossman in this chapter were gathered via personal email exchanges over February 17 and 18, 2015.

4 D. Michael Lindsey, *Faith in the Halls of Power: How Evangelicals Joined the American Elite* (New York: Oxford University Press, 2007).

5 Elisabetta Povoledo, "Pope Calls for 'Peace in All the World' in First Easter Message," *The New York Times*, 2013, March 31, 2013, http://www.nytimes.com/2013/04/01/world/europe/pope-francis-calls-for-peace-in-all-the-world-in-first-easter-message.html.

6 David H. Weaver, Randal A. Beam., Bonnie J. Brownlee, Paul S. Voakes and G. Cleveland Wilhoit, *The American Journalist in the 21st Century: U.S. News People at the Dawn of a New Millennium* (New York: Lawrence Earlbaum, 2007).

7 Donna Abu-Nasr, "Nike Inc. Will Recall 38,000 Pairs of Shoes," Associated Press, June 24, 1997, http://www.apnewsarchive.com/1997/WASHINGTON-AP-Nike-Inc-will-recall-38–000-pair-of/id-5ac81076969742d66fb4082b55c82dbf

8 Bernardo Vizcaino, "Online Ventures Target Global Muslim Consumer Market," Reuters, December 16, 2014, http://www.reuters.com/article/2014/12/16/islam-consumers-idUSL6N0SX06G20141216.

9 "United Arab Emirates," Freedom House, 2013, https://freedomhouse.org/report/freedom-press/2013/united-arab-emirates#.VOK0erDF9F8.

10 "U.S. Religious Prejudice Stronger Against Muslims," *Gallup Center for Muslim Studies*, January 21, 2010, http://www.gallup.com/poll/125312/religious-prejudice-stronger-against-muslims.aspx.

11 Scott Keeter and G. Smith, "Public Opinion about Mormons: Mitt Romney Discusses his Religion," Pew Research Center, December 4, 2007, http://www.pewresearch.org/2007/12/04/public-opinion-about-mormons/.

12 Julia Talanova, "As 'Book of Mormon' Takes New York, City Gets Mormon Church Ad Campaign," CNN, June 17, 2011, http://religion.blogs.cnn.com/2011/06/17/as-book-of-mormon-takes-new-york-city-gets-mormon-church-ad-campaign/.

13 "Westboro Baptist Church," Anti-Defamation League, 2013, http://archive.adl.org/learn/ext_us/wbc/default.html?LEARN_Cat=Extremism&LEARN_SubCat=Extremism_in_America&xpicked=3&item=WBC.

14 "Statement about Westboro Baptist Church," *American Baptist Church (USA)*, December 16, 2012, http://www.abc-usa.org/2012/12/16/statement-about-westboro-baptist-church/.

15 Juliet Eilperin, "Critics Pounce after Obama Talks Crusades, Slavery at Prayer Breakfast," *Washington* Post, February 5, 2015, https://www.washingtonpost.com/politics/obamas-speech-at-prayer-breakfast-called-offensive-to-christians/2015/02/05/6a15a240-ad50-11e4-ad71-7b9eba0f87d6_story.html.

16 Barbara Mueller, Communicating with the Multicultural Consumer: Theoretical and Practical Perspectives (New York: Peter Lang, 2008).

17 "Hate Speech: A Five-Point Test for Journalists," *Ethical Journalists Network*, 2014, http://ethicaljournalismnetwork.org/en/contents/hate-speech-infographic.

▶ ADDITIONAL READINGS

Buddenbaum, Judith. *Reporting News about Religion: An Introduction for Journalists.* Ames, IA: Iowa State University Press, 1998.

Connolly, Diane. *Reporting Religion: A Primer on Journalism's Best Beat.* Westerville, OH: Religion Newswriters Foundation, 2006.

Einstein, Mara. *Brands of Faith: Marketing Religion in a Commercial Age.* New York: Routledge, 2008.

Journal of Media and Religion. Taylor & Francis. http://www.tandfonline.com/action/journalInformation?show=aimsScope&journalCode=hjmr20#.Vf8gn5cutsk

Kraybill, Donald. "Fake Amish and the Real Ones." *Huffington Post*, July 18, 2013. http://www. huffingtonpost.com/donald-kraybill/fake-amish-and-the-real-o_b_3617736.html.

Mason, Debra, ed. *Investigating Religion*. Columbia, MO: Investigative Reporters and Editors, 2013.

Matlins, S. M. and Arthur J. Magida, A. J. eds. *How to Be a Perfect Stranger: The Essential Religious Etiquette Handbook*, 4th ed. Woodstock, VT: Skylight Paths Publishing, 2006.

Stout, Daniel. *Media and Religion: Foundations of an Emerging Field*. New York: Routledge, 2012.

Winston, Diane, ed. *Handbook of Religion and the American News Media*. New York: Oxford University Press, 2013.

8

Reporting and Strategic Communication Across Borders

Beverly Horvit and Yulia Medvedeva

One photograph showed a roadway scarred with potholes. Another showed a pristine eight-lane highway. The game: "Spot the Africa." The contestant: Jon Stewart in a December 2014 broadcast of *The Daily Show*. His job—compliments of Trevor Noah, a South African comedian who now hosts the show—was to decide which photograph depicted Africa and which the United States. Round two showed young black men working on computers in a clean, well-lit classroom; the other photograph showed two black children—a young girl sleeping atop a stained mattress placed on a filthy, uneven couch and a young boy eating a snack as he rested on an empty desktop attached to an equally barren bookshelf. As most Americans probably would have, Stewart bombed the test. The nice facilities were in Africa, the pitted roadway was in New York City and the two children live in Detroit. As Noah told Stewart, "To a lot of Americans, Africa is just one giant village full of AIDS, huts and starving children, who you can save for five cents a day."[1] Of course, Africa, like the United States, is not without its problems, and round three of "Spot the Africa" showed a grim image that indeed was taken in a slum in Johannesburg. Still, the point is that because most U.S. citizens'

157

image of the world beyond the United States' borders hinges largely on the media they consume, their answers would unlikely differ from Stewart's.

Unfortunately, over the last decade, U.S. newspapers and television networks have closed bureaus outside the United States and drastically reduced their numbers of full-time international correspondents.[2] So, rather than have full-time correspondents based in a location, when a crisis erupts, news organizations quickly fly a correspondent in to cover that particular episode. The practice, called parachute journalism, may sound glamorous, but critics worry that journalists who have not been able to invest a lot of shoe leather into covering a beat will miss important context. Parachute journalists, former *New York Times* executive editor Bill Keller wrote in a December 2, 2012, op-ed piece, "give us spurts of coverage when an Arab Spring breaks out or Hamas fires rockets into Israel, but much less of the ongoing attention that would equip us to see crises coming and understand them when they erupt." Despite issues posed by the so-called legacy media's declining resources, opportunities exist for those individuals who want to explore the world beyond the U.S. borders and tell its stories. Whether you plan to go into journalism or strategic communication, the tenets of excellent journalism are the same: Excellent journalism provides context, embraces complexity, highlights a range of voices and offers a proportional image, all adding up to authenticity. Producing excellent journalism means doing your homework first and doing as much homework as possible.

▶ UNDERSTANDING AND PROVIDING CONTEXT

Sometimes international correspondents discover their calling early in life and start preparing well before they ever take that first assignment abroad. For veteran journalist Kevin Drew, who has worked for CNN, the *Christian Science Monitor*, the Associated Press and *The New York Times*, that preparation started in middle school when he began studying Russian language and literature. It continued in college when he majored in political science and specialized in European politics. "When the [Berlin] Wall came down in 1989, I knew it was just a matter of time until I was in that part of the world," Drew said. Indeed, less than three years later, he was working full time in Czechoslovakia to help tell the story of the breakup of the Soviet Union and the challenging transitions faced by the former Soviet Bloc members. He knew the history, and he knew the culture.

Although it may be too late to add a major or minor in history or political science, don't disregard the benefits of doing your homework. Before tackling the international assignment, whether in journalism or strategic communication, study the area's history, recent events, press system and culture.

History Lessons

For starters, the U.S. State Department offers in-depth country histories provided by the Library of Congress, but be wary of spending too little time researching a country's history—especially if the United States has been involved. A quick introduction to El Salvador in the Central Intelligence Agency's World Factbook, for example, states, "A 12-year civil war, which cost about 75,000 lives, was brought to a close in 1992 when the government and leftist rebels signed a treaty that provided for military and political reforms."[3] What that brief summary does not include is the role the U.S. government played in that civil war, sending billions of dollars in military aid to help the Salvadoran government, despite gross human rights abuses committed by the Salvadoran military.[4] The legacy of war has repercussions for El Salvador and the United States today, as well. In an in-depth July 2014 piece about U.S.-born gangs, Scott Johnson of *National Geographic* reported that gang violence in Central America dates back the 1980s when people tried to flee the civil wars in their countries. "Some of those immigrants found their way into gangs in Los Angeles that wound up seeding drug-related violence back home, often after their members were deported by the United States," Johnson wrote.[5] Many of the Central-American children trying to enter the United States in 2014 did so to try to escape the gang violence that, in a way, had been exported from the United States. One wonders how many U.S. citizens know that context.

Of course, nation-states should not be the only unit of analysis. In *The Al Jazeera Effect*, journalism Professor Philip Seib calls attention to the importance of virtual states, imagined communities based on a common identity.[6] By imagined, he means that the communities have self-identified as states. "Particularly in parts of the world where states and borders are vestiges of faded empires, reality may give birth to new states that lack diplomatic and cartographic recognition but nevertheless possess significant political dynamism," Seib writes.[7] In other words, although Hezbollah is not a country, Hezbollah operated as one, Seib argues, when in 2006 it challenged Israel from its base of Lebanon. Similarly, Kurdistan is not a country recognized by world powers, but rather a 25 million person–strong community of Kurds living in Iraq, Turkey and Syria. The Kurds' presence contributed to Turkey's reluctance to join efforts to fight the Islamic State in the summer of 2014. Understanding the power of virtual states to unite people might have helped U.S. policy-makers and others better predict—and perhaps stop—the rise of the Islamic State, also known as ISIS or ISIL, which is trying to become more than a virtual state as it captures territory in Iraq and Syria. Maps produced by *The New York Times* (see, for example, http://www.nytimes.com/interactive/2014/06/12/world/middleeast/the-iraq-isis-conflict-in-maps-photos-and-video.html?_r=0) help illustrate the mismatch between where people with the same ethnic or sectarian backgrounds have lived for centuries and where national borders exist. That history provides much-needed context for better understanding the Islamic State's appeal to some of its followers.

Following the News

Just as history, whether decades or centuries old, can help journalists add context to their stories, so can a working knowledge of recent significant events and issues in an unfamiliar locale. Again, do your homework. On its website, *The New York Times* offers a "Times Topic" page for most of the world's countries that includes a timeline and links to *Times* articles and other sites. Similarly, search the BBC website for a particular country, and you'll find a "profile."

South African journalism scholar Eric Louw would heartily agree about the need to find multiple sources of international news. Louw argues that not only do the Western media misread and distort international issues, [8] but he says their inaccurate reporting also becomes the basis for future interpretations:

> These 'partial pictures' acquire a reality that then serves to frame the way the next generation of foreign correspondents and their news editors look at (and hence report) the distant places. Once a prejudice (whether negative or positive) has rooted itself within a newsroom culture, that prejudice will (unconsciously) inform future newsmaking about that particular group of people.[9]

We all have a hard time knowing what we don't know. Examining news events and issues from multiple perspectives provides an antidote for bias and ignorance. One good resource is worldpress.org, which offers links to the newspapers throughout the world and curates an ever-changing list of top stories worldwide. Also important, worldpress. org offers some background on the newspapers' ideologies so that you can better evaluate the lens through which the newspaper is reporting.

Of course, correspondents will need to do more than just read about a country before parachuting in. CNN correspondent Robyn Kriel (See Figure 8.1) is honest about not always having had enough time to fully prepare. She remembers reporting from Sudan in 2012, when she was covering more than 12 African countries for eNCA, a 24-hour-news channel based in South Africa. Kriel, a 2005 graduate of Texas Christian University, recounts the experience:

> The South and North were fighting each other over oil, and we went in with little clue of the realities on the ground, the dangers, the politics, the

FIGURE 8.1 Correspondent Robyn Kriel interviews refugees at the Dadaab refugee camp in Kenya with the help of cameraman Orto Sori in October 2011. At the time, Kriel was working as a correspondent for eNCA, a 24-hour-news channel based in South Africa. In April 2015, she started working for CNN. Photo courtesy of Robyn Kriel

nuances of the various tribes and the culture. How do we cope in these types of situations? Ask a lot of questions. Be tenacious, but know when to keep your mouth shut. Don't be antagonistic, and always get a second, third, fourth opinion. Ask other journalists who have been in the region for their advice. Foreign correspondents are usually very helpful to others and will share with you their phone numbers of key players on the ground who can help you get what you need.

Having a working knowledge of key issues is critical, but Kriel says journalists also need to contact other journalists, NGOs and U.N. staffers to find out other key information, such as:

Is there a cellphone network? How are the roads? Will you need a 4x4 vehicle? Will you have electricity? Should you take/rent a generator? Should you take a satellite phone? Will you be staying in tents? Do you need a sleeping bag? Malaria meds? Special equipment such as body armor?

In other words, be smart, and think ahead.

Knowing the Media System

Another practical piece of knowledge to arm oneself with is how journalists are treated in the country where you plan to work. Kriel, a native of Zimbabwe who is now based in Nairobi, Kenya, has learned about government restrictions firsthand. In 2008, Kriel and her photographer had to flee Zimbabwe in the middle of the night because Robert Mugabe's government was not thrilled with her reporting, and Kriel's mother, who did not escape, spent a week in jail. Indeed, most of the world's population does not enjoy the freedoms U.S. citizens take for granted—freedom of speech and freedom of press. According to Freedom House's 2014 report "Freedom of the Press," fewer than 1 in 5 of the world's citizens enjoy a free press.[10] Instead, the media systems in their countries are controlled by their country's governments or unduly influenced by other entities, whether big corporations or organized crime syndicates. When you're doing your homework, be sure to review the Freedom House reports, as well as reports by such entities as the Paris-based Reporters Sans Frontières (Reporters Without Borders at http://en.rsf.org/) or the Committee to Protect Journalists (http://cpj.org/). As an international correspondent, you will want to know how both domestic and international correspondents fare in a given country, and from where, if anywhere, threats might arise. Forewarned is forearmed.

Sometimes the threats originate with a government, and sometimes not. In June 2014, for example, an Egyptian court sentenced three journalists working for Al Jazeera to seven or more years in prison, allegedly for conspiring with the Muslim Brotherhood to write false reports.[11] The not-so-subtle message: Be careful what you write, and don't write anything that reflects badly on the military government. The "evidence" against the journalists appeared pretty sparse. Elsewhere, in July 2014, the Chinese government told its domestic journalists they were not allowed to help non-Chinese news agencies; a journalist who wrote for a website based in Hong Kong said he was fired for doing so.[12] In more extreme cases, journalists have been kidnapped, assaulted and even killed. Often, the oppressors are what Freedom House classifies as "extra-legal," "extra" meaning operating outside the law. Sadly, examples are not difficult to find. In June and July 2014, for example, the Committee to Protect Journalists issued the following news alerts: "Radio host gunned down in Paraguay," and "Armed men raid Sudanese newspaper, beat editor."[13] The Islamic State has also struck terror with its videos showing journalists being beheaded and burned to death. Although some violence is unexpected—for example, the killings of Charlie Hebdo journalists in Paris in January 2015—in known conflict zones, journalists can take steps to prepare. The International News Safety Institute based in London offers numerous safety tips at http://www.newssafety.org/safety/advice/.

In some countries, religious and other sectarian alliances can affect coverage. The rulers of Saudi Arabia, for example, ban journalists from reporting news that contradicts Sharia (Islamic) law or defames religious leaders.[14] Somewhat similarly, when U.S. journalist Tom O'Hara worked for *The National*, a government-owned newspaper in Abu Dhabi, he encountered all sorts of prohibitions: no photos of Bahraini authorities firing tear gas at protesters because the rulers of Bahrain were related to the rulers of the United Arab Emirates; no briefs about gay rights and no identification of the Persian Gulf by that name.[15] Explained O'Hara: "In the Arab world, it's the Arabian Gulf. The Iranians are Persians. The Gulf Arabs despise and fear Iran. So, even though the rest of the world calls that body of water the Persian Gulf, *The National* does not."[16]

Not only will knowing about the climate for journalists in a country help you avoid and/or prepare for difficulties, but such knowledge also will allow you to evaluate more critically the news coverage produced in that country. Self-censorship can be as problematic as outright government censorship. Journalists who face strict punishments often choose to censor themselves rather than put themselves at risk. If self-censorship is likely in the country you're reporting on, then know the local media coverage probably paints a more positive picture of life in that country than is realistic.

The Media Climate for Strategic Communication

Those working in strategic communication have to do their homework, as well. The savvy strategic communicator will stay on top of current events and trends—for starters, which political faction is in control, how well the economy is doing and how involved the government is in the private sector. Don't think free-press issues don't affect you. In June 2014, Next Media Limited, a huge media company in Hong Kong, got some bad news: Two large British banks had decided to stop advertising in the *Apple Daily* because, a Next Media Limited executive said, they were told to by the Chinese government.[17] Exactly what role the Chinese government played is unclear, but other Hong Kong media also have suggested the Chinese government put pressure on advertisers.

Regulations and professional practices vary by country, and if your clients want to expand, you cannot afford to ignore the world beyond the U.S. market. *AdAge* reports that Latin America has enjoyed the fastest growth in ad revenue since 2010 and will remain the fastest through 2016, and China, the third largest ad market, also is expected to grow about 10 percent a year through 2016.[18] (By 2015, *AdAge* predicts, three of the four so-called BRIC countries—Brazil, Russia and China—will be among the top 10 advertising markets in the world, while Brazil will be among the 10 fastest growing.[19] (India is the other BRIC country.)

It will also pay to know the rules. Can alcohol and tobacco be advertised? What about e-cigarettes? Can children be targeted by ad campaigns? In the European Union, companies are not allowed to advertise tobacco products, and in 2016, that prohibition will extend to e-cigarettes.[20] In case you're wondering, the World Health Organization maintains a database of the advertising restrictions on alcohol by country. The WHO site[21] outlines the restrictions worldwide for television, radio, print, film, billboards, point-of-sale, the Internet and social media. In the United Kingdom, the Advertising Standards Authority works to protect children by monitoring ads and responding to citizen complaints. In December 2012, for example, the ASA told American Apparel to stop using a print ad that regulators believed sexualized a model who looked like a child.[22]

In addition to understanding the varied regulatory environments, strategic communicators seeking to get their message to the media must understand how the media work. In many countries, journalists make such pitiful salaries that it's common for sources to pay journalists to write positive stories. For example, in some Middle Eastern countries, Pintak and Ginges report, what's known as an "envelope culture" prevails.[23] Pintak and Ginges said companies in the Middle East often provide "taxi money" to Arab journalists so they will attend news conferences.[24] A report for the Center for International Media Assistance provides similar examples from other regions of what professors Dean Kruckeberg and Katerina Tsetsura term "cash for news coverage."[25] The report advises public relations practitioners, nonprofits and corporations to adopt a policy of never agreeing to pay for coverage,[26] and offering financial rewards to the media is clearly contrary to the International Public Relations Association's Code of Conduct.[27] Still, practitioners should not be caught off guard by different expectations in differing parts of world.

▶ DEVELOPING CULTURAL COMPETENCY

Beyond knowing about history, current events and the current media climate, journalists and strategic communicators who want to craft authentic stories and media messages also will need to work to understand the local culture. For journalists, being able to interact successfully with a range of people allows journalists to capture the most complete version of any story—the story with the largest range of voices.

For starters, consider what anthropologist Edward T. Hall called a culture's "silent language," including its rules for handling time and space.[28] For example, how close does one stand to someone else when engaged in conversation? How much—and what kind of physical contact—is customary when meeting someone for the first time?

A kiss? A handshake? Those of us from North America might want our space; we might feel someone from another culture is crowding us. If we back up, that individual might assume we're standoffish. Similarly, consider the various approaches to time. One of Hall's key points is that what we take for granted as human nature is not human nature; it's learned behavior. What does it mean to be "on time," for example? Do all cultures worry about being "on time"? Of course not. Indeed, you probably know people in your own circle who are late to most events, and you know that being "on time" for a college course is not the same thing as being "on time" for a wedding versus being "on time" for a late-night party. You might think someone who comes late to class is rude and/or unorganized, but how you perceive that lateness depends on your own culture—how you've been conditioned to respond. So, if you set up an interview for noon and your source doesn't arrive at noon, don't take it personally. Consider the culture. (Read up on the culture beforehand.)

Carolina Escudero, an experienced journalist who has helped run University of Missouri School of Journalism programs in Argentina and Spain, says U.S. students coming to Argentina have to make several cultural adjustments: For example, it's normal there to receive kisses and hugs from one's boss, and it's normal for others (but not U.S. students) to be late for appointments. And, whether U.S. students are heading to the Czech Republic's capital of Prague or to Tokyo, mentor Sandy Kornberg offers them the same advice: Pipe down. What U.S. citizens might assume is a normal volume level doesn't always translate well in another culture.

Likewise, if you're used to calling a source and getting immediate, concise answers to your questions, don't consider that the norm around the globe. Whether you're a journalist trying to report a story or a strategic communicator trying to identify what your client needs, you'll need to understand the importance a particular culture places on building relationships and showing politeness. Kornberg, who worked in Asia for decades as an executive with the McCann-Erickson World Group advertising firm, offers this advice to University of Missouri journalism students about to team up with Japanese students in Tokyo for an integrated marketing campaign: Be patient. Although all the Japanese students speak English, they are not necessarily fluent. The U.S. students also have to try to guard against misunderstandings.

How much small talk is necessary before "getting down to business"? Again, the answer may vary with culture. When journalism scholars Jerry Palmer and Victoria Fontan interviewed international correspondents' interpreters in Iraq, the interpreters said the Western journalists didn't understand the importance of just talking—not interviewing—first.[29] If a journalist doesn't respect one's culture, why cooperate?

Of course, reporting involves more than interviewing. Reporting also involves observing. Again, be careful not to assume that what you're seeing is what you think you are seeing. Do we laugh because we think something's funny? Do we

smile because we're happy? Perhaps. But in some cultures—Japan, for example—
a smile or laughter may mean what you think or it may be used as a way to hide
other emotions, such as anger or embarrassment. Similarly, some cultures tend to
be more collectivist, as opposed to the more individualistic U.S. culture, and place
a high value on consensus, making it less likely that someone who opposes one of
your ideas will say so publicly or directly. So, you can't assume silence equates to
agreement.

Cultural expectations may also vary for men vs. women in any given society. Your
own gender may preclude you from talking to some sources. A male journalist, for
example, may not be permitted to interview a female in some Islamic societies because
doing so would violate a cultural norm. A female journalist would likely be more able to
talk to the women and children. In 2001, Cheryl Diaz Meyer, a Pulitzer Prize–winning
photojournalist, took a photograph of a woman begging outside a mosque in northern
Afghanistan. "I wanted to interview Momo Juma, but my translator, a male, thought
it would not be respectful for him to speak with her," Meyer said of the woman in the
photograph.[30] In Africa, Kriel says, the cultures vary greatly. "In Somalia, sometimes
I put out my hand to shake a man's hand, and culturally, some men think it's not polite
at all," she says. "Others don't mind, but it's not really a good thing for a woman to shake
a man's hand in a stricter Islamic society. I'm always mad at myself for doing it. In some
places, you must cover your hair and wear long clothes that cover your legs and arms."
In other words, show you respect local customs.

Of course, the same applies to strategic communicators. Judy Phair, president of
independent consulting firm PhairAdvantage Communications LLC, remembers helping to open a client's first office in India and arranging meetings with the media. In one
awkward moment, a male colleague offered his hand to greet a female reporter and she
immediately drew back. Her religion forbade touching a man who was not her spouse
or a family member, so she could only shake hands with a woman. Partners assisting
Phair's team didn't warn them of the reporter's religious strictures. Respect for local
journalists is top priority, Phair says. After that incident, she always insisted on being
fully briefed on local customs and restrictions well in advance.

In addition to understanding gender roles in a given society, don't let your preconceptions of class lead you to do something rude. Individuals may be more willing to
share their thoughts and feelings with journalists if they've shown they understand
the importance of cultural niceties. What should you do when a poor family in rural
Afghanistan offers you a meal, you're not hungry and you're worried about using up
their precious resources? Accept it graciously. Custom dictates that guests be treated
well; to decline the meal would be an insult. Kriel got the same advice when reporting
from the Democratic Republic of Congo. She had been interviewing rebels in the DRC
when they invited her and her crew for beer and barbecued meat. "I didn't want to stay,

and it was early in the morning and I certainly didn't want beer, but my fixer warned me that it might be considered offensive if we didn't stay," recalls Kriel.

> So, we stayed, we ate and we drank warm Heineken. Then we had to continue on with our full work day. It wasn't easy. The situations vary from country to country. You have to be ready to roll with whatever is thrown your way and always maintain a healthy sense of humor.

▶ SHOWCASING A RANGE OF VOICES

Capturing the complexity of any given situation or issue requires more than interviewing those on "both sides" of a story, and it requires more than a sound bite. You will want to be able to engage in meaningful conversations with individuals with multiple backgrounds and points of view—in Kriel's case, the DRC rebels *and* the civilians. You will need to give voice to people who often are left without an opportunity to tell global audiences what they think. Don't underestimate the value of knowing the language. Fortunately for native English speakers, English tends to be the language of international commerce. Dan Pierce, who worked for Anheuser-Busch on the Budweiser brand in China, India, Russia and the U.K., says in public relations language is not a requirement, but the added value. Still, Kornberg says, even when U.S. students work with their Japanese peers in Tokyo, conducting all their meetings in English, the final creative work will ultimately be in Japanese. Authenticity depends on working with Japanese practitioners, he said.

However, for journalists, unless you plan only on interviewing government officials or a country's most elite citizens, English is not sufficient. So, consider yourself lucky if you've been required to learn another language in school or you've spent a semester or two outside the United States soaking in another culture and working on your fluency. And, if you've learned another language at home, that's even better. Both Gareth Harding, director of the Missouri School of Journalism's Brussels program, and Escudero are emphatic about the need for U.S. journalism students who want to work internationally to learn other languages. Harding, a native of Wales who has written extensively about the European Union, speaks French and Spanish, and also some German, Norwegian, Dutch and Italian. He said U.S. students arriving in Brussels will find that most people there speak an average of three languages. "It wakes them up very quickly that it's a multilingual, multicultural environment. They feel very inadequate in terms of language," Harding said. Escudero, who has reported from Belgium, France, Spain, the Netherlands, China and Bolivia, also speaks multiple languages: French, Spanish, English, Italian, Portuguese and some Dutch.

Their language skills have proved invaluable. Harding, who straddles the fields of journalism and strategic communication, recalls a time when he was working on video news releases for the European Union about climate change. "I was filming a lot in Spain, and I'd be in a field talking to a farmer about climate change. I had to speak Spanish. You couldn't always afford a translator," Harding said. Likewise, Drew found his many years learning Russian, beginning in junior high, paid off. When most journalists started reporting on the privatization of the formerly communist countries of Eastern Europe, Drew opted instead to move from central Europe and cover Russia's withdrawal of troops from Estonia, Latvia and Lithuania. A big bonus was he could use his Russian language skills because roughly a third of the three countries' populations were non-Baltic, coming from other parts of the former Soviet Union.

If you're wondering which language to learn next, consider what the global news agency Reuters tells potential applicants for its training program: "Fluency in more than one language is a distinct advantage. Arabic, Russian or Mandarin are particularly welcome."[31] Language skills are invaluable at home, as well, Drew says. "If I were beginning my journalism career in the U.S. today, I would absorb Spanish, given the demographic projections for the future," he said.

When correspondents do not have the necessary language skills, they often turn to individuals known as "fixers." Kriel calls fixers a "lifeline into a society" because they can help journalists navigate all sorts of issues, including security. During the 2003–2011 U.S.-led military effort in Iraq, Western journalists often employed Iraqi fixers. The vast majority of the journalists Palmer and Fontan interviewed spoke little to no Arabic, and the one native Arabic speaker found that the Iraqi version differed enough that he also needed help interpreting.[32] Although many Iraqis can speak French or English, those language skills go hand in hand with education—and the fault line of class. For journalists wanting to speak to Iraqis of lower socioeconomic status, having Arabic-speaking translators was imperative. In addition, in Iraqi society, "religious, tribal, political and personal affiliations are crucial in the creation of trust," and fixers had to be aware of those affiliations as they looked for a range of individuals who could be coaxed into being interviewed by Western media.[33]

▶ EMBRACING COMPLEXITY: AVOID GOOD GUYS VS. BAD GUYS

Of course, the more homework you do on most issues, and the more people whose views you consider, the more you realize how most issues are not black and white. Life is complex. Producing meaningful work requires embracing complexity, and embracing complexity requires boycotting simplistic frames. Political scientist Robert M. Entman defines framing as "selecting and highlighting some facets of events or issues, and making connections among them so as to promote a particular interpretation, evaluation, and/or solution."[34] In international reporting, the most natural frame for a conflict is good guys vs. bad guys. This frame is especially prevalent in war reporting, but it can appear in everything from environmental reporting to business reporting.

When one's own country is involved in a dispute with another, it may seem only natural to trust—and quote—officials from one's own government more than officials from another country. When a bomb kills dozens of civilians, the most expedient narrative would be that the bad guys are at it again. The hijackers who crashed jets into the World Trade Center in 2001 belonged to al-Qaida, which had operated training camps in Afghanistan with the blessing of the ruling Taliban. In the U.S. media, the Taliban often were collectively vilified as religious extremists who, among other things, repressed women's rights. Were all the Talibs extremists bent on spreading their own religious views and physically attacking Western interests? Former *New York Times* correspondent Dexter Filkins, who spent extended time in both Iraq and Afghanistan, offers a more complex portrayal:

> Men fought, men switched sides, men lined up and fought again. War in
> Afghanistan often seemed like a game of pickup basketball, a contest among
> friends, a tournament where you never knew which team you'd be on when
> the next game got under way. Shirts today, skins tomorrow. On Tuesday,
> you might be part of a fearsome Taliban regiment, running into a minefield.
> And on Wednesday you might be manning a checkpoint for some gang of
> the Northern Alliance. By Thursday you could be back with the Talibs again,
> holding up your Kalashnikov and promising to wage jihad forever. War was
> serious in Afghanistan, but not that serious. It was part of everyday life. It was
> a job.[35]

Filkins' observation—indeed, his entire book—illustrates the folly of making assumptions about motivations—and who's good and who's bad. Filkins, who at times depended on the U.S. military for his security while he embedded with American troops, offers a nuanced view of the U.S. troops and their leaders. Their actions were not all heroic, just as the people he encountered in Iraq and Afghanistan were not all extremist.

Sometimes, journalists covering breaking news seem unable to stop themselves from making assumptions. When a bomb blast levels a busy Western hotel during the height of the tourism season on Egypt's Sinai peninsula, journalists feel compelled to offer whatever tidbits of information they think they have. A broadcast correspondent filing an immediate report about a 2004 bomb blast at the Hilton Hotel in Taba, Egypt, that killed dozens told viewers: "As yet, there is no claim of responsibility, but one of the usual suspects, Hamas, has recently threatened to hit Israeli targets outside of Israel."[36] Assumption: Hamas is bad. Implication: Hamas may be responsible for the blast. In an update the same day, the journalist said Israeli and Egyptian investigators were "pointing to al-Qaida" and included this soundbite from an Israeli official: "Most of the evidence points to al-Qaida. The fingerprints look like al-Qaida."[37] The journalist did not ask follow-up questions on air, leaving the implication that al-Qaida was responsible. So, who was responsible? Al-Qaida or Hamas? The viewer will not know. The truth likely was more complicated; that first draft of history was not quite right. Writing for *National Geographic Magazine* nearly five years later, Matthew Teague recounts the events—large and small—leading up to the attacks, and nowhere does he mention al-Qaida or Hamas. Instead, he reports on a dentist who, upset with Egypt's peace deal with Israel among other things, created a terrorist group called Tawhid wa Jihad (translated as Unity and Holy War).[38] Among the small group of bombers were jobless men and Bedouins, a tribal, nomadic people the Egyptian government had forcibly relocated beginning in 1982. The dentist, Teague writes, "needed followers—disaffected young men willing to strike out against authorities, against tourists, against Israel, against Egypt itself."[39] For the average viewer of broadcast news, the initial reports pointed to clear bad guys and likely forced most viewers to a somewhat circular conclusion: Bad guys kill innocent civilians because that's what bad guys do. While not excusing the bombers, Teague captures the complexity of the issues leading to their fateful choices. The Norwegian scholar Johan Galtung would likely label Teague a "peace journalist." Galtung compares typical war reporting to sports journalism, reporting who won and who lost and the score, and likens peace journalism to health journalism, a more holistic approach to reporting that explains the causes and consequences of conflict—or, as it were, illness.[40]

▶ ENSURING PROPORTIONALITY

Once you've done so much homework and have been able to consider so many perspectives in your reporting, the next element for ensuring authenticity in international coverage is remembering proportionality. Does U.S. news coverage provide a mirror image of international events and issues? Research shows it doesn't. Instead, journalists tend to focus on negative news—and on only a handful of countries. In 2006, for example, even though there are about 200 countries in the world, more than 50 percent of four non-elite newspapers' international coverage focused on between four and nine countries and, understandably given the timeframe, the country garnering the most coverage was Iraq, where U.S. troops had been engaged in combat since 2003.[41] The United States has economic, cultural and other ties to countries across the globe. Ideally, U.S. citizens would be provided a wider scope of coverage in their typical news diet.

Journalists also seem conditioned to focus on the negative, whether it's an Ebola outbreak in West Africa or another bomb blast in the Middle East. As Galtung and Ruge noted in 1965, journalists have an easier time reporting negative news because those events tend to fit their news cycles.[42] The bomb, for example, goes off in an instant, and the carnage is immediate. The breaking news story of how many people were killed when and where can be reported and told within a 24-hour news cycle. The positive stories—the steps civic and other groups are taking to encourage peaceful interactions, an improving business climate and stability—require more digging and more time. The positive stories can be rewarding for all involved, though.

In 2012, Jeffrey Gettleman of *The New York Times* won a Pulitzer Prize "for his vivid reports, often at personal peril, on famine and conflict in East Africa, a neglected but increasingly strategic part of the world."[43] His reporting put a spotlight on the hardships faced by the people of Somalia, painting a depressing picture that he hoped would encourage Americans to open their wallets to help correct. When Kriel returned to Somalia in 2014, she was able to spotlight progress—an art exhibition in Mogadishu, for example, that celebrated culture and conveyed a sense of normalcy. The payoff: "It's so much more fun than the gloom and doom, and people, in this case ordinary Somalis, really appreciated that we had told a positive story about their country," Kriel says. "It got a lot of attention."

Just as excellent journalism requires a sense of proportionality—covering the good and bad and a wider geographic scope—so do strategic communicators want to make sure their market research is wide enough in scope to be reliable. Just as an excellent story requires more than one interview, getting one expert opinion or analyzing data from one source is not enough in strategic communication. Fault lines can prove especially helpful. When considering the target audience, strategic communicators want to carefully examine gender, generation, geography, ethnicity and class. Societies in different countries often differ across the fault-line divides. India is a great example. Varsha Jain, professor of integrated marketing communications at the Mudra Institute of Communication, notes that India is a heterogeneous country with 780 spoken and 22 official languages, a large geographical area, and different tastes and preferences. India is also moving from a collectivist to more individualistic culture, and this is particularly clear among younger generations of Indians. Jain adds that strategic communicators also need to consider the urban vs. rural mix in the country. One can never assume one message or strategy will work for all audiences.

▶ CHAPTER SUMMARY

Successfully working across cultures requires a willingness to work hard to learn what you don't know and unlearn what you think you know. Those in global strategic communication, Jain says, "need to be flexible and open for different cultures and people. They need to understand the nuances of local culture, product and brand usage and lifestyle of the consumers." Kriel agrees about the need to work hard and be open-minded and adventurous. But for her, the payoff is worth it:

I have covered stories from Zimbabwe to Afghanistan, South Africa and Somalia. I've lived in a lot of wonderful places. I've eaten a lot of different types of food and drunk a lot of bad and, occasionally, good wine. I feel very privileged to have seen what I have seen, spoken to the people I have spoken to, told the stories I have told and all while getting paid to do it. While there is something really depressing about checking into another horrible hotel room with a filthy bathroom, there is also something amazing and truly exhilarating about it, too. When I'm not there, I want to be there. I need to be there. I am a news addict.

BOX 8.1   From the Field: Advertising Across Cultures

Varsha Jain

Advertisers love to use "slice of life" vignettes to help sell a product. But people from two distinctive cultures are likely to interpret the same situation from different points of view. For this reason, 95 percent of commercials do not translate across cultures well enough to convey their special meanings to Cannes Lions judges.[44] This is true even for commercials such as ones for the chocolate giant Cadbury. For example, in a 2009 Cadbury's 60-second commercial,[45] two postmen, unhappy with how isolated families in their neighborhood have become, deliberately deliver mail to wrong addresses. Neighbors learn each other's news and reunite to return the letters to the proper recipients, discuss the news and treat neighbors to Cadbury.

What might seem to be a breach of professional conduct and intrusion of privacy in the eye of a strategic communicator raised in the U.S. became a much-loved television ad in India.

Varsha Jain, professor of integrated marketing communications at the Mudra Institute of Communications in Ahmedabad in India, explains why the Cadbury "Postman" ad works for the Indian audience:

> In India, people like celebrations as there are many festivals. Diwali is the biggest festival in India where people come together and celebrate. They distribute sweets and enjoy [them] in a community. However, they just want a trigger that can make this happen, and it was given by Cadbury. Initially, people do not talk to each other, but

(Continued)

BOX 8.1 Continued

when the postman exchanges the letters where the good news was written, it worked for the individuals. When they read the good news, then they want to celebrate. This happiness and the sweet moments were exaggerated by Cadbury.

When presented with a storyboard for such an advertisement, companies should know the culture of the country well enough to understand if it will be successful with the Indian audience. "If the ads are not developed from 'Indian DNA and local culture,' then they will reject the campaign and will not connect with the brands," Jain says. "If foreign brands want to be successful, they should know the Indian culture, lifestyle and thought process." It might hurt to know that your work in India might not land a Cannes Lion award, but knowing that you've decoded "Indian DNA" is probably more rewarding.

 BOX 8.2   From the Field: Listening to the Voices of the Target Audience

In strategic communication, professionals work hard to learn how a product will be perceived and used by the target audience in the new market. Focus groups and in-depth interviews are held to elicit opinions about the product and the context in which potential customers will purchase and use it. Strategic communicators also turn to experts—people who are familiar with the region—for their opinion about habits, values, business climate and infrastructure in the country.

When Judy Phair, president of consulting firm Phair-Advantage Communications LLC, worked on increasing enrollment of students from India in liberal arts colleges in the Midwest, she took advantage of talking to Indian students already attending colleges in the U.S., Indian alumni in the U.S. and India and high

Judy Phair

school students in India. This gave her insights into how they chose a school, as well as testimonials to include in promotional materials.

She says she learned that in India, parents and other family members tend to participate more in making decisions about a child's education than they might in

(Continued)

BOX 8.2 Continued

other countries. She adds that she found this an interesting contrast to Chinese students she had worked with earlier for another organization. The Chinese students wanted to attend school in the U.S. to gain a broader view of the world and to better understand business practices in the West. Parents in China see a great value in American education and are willing to sacrifice a lot to make sure that their child—often their only child—attends a university abroad. She said parents also expect their child to return to China after graduation.

Talking to Indian students allowed Phair to discover that they often encounter less culture shock than Chinese students because English is one of their country's official languages. For Chinese students, she says, language is often more of a barrier. Indians also knew more about Western culture before coming to the United States, she says, because they came from a democratic country that allowed more exposure to Western ideas. Such insights helped Phair address students' expectations and concerns in texts and images in promotional materials. "I think one of the biggest wake-up calls for the U.S businesses has been, whether it's education or business, that you cannot take the same materials that you use here and just change language or color scheme," Phair says. "You really have to learn about the culture and develop your materials specifically for that country. It's also a mark of respect." Not surprisingly, Phair includes interpersonal skills among the skills strategic communicators should master. She explains that they should have good listening skills, be able to fully engage and interact with people, and to be considerate of others.

FOR DISCUSSION

1. What would you need to research before promoting WeightWatchers in the Czech Republic? Smucker's jam? Samuel Adams beer? How would you use the framework of excellence in journalism and strategic communication to guide you in your research?

2. What are the online resources available for journalists and strategic communicators for background research on countries? Would you want to only use U.S. media sources? Why or why not?

3. If you were writing a piece on relations between Turkey and Armenia, what sources would you use? Would you need to write about something that happened more than 100 years ago?

▶ SUGGESTED ACTIVITIES

1. Choose a country with strong political and economic ties with the United States Search the website of a U.S. news organization to see how your country is covered. Aim for 10 distinct stories. How much coverage appeared over time? Which topics made news? How would you rate the quality of the reporting?

2. In *The World News Prism*, William A. Hachten compared the global system of news distribution to a crystal prism: "One person's truth becomes, to another, biased reporting or propaganda, depending on where the light strikes the prism and where it emerges."[46] Select an international issue involving a country that recently received substantial news coverage. Find stories about the issue from two news organizations based in different countries. Do they quote the same people? Do they describe the issue in similar ways? How do they differ?

3. Using the Freedom House report on press freedom[47] as your starting point, evaluate the economic, political, legal, media and cultural barriers facing journalists and strategic communicators, both domestic and international, in the country of your choice.

4. Pick up a popular U.S. magazine and find an advertisement for a product you like. How, if at all, would you have to modify the ad campaign to be successful in India or Saudi Arabia? Explain your answer.

▶ NOTES

1 "Spot the Africa," *The Daily Show with Jon Stewart*, December 4, 2014, http://thedailyshow.cc.com/videos/myb4mb/spot-the-africa.

2 Priya Kumar, "Foreign correspondents: Who covers what," *American Journalism Review*, December/January 2011, http://ajrarchive.org/Article.asp?id=4997.

3 "El Salvador," Central Intelligence Agency, https://www.cia.gov/library/publications/the-world-factbook/geos/es.html.

4 Mark Danner, "Staying on in El Salvador," *Index on Censorship*, 2006, 32–39, Available: http://www.tandfonline.com/doi/full/10.1080/03064220600608765)

5 Scott Johnson, "American-Born Gangs Helping Drive Immigrant Crisis at U.S. Border," *National Geographic*, July 23, 2014, http://news.nationalgeographic.com/news/2014/07/140723-immigration-minors-honduras-gang-violence-central-america/.

6 Philip Seib, *The Al Jazeera Effect: How the New Global Media Are Reshaping World Politics* (Virginia: Potomac Books, 2008), 65–90.

7 Ibid., 66.

8 P. Eric Louw, "Reporting Foreign Places," in *Global Journalism: Topical Issues and Media Systems*, ed. Arnold S. de Beer (Boston: Pearson, Allyn and Bacon, 2009), 153–164.

9   Ibid., 154.

10 "Freedom of the Press," Freedom House, http://www.freedomhouse.org/report-types/free dom-press#.U9KtYPldWSo.

11 "Egypt Sentences Al-Jazeera Trio to at Least Seven Years' Jail," British Broadcasting Corporation, June 23, 2014, http://www.bbc.com/news/world-middle-east-27972181.

12 "Chinese Journalist Dismissed After Writing on Hong Kong News Website," Committee to Protect Journalists, July 22, 2014, https://cpj.org/2014/07/chinese-journalist-dismissed-after-writing-on-hong.php#more.

13 "Alerts," Committee to Protect Journalists, 2014, https://cpj.org/news/2014/.

14 "Saudi Arabia," Freedom House, http://www.freedomhouse.org/report/freedom-press/2013/saudi-arabia#.U9LQOfldWSo.

15 Tom O'Hara, "Just Make Sure You Don't Call it the Persian Gulf!" *American Journalism Review*, December 2012/January 2013, http://ajrarchive.org/article.asp?id=5460.

16 Ibid.

17 Enda Curran, "Hong Kong Newspaper Says HSBC, Standard Chartered Pulled Ads," *Wall Street Journal*, June 16, 2014, http://www.wsj.com/articles/apple-daily-says-hsbc-standard-chartered-pulled-ads-due-to-chinese-government-pressure-1402923219.

18 Bradley Johnson, "Global Marketers 2013," December 9, 2013, 84(43): 16. http://adage.com/datacenter/globalmarketers2013.

19 Ibid.

20 "Questions & Answers: New Rules for Tobacco Products," European Commission, February 26, 2014, http://europa.eu/rapid/press-release_MEMO-14–134_en.htm.

21 "Alcohol Control Policies: Advertising Restrictions," World Health Organization, http://apps.who.int/gho/data/node.main.A1131?lang=en&showonly=GISAH.

22 "Children and Advertising," Advertising Standards Authority, http://www.asa.org.uk/News-resources/Hot-Topics/Children-and-advertising.aspx#.U9QVIPldWSo.

23 Lawrence Pintak and Jeremy Ginges, "Inside the Arab Newsroom: Arab Journalists Evaluate Themselves and the Competition," *Journalism Studies* 10, no. 2 (2009): 164–165.

24 Ibid., 166.

25 Bill Ristow, "Cash for Coverage: Bribery of Journalists Around the World," Center for International Media Assistance, 2010, http://cima.ned.org/sites/default/files/CIMA-Bribery_of_Journalists-Report.pdf.

26 Ibid.

27 "IPRA Code of Conduct," International Public Relations Association, http://ipra.org/images/English.pdf.

28 Edward, T. Hall, *The Silent Language* (Greenwich, CN: Fawcett, 1959).

29 Jerry Palmer and Victoria Fontan, "'Our Ears and Our Eyes': Journalists and Fixers in Iraq," *Journalism* 8, no. 1 (2007): 5–24.

30 Verve Photo, http://www.ohio.edu/people/bt126509/vico361/redesign/photographer.html.

31 "Reuters Journalism Program," Thompson Reuters, http://careers.thomsonreuters.com/Students/Bachelors/Europe/Reuters-Journalism-Program/.

32 Palmer and Fontan, "*Our Ears and Our Eyes.*"

33 Ibid., 12.

34 Robert M. Entman, *Projections of Power: Framing News, Public Opinion, and US Foreign Policy* (Chicago, IL: University of Chicago Press, 2004), 5.

35 Dexter Filkins, *The Forever War* (New York: Random House, 2008), 51.

36 "Deadly Resort Blast in Egypt," CBS News, October 25, 2004, http://www.cbsnews.com/videos/deadly-resort-blast-in-egypt/.

37 "Egypt blast aftermath," CBS News, October 25, 2004, http://www.cbsnews.com/videos/egypt-blast-aftermath/.

38 Matthew Teague, "A Separate Place," *National Geographic Magazine*, March 2009, http://ngm.nationalgeographic.com/print/2009/03/sinai/teague-text.

39 Ibid.

40 Annabelle McGoldrick and Jake Lynch, "Peace Journalism—What Is It? How to Do It?" Transcend, 2000, 26–27, http://www.transcend.org/tri/downloads/McGoldrick_Lynch_Peace-Journalism.pdf.

41 Beverly Horvit, Peter Gade and Elizabeth A. Lance, "News Wire Greatest Predictor of Papers' International News," *Newspaper Research Journal* 34, no. 1 (2013), 95–96.

42 Johan Galtung and Marie Hombue Ruge, "The Structure of Foreign News: The Presentation of the Congo, Cuba and Cyprus Crises in Four Norwegian Newspapers," *Journal of Peace Research* 2, no. 1 (1965): 69, doi:10.1177/002234336500200104.

43 "The 2012 Pulitzer Prize Winners: International Reporting," The Pulitzer, http://www.pulitzer.org/citation/2012-International-Reporting.

44 "Cannes Lions 2014: Ad Campaigns that are 'Too Indian' to Bring Home Even a Bronze," *The Economic Times*, June 12, 2014, http://economictimes.indiatimes.com/magazines/brand-equity/cannes-lions-2014-ad-campaigns-that-are-too-indian-to-bring-home-even-a-bronze/articleshow/36356175.cms.

45 Cadbury Advertisement. https://www.youtube.com/watch?v=aAXu_2RFPTc.

46 William A. Hachten and James F. Scotton, *The World News Prism: Global Information in a Satellite Age*, (Malden, MA: Blackwell, 2007), xxi.

47 "Freedom of the Press," Freedom House, 2014, https://freedomhouse.org/report-types/freedom-press.

▶ ADDITIONAL READINGS

Barboza, David. "Billions in Hidden Riches for Family of Chinese Leader." *The New York Times*, October 25, 2012. http://www.nytimes.com/2012/10/26/business/global/family-of-wen-jia-bao-holds-a-hidden-fortune-in-china.html?_r=0.

Chen, Huan and Eric Haley. "Product Placement in Social Games: Consumer Experiences in China." *Journal of Advertising* 43, no. 3 (2014): 286–95. doi:10.1080/00913367.2013.858086.

Curtin, Patricia A. and Thomas Kenneth Gaither. *International Public Relations: Negotiating Culture, Identity and Power*. Thousand Oaks, CA: Sage, 2007.

Erzikova, Elina. "Practitioners in Russia's Provinces: Affectionate and Unpredictable." *Public Relations Review* 38, no. 3 (2012): 454–57. doi:10.1016/j.pubrev.2012.04.002.

Ford, John B., Barbara Mueller and Charles R. Taylor. "The Tension Between Strategy and Execution: Challenges for International Advertising Research." *Journal of Advertising Research* 51 (2011): 27–44.

Hall, Emma. "In YouTube World, Humor Can Get Lost in Translation." *AdAge* 79, no. 31 (2008): 3–21.

Holtz-Bacha, Christina, Benot Johansson, Jacob Leidenberger, Philippe J. Maarek and Susanne Merkle. "Advertising for Europe." *Nordicom Review* 33, no. 2 (2012): 77–92.

Horvit, Beverly, Peter Gade and Elizabeth A. Lance. "News Wire Greatest Predictor of Papers' International News." *Newspaper Research Journal* 34, no. 1 (2013): 89–103.

Horvit, Beverly. "International News Agencies and the War Debate of 2003." *International Communication Gazette* 68, no. 5/6 (2006): 427–47. doi:10.1177/1748048506068722.

"How Lynx Changed Cultural Notions About Men and Fragrance in China." *AdAge* 83, no. 3 (2012): 1–20.

Hubbard, Ben. "Syrian Civilians Hit Hard by Spreading Violence." Associated Press, June 23, 2012. http://www.ap.org/Images/Syria_%20final_tcm28–12511.pdf.

Jain, Rajul, Maria De Moya and Juan-Carlos Molleda. "State of International Public Relations Research: Narrowing the Knowledge Gap About the Practice Across Borders." *Public Relations Review* 40, no. 3 (2014): 595–97. doi:10.1016/j.pubrev.2014.02.009.

Kineta, Hung, Kimmy W. Chan and Caleb H. Tse. "Assessing Celebrity Endorsement Effects in China." *Journal of Advertising Research* 51, no. 4 (2011): 608–23. doi:10.2501/JAR-51-4-608-623.

Martin, Justin D. "Which Country Jails the Most Journalists?" *Columbia Journalism Review*, April 2, 2012, http://www.cjr.org/behind_the_news/which_countries_jail_the_most.php.

McDevitt, Michael. "Journalistic Influence in Moral Mobilization." In *The Geopolitics of Representation in Foreign News: Explaining Darfur*, ed. Bella Mody, 445–63. New York: Lexington Books, 2010.

McGoldrick, Annabelle and Jake Lynch. "Peace journalism—What is it? How to do it?" Transcend, 2000. http://www.transcend.org/tri/downloads/McGoldrick_Lynch_Peace-Journalism.pdf.

McPhail, Thomas L. *Global Communication: Theories, Stakeholders, and Trends.* Hoboken, NJ: Wiley Blackwell, 2014, chap. 7–12, 15.

Mueller, Barbara. *Communicating with the Multicultural Consumer: Theoretical and Practical Perspectives.* New York: Peter Lang, 2008, 23–54.

Neff, Jack. "Walmart, P&G, Unilever Learn from Their Mistakes." *AdAge* 80, no. 22 (2009): 3–26.

Nieman Reports. "The Future of Foreign News." Fall 2014. http://nieman.niemanfoundation. netdna-cdn.com/wp-content/uploads/2014/12/NiemanReportsFall2014.pdf.

Quelch, John A. and Katherine E. Jocz. *All Business Is Local: Why Place Matters More Than ever in a Global, Virtual World.* New York: Penguin, 2012.

Ricchiardi, Sherry. "The Limits of the Parachute." *American Journalism Review* 28, no. 5 (October/November (2006): 40–47.

Sinclair, John. "The Advertising Industry in Latin America." *International Communication Gazette* 71, no. 8 (2009): 713–33.

Trotta, Liz. *Fighting for Air: In the Trenches with Television News.* New York: Simon & Schuster, 1991.

Valentine, S. R. and T. L. Rittenburg. "The Ethical Decision Making of Men and Women Executives in International Business Situations." *Journal of Business Ethics* 71, no. 2 (2007): 125–34. doi:10.1007/s10551-006-9129-y.

Wanta, Wayne, Guy Golan and Cheolhan Lee. "Agenda Setting and International News: Media Influence on Public Perceptions of Foreign Nations." *Journalism & Mass Communication Quarterly* 81, no. 2 (2004): 364–77.

Ward, Stephen. "Global Journalism Ethics." In *Global Journalism Ethics*, 153–183. Montreal, Quebec and Kingston, Ontario: McGill-Queen's Press, 2010.

Wentz, Laurel. "See Some of the Best Latin American Work Going to Cannes." *Advertising Age*, June 19, 2015. http://adage.com/article/global-news/latin-american-work-cannes/299141/.

Wentz, Laurel. "P&G Whisper's 'Touch the Pickle' Wins Glass Grand Prix" *Advertising Age*, June 23, 2015. http://adage.com/article/special-report-cannes-lions/p-g-whisper-s-touch-pickle-wins-glass-grand-prix/299182/.

9

Immigrants and Immigration: Reporting the New America

Melita M. Garza

As tens of thousands of children fleeing violence and poverty in Central America crossed the southwestern border into the United States in 2014, one boy among the multitude in an emergency shelter at San Antonio's Lackland Air Force Base caught the eye of ABC News reporter Gina Sunseri. What stood out for her was his crayon drawing, movingly captioned, 'echo [sic] de menos a mi familia', meaning, "I miss my family." [1]

The influx that President Barack Obama declared "an urgent humanitarian situation" became a breaking news story that national, regional and local media rushed to cover. [2] Reporters chronicling the fate of these desperate children narrated another important episode in the country's lengthy immigration history. This chapter will help you gain the skills to contribute insightfully to the ongoing saga that defines the nation.

Who are immigrants? What is "the immigration beat?" What makes immigrants an important public in marketing and strategic communication? More immigrants come to the United States than any other country, making the ability to report, write and reach this growing group essential.[3] Immigrants are changing the face of the United States, while in many instances both high- and low-skilled immigrants are boosting the country's economic vitality.[4] The black–white race binary, the idea that

FIGURE 9.1 A youngster who crossed the border looks out the door window from the room in which he is staying in at the Brownsville, Texas, port of entry.
Credit: Eduardo Perez, U.S. Customs and Border Protection

race in the United States consists of only two groups, black and white, once defined the nation. As recently as 1960, the country was 85 percent white. By 2060, the nation will be less than 45 percent white, according to Pew Research.[5]

More than 90 national and local print, television, radio and online news organizations had journalists covering immigration as a beat or part of their beat in 2014.[6] These included *The New York Times*, the *Los Angeles Times*, the *Dallas Morning News* and the major networks, among others. Marketers are growing savvier about the transformation of their audience. One of America's most iconic enterprises, The Coca-Cola Company, aired a television advertisement during Super Bowl 2014 that featured young women singing "America the Beautiful" in several languages. The ad went viral, stirring praise and criticism. Despite the mixed reaction, Coca-Cola ran an even longer version of the same ad during the 2014 Sochi Winter Olympics.[7]

Business is following the numbers. In 2012 alone, 1.03 million legal immigrants were admitted to the United States, with 80 percent coming from Asia and the Americas.[8] Since 1980, more immigrants have come to the United States from Mexico than from any other country.[9] News coverage tends to pivot off conflict and controversy. In the case of immigrants, this makes being unlawfully in the country a news peg.

In writing about immigration much of what is publicly debated relates to the issue of illegal immigration. However, communicators should understand that more than two-thirds of the 40.7 million immigrants living in the United States are here legally.[10]

Immigration enforcement is only one component of the beat. Consider the role of immigrants in education, health, economic and business news, public policy and culture and the arts, among other things. Think about the way language, culture and Robert Maynard's fault lines of race, geography, gender, class and the age of various immigrant groups, might inform and shape strategic communication plans and journalism interviews.

Take geography. Refugees—people who are forced to flee their country because of persecution, war or violence—are legally admitted each year to the U.S. from all over the world. In 2012, some 46.7 percent of all refugees came from the Near East and South Asia, more than from any other region.[11]

Refugees and other immigrants are revitalizing towns and cities throughout the United States. Burlington, Vermont, for example, elected its first "new American" to the City Council in 2014. The council member, Bianka LeGrand, arrived as a refugee from war-torn Bosnia in 1997.[12] Minnesota, long called "the land of 10,000 lakes," is now also known for hosting the largest community of Somalis in the United States. The flourishing community produced Barkhad Abdi, the Oscar-nominated actor who upstaged Tom Hanks in the 2013 Sony Pictures adventure biopic, *Captain Phillips*.[13]

Such triumphs are often overshadowed by media coverage that focuses on conflict and controversy, as immigrants and refugees find tension between the language and customs of their homeland and their new lives and neighbors. These issues are not limited to the United States. Many countries struggle to absorb the foreign-born, with xenophobic attitudes often sharpening in periods of economic calamity. A Pew Research survey of seven European countries, taken on the eve of the 2014 elections for the European Union Parliament, showed high levels of anti-immigrant sentiment. This was most pronounced in countries in economic upheaval, such as Greece, which was reeling from tough economic sanctions imposed by the European Central Bank.[14]

▶ THE HISTORICAL BACKDROP: AMERICA, A NATION OF IMMIGRANTS FROM THE 16TH CENTURY THROUGH TODAY

TABLE 9.1 Three great waves of immigration to the U.S.

Era and Country	Total (in thousands)	Percent
Modern Era (1965–present)	**44,495**	**100**
Mexico	12,416	28
China*	2,479	6

(Continued)

TABLE 9.1 Continued

Era and Country	Total (in thousands)	Percent
India	2,077	5
Philippines	1,990	4
Korea	1,391	3
Vietnam	1,291	3
Former U.S.SR	1,272	3
El Salvador	1,101	2
Cuba	1,090	2
Dominican Republic	912	2
Region totals		
Latin America	22,111	50
South/East Asia	11,811	27
Europe, total	5,373	12
Canada**	880	2
Africa/Middle East	3,211	7
All other	1,110	2
Southern-/Eastern-Europe Wave (1890–1919)	**18,244**	**100**
Italy	3,764	21
Austria-Hungary	3,690	20
Russia & Poland	3,166	17
United Kingdom	1,170	6
Germany	1,082	6
Ireland***	917	5
Region totals		
Europe, total	16,134	88
North/West Europe	4,757	26
South/East Europe	11,377	62
Canada	835	5
Latin America	551	3
South/East Asia	315	2
Africa	332	2
Other/Not specified	77	<0.5
Northern-Europe Wave (1840–1889)	**14,314**	**100**
Germany	4,282	30
Ireland***	3,209	22
United Kingdom	2,586	18
Norway-Sweden	883	6
Region totals		

Era and Country	Total (in thousands)	Percent
Europe, total	12,757	89
North/West Europe	11,700	82
South/East Europe	1,058	7
Canada	1,034	7
Latin America	101	1
South/East Asia	293	2
Africa/Middle East	5	<0.5
Other/Not specified	124	1

Notes: Data for 1965–2011 include legal and unauthorized immigrants in the total population. Data for 1840–1919 include only legal admissions. *China includes Hong Kong, Taiwan and Macao. **Includes other North America. ***Ireland incudes Northern Ireland. Persons from Puerto Rico not included.

Source: For 1965–present. Pew Hispanic Center tabulations from Integrated Public Use Microdata Samples for 1980, 1990 and 2000 censuses and 2005–2011 American Community Surveys (with 2010-based weights); for 1840–1919, Table 2 from Office of Immigration Statistics. *Yearbook of Immigration Statistics, 2008*

▶ **PEW RESEARCH CENTER**

To report and write about immigrants, and reach them in strategic communication campaigns, it is imperative to understand the historical role of immigrants in building the nation. "Good journalists should not be weighted down by their own assumptions," said award-winning reporter Maria Hinojosa, whose PBS Frontline special, *Lost in Detention*, uncovered abuse of immigrants in U.S. government facilities. As much as learning about immigrants, "realize that you have to unlearn" and "challenge the mindset that immigrants are less than," Hinojosa said.

For the immigration beat, this means identifying experts, reading background material, and most importantly, checking your pre-conceived ideas. Doing your history homework will help you achieve all three. Immigration history is complex. Immigrants have been sought after, celebrated and vilified—in some periods these sentiments have surfaced simultaneously.

Spanish-Speaking Immigrants: A 400-Year-Old Tradition

The trend toward immigration from Asia and Latin America, which started in the late 20th and early 21st centuries, is a clear demographic shift for the United States.

These new settlers are only the latest participants in a 400-year-old tradition that started with the Spaniards, the first Europeans to immigrate and build a permanent continuous settlement in what is now the United States. The Spanish colonization of Puerto Rico in 1505, more than 100 years before Jamestown's founding in 1607, is the starting point, according to the historian Felipe Fernández-Armesto.[15] El Paso, Texas, and Santa Fe, New Mexico, "were in Spanish hands" by 1598, a decade before Jamestown. The Spaniards took over San Agustin, Florida—in English, St. Augustine—even earlier, after ousting the French in 1567.[16]

The Spaniards, like the French, the English and the Dutch, who founded New Amsterdam, later renamed New York, voyaged to the New World for many of the same reasons immigrants continue to come to the United States. They came to make their fortune, to flee persecution and to freely practice their faith.[17] In short, they were seeking a better life. From the beginning, media played an important role in attracting immigrants, with Sir Walter Raleigh employing persuasive communication tactics, including promotional brochures, to attract English colonists to Roanoke Island off the coast of North Carolina.[18] Spanish explorers described cities of gold in the New World to lure government backing for expeditions, new recruits and settlers willing to gamble on a new life.[19] Although many of these immigrants pre-dated the American Revolution and the formation of the U.S. constitution, their pioneering efforts have left an indelible mark on U.S. culture.

Mexicans: Americans and Immigrants

From the early days of the Republic, starting in the 1800s, the United States had a policy of admitting European immigrants. As the country expanded westward, the United States fought a war against Mexico that ended with the Treaty of Guadalupe Hidalgo in 1848. Mexico lost half of its territory, including previously annexed Texas and land that is now California, Arizona, Nevada, Utah, Wyoming, Colorado, Kansas, Oklahoma and New Mexico.[20]

Under the treaty, Mexicans were guaranteed that legal rights and property would be preserved. Despite the treaty, many Mexicans lost property and other rights.[21] Mexicans became "strangers in a strange land, a minority struggling for acceptance in a sea of Americans."[22] This longtime historic connection between Mexicans and Americans is often forgotten in the current debate and news stories about Mexican "immigrants."

Immigrants and Identity

Tensions between an immigrant identity and a U.S. identity characterize most immigrants groups, not just those from Mexico. Historian Oscar Handlin traced the impact of hate groups, such as the Know-Nothing Party, on immigrants' sense of alienation. The Know-Nothings of the mid-1850s spewed nativist, anti-immigrant and anti-Catholic attitudes, with the latter mainly aimed at Irish immigrants. By the late 1800s, after several decades "that the melting pot had been simmering . . . the end product seemed no clearer than before."[23] Despite their time living in the United States, Irish and Germans were still observably distinctive "from other Americans," Handlin wrote.[24]

Just who might be considered truly American was hotly debated, with most Anglo-Saxons claiming the title. In Handlin's account, this left out the Irish, not to mention Chinese and Mexicans. But some celebrated this diversity. And while the Know-Nothing movement preached that immigrants represented the decline of American civilization, poet Walt Whitman took a different view. "The United States themselves are essentially the greatest poem. Here is not merely a nation, but a teeming nation of nations," Whitman wrote in 1855.[25]

European immigration to the United States predominated for decades. Between 1900 and 1909, more than 8.2 million immigrants came to the United States.[26] Mexicans in the United States had a low profile until the late 19th century, when economic and cultural integration increased with Mexico.[27] An increase in agricultural and industrial productivity, coupled with the Mexican Revolution of 1910, boosted Mexican immigration in the early 20th century.[28]

Restricting Asians; Denouncing Ethnic Europeans in Wartime

Laws that restricted Asian laborers also fueled an increase in Mexican immigrants. These included the Chinese Exclusion Act of 1882, and the subsequent Gentlemen's Agreement of 1908, which restricted Japanese immigrants prior to World War I. Many Japanese were ousted after they moved from contract farm labor and formed cooperatives, bought their own land and competed with their former employers.[29] Unlike Asian immigrants, U.S. business perceived Mexicans as low-cost, controllable and mobile workers.[30]

Europeans were not always wholeheartedly accepted either. For instance, during World War I, a time of intense political turmoil, Germanic culture became taboo in the United States. Boston banned the playing of Beethoven's music; Iowa governor William L. Harding outlawed uttering German in public or on the telephone and Wisconsinites burned German books.[31] Later, during World War II, some Italian- and German-Americans were placed in internment camps. But Japanese Americans took the brunt of that xenophobia—120,000 were incarcerated without due process.[32] In 1988, during the administration of President Ronald Reagan, they were issued an apology and each surviving internee received $20,000 in reparations.[33]

Economic Pressures Spur Immigration Laws

An agricultural downturn in the early 1920s spurred immigration restrictions that led to the 1924 Immigration Act. The act was the first comprehensive law that numerically limited the immigrant groups that would be welcomed to live in the United States. It also established a "global racial and national hierarchy that favored some immigrants over others."[34]

> The famous words of Emma Lazarus on the pedestal of the Statue of Liberty read: "Give me your tired, your poor, your huddled masses yearning to breathe free." Until 1921 this was an accurate picture of our society. Under present law it would be appropriate to add: "as long as they come from Northern Europe, are not too tired or too poor or slightly ill, never stole a loaf of bread, never joined any questionable organization, and can document their activities for the past two years."
>
> John F. Kennedy, *A Nation of Immigrants*, 1958[35]

Literacy tests and other measures were employed starting in 1924 to keep out immigrants from southern and eastern Europe, as well as those from Asia and Africa.[36] During the Great Depression, 1929 to1934, state and local governments, spurred by the federal government and supported by social service agencies, repatriated almost 500,000 Mexicans and Mexican-Americans. The expulsion and voluntary return of so many Mexicans and their U.S.-born children led to a humanitarian crisis on the Mexican border akin to the 2014 crisis sparked by Central American children fleeing to the United States. Massive removals of Mexicans from the United States in the aftermath of the Great Recession, which ran from December 2007 to June 2009, is also reminiscent of the Depression era.

Until 1960 most immigrants to the United States came from European countries, first northern Europe, and then later southern Europe. Italian-born immigrants accounted for 13 percent of all foreign-born in 1960; Germans and Canadians followed closely at roughly 10 percent each. Early in 1963, the year he was assassinated, President John F. Kennedy proposed legislation to abolish the national origin quotas imposed in the 1924 Act. In 1965, President Lyndon B. Johnson signed the law that eliminated the numerical immigration restrictions that had been in place for more than 40 years. As a grandson of Irish immigrants, Kennedy was a compassionate defender of U.S. newcomers, revising his book, *A Nation of Immigrants*, shortly before his death.

> **Activity:** Using family interviews, databases such as ancestry.com and government records, trace your family history in the United States to the first arriving immigrant. What records of their entry, legal or otherwise, did you find?

Highlights of More Recent Immigration Law

Immigration laws have continued to evolve. For instance, in 1980, in the aftermath of the Vietnam War, Congress streamlined admission of refugees and asylum seekers. Later that decade, Congress passed the Immigration Reform and Control Act of 1986, which legalized the status of about three million immigrants while imposing tough new requirements that made workers prove they were eligible to hold jobs in the United States. Ten years later, in 1996, Congress imposed harsh new penalties on immigrants illegally in the country, requiring detention and deportation for many immigration violations.[37]

The terrorist attacks of September 11, 2001, led to the absorption of the Immigration & Naturalization Service into a new government agency, the Department of Homeland Security. This reframed immigration as a national security issue and contributed to expedited deportations. The Obama administration "deported more people more quickly than any other president."[38] In 2012, deportations reached a record 419,384 for the fiscal year, according to the Department of Homeland Security. The emergence of Latinos as the largest U.S. minority added political pressure for immigration reform, with more than half of Hispanics supporting policies that would enable undocumented immigrants to work without fear of deportation, according to a 2013 Pew study.[39] Latino political clout, however, lags their numbers. Because of age and citizenship, fewer than half of Hispanics are eligible to vote. Overall, they accounted for only 11 percent of the potential electorate in 2014.[40]

Obama, as of mid-2015, had not succeeded in gaining passage of comprehensive immigration reform legislation. In the legislative vacuum, several states, including Arizona in 2010, passed their own laws. Arizona, which shares a 370-mile border with Mexico, required police to verify the legal status of any person they stop or arrest if they have "reasonable suspicion" the individual entered the country illegally.[41] Arizona's statute, known as SB 1070, was rapidly challenged. But it also led five other states to enact similar laws by August 2011.[42] The U.S. Supreme Court ruled on the constitutionality of Arizona's law in June 2012, upholding this key "show me your papers" provision, while striking other sections.[43]

Changes in immigration law make compelling and important news stories, but they also have implications for public relations, as Elizabeth S. Mitchell pointed out in PRNewser in 2013.[44] Outrage over Arizona's law fueled state boycotts, leading to a loss of $141 million in tourism revenue in 2010. The negative PR effects persisted even three years later, with 2012 bookings at the Phoenix Convention Center estimated at one-third fewer than in 2009.[45] Mitchell concluded that possibly only the law's repeal would restore Arizona's image.

Despite Obama's failure at immigration reform, he initiated an immigration program in September 2012 known as deferred action. The program aimed to give a reprieve to certain illegal immigrants brought to the country as children. It protected them from deportation, allowed them to work and, in some states, enabled them to get a driver's license. This fell short of the proposed Dream Act, which would permit certain immigrants who were brought to the United States as children, known as "Dreamers," to achieve permanent legal status.[46]

The dashed hopes of these young people failed to deter thousands of children from Honduras, El Salvador and Guatemala from making the perilous journey to the United States. Between October 1, 2013, and June 15, 2014, 52,000 children were apprehended at the southwestern border with the United States, a 99 percent jump from the prior year period.[47] The surge led the U.S. Border Patrol to launch a $1 million international print, radio and television public relations campaign in Spanish to warn families it would be safer for young people to stay home.

BOX 9.1   Putting Your Reporting in Historical Context

- Statistics: Numbers of immigrants in one historical context may be smaller numerically, but more significant as a proportion of the population at that time. Check U.S. census data.

- Laws: Consider how legal measures, including treaties, may have been used to achieve the same ends in different eras.

- International history: Understand how armed conflicts, economic disruptions and natural disasters may spur immigration to the United States.

Activity: Immigration history: Start a file of historical resources. Categorize each entry and annotate them with brief paragraph descriptions so that you can quickly retrieve important background to put your stories in context for readers.

FOR DISCUSSION

1. How might you use an understanding of fault lines and fissures to guide your reporting, research and writing about immigrants?

▶ TERMINOLOGY

In journalism, getting someone's name right is crucial. Naming, categorizing or otherwise labeling a group of people is equally critical. In this case, the proper way to refer to immigrants who are in the country without permission from government authorities is one of the most hotly debated issues in reporting and writing about newcomers to the United States. As George Lakoff, a linguistics professor at the University of California at Berkeley noted, the language of immigration is anything but neutral. These terms, or linguistic expressions, frame "immigration." In other words, they define immigration as a narrow set of issues or problems, which then limits political discourse and solutions.[48]

The Associated Press (AP), the Society of Professional Journalists (SPJ) and the National Association of Hispanic Journalists (NAHJ) are among the journalism organizations that have revamped recommendations for the best way to describe a person who is in the country without authorization. In 2013, AP executive editor Kathleen Carroll announced that "the Stylebook no longer sanctions the term 'illegal immigrant' or the use of 'illegal' to describe a person. Instead, it tells users that 'illegal' should describe only an action."[49] Reflecting this idea that the term "illegal" should not refer to people, the AP also changed the title of the Stylebook entry from "illegal immigrant" to "illegal immigration."[50]

The AP's decision came two years after the SPJ approved a resolution urging journalists to stop using "the politically charged phrase 'illegal immigrant' and the more offensive and bureaucratic 'illegal alien' to describe undocumented immigrants, particularly Latinos."[51] Among other things, SPJ noted, "only the court system, not reporters and editors, can decide when a person has committed an 'illegal' act."[52]

Newspapers and television networks, even if they are members of the AP, usually set their own stylebook standards. Among those were *The New York Times*, Fox News, Fox News Latino, the *Wall Street Journal* and the *Los Angeles Times*.

The New York Times also changed its policy on the term in 2013. The newspaper stated that illegal immigrant was permissible but asked reporters to consider more specific alternatives. These included describing the immigrant as someone "who crossed the border illegally; who overstayed a visa; who is not authorized to work in this country."[53] *The New York Times* stylebook entry went on to advise its journalists to take:

> particular care in describing people whose immigration status is complex or subject to change—for example, young people brought to this country as children, many of whom are eligible for temporary reprieves from deportation under federal policies adopted in 2012. Do not use *illegal* as a noun, and avoid the sinister-sounding *alien*.[54]

The Fox News channel policy calls for the use of "illegal immigrant," according to a spokeswoman for the channel. Similarly, "illegal immigrant remains the preferred term for a person who enters the U.S. illegally," for the *Wall Street Journal*, which, like Fox, is majority-owned by media titan Rupert Murdoch. In a 2012 style note, the *Journal* stated that the term "illegal immigrant" was "less extraterrestrial" than "illegal alien" but "less euphemistic" than "undocumented worker." For second references, "undocumented worker" would be considered acceptable, the *Journal* stated. "Don't use illegal or illegals as nouns," the style note further advised.[55]

Not all News Corp. properties abide by the *Journal* and Fox News policy. Fox News Latino uses "undocumented" immigrant. Alberto Vourvoulias-Bush, former managing editor for Fox News Latino, explained the policy: "The word illegal is an accurate description for actions, but not individuals. We don't use it to describe people who commit other crimes. We write about unlicensed drivers, for example, not illegal drivers."[56]

The National Association of Hispanic Journalists prefers the term "undocumented worker."[57] Moreover, NAHJ urged the news media to quit using the word "illegals" as a noun or shorthand for "illegal aliens." The NAHJ noted this is not only ungrammatical, but also "crosses the line by criminalizing the person, not the action they are purported to have committed."

FOR DISCUSSION

1. How would changing the words we use to talk about immigrants change the way we think about immigrants?

2. What is being left out of our thinking about immigrants because of the way they are framed?

▶ REPORTING AND WRITING IMMIGRATION

"Deportation": Numerous news organizations have reported that President Barack Obama deported a record number of immigrants. It is true that large numbers of immigrants have been apprehended, mostly at the border, and returned to their country of origin. This makes deportation and border enforcement a big story, one that cannot be ignored.

However, there is a danger in making statistical comparisons, particularly when immigration law and terminology have changed. The 1996 Illegal Immigration Reform and Responsibility Act, created three ways for authorities to send immigrants out of the country.[58] Collectively known as "summary removal," two of these procedures, "expedited removal" and "reinstatement of removal" put immigration officers in charge of investigating and deciding cases, often within a 24-hour period. Unlike the case of deportation, immigrants have no access to lawyers and do not appear before a judge. About 75 percent of all immigrants leave the United States through "removal."

BOX 9.2   Short Interview: Dianne Solis, *Dallas Morning News* "Changing the Camera Angle"

THREE KEY TIPS FOR REPORTING ON LEGAL ISSUES AND IMMIGRATION

Dianne Solis is an award-winning senior writer at the *Dallas Morning News*, where, as her Twitter feed states, she is "a specialist in immigration, education and the under-told story." She joined the *Dallas Morning News* in 1997. Prior to that, she was a correspondent for the *Wall Street Journal* in Houston and Mexico City. She is a senior fellow at the Oakland, California-based Institute for Justice and Journalism.

"It is important to change the camera angle," Solis said. "Think deeply about your choice of lead character." That might mean telling the story through the eyes of the policeman who has to enforce the laws. Or relaying it from the point of view of the school principal or teacher, and how they deal with an influx of students from other countries.

Legal issues can be complicated and dry, but their impact on people is anything but. "Remember that the essence of the writer's craft is often finding the humanity in the story," Solis says. Her top three tips for reporting on legal issues and immigration are as follows:

1. Take time to learn the nuances. Immigration law is complex. "Even if you understand it well, it is hard to distill it for readers and keep them engaged," says Solis.
2. Be prepared for a court system that is unlike the municipal, county and federal circuit courts with which most reporters are familiar. One significant difference is that the immigration process lacks transparency. The Immigration Court is run by the U.S. Justice Department. There is no docket and no way to know what is scheduled unless someone tells you.
3. Get to know the attorneys for Immigration and Customs Enforcement, I.C.E., and the attorneys in the immigration legal community. "It is crucial to have a relationship with lawyers on both sides," Solis says.

BOX 9.3   Covering Immigrants: Two Approaches

INTERVIEW: BOB ORTEGA, REPORTER *ARIZONA REPUBLIC*

Covering the Border and Enforcement Issues

Bob Ortega
Credit: Rob Schumacher, *Arizona Republic*

Bob Ortega's career proves that the skills that make a top immigration reporter covering the border are the same needed to become a groundbreaking reporter on any beat. Fluent in Spanish and English, Ortega also has working knowledge of Georgian and Russian. Ortega's language abilities reflect his non-linear journalism career, which has taken him from Ecuador to Ukraine, and from Alaska to Arizona, where he began covering border issues for the *Arizona Republic* in 2011. Ortega has been managing editor of the *Homer News*, a small-town weekly in Alaska, and an investigative reporter for the *Wall Street Journal*. He has worked in television, radio, print and online.

Ortega takes the same investigative skills he used on the business beat and applies them to the subject of immigration. A prime example is a three-day series, published in December 2013, documenting the use of force by Border Patrol agents.[59] The data-driven project opens with a line describing shooting victim Jose Antonio Elena Rodriguez, 16, as the "ghost" that is "haunting Nogales." Shot 10 times as he walked to a convenience store on the Mexican side of the border in Nogales, Sonora, the teen appears everywhere in town on billboards and handbills. U.S. Border Patrol agents, who said they were responding to rocks thrown at them from across the border, fired at him from the U.S. side of the fence. Portraits of others killed in similar incidents are found all along the border.

"We made 120 Freedom of Information Act requests and appeals with six agencies in seven states," Ortega said. The attorney for *USA Today*, the flagship paper of Gannet Co., which also owns the *Arizona Republic*, stepped in. "It still took more than a year to get the data. It arrived as 12,000 pages of records contained in 1,600 individual, non-searchable pdfs."

After six weeks converting the data into searchable form, Ortega and co-author Rob O'Dell were able "to document the level of force—what kind of deadly and

(Continued)

BOX 9.3 Continued

less lethal force was used and under what circumstance," Ortega said. They found that since 2005, on-duty Border Patrol agents and Customs and Border Protection officers had killed at least 42 people, including 13 U.S. citizens. They created an online searchable database and interactive map allowing readers to locate and learn more about each incident.[60]

"Nobody has ever been held accountable," Ortega said. Movement toward that occurred in June 2014, when the FBI took over internal affairs for the Customs and Border Protection agency. Simultaneously, the Homeland Security department's inspector general began investigating the agency's hundreds of sexual abuse and excessive force complaints.[61]

Reporting on Immigrants in American Life

Interview: Anh Do, reporter, *Los Angeles Times*

Anh Do is an award-winning journalist specializing in little-covered and little-served communities for the *Los Angeles Times*. Do, who was born in Vietnam, is fluent in English, Spanish, and Vietnamese. She was vice president of the *Nguoi Viet Daily News*, a paper founded by her father that is the largest Vietnamese newspaper in the United States. She has reported for the *Dallas Morning News*, the *Seattle Times* and the *Orange County Register*, where she also wrote a column on Asian affairs. She also lived in Mexico, where she was a freelance writer.

Anh Do
Credit: Anh Do

Guiding Do's work is the question: "Who is being left out?" One way she tackles this challenge is to take a national issue and localize it with an under-covered community. When insurance became available under Obama's Affordable Care Act, Do immediately wondered: "What about the people who do not understand what insurance is?"

That question led her to produce a *Times* story featuring a Bangladeshi community that numbers about 6,000 immigrants and lives on the edge of Los Angeles.[62] "They are the opposite of assimilated in America," Do said. When she learned that the local South Asian Network planned to do outreach in Little Bangladesh, Do went along. Her story took readers inside the Deshi Restaurant and Grocery where workers conducted interviews "near bags of lentils, chickpeas and curry leaves."

(Continued)

BOX 9.3 Continued

More often than not, Bangladeshis had not heard of healthcare reform, even by its nickname, Obamacare.

Do also uncovers untold stories by looking at how "ordinary lives are made in some way extraordinary through personal experience." As Do put it: "I find a lot of beauty in the everyday of how people live." Vietnamese immigrants own the majority of nail salons in California, leading Do to a slice-of-life story that evoked the humanity of a community with little visibility. Her driving question: "What do people talk about in nail salons?" Her story: "In Vietnamese salons, nails, polish and unvarnished opinions," took readers inside salons to hear the gossip, chatter and hopes and dreams of immigrant estheticians.

 BOX 9.4   Getting to the Heart of the Story: Tips from *Los Angeles Times* Reporter Anh Do

1. Be patient and be prepared to learn to interview people in groups.

"I'm in the position of dealing with people who have never dealt with the press. They may be either scared or worried, or both. They don't do interviews one-on-one. I have to conduct interviews in a way that I can hear from everyone. Even if I have a strong feeling about who may be a source, I don't want to make the so-called 'least useful' feel ignored."

2. Manners

- For Do, it is not about showing respect; it is about "sharing respect."

"I use 'ma'am.' I always mind my 'p's' and 'q's.' I always give sources a chance to ask questions. These are ordinary people and they do have extraordinary lives. Share the right amount of respect, and in return they will give you things that will illuminate the story."

- Say thank-you.

Do sends thank you notes to people she's interviewed. Often she writes these by hand, using one of the five styles of stationary she keeps at her desk. Some are designed for men, others for women and another style, with flowers, is geared for older Asians. She puts the cost of the stationary on her *Times* expense account. "Sometimes sending thank-you notes by email is better because it is easier for them to respond." Do also makes sure she sends them a copy of the story once it

(Continued)

BOX 9.4 Continued

has been published, and makes sure to ask whether they would like it emailed or on hard copy. Sometimes she hand-delivers the copies.

3. Language is not necessarily a barrier.

- Interpreters

"If we don't speak Spanish or Hindi, we can still get the story. There are ways to vet translators. You can ask them questions that don't relate to your story and check the translation. Or ask them some basic questions about their background and see how they translate that."

- Drawings

"Say someone was jailed in a cubicle. I ask them to draw the cubicle and the way they were positioned in the cubicle. I use that as a basis for the conversation."

- Listen

"Sometimes I put away the pen and say: 'Let's just walk in your garden. You are creating art and you don't have to color in the lines. Let me soak up the information at the same time you are releasing it. I will tell you later which parts I am more interested in learning more about.'"

Activity: Draft a thank-you note for the next person you interview, explaining why you appreciated their time and willingness to talk.

▶ ETHICS ON THE IMMIGRATION BEAT

1. Ensure that vulnerable sources understand the consequence of speaking to a reporter. Zita Arocha, executive director of the multimedia Borderzine Project at the University of Texas El Paso, advises: "Only mention someone's legal status if it pertinent to the story. Practice SPJ's golden rule: Do no harm. You may not want to use someone's name or personal details if it might lead to detention and deportation."

2. Balance the journalist's role to speak for those who cannot speak for themselves with the journalist's requirement to remain neutral. Journalism has a long tradition of public service aimed at righting wrongs and shedding light on injustice. Temper that crusading spirit with fairness.

3. Avoid false equivalence. Sometimes there are many sides to a story. Sometimes one or more sides are wrong. A prime example is *Arizona Republic* reporter Bob Ortega's investigation into the shooting death of Jose Antonio Elena Rodriguez, 16, in 2012.

Border Patrol agents justified their use of force, saying the boy threw rocks from Mexico over the U.S. side of the fence. Ortega went to the scene and walked it. He found that scenario would be "all but impossible" because the Mexican side of the fence is 25-feet lower than the U.S. side at the spot where Elena Rodriguez died.[63] "Go down there and do the shoe-leather reporting," Ortega said. It is a disservice to readers to provide "on the one hand" and "on the other hand" reporting. If it is clearly wrong, explain why it is wrong.

 BOX 9.5   From the Field: Q&A with Maria Hinojosa

BROADCAST AND MULTIMEDIA

Maria Hinojosa
Credit: Benjamin Chasteen/Echo Times

Maria Hinojosa is an award-winning multi-platform journalist. Born in Mexico and raised in Chicago, she holds a bachelor's degree from Barnard College. She is the anchor and executive producer for NPR's weekly "Latino USA" show and the anchor of *Maria Hinojosa: One-on-One*. In 2010, she started her Harlem-based company, the Futuro Media Group, to produce community-based, multi-media journalism that will tell America's untold stories. In 2013, she was named the *Sor Juana Ines de La Cruz* chair of DePaul University's Latin America and Latino Studies program.

Q. *What do reporters need to be aware of as they start the immigration beat?*

A: "I worry that a dehumanization of immigrants has already been internalized by reporters working for major news organizations. We do carry perspectives and bias. The coverage around immigration has been almost non-existent until the last couple of years."

Q: *What are some of the biggest stumbling blocks facing newsrooms today as they cover this issue?*

A: "Newsrooms are inherently un-diverse. Immigrants in journalism today are a rarity. During the recession, we probably lost many journalists from immigrant backgrounds."

Q. *Why is the lack of newsroom diversity problematic for immigration coverage?*

A: "It is about who controls the agenda and what kind of insights go into the reporting."

BOX 9.6   From the Field: Reporting Tips from BorderZine's Zita Arocha

Zita Arocha is a bilingual journalist and has been senior lecturer in the University of Texas El Paso (UTEP) Department of Communication since 2004. She is director of borderzine.com, an award-winning multi-media web magazine at UTEP that prepares Hispanic college journalists for jobs in 21st-century newsrooms. In more than two decades in journalism, she worked for the *Washington Post*, the *Miami Herald*, the *Miami News* and the *Tampa Times*. She was execu-tive director of the National Association of Hispanic Journalists (NAHJ) from 1993–1997.

Zita Arocha
Credit: David Smith

Pointers for the immigration beat:

- Learn who lives there. Create a demographic portrait of the community using the U.S. Census Bureau's American Factfinder: http://factfinder2.census.gov/faces/nav/jsf/pages/index.xhtml. Here you can drill down from overall city stats, to specific neighborhoods and even blocks, and obtain information on income, education, jobs, even language spoken at home.

- Get to know where immigrants buy groceries, send money home, wor-ship, seek medical assistance or go for other help. Visit these places regularly and introduce yourself and your media outlet.

- Investigate which immigrant advocacy groups and community centers work with immigrants. Get to know the key players. These folks have their ears close to the ground and probably know what is going on with workplace raids, law enforcement, asylum seekers, deportations, etc.

- Interview local immigration lawyers and find out what cases they are working on. Sometimes there will be a local spike in asylum claims. Attor-neys will know because they typically take on these cases.

- Gain access to detention facilities and immigration courts by accompany-ing an immigration lawyer on client visits.

- Familiarize yourself with the language and culture of the people you are covering. One way is to take a beginner's language class. Although you

(Continued)

BOX 9.6 Continued

will probably not become fluent, it will be easier to establish rapport with an immigrant you are interviewing if you know a few words and key phrases. If language is a barrier, ask a fellow journalist, or an immigrant advocate who speaks the language, to join you.

Activity: Use the U.S. Census Bureau's American Factfinder to create a demographic portrait of your own hometown, neighborhood and block.

▶ STRATEGIC COMMUNICATION AND IMMIGRANTS

Today's interconnected, global world means that there are no borders between advertisements, even those carefully crafted to appeal to the tastes, consumer preferences and culture of a specific market. Absolut Vodka, a Swedish brand owned by Pernod Ricard, developed an ad for Mexican consumers in 2008 that failed to translate well to some of its northern neighbors.

Part of its "In an Absolut World" campaign depicted an 1830s map of Mexico showing the country's original boundaries, before it lost half its territory in the U.S.–Mexican War. The ad played well in Mexico where bitter memories remain of the war.

Though not aimed at U.S. audiences, images of the whimsical ad spread through the Internet. Americans for Legal Immigration PAC, a North Carolina–based political action committee, denounced the ad, suggesting that it legitimized the aspirations of Mexican immigrants to stage a *reconquista*, or a reconquering, of U.S. territory. Absolut apologized for the ad and then withdrew it.[64]

Absolut's experience highlights the volatility of the immigration debate. It also illustrates the complexity of advertising across cultures, underscoring how messages can have unintended consequences.

"Immigrant is a word that makes you think of immigration, but basically all companies that do ethnic marketing are marketing to immigrants, whether first generation, the 1.5 generation or to consumers who have been here for generations," said Lisa Skriloff, president of New York–based Multicultural Marketing Resources Inc.

"Immigrants, or 'so-called' minorities, are now expected to be the majority population by 2042, according to census predictions," said Skriloff, who publishes *The Source Book of Multicultural Experts* directory, www.multicultural.com.

Five states are already majority-minority, noted Skriloff, a former *New York Times* marketing director. "The multicultural market is the new general market and companies are creating outreach campaigns based on multicultural insights, a practice being looked at as a 'total market' concept."

Spotlight on Asian-Americans

Defining any target market, including the immigrant and ethnic market, requires careful research and a clear understanding of a group's culture, consumer preferences, and the metrics of its market size. Consider Asian-Americans. Many diverse nationalities make up this group of 18.3 million people, and the multiplicity of languages and ancestries is ideal for niche marketing efforts, according to the Selig Center for Economic Growth. Torrance, California-based H&Y Planning fields a marketing team with native speakers from several Asian countries. This gives H&Y valuable insights "because each Asian subgroup shares some common values but has different characteristics, mindset and attitudes," said Rin Ueno, H&Y's president, who is a Japanese immigrant.

"The Asian-American market stands out from all other segments as a true market of superlatives," said Saul Gitlin, chief marketing and strategy officer for New York–based GlobalWorks. Asians were the fastest growing racial group between 2000 and 2010,

PHOTO 9.6 Rin Ueno, president, H & Y Planning, Torrance, California.
Credit: Nader Nakhla

increasing by 43.7 percent, according to Pew Research. California, New York and Texas, three of the largest states, are home to half of the nation's Asians, Gitlin noted.

Asians, however, number 18.3 million compared to 50 million Hispanics. "Don't look at just total population numbers," advises Gitlin, whose agency includes Allstate, U.S. Bank and Verizon among its clients. "If you want to reach people with annual incomes of $250,000 or more, there are more high net–worth Asian-Americans than Hispanics."

FOR DISCUSSION

1. What kind of information would you need to gather to build a marketing campaign targeting a newly emerged ethnic group?

 BOX 9.7   Key Terms

Know and understand the legal definitions of terms concerning immigration and naturalization. News organizations, as noted earlier in this chapter, may establish a different style for publication, but reporters must understand the language of law enforcement and the courts to report effectively.[65]

Immigrant: The *Oxford English Dictionary* describes an immigrant as a person who migrates into a country as a settler. "Permanent resident alien" is the U.S. government term for immigrants who entered the country legally. The government term for those without permission to be in the country is "illegal alien."[66]

Black–white race binary: The historical paradigm that defined the United States as having only two races: black and white.

Deportation: The formal removal of an immigrant found violating U.S. immigration law.

Refugee: A person who has fled his or her home country and is unable to return because of a "well-founded fear of persecution based on religion, race, nationality, political opinion or membership in a particular social group."[67]

Removal: The expulsion of an immigrant from the United States based on inadmissibility or deportability.

Asylum: Someone seeking asylum fits the same characteristics as a refugee, except that this person is already in the United States. Asylum seekers must file a petition for asylum at their port of entry or within one year of their arrival in the country.[68]

Xenophobia: The *Oxford English Dictionary* defines xenophobia as a deep antipathy to foreigner.

▶ CHAPTER SUMMARY

The story of the United States is a story of immigrants. Other than Native Americans, everyone, starting in the 1500s with the arrival of the Spanish, has been a newcomer. The rich national narrative of how successive waves of immigrants have been absorbed, assimilated and accepted—or not—is often fraught with tension and filled with drama.

To be a competent cross-cultural communicator in the 21st century requires understanding U.S. history, grasping the nuances of diverse immigrant communities from various parts of the world and developing sensitivity and humanity in reporting and writing about people whose experiences may be far removed from the typical U.S. journalist, public relations professional or advertising copy writer.

▶ NOTES

1 Gina Sunseri, "Surge of Children Crossing Border Alone Filling Lackland AFB," ABC News, June 5, 2014, http://abcnews.go.com/US/surge-children-crossing-border-filling-lackland-afb/story?id=24013460. For information about the reasons for the surge in unaccompanied minors entering the U.S. from Central America see, Ana Gonzalez-Barrera, Jens Manuel Krogstad, and Mark Hugo Lopez, "DHS: Violence, Poverty is driving children to flee Central America to U.S.," Pew Research Center, http://www.pewresearch.org/fact-tank/2014/07/01/dhs-violence-poverty-is-driving-children-to-flee-central-america-to-u-s/.

2 "Presidential Memorandum—Response to the Influx of Unaccompanied Alien Children Across the Southwest Border," The White House, Office of the Press Secretary, June 2, 2014, http://www.whitehouse.gov/the-press-office/2014/06/02/presidential-memorandum-response-influx-unaccompanied-alien-children-acr.

3 "Legal Immigration to the United States, 1920 to the Present," Migration Policy Institute, http://www.migrationpolicy.org/programs/data-hub/us-immigration-trends#history.

4 Pia Orrenius and Madeline Zavodny, "From Brawn to Brains: How Immigration Works for America," Federal Reserve Bank of Dallas, Annual Report, 2010, http://www.dallasfed.org/assets/documents/fed/annual/2010/ar10.pdf.

5 Paul Taylor, "The Next America," Pew Research Center, April 10, 2014, http://www.pewresearch.org/next-america/#Two-Dramas-in-Slow-Motion.

6 "Immigration Reporters," Business Wire, http://www.businesswire.com/portal/site/home/template.MAXIMIZE/40174/?javax.portlet.tpst=240afb847939ee8235f69d70098a8b0b_ws_MX&javax.portlet.prp_240afb847939ee8235f69d70098a8b0b_catmvcid=40478&javax.portlet.prp_240afb847939ee8235f69d70098a8b0b_viewID=media_view&beanID=1594717458&viewID=media_view&javax.portlet.begCacheTok=com.vignette.cachetoken&javax.portlet.endCacheTok=com.vignette.cachetoken.

7 Grace Chung, "Coke's 'America the Beautiful' Tops Viral Chart as Super Bowl Ads Dominate Online," Advertising Age, February 12, 2014, http://adage.com/article/the-viral-video-chart/coke-s-america-beautiful-tops-viral-chart/291631/.

8 "Largest US Immigrant Groups Over Time, 1960–Present," Migration Policy Institute, http://www.migrationpolicy.org/programs/data-hub/us-immigration-trends#history.

9 Ibid.

10 Jens Manuel Krogstad and Michael Keegan, "15 States with the Highest Share of Immigrants in their Population," FactTank, Pew Research Center, May 14, 2014, http://www.pewresearch.org/fact-tank/2014/05/14/15-states-with-the-highest-share-of-immigrants-in-their-population/.

11 "FY12 Refugee Admission Statistics," U.S. Department of State, February 28, 2013, http://www.state.gov/j/prm/releases/statistics/206319.htm.

12 Matt Austin, "A Changing Community: Refugees Moving to Vt.," MyChamplainValley.Com, May 15, 2014, http://www.mychamplainvalley.com/story/d/story/a-changing-community-refugees-moving-to-vt/88671/WkvUGJ3RM02q98y_-CF35A.

13 Jamal Abdulahi, "Somalis in Minnesota: Still Misunderstood," *StarTribune*, March 3, 2014, http://www.startribune.com/opinion/commentaries/247927831.html.

14 Richard Wike, "In Europe, Anti-Immigrant, Anti-Minority Sentiment Runs High," FactTank, Pew Research Center, May 14, 2014, http://www.pewresearch.org/fact-tank/2014/05/14/in-europe-sentiment-against-immigrants-minorities-runs-high/.

15 Felipe Fernández-Armesto, *Our America: A History of the United States* (New York: Norton, 2014), 3.

16 Ibid., 4.

17 John F. Kennedy, *A Nation of Immigrants* (1965; repr., New York: Harper, 2008), 6.

18 Ron Smith, *Public Relations: The Basics* (New York: Routledge, 2014), 44.

19 Ibid.

20 David Gutiérrez, *Walls and Mirrors: Mexican Americans, Mexican Immigrants, and the Politics of Ethnicity* (Berkeley: University of California Press: 1995), 13, 40.

21 Ibid.,17, 18.

22 Zaragosa Vargas, *Crucible of Struggle: A History of Mexican Americans from Colonial Times to the Present Era* (New York: Oxford University Press, 2011), 106.

23 Oscar Handlin, *The Uprooted*, 2nd ed. (1951; repr., Boston: Little, Brown, 1973), 240.

24 Ibid., 241.

25 Walt Whitman, "Preface," *Leaves of Grass* (Brooklyn, N.Y., 1855), http://www.english.illinois.edu/maps/poets/s_z/whitman/preface.htm.

26 "Legal Immigration to the United States, 1920 to the Present," Migration Policy Institute, http://www.migrationpolicy.org/programs/data-hub/us-immigration-trends#history.

27 Ibid., 39.

28 Ibid., 41.

29 Ibid., 43. For a fuller discussion of the forces militating against Asian immigrants, see, for example Mae M. Ngai, *Impossible Subjects: Illegal Aliens and the Making of Modern America* (2004; repr., Princeton, NJ: Princeton University Press, 2005), 21–55. Also see Erika Lee, *At America's Gates, Chinese Immigration During the Exclusion Era, 1882–1943* (Chapel Hill: University of North Carolina Press, 2003). For more on restrictions against Japanese immigration, see Roger Daniels, *Guarding the Golden Door* (New York: Hill and Wang, 2004), 44–52.

30 "Statement of Harry Chandler, President Los Angeles Times Co," *Hearings Before the Committee on Immigration and Naturalization, Western Hemisphere Immigration* 71st Congress, 2nd Session, 1930, 61, 63–75. See, for instance, page 61: "So you have to consider fundamentally that these Mexican men are practically Indians, they are of Indian blood, these peons who come in; and there is no more problem with them than with our original Indians. And we Americans who look back to the time we were among the Indians know there were fewer problems then. But they were not Americans, and they were not our race. They did not make the problem that the negro has made or that the Filipino would make if we brought him in."

31 Daniel Okrent, *Last Call: The Rise and Fall of Prohibition* (New York: Simon & Schuster, 2011), 101.

32 "Brief Overview of the World War II Enemy Alien Control Program," National Archives, http://www.archives.gov/research/immigration/enemy-aliens-overview.html.

33 Bilal Qureshi, "From Wrong to Right: A US Apology for Japanese Internment," NPR, August 9, 2013, http://www.npr.org/blogs/codeswitch/2013/08/09/210138278/japanese-internment-redress.

34 Ngai, *Impossible Subjects*, 3.

35 Kennedy, *A Nation of Immigrants*, 45.

36 Ngai, *Impossible Subjects*, 3.

37 Mary Giovagnoli, "Overhauling Immigration Law: A Brief History and Basic Principles of Reform," Immigration Policy Center, American Immigration Council, www.immigrationpolicy.org/perspectives/overhauling-immigration-law-brief-history-and-basic-principles-reform.

38 "Adding Delay to Immigration Failure," *The New York Times*, May 28, 2014, http://www.nytimes.com/2014/05/29/opinion/adding-delay-to-immigration-failure.html?hp&rref=opinion.

39 Mark Hugo Lopez, Paul Taylor, Cary Funk and Ana Gonzalez-Barrera, "On Immigration Policy, Deportation Relief Seen as More Important than Citizenship," Pew Research Hispanic Trends Project, December 19, 2013, http://www.pewhispanic.org/2013/12/19/on-immigration-policy-deportation-relief-seen-as-more-important-than-citizenship/.

40 Nate Cohn, "Why Hispanics Don't Have a Larger Political Voice," *The New York Times*, June 15, 2014, http://www.nytimes.com/2014/06/16/upshot/why-hispanics-dont-have-a-larger-political-voice.html?module=Search&mabReward=relbias%3As%2C[%22RI%3A5%22%2C%22RI%3A18%22.

41 Greg Stohr, "Arizona Illegal-Immigration Legislation Given US Supreme Court Review," Bloomberg, December 12, 2011, http://www.bloomberg.com/news/2011–12–12/supreme-court-to-hear-arizona-s-appeal-of-ruling-against-immigration-law.html.

42 Andrew Harris, "Alabama Immigration Law Improperly Encroaches on Federal Power, US Says," Bloomberg, August 1, 2011, http://www.bloomberg.com/news/2011–08–01/alabama-immigration-law-imporperly-encroaches-on-federal-power-u-s-says.html.

43 Greg Stohr, "Arizona Immigration Law Partially Struck by High Court," Bloomberg, June 25, 2012, http://www.bloomberg.com/news/2012–06–25/arizona-illegal-immigration-law-gets-mixed-top-court-decision.html.

44 Elizabeth S. Mitchell, "Arizona Deals with Negative PR Effects of Immigration Law," PRNewser, January 4, 2013, http://www.mediabistro.com/prnewser/arizona-deals-with-negative-pr-effects-of-immigraton-law_b53840.

45 Ibid.

46 "Get the Facts on the Dream Act," The White House Blog, http://www.whitehouse.gov/blog/2010/12/01/get-facts-dream-act.

47 U.S. Department of Homeland Security, U.S. Customs & Border Protection, Southwest Border Unaccompanied Alien Children, http://www.cbp.gov/newsroom/stats/southwest-border-unaccompanied-children. For more information on the media campaign, see "CPB Commissioner Discusses Dangers of Crossing US Border," Awareness Campaign, CPB, July 2, 2014, http://www.cbp.gov/newsroom/national-media-release/2014–07–02–000000/cbp-commissioner-discusses-dangers-crossing-us.

48 George Lakoff and Sam Ferguson, "The Framing of Immigration," The Rockridge Institute, 2006.

49 Paul Colford, " 'Illegal Immigrant No More,' " The Definitive Source, April 2, 2013, http://blog.ap.org/2013/04/02/illegal-immigrant-no-more/.

50 Ibid.

51 "Resolution No. 7: The Use of 'Illegal Immigrant' and 'Illegal Alien' in News Stories," Resolutions, submitted to the Excellence in Journalism Conference in New Orleans, LA, for Passage on September 27, 2011, Society of Professional Journalists, http://www.spj.org/res2011.asp.

52 Ibid.

53 Christine Haughney, "The Times Shifts on Illegal Alien, but Does not Ban its Use," *The New York Times*, April 23, 2013, http://www.nytimes.com/2013/04/24/business/media/the-times-shifts-on-illegal-immigrant-but-doesnt-ban-the-use.html.

54 Ibid.

55 "Style & Substance, Iconic Vogue Words, Vol. 25, No. 9," *Wall Street Journal*, September 28, 2012, http://blogs.wsj.com/styleandsubstance/search/immigrant/?s=immigrant.

56 Andrew O'Reilly, "Undocumented or Illegal: Media Outlets Battle Over Immigration Terms," Fox News Latino, September 25, 2012, http://latino.foxnews.com/latino/news/2012/09/25/undocumented-or-illegal-media-outlets-battle-over-immigration-terms/.

57 "NAHJ Urges News Organizations to Stop Using Dehumanizing Terms When Covering Immigration," NAHJ, http://www.nahj.org/nahjnews/articles/2006/march/immigrationcoverage.shtml.

58 Beth Werlin, "Summary Removal Procedures and Their Role in Rising Deportations," American Immigration Council, May 28, 2014.

59 Bob Ortega and Rob O'Dell, "Deadly Border Agent Incidents Cloaked in Silence," AZCentral.com, March 28, 2014, first published December 15, 2013, http://www.azcentral.com/story/news/arizona/2014/03/28/arizona-border-force-deadly-incidents/7013023/.

60 "Force at the Border" interactive map, http://www.azcentral.com/news/immigration/border/; "Force at the Border," database, http://www.azcentral.com/news/projects/border-deaths/.

61 Brian Bennet, "Border Agency Ousts Head of Internal Affairs, Will Investigate Unit," *Los Angeles Times*, June 9, 2014, http://www.latimes.com/nation/nationnow/la-na-nn-border-patrol-internal-affairs-20140609-story.html.

62 Anh Do, "Team Takes Healthcare Plan to Ethnic Areas," *Los Angeles Times*, October 1, 2013, http://articles.latimes.com/print/2013/oct/01/local/la-me-ff-health-care-neighborhoods-20131002.

63 Bob Ortega and Rob O'Dell, "Deadly Border Agent Incidents Cloaked in Silence," AZCentral. com, March 28, 2014, first published December 15, 2013, http://www.azcentral.com/story/ news/arizona/2014/03/28/arizona-border-force-deadly-incidents/7013023/.

64 "Anti-Illegal Immigration Group Calls for 'Absolut' Vodka Boycott," Fox News, April 8, 2008, http://www.foxnews.com/story/2008/04/08/anti-illegal-immigration-group-calls-for-absolut-vodka-boycott/.

65 The U.S. Internal Revenue Service offers a general summary of terms, which can be found here: http://www.irs.gov/Individuals/International-Taxpayers/Immigration-Terms-and-Definitions-Involving-Aliens. The Department of Homeland Security offers an alphabetized sourcebook for "Definition of Terms," which can be found here: http://www.dhs.gov/definition-terms#3.

66 See the Department of Homeland Security's Alphabetized Definition Source List: http:// www.dhs.gov/definition-terms#3.

67 "Refugee Admission," Department of State, http://www.state.gov/j/prm/ra/index.htm.

68 "How the United States Immigration System Works: A Fact Sheet," Immigration Policy Center, American Immigration Council, http://www.immigrationpolicy.org/just-facts/how-united-states-immigration-system-works-fact-sheet.

Resources for Journalists and Strategic Communicators

Government

Department of Homeland Security

Immigration statistics: http://www.dhs.gov/immigration-data-statistics
Immigration enforcement: http://www.dhs.gov/topic/immigration-enforcement
U.S. Citizenship and Immigration Services, Refugees and Asylum: http://www.uscis.gov/ humanitarian/refugees-asylum/refugees
U.S. Immigration & Customs Enforcement: http://www.ice.gov/about/overview/

Other Government Resources

United States census data about the foreign-born in the U.S.: http://www.census.gov/population/ foreign/
UN High Commission on Refugees: http://www.unhcrwashington.org/
U.S. Department of State, Bureau of Population, Refugees and Migration: http://www.state.gov/j/prm/

Immigration Research Organizations

Pew Research Center

Pew, a nonpartisan subsidiary of the Pew Charitable Trusts, provides a wide variety of research on "attitudes and trends shaping America and the world." These include immigration, citizenship, remittances, migration, unauthorized immigration, Hispanics/Latinos and population trends.

Immigration
http://www.pewresearch.org/topics/immigration/

Hispanic/Latino Demography
http://www.pewresearch.org/topics/hispaniclatino-demography/

Pew Research Hispanic Trends Project
http://www.pewhispanic.org/

The Rise of Asian-Americans
http://www.pewsocialtrends.org/2012/06/19/the-rise-of-asian-americans/

Demographics of Asian-Americans
http://www.pewsocialtrends.org/2013/04/04/asian-groups-in-the-u-s/

American Immigration Council—Immigration Policy Center

The nonpartisan council offers a variety of research on immigration policy, initiatives and the economic impact of immigrants on a state-by-state-level. The policy center also offers a helpful primer on how the U.S. immigration process works. http://www.immigrationpolicy.org/.

Migration Policy Institute
http://www.migrationpolicy.org/

The VERA Institute of Justice—Center on Immigration and Justice
http://www.vera.org/centers/center-immigration-and-justice

Bancroft Library—Timeline on Italian Americans in California
http://bancroft.berkeley.edu/collections/italianamericans/timeline_spanishmexican.html

Immigrant Advocacy Organizations

Sources Advocating Curtailment of Immigration

Federation for American Immigration Reform (FAIR)
http://www.fairus.org/

Center for Immigration Studies (CIS)
http://cis.org/

Social Service and Policy Organizations Supporting Immigrants

United States Conference on Catholic Bishops—Migration and Refugee Services
http://www.usccb.org/about/migration-and-refugee-services/

Catholic Charities (various locations nationwide)
Catholic Charities Fort Worth, Texas: http://www.ccdofw.org/immigrationservices

American Civil Liberties Union ACLU—Immigrants' Rights Project
https://www.aclu.org/immigrants-rights/about-aclus-immigrants-rights-project

U.S. Committee for Refugees and Immigrants
http://www.refugees.org/

Center for Gender and Refugee Studies—UC Hastings
http://cgrs.uchastings.edu/request-assistance/requesting-assistance-cgrs

Muslim Public Affairs Council
http://www.mpac.org/issues/immigration.php#.UyYo41FdVgM

Asian Americans Advancing Justice
http://www.advancingjustice-aajc.org/

The International Rescue Committee
http://www.rescue.org/irc-a-glance

Alliance for Citizenship
http://allianceforcitizenship.org/#sthash.oldXQK2i.dpbs

United We Dream
http://unitedwedream.org/about/our-missions-goals/

Reform Immigration for America
http://www.reformimmigrationforamerica.org/#content-news

Americans for Immigration Justice
http://www.aijustice.org/

America's Voice
http://americasvoice.org/about/

Center for American Progress
http://www.americanprogress.org/issues/immigration/view/

National Council of La Raza
http://www.nclr.org/

National Immigrant Justice Center
http://immigrantjustice.org/

National Immigration Forum
http://www.immigrationforum.org/

Immigration and the Media Resources

Dart Center for Journalism & Trauma, Columbia Journalism School
"Covering Immigrants," full workshop resources: http://dartcenter.org/event/workshop-covering-immigrants-and-mental-health#.U3zQ4FhdV30

CCEM: Center for Community and Ethnic Media
City University of New York: http://ccem.journalism.cuny.edu/

Multicultural Marketing Resources (MMR)
http://multicultural.com/

America Reimagined
http://www.americareimagined.com/

EthniFacts
http://www.ethnifacts.com/

Chicago Area Ethnic Resources (CAER)
http://www.chicagoethnic.org/

Media Matters for America—Immigration
http://mediamatters.org/issues/immigration

The Institute for Justice & Journalism
http://justicejournalism.org/

Colorlines: News for Action—Immigration
http://colorlines.com/immigration/

Islam for Reporters
http://islamforreporters.com/

 ## ADDITIONAL READINGS

Bennett, Samuel, Jessika Ter Wal, Artur Lipinski, Malgorzata Fabiszak and Michal Krzyzanowski. "The Representation of Third-Country Nationals in European News Discourse." *Journalism Practice* 7, no. 3 (2013): 248–65.

Cuadros, Paul. *A Home in the Field: How One Championship Soccer Team Inspires Hope for the Revival of Small Town America*. New York: Harper, 2007.

de Zúñiga, Homero Gil, Teresa Correa and Sebastian Valenzuela. "Selective Exposure to Cable News and Immigration in the U.S.: The Relationship between Fox News, CNN, and Attitudes Toward Mexican Immigrants." *Journal of Broadcasting & Electronic Media* 56, no. 4 (2012): 597–615. doi:10.1080/08838151.2012.732138.

Domke, David and Kelley Mccoy. "News Media, Racial Perceptions, and Political Cognition." *Communication Research* 26, no. 5 (1999): 570

Frontline. "Lost in Detention." 2011. http://www.pbs.org/wgbh/pages/frontline/lost-in-detention/.

Frontline. "Rape in the Fields." June 25, 2013. http://www.pbs.org/wgbh/pages/frontline/rape-in-the-fields/.

Humphreys, Jeffrey M. *The Multicultural Economy 2013*. Athens, GA: The University of Georgia, Terry College of Business Selig Center for Economic Growth, 2013.

Ina, Satsuki, *Children of the Camps*, 1999. http://www.children-of-the-camps.org/default.htm.

Mastro, Dana, Riva Tukachinsky, Elizabeth Behm-Morawitz and Erin Blecha. "News Coverage of Immigration: The Influence of Exposure to Linguistic Bias in the News on Consumer's Racial/Ethnic Cognitions." *Communication Quarterly* 62, no. 2 (2014): 135–54. doi:10.1080/01463373.2014.890115.

Nazario, Sonia. *Enrique's Journey: The Story of a Boy's Dangerous Odyssey to Reunite With his Mother*. New York: Random House, 2006.

Pew Research Center. *The Rise of Asian Americans*, updated ed., April 4, 2013. http://www.pew-socialtrends.org/2012/06/19/the-rise-of-asian-americans/.

Ramos, Jorge. "Why Neither Party Speaks Our Language Yet." *Time*, March 5, 2012, 30.

Santa Ana, Otto and Celeste González de Bustamante. *Arizona Firestorm: Global Immigration Realities, National Media, and Provincial Politics*. Lanham, MD: Rowman & Littlefield, 2012.

See, Lisa. *On Gold Mountain*. New York: Vintage Books, 1996.

Suarez-Orozco, Marcelo M., Vivian Louie and Roberto Suro. *Writing Immigration: Scholars and Journalists in Dialogue*. Berkeley: University of California Press, 2011.

10

Achieving Excellence in Crime Coverage

Earnest L. Perry and Teri Finneman

The television reporter begins his story by introducing one of the victims of a home invasion that occurred in the early morning hours. The victim describes how the intruders forced their way into the home and held his family at gunpoint. Throughout the roughly 1-minute-30-second story, two other family members talk about what was running through their minds during the crime. At the end of the story, the reporter provides a description of the suspects: "The Salman family described the suspects as three black males. They said the suspect with the gun is tall with dark clothing, gloves and glasses."

The reporter did not provide any further information from law enforcement about the suspect or whether there had been other home invasion robberies in the area. This story is not unusual. Many local newscasts around the country lead their programs with similar stories. Most of those stories provide a similar vague description of the suspect. A common descriptor used in most of them is race.

The phrase "if it bleeds, it leads" is well known in television news, but newspapers provide just as much coverage of

LEARNING OBJECTIVES

By the end of this chapter, you should be able to:

- understand the impact of the news media's over-reporting of crime.

- explore the historical relationship between people of color and the criminal justice system.

- recognize bias in the use of description in crime reporting.

- develop the skills necessary to write and report on crime in a way that minimizes bias and accurately represents the impact of crime in the community.

crime. Researchers have determined that the amount of crime reported by the news media is exaggerated. The stories usually show people of color as the perpetrators of crime, despite the fact that statistics show that in 2012, blacks represented 39 percent of arrests for violent crimes and 29 percent of arrests for property crimes. However, blacks represent only 13 percent of the U.S. population. During a four-month period in 2014, the nightly newscast of the four major local television stations in New York City overrepresented, based on population, the percentage of African-American suspects in murders, thefts and assaults.[1] This type of coverage leads to the perception that African-Americans, particularly men, are violent and prone to criminal activity despite evidence to the contrary.

Most Americans rely on television for their local news. Studies have shown that local crime news focuses on violent and drug-related crimes. A disproportionate number of people in those stories are non-white, and mainly male.[2] This type of reporting influences the audience perception of people of color. The overrepresentation of men of color in crime coverage not only impacts what people think, but how they think and what steps should be taken to alleviate their fears of the "other." Black men and Hispanic men are seen as "criminal and violent."

When news media carry sensationalized crime reporting that features black or Hispanic men as violent criminals, the journalism can lead the audience to assume that all black and Hispanic men are a possible threat. The news media forge this idea into the minds of viewers despite the fact that violent crime is down. Further, most crime, when it does happen, occurs when the assailants are often known by their victims. However, because crime news is seen by the audience as an incident happening to someone else, the stranger who is not "us," the fact that the person accused is of a different race, ethnicity, class or community further feeds the negative stereotype.[3] A 2011 study of Pittsburgh television newscast and newspaper articles showed that African-American men and boys were featured in crime stories more than any other topic in the media, which raises the question of why African-American men are not featured in other news categories. Indeed, the authors note:

> Scant coverage exists featuring African-American men and boys in the "quality of life" topics: education, business/economy, environment, leadership/community and the arts. And coverage of young African-American men and boys ages 15–30 was all but nonexistent, with only 60 stories, or 2.7 percent, outside of the crime context in the three-month period.[4]

The preponderance of crime coverage reinforces the "culture of fear" that leads people to overestimate the real occurrence of crime in their communities. Black and Hispanic males are more likely to be featured in mug shots or paraded through arraignment hearings wearing jail uniforms. Studies show that heavy viewing of these images affect the public's views on criminal punishment for both adults and juveniles.

FOR DISCUSSION

1. If sensationalized crime coverage leads to a "culture of fear," what steps should media outlets take to more accurately reflect the level of crime in their communities?

▶ IMPACT OF STEREOTYPICAL NEWS COVERAGE ON RACIAL PROFILING

Media coverage of racial profiling has increased in the past 15 years, but controversy still exists over what racial profiling even means.[5] The term gained popularity in the late 1980s when it became clear that police were stopping blacks for traffic violations at suspiciously high rates, prompting discussion of a new "crime" of "driving while black."[6] In other words, the black community believed law enforcement was continuing to target minorities for false or minor crimes just as officers had in the 1800s and early mid-1900s.

More recently, researchers analyzed news coverage of high-profile cases to understand the status of racial profiling in 2013. The study found law enforcement and its defenders and racial justice advocates and minorities disagree on what racial profiling means. The former groups focus on a narrower perspective based on individuals, while the latter groups have a broader definition that encompasses institutional racism. The study found journalists are focusing stories more on institutional racism and subconscious bias, as was evident in coverage of the Trayvon Martin/George Zimmerman case and the New York Police Department's controversial stop-and-frisk policy.[7]

In February 2012, black high-school student Trayvon Martin was shot by George Zimmerman, a mixed-race Hispanic man, in Sanford, Florida. Zimmerman said he was acting in self-defense, but critics noted Martin was unarmed. During the trial, media took a closer look at subconscious bias and institutional racism, quoting sources who said that black men are stigmatized and automatically assumed to be criminals.[8] These arguments also played out in coverage of New York's stop-and-frisk policy. Although officers denied they were racial profiling, the New York Civil Liberties Union conducted an analysis of police data and found blacks and Latinos were predominantly targeted.[9] In nearly 90 percent of all cases, the person targeted was innocent, according to the New York Civil Liberties Union.[10]

FOR DISCUSSION

1. How does the news media's overexposure of crime involving men of color contribute to racial profiling?
2. Coverage of the "War on Terror" created a similar environment for Muslim Americans. What can the media do to present a more authentic picture?

▶ SEEDS OF MISTRUST BETWEEN COMMUNITIES OF COLOR AND LAW ENFORCEMENT

To understand the context for the relationship between law enforcement and the black community, you need to look at history. In the late 1800s, blacks in the South could be arrested simply for being disliked by white officials, who would come up with trivial reasons for pressing charges and then orchestrate biased trials. Laws prevented blacks from assimilating into white society and criminalized them for little or no reason. Blacks arrested for minor offenses faced significant punishment, such as being sent to a prison mine to perform hard labor in inhumane conditions. Others had their bodies twisted and bound to poles while others were repeatedly whipped while serving out their sentences. It was not uncommon for blacks' sentences to be extended by white officials who made up additional charges against them, or for blacks to be assigned the blame for an offense committed by a white person.[11] Although technically free from slavery, the lives of blacks were still largely controlled by whites, and distrust of law enforcement grew with every new story of injustice.

The troubled relationship between law enforcement and the black community did not end with slavery in the 1860s. From the late 1800s through the early 1900s, blacks also faced mobs and street violence. Yet white authorities did not always prosecute whites for crimes against blacks even when they were clearly responsible for lynching, shootings or destruction of blacks' property. Jim Crow laws that segregated blacks and punished them for challenging the white-dominated status quo remained in force in the United States until the 1960s. Most Americans nowadays are familiar with the police brutality that occurred in the 1960s when peaceful black protestors were attacked by police dogs, batons and hoses. Yet the Civil Rights Act of 1964 did not end the tension between the black community and law enforcement. Reports in recent decades indicate blacks continue to be imprisoned at rates significantly higher than whites.[12]

More recently, the troubled history between blacks and law enforcement was evident in Missouri, where some residents viewed the shooting of Michael Brown, a black teenager, as the final straw after decades of law enforcement injustice. Following the highly publicized shooting of Brown by a white police officer in Ferguson in 2014, the *Washington Post* ran an in-depth story outlining the institutional disadvantages faced by blacks in St. Louis County in particular. This includes predominantly white police departments serving predominantly black communities and a governmental system reliant on money from law enforcement fines. The *Post* found that some cities earned 40 percent of their revenue from court fines and fees. As a result, local residents felt like they were being charged with offenses simply to boost the city's finances, with statistics indicating that blacks were targeted by police much more often than whites. "To many residents, the cops and court officers are just outsiders who are paid to come to their towns and make their lives miserable," the *Post* reported. "There's also a widely held sentiment that the police spend far more time looking for petty offenses that produce fines than they do keeping these communities safe."

It is critical for new journalists to understand the importance of the context provided by this *Post* report as well as to understand the nation's broader history of race. In order to produce excellent journalism when assigned a racially charged topic, you must have knowledge about the context and complexity of race relations in America and in the particular city involved. Too many media outlets simplified the Michael Brown story—black teen, white cop—without explaining why Ferguson boiled over like it did and the underlying systemic problems not only within the St. Louis area but the nation. By not providing context of the facts, the media can make a situation worse and perpetuate stereotypes of blacks in America as well as decrease the odds that the real root of a problem will be addressed.

The news media must also ward against assuming that because there was violence in one city after a racially charged incident, the same will occur whenever there is a similar situation. "In a very profound way, Michael Brown and Eric Garner force the media to change the way that we cover the shootings of black men by police," said Joy Reid, a national correspondent for MSNBC. "There was a point in the coverage when part of the media were trying to spin the entire Ferguson story into one of out-of-control black people rioting."[13]

FOR DISCUSSION

1. What aspects of history should you know about the communities you are assigned to cover?
2. How can journalists determine the relationship between law enforcement and the communities they are sworn to protect and serve?

BOX 10.1

From the Field: When Crisis Strikes Your Community, Be Ahead of the Pack

Jason Rosenbaum
St. Louis
Public Radio

When Michael Brown was shot and killed on August 9, 2014, it may have been safe to assume that the news of his death would have a fairly short shelf life.

That assumption turned out to be very wrong.

What happened after the 18-year-old's death became a vital moment for the St. Louis region. It led to months of intense protests and jarring destruction. It produced searing questions about relations between police and citizens—and faith in the U.S. judicial system. And it was a watershed moment for Missouri's political class—and how ordinary St. Louis residents view race and economic disparity.

Brown's saga received wall-to-wall coverage from respected national news outlets. But the Brown story proved a very different challenge for journalists from the St. Louis region. We already knew about the systemic racial, economic and educational divides within our community—we saw it every day. With the world watching, we had the knowledge and the insight to tell the Ferguson and St. Louis story in a more distinctive manner than did national or international reporters.

It wasn't easy. Contrary to popular belief, covering the unrest in Ferguson wasn't adventurous or exciting. Journalists were thrust into volatile and dangerous situations with little rest or time off. The constant demand for coverage required personal sacrifice—especially for journalists with spouses and young children. And there's something inherently distressing about watching your community disintegrate—especially when you know there are no snap solutions.

But challenge also brings opportunity. And while I may be biased, I truly believe St. Louis Public Radio joined outlets like the *St. Louis Post-Dispatch*, KMOX, *St. Louis Magazine*, the Nine Network and KSDK in rising to the occasion amid turmoil.

This was a critical duty for us for more than just pride or ratings. While some national reporters—such as *Los Angeles Times'* Matt Pearce, *Huffington Post's* Ryan Reilly and the *Washington Post's* Wesley Lowery—did exceptional work from Ferguson, other media outlets presented general and assumptive coverage. Outside-media outlets were often more interested in the conflict in the streets

(Continued)

BOX 10.1 Continued

than in why or what prompted St. Louis' powder keg to burst. Some journalists used unreliable anonymous sources dishing out bad information. They often failed to grasp basic historical or geographical facts about the region.

The heart of Brown's story was how ordinary citizens felt disengaged with the greater St. Louis community. Many of these people were willing to share their stories with local reporters who had the expertise to present their experience in a candid and authoritative manner. When black St. Louisans talked to us about how they had been profiled, denigrated and disrespected by police, we knew what they were talking about—because we had been writing about the segregated nature of our region for years, if not decades. Local reporters provided context and knew where to go to demand answers.

To be sure, St. Louis' media outlets didn't provide pristine news coverage. Some took a boosterish approach, implicitly glossing over some of the St. Louis region's big divides in the name of "coming together." Others fell into the trap of focusing on loud and dangerous conflict without the nuance or distinctiveness that was lacking nationally. This had an impact, as some sources that were eager to talk with local reporters earlier on in the crisis became more guarded as time went on, making follow-up stories more difficult to write.

I can't speak for every member of the news media, but I know that I probably interacted with police officers differently than national media. I remember vividly a Canadian reporter getting arrested for running up to Highway Patrol Capt. Ron Johnson during the height of the protests. I'm not sure I would have done that—especially knowing that both high-ranking and rank-in-file officers were undergoing immense stress. Would I have been better to be more detached and less emphatic? Possibly. And it was probably easier for outside outlets to be critical of institutions that they don't interact with on a daily basis.

Still, there were some practical advantages to my local status. Many nonlocal reporters arrived in St. Louis with an expectation to cover the big events—nighttime protests, marquee press conferences and any big-ticket developments. They couldn't spend a lot of time milling around Ferguson or the St. Louis area looking for distinctive threads to weave a dynamic story. Since local news had more people covering more ground, they could uncover distinguishing stories.

One example: In mid-August, I went to a St. Louis County Council meeting, something I have done for more than three years. No other reporters were there for most of the meeting. It was a good thing I was there, because that's where an 11-year-old boy named Marquis Govan made an impassioned and brilliant speech

(Continued)

BOX 10.1 Continued

about the Ferguson unrest. People with advanced college degrees hadn't articulated the despair and anguish of black St. Louis as well as Govan.

The day after I posted the audio of his address on YouTube, one of my colleagues—Tim Lloyd—suggested I contact Govan for a follow-up interview. That led to a well-received feature for St. Louis Public Radio. Once that aired, NPR's Weekend Edition asked me to produce a story about Govan—which aired a couple weeks after the original version. The piece was well received enough to prompt Jane Pauley to effectively recreate my story for CBS Sunday Morning. All of this happened because I went off the beaten path instead of following the crowd and gave a voice to those in the community that in most cases are ignored.

Far from being a fleeting spot news story, what happened after Brown's death was unlike anything else I've ever covered. It was an unprecedented opportunity to examine a community in crisis and candidly shine a light on long-held racial divides. Being an effective reporter in this high-pressured situation required patience and the ability to listen. It also reinforced the importance of upholding the basic journalistic standards of fairness and accuracy—even when the desire to be first and fast was very real.

▶ COVERING CRIME IN THE AGE OF SOCIAL MEDIA

Another issue facing law enforcement and journalism is the extensive use of cell phone and surveillance cameras. In most crime stories, journalists rely on information provided by police officials. In 2014, a Cleveland police officer shot and killed 12-year-old Tamir Rice, who was carrying a toy gun. About six months later, a North Charleston, South Carolina, police officer shot and killed Walter Scott as he was running away. Both incidents were caught on camera and the police version of events did not match. Local news reports reflected the police version, but once the bystander videos surfaced, the narratives changed. Meanwhile, social media, especially those sites frequented by African-Americans, accused law enforcement of a cover up and the media for failing to seek the truth. *Columbia Journalism Review*'s David Uberti outlined in the following web post the challenges facing journalists in an era of smartphones: http://www.cjr.org/analysis/smartphone_video_changes_coverage.php.

▶ USE OF DESCRIPTORS IN NEWS STORIES

Using race or ethnicity as a descriptor in stories—crime stories in particular—continues to be one of the most vexing issues in journalism. Many news organizations have guidelines on when race should be used to describe people in stories. It comes down to, "is it pertinent to the story?" The problem is that much of our audience has been conditioned to see race as a primary descriptor. Keith Woods, vice president of diversity at NPR and author of Chapter 2, said "race carries no true color and offers a mind-boggling range of eye/ear/nose/mouth/skin color combinations from which to choose. It is imprecise, often bordering on inaccurate, to describe someone by race." Racial IDs, just as the use of any social category, should be included in stories when there is a reason to do so. Many people argue that racial IDs are important to the story. Think. Why are IDs kept in the story? To help the police catch the alleged perpetrator? To keep the public safe? How would it help you to find out the burglar was a young, black male in his early 20s who wore a white t-shirt and a black hoodie? Would you be able to identify this person? Or just look suspiciously at anyone who fit that description? The unhelpful, nonspecific use of IDs could be considered racial profiling by journalists. And remember—that is what the terrorized victims *think* they saw . . . we know bystander identification is not highly accurate. Also, remember, the police report is based on what police officers choose to write down. While the police report could be highly accurate, police officers can be prone to human error. The problem is, when it comes to topics like crime, health or journalism, some errors can have grave consequences.

While at the Poynter Institute, Keith Woods developed a method journalists could use to help them determine when race and/or ethnicity is relevant to a story.

The Inexplicable ID: These IDs have no obvious connection to the story. They appear in a quote or a sound byte, or are placed in a story by the journalists as a superficial way of distinguishing one person from another. Ethnicity is inexplicably included unless relevance is provided. The solution to this problem is to demonstrate why its use is necessary or take it out.

The Unexplained ID: Race or ethnicity is relevant to the story, but the communicator has left it up to the audience to determine why. The solution is to clearly explain to the audience why race is relevant.

The Misplaced ID: Where race or ethnicity is placed in a story determines its significance to the audience. If the journalist places it too high in a story the audience is more likely to believe race or ethnicity is the focus. Journalists should give the audience a more accurate idea of the significance in stories by making sure it is in its proper place.

The Uneven ID: Race and ethnicity plays a central role in many stories about conflict, disparities, group pathology or discrimination. However, journalists will identify the race/ethnicity of some characters, but not others. In most cases, people of color are identified while whites are not. If race/ethnicity is relevant for some, it should be for all.

The Suspect ID: Journalists often use race or ethnicity to describe how people look. These are inadequate descriptors and should only be used when they are central to the story.

Take a look at the following story. The use of race is problematic. Let's read it first and then discuss:

> Police are looking today for three suspects in connection with an armed robbery yesterday evening at a fast food restaurant at 2210 Market Road.
>
> Officers were dispatched to the fast-food restaurant just after 8 p.m. and arrived to find three white male employees, ages 16, 20 and 21, who reported that they had been robbed by three suspects, one armed with a shotgun.
>
> Police described the suspects as three black males, ranging in age from 18 to 25, dressed in dark clothing and ski masks.
>
> The suspects entered the business through an unlocked door and confronted the employees, police said. During the robbery, one of the employees was struck in the face with the weapon, which caused a laceration. The employee did not require medical attention.
>
> The suspects fled with an undisclosed amount of cash from the rear of the business on foot in an unknown direction, police said.

The reporter used race as an identifier in his description of the restaurant employees and the robbery suspects. The reporter should tell the reader why it was necessary to tell the reader the employees were white (inexplicable ID). In describing the suspects, the writer describes them as black, provides a wide age range and vague information about what they were wearing. The public will have a difficult time identifying the suspect because not enough information was provided. Race is the only specific identifier used and it does not explain the suspects' appearance.

This story needs a good reporter. When you receive a police report that provides little descriptive information, you should treat it as any other source. Question it as if it were a person. What were the three employees doing at the time of the robbery? Why was the door unlocked? Did all three see the suspects and if so, why the vague description? Had they seen the suspects before? Were there customers present at the time of the robbery? In what direction did they leave? These are just a few questions to get the conversation started. Asking questions can help you write a more effective story.

The use of race as a descriptor in this story does not help the identification process, but does perpetuate the stereotypical black suspect/white victim narrative that is pervasive in crime reporting. News organizations need to consider whether the use of race as a main descriptor is worth the loss of credibility in communities of color.

BOX 10.2   Why is Scrutinizing Citizens, But Not Officers, in Police Shootings Now the Norm?

March 10, 2015

Reprinted by permission of alldigitocracy.org

Questioning the police and their account of events should be standard in newsrooms. But too often, journalists seem to readily accept police narratives at face value.

This has become the case with the narrative in the shooting of Tony Robinson, an unarmed man fatally shot by police Officer Matt Kenny in Madison, Wisconsin over the weekend. The type of journalism emerging in this case has led to an over-reliance on official sources, and an emphasis on conflict that has pushed concerns about protest to the forefront and has given police control of the narrative.

Jean Marie Brown, Texas Christian University

Unlike the police chief in Ferguson, Missouri, Madison Police Chief Mike Koval understands the fundamentals of crisis management and responded quickly to news that Kenny, a white officer, had shot Robinson, who is black. While Koval's transparency is laudable, two of the first things you're taught in journalism school are (a) don't rely solely on official sources and (b) find as many sources as possible.

News reports in the *Wisconsin State Journal, The New York Times, USA Today*, the *Huffington Post, BuzzFeed* and *NBC Nightly News* show that those two rules, and other basic principles of reporting, may not be getting followed in this case. The voices of neighbors and other witnesses to the events leading up to Robinson's death have been ignored.

According to police, officers responded to three complaints that Robinson was being disruptive, but it is unclear whether journalists are trying to find out who may have made those calls or if anyone was aware of Robinson's behavior. There is also a lack of skepticism by journalists regarding police procedure in this case. Accounts of the incident in the news relay, without question, that Officer Kenny "forced" his way into the home where Robinson was and that Robinson then "attacked" him.

Is it typical for officers to "force" their way into homes without a warrant? Is this even legal? If the officer "forced" his way into the home, is it accurate to describe Robinson as the aggressor? Following only the chief's narrative puts Robinson in the role of the villain. Journalists appear to have quickly—too quickly—accepted police

(Continued)

BOX 10.2 Continued

accounts that Robinson was the aggressor and/or the bad guy. Is this accurate reporting or just the police narrative? The two are not necessarily one-in-the-same [sic].

Robinson's character is also scrutinized with reports on his police record and a diagnosis of attention deficit disorder. But no such scrutiny is given to Officer Kenny's last fatal shooting, one characterized by Chief Koval as "suicide by cop." Unfortunately, scrutinizing citizens, but not the police in officer shootings, has become the norm. When 12-year-old Tamir Rice was shot and killed by a police officer in Cleveland, Cleveland.com initially reported on Tamir's father's police record and other parental shortcomings rather than focus on the police officer, a man who had been fired from his previous police department job due to performance issues.

Rather than seeking out people with knowledge of Robinson's behavior that night and the confrontation in order to tell a more comprehensive story, journalists have turned their attention to making predictions about what those protesting the shooting may or may not do. This does readers a disservice because there are still a number of unanswered questions about how and why Robinson died.

Delving into what happened and police attitudes about enforcing the law could not only add depth to the underlying tensions that provoke protests when shootings such as this one occurs, but also helps the public, and public officials, better understand the dynamics of these shootings and how they can be prevented, which is our job as journalists.

Journalists reporting on incidents like the Robinson shooting need to do the following to ensure that they get the most accurate information possible:

- Seek out witnesses;
- Look for patterns of behavior on the part of the police, not just the victim;
- Make sure that those patterns of behavior relate to the situation at hand for both parties;
- Question police procedure; and
- Choose your words carefully.

▶ CRISIS COMMUNICATIONS AND CRIME COVERAGE

Crisis communication experts working on either side of an incident involving law enforcement face a brave new world. Gone are the days of gathering all the facts, speaking to the key players, calling the media together and holding a press conference. All of that takes time, something social media does not allow. When George Zimmerman shot and killed Trayvon Martin, Martin's family hired a public relations expert to generate media attention. He reached out to prominent African-American journalists in mainstream media, but it was the tweets, Facebook postings and other forms of social media that caught the attention of the nation. Since that time, it has become standard procedure for the victim's family to hire an attorney who comes equipped with a public relations expert. Their goal is to garner support and media coverage that counters the narrative from official sources. As stated previously in this chapter, the official story, as in the case of Walter Scott, the suspect fatally shot in the back by a police officer in South Carolina in 2015, is what the public sees first because the local media is conditioned to go with that version first. It's not until that narrative is disputed with contradictory facts (such as the video of Scott being shot in the back) that it changes.

However, in the Michael Brown / Darren Wilson shooting in Ferguson, Missouri, the aggrieved community controlled the narrative using Twitter and other forms of social media. Ferguson police waited several days before holding a press conference, and by that time the "hands up, don't shoot" narrative had taken hold. That narrative proved to be false, but the conversation had moved from the initial fatal shooting to the perceived injustice of the criminal justice system locally and nationally.

Not only should police departments have experts who are good in front of a camera, they also need to be proficient in the use of social media. They should also understand that the narrative created from inside their departments could not be the only one out there. Always expect the unexpected and be prepared to respond.

FOR DISCUSSION

1. What should a public affairs officer do when she/he discovers that the information they were told by officers at the scene contradicts what the media has heard from eyewitnesses? What if partial video evidence has been posted to social media?

▶ **CHAPTER SUMMARY**

Practicing excellence can be a challenge in the criminal justice arena. The complex relationship between law enforcement and communities of color calls on journalists and crisis communicators to have an understanding of people involved and the history of that relationship. When a crisis occurs, it is important to make sure you understand the context of the situation and relay that to your audience. Journalists and public relations experts who gain the trust of the community members and law enforcement officials will be rewarded in times of trouble. Those voices will help craft a narrative that more accurately reflects the situation on the ground.

Crime receives the most local news coverage, other than the weather. In many communities, the coverage does not reflect the amount of crime that occurs, especially as it relates to communities of color. When men of color appear in media mainly as crime suspects or victims, it creates a climate of fear among those in the community and society in general. As we have read in this chapter, studies indicate that this continued overexposure exacerbates the mistrust between many ethnic minority communities and law enforcement.

▶ SUGGESTIONS FOR IMPROVEMENT

- Expand sources beyond police and courts.

- Provide context for crime in regular reporting.

- Bolster enterprise and increase investigative reporting.

- Balance stories about crime and the areas where it occurs.

- Conduct periodic audits of news content.

- Examine the story selection process and use restraint when necessary.

- Cover crime victims and suspects as individuals.

▶ SUGGESTED ACTIVITIES

1. Imagine that you are the cops-and-courts reporter for a local media outlet. You just received this news release from the local police in your email:

At 5:21 a.m., officers were dispatched to the 200 block of Hickman Avenue in reference to an assault. Upon officers' arrival, they located a male victim with a gunshot wound who was unresponsive. The victim was transported to a local hospital for treatment. Officers spoke with residents of the home who advised that an intruder, described as a black male, made his way into the home and shot the victim. The victim's current medical condition is unknown at this time. The investigation is ongoing.

Focus closely on the suspect description. What information is missing from the description that you need in order to write a fair and effective news brief?

2. You're working as night reporter, and your boss just handed you this news release from the police department. She wants you to write up a breaking news report for the web:

> At approximately 10:17 p.m., officers were dispatched to 2402 Paris Road, the Break Time convenience store, in reference to a robbery. Investigation revealed the clerk emerged from the back of the business to find a white male near the counter wearing dark clothing and a covering over his head. The suspect demanded money and the clerk provided the drawer from the register. The suspect took an undisclosed amount of money from the drawer and ran southbound from the business. No one was injured in the robbery.

Again, focus on the suspect description. What questions about this description should you ask the police spokesperson in order to provide a fairer and more effective news brief?

▶ NOTES

1 Daniel Angster and Salvatore Colleluori, "New York City Television Stations Continue Disproportionate Coverage of Black Crime," Media Matters for America, 2015.
2 Franklin D. Gilliam Jr. and Shanto Iyengar, "Prime Suspects: The Influence of Local Television News on the Viewing Public," *American Journal of Political Science* 44, no. 3 (July, 2000): 560–574.
3 Lori Dorfman and Vincent Schiraldi, "Off Balance: Youth, Race and Crime in the News," Justice Policy Institute, 2001.
4 "Portrayal and Perception: Two Audit of News Media Reporting on African American Men and Boys," Heinz Endowment, Pittsburgh, PA, 2011.
5 Larry J. Siegel, *Introduction to Criminal Justice*, 14th ed. (Belmont, CA: Wadsworth, 2014).
6 Ibid.
7 Ibid.
8 Ibid.
9 "Stop-and-Frisk data," New York Civil Liberties Union, http://www.nyclu.org/content/stop-and-frisk-data.
10 Ibid.
11 Douglas A. Blackmon, *Slavery by Another Name: The Re-enslavement of Black Americans from the Civil War to World War II* (New York: Anchor Books, 2008).
12 Michelle Alexander, *The New Jim Crow: Mass Incarceration in the Age of Colorblindness* (New York: The New Press, 2010).
13 Aaron Morrison, Journalists Grade Race-Based Media Coverage: Walter Scott, Michael Brown Discussed at Al Sharpton's Civil Rights Convention (International Business Times,

April 12, 2015) http://www.ibtimes.com/journalists-grade-race-based-media-coverage-walter-scott-michael-brown-discussed-al-1877930.

▶ **ADDITIONAL READINGS**

Blackwell, Brandon. "Tamir Rice's father has history of domestic violence." *Cleveland.com* (November 26, 2014). http://www.cleveland.com/metro/index.ssf/2014/11/tamir_rices_father_has_history.html

Brennan, Pauline K. and Abby L. Valdenberg. "Depictions of Female Offenders in Front-Page Newspaper Stories: The Importance of Race/Ethnicity." *International Journal of Social Inquiry* 2, no. 2 (2009): 141–175.

Ellis, Ralph, Joe Sutton, and Greg Botelho. "Wisconsin man killed by officer was not armed, police say." *CNN.com* (March 7, 2015). http://www.cnn.com/2015/03/07/us/wisconsin-protests/.

Entman, Robert M. and Kimberly A. Gross. "Race to Judgment: Stereotyping Media and Criminal Defendants." *Law & Contemporary Problems* 71, no. 4 (2008): 93–133.

Johnson, Kirk A. and Travis L. Dixon. "Change and the Illusion of Change: Evolving Portrayals of Crime News and Blacks in a Major Market." *Howard Journal Of Communications* 19, no. 2 (2008): 125–143.

McCarthy, Tom. "Cleveland officer who fatally shot Tamir Rice judged unfit for duty in 2012." *The Guardian* (December 4, 2014). http://www.theguardian.com/us-news/2014/dec/03/officer-who-fatally-shot-tamir-rice-had-been-judged-unfit.

Morrison, Aaron. "Journalists Grade Race-Based Media Coverage: Walter Scott, Michael Brown Discussed at Al Sharpton's Civil Rights Convention." *International Business Journal* (April 10, 2015). http://www.ibtimes.com/journalists-grade-race-based-media-coverage-walter-scott-michael-brown-discussed-al-1877930.

Oliver, Mary B. "African American Men as "Criminal and Dangerous": Implications of Media Portrayals of Crime on the "Criminalization" of African American Men." *Journal of African American Studies* 7, no. 2 (2003): 3–18.

Schlesinger, Phillip and Howard Tumber. *Reporting Crime: The Media Politics of Criminal Justice.* Oxford, England: Oxford University Press, 1994.

11

The Complexity of Disability

Chad Painter

Temple Grandin is one of the world's foremost experts in the design of more humane slaughterhouses. Such slaughterhouses are important to business because consumers demand animals to be reared, handled, transported and even slaughtered in ways that minimize pain and suffering.[1] Grandin, who has taught as an animal sciences professor at Colorado State University in Fort Collins for more than 20 years, regularly consults with companies such as McDonald's and Burger King about animal welfare. She also has designed corrals for handling cattle on ranches, as well as systems for handling cattle and hogs during veterinary procedures. Nearly 50 percent of cattle and 33 percent of hogs in the United States are handled by systems she designed. Grandin's work has revolutionized animal welfare.

Grandin was diagnosed with autism in 1950. The Centers for Disease Control classify autism spectrum disorders as a group of lifelong developmental disabilities caused by an abnormality of the brain. Impairments, which can range from very mild to very severe, include problems with social interaction and communication skills, as well as repetitive behaviors. Grandin's autism, she has said, enables her to excel in visual spatial skills while it leads

> **LEARNING OBJECTIVES**
>
> By the end of this chapter, you should be able to:
>
> - appreciate the individual and group complexity of defining disability.
>
> - develop authentic stories that include people with disabilities and address issues that are of concern to people with disabilities.
>
> - acquire the analytical capacity to select and decide whether advertising is inclusive or stereotypical.

her to perform poorly verbally. She says that she thinks in pictures, and she credits her visual thinking with helping her understand animals.

The animal-welfare and autistic-rights activist is hailed as the most famous person with autism in the world. The 2010 HBO film *Temple Grandin*, a semi-autobiographical biopic, won a Golden Globe and seven Emmy awards. Grandin is the author of six books, most notably the bestsellers *Thinking in Pictures: My Life with Autism* and *The Autistic Brain: Helping Different Kinds of Minds Succeed*. Finally, she was named one of *Time* magazine's 100 Most Influential People in the World in 2010.

Grandin has a disability. However, she is not defined by her disability. In this chapter, you will learn the tools to report effectively about people with disabilities, as well as learn how to include people with disabilities in advertising and public relations campaigns.

 BOX 11.1   Defining Disability

KEY TERMS

There is no one accepted definition of disability. Disability is defined in the 1990 Americans with Disability Act to mean:

1) a physical or mental impairment that substantially limits one or more major life activities. Major life activities include caring for oneself, performing manual tasks, seeing, hearing, eating, sleeping, walking, standing, lifting, bending, speaking, breathing, learning, reading, concentrating, thinking, communicating and working. A major life activity also includes the operation of a major bodily function, including functions of the immune system, normal cell growth, digestive, bowel, bladder, neurological, brain, respiratory, circulatory, endocrine and reproductive functions.
2) a record of such an impairment.
3) being regarded as having such an impairment. An individual meets the requirement of "being regarded as having such an impairment" if the individual has been subjected to an action because of an actual or perceived physical or mental impairment whether or not the impairment limits or is perceived to limit a major life activity. However, impairments must not be transitory or minor, meaning that the impairment must have an actual or expected duration of six months or more.

More than 56.7 million Americans—or about 2 in 10 adults—live with a disability, according to the U.S. Census Bureau. Worldwide, more than 650 million people—or 10 percent of the total world's population—live with a disability, according to the United Nations. Those disabilities include disabilities one is born with, disabilities one develops through age, disabilities one incurs due to genetic health issues, disabilities related to accidents and war and disabilities related to job hazards. As such, disability intersects with the five major fault lines of age, geography, class, race and gender.

▶ FACTORS THAT LED TO INCREASE IN IMAGES OF DISABILITY IN THE UNITED STATES

Four factors directly or indirectly influenced mass media to include more images of people who have disabilities in news stories and advertisements. Knowing the history of people with disabilities can help journalists and strategic communication professionals add context to their stories and campaigns.

The first factor was the independent living movement, which started in the 1960s. Members of the independent living movement seek to establish a new philosophy about people with disabilities. This philosophy is distinguished from the medical model of disability, which sees a person's body as a "machine" to be fixed in order to fully participate in society. The medical model focuses on an individual's limitations and how to adapt technology and society to reduce those limitations. Negative stereotypes and connotations associated with the medical model of disability contribute to fewer occupational and familial opportunities for people with disabilities. Instead, people in the independent living movement subscribe to the social model, which places systematic barriers, negative attitudes and societal exclusion as the main factors in disabling people.

The second factor that has led to better representation and rights for people with disabilities was the Rehabilitation Act of 1973, sponsored by Indiana representative John Brademas. In the bill, lawmakers sought to extend and revise services that help people with physical or mental disabilities get or keep a job, to expand research and training programs for people with disabilities and to coordinate federal programs to better help and serve people with disabilities.

The third factor that increased information access and the awareness of the needs of people living with disability was television's introduction of open captioning and closed captioning. Open captioning, which is visible to all viewers, first appeared on the Public Broadcasting System in 1972. Shortly thereafter, closed captioning, or captions that are not visible until activated by the viewer, first appeared on PBS station WGBH-Boston. These text subtitles were created to assist people with partial hearing loss or people who are deaf to enjoy television programming.

The fourth factor that increased media awareness of people with disabilities was the Americans with Disability Act of 1990. The act, sponsored by Iowa Senator Tom Harkin, is a wide-ranging civil rights bill that prohibits job discrimination by employers, employment agencies, labor organizations and local, state and federal government entities against people with disabilities. The ADA also requires state and local governments to give people with disabilities an equal opportunity to benefit from all of their programs, services and activities. Further, businesses and nonprofit agencies must comply with basic nondiscrimination requirements—such as placing wheelchair ramps next to stairs—that prohibit exclusion, segregation and unequal treatment.

▶ FRAMING DISABILITY

Media shape public perceptions and attitudes. Media, therefore, can influence how the public feels toward people with disabilities. Members of news media "select the content and frame of the news, thereby constructing reality for those who read, watch, or listen to their stories."[2]

Some academics argue that media still do not use acceptable language when describing people with disabilities.[3] Paul Darke argues that "The representation of disability in the media in the last ten years is pretty much the same as it has always been: clichéd, stereotyped and archetypical."[4]

Media framing can be seen in several predictable stereotypes for people with disabilities.[5] The first stereotype is that they are "others"—that they are partial, limited and less than fully human. The second stereotype is that they are superhuman, overcoming overwhelming odds to live a normal life in a way that can serve as an example to others. Former Major League Baseball pitcher Jim Abbott is a prime example of this stereotype. Abbott, who pitched for four teams during his 11-year career, made the majors despite being born without a right hand. The third stereotype is that the burden or disability is unending, that a person living with a disability must rely on family, friends and society for support. The fourth stereotype is that disability is a sickness needing to be fixed or cured. This medical model, which often may be seen in telethons such as Jerry Lewis' MDA telethon, shows people with disabilities as broken humans that can contribute to society once medical professionals "fix" them. The fifth stereotype is that people with disabilities, especially mental disability, are a menace to others, to themselves and to society. This "villain" stereotype, which is shown repeatedly in superhero movies such as *X-Men*, shows people with disabilities as evil and warped creatures that must be controlled or killed. The sixth stereotype is that people with disabilities, especially cognitive disabilities, are innocents who inspire others to value life. This stereotype can be seen in the eternally innocent portrayals of movie characters such as Forrest Gump and *Rain Man*'s Raymond Babbitt.

FOR DISCUSSION

1. What images of people with disabilities have you seen in popular culture? How are the people represented and depicted?
2. As journalists, how can we use the elements of excellent journalism to overcome negative stereotypes of people with disabilities?

By embracing the elements of excellent journalism, media professionals can overcome these predictable stereotypes. As a journalist or strategic communicator, the best—and, really, only—way to frame people with disabilities is to rise above one-dimensional characterizations and explanations to show the complexity of their lives. People with disabilities are more than the six stereotypes listed previously. Further, people with disabilities are not defined by their disability—just like a person is not defined by his or her race, gender, sexual orientation or any other *one* factor. Journalists and strategic communicators must recognize and embrace the full life of a person, not just one aspect. John Clogston and Beth A. Haller proposed a set of media models that represent people with disabilities as full and active members of society instead of the more stigmatizing traditional models.[6] Their models are:

- *Minority/Civil Rights*: A person with a disability is shown as a member of a minority group with legitimate political grievances.

- *Cultural Pluralism*: A person with a disability is considered a multi-faceted individual whose disability is considered one aspect of many. No unwarranted attention is paid to the disability.

- *Consumer*: People with disabilities are presented as an untapped consumer group that could be profitable to business and society.

The Poynter Institute offers several tips for journalists and strategic communicators looking to report a fuller, non-stereotypical, picture of people with disabilities. First, understand who falls under the definition of a person with a disability. Next—this one seems like a no-brainer, but you would be surprised—talk to people with disabilities when doing stories about disability. Finally, focus on the person, not the disability.[7]

The best news for aspiring journalists and strategic communicators: Disability issues are rich territory for unusually rewarding stories.[8] Disability issues still receive very little coverage by the media, and most disability coverage is clichéd, despite disability issues being interesting and complex. As a result, thoughtful stories that embrace excellent journalism can stand out from the crowd and change the way people think about these issues.

ProPublica reporter Jennifer LaFleur suggests some handy tips for someone trying to cover disability better. First, become extremely familiar with laws such as the Americans with Disability Act, which are extremely complex. Second, uncover issues in your area. You can do this by talking to disability advocates, learning about complaints by sending Freedom of Information Act requests to government agencies, checking for Americans with Disability Act lawsuits in your area and—probably most importantly—observing what is happening around you. Third, practice. Like all types of journalism, you will become better at reporting about disability issues the more you actually report about these issues.

BOX 11.2   From the Field: Chris Hamby

Chris Hamby, BuzzFeed

Chris Hamby won the 2014 Pulitzer Prize for Investigate Reporting for his series "Breathless and Burdened," which he wrote while at the Center for Public Integrity. In the series, Hamby wrote about how some lawyers and doctors rigged a system to deny benefits to coal miners stricken with black lung disease. His reporting led to remedial legislative efforts.

Q: *What challenges did you face reporting the story—especially in terms of reporting on people with disabilities?*
A: When you're reporting on a population like coal miners in West Virginia, they are skeptical about people from Washington or New York coming in and writing about them. There have been a lot of negative portrayals. The negative points are not true, but they are sensitive about how they are portrayed. I tried to get past that by being around and learning a lot about coal mining. I started by talking about their work. They can see you're legitimately interested. I was surprised about how forthcoming people were about their disease.

It is very difficult to be talking to someone who is 46 and looks in good shape, and then after 15 minutes they start making this horrible gasping sound. I didn't know the appropriate thing to do: going on with the interview, leaving them alone,

(Continued)

BOX 11.2 Continued

taking a break or stopping. They wanted to press on because this was the first time anyone really listened to what they had to say. I interviewed the family of Steve Day. At the end of my interview, I asked the standard question: "Is there anything I didn't ask you?" His wife was sitting there crying; she said, "Thank you so much for listening to us. No one ever has." I didn't know how to respond, but that's what makes this type of journalism challenging but rewarding. There were a lot of moments like that.

You don't want to portray people as caricatures. They gave me a lot of trust. It was important to me to portray their stories with sensitivity. These people didn't need to talk to me. It shook them up for a while.

Q: *What tips do you have for journalists who are reporting similar stories?*
A: Don't assume that people don't want to talk to you.

Don't put on airs. They will sniff out an artifice immediately. Don't sweet-talk them. Just be genuine. Tell them the good and bad of talking to you. If they're hesitant, kindly ask them what they're concerned about. Sensitivity is important here. Be genuine.

Don't immediately sit down and start talking about how their lives are ruined. Learn about the world they inhabit, even if it won't go into the story. The interview will be better if you connect with sources.

▶ GROUP COMPLEXITY: THERE ARE MANY TYPES OF DISABILITY

Disability culture is not any different from many other cultures because "persons with disabilities share a common bond of experiences and resilience."[9] There is not one monolithic group called the "disabled." Instead, disabilities are individual and differ in the adjustments required. Further, some people do not identify as people with disabilities. Instead, there is a myriad of types of disability. For example, the American Community Survey includes six different questions to distinguish between visual (blindness or difficulty seeing), hearing (deaf or difficulty hearing), ambulatory (walking or climbing stairs), cognitive (difficulty concentrating, remembering or making decisions), self-care (ability to dress or bathe) and independent living (activities such as running errands, visiting a doctor's office or shopping) disabilities.

Embracing complexity and understanding the plethora of disabilities and people with disabilities is important to achieving excellent journalism. Journalists also can add context such as social and cultural backgrounds, political and legal history and economic implications. Finally, journalists can tell the story from the point of view of the interviewee, bringing the voice of the people to the listener, reader and viewer.

The prevalence of disability increases as one ages, and the combination of rising life expectancy and lower birth rates is creating an aging population worldwide—especially in European countries such as Italy and England, Asian countries such as Japan and China and North American countries such as Canada and the United States. While the trend has not yet impacted the Middle East and sub-Saharan Africa, the United Nations expects the vast majority of people 65 and older to live in what it terms "developing countries" by 2050.

According to the 2012 American Community Survey, 0.8 percent of people under the age of 4 reported a disability, compared to 5.3 percent of people 5–15, 5.5 percent of people 16–20, 10.4 percent of people 21–64, 25 percent of people 65–74 and 50 percent of people over the age of 75. The American Community Survey (ACS) is a mandatory, ongoing statistical survey conducted by the U.S. Census Bureau that samples a small percentage of the population every year—giving communities the information they need to plan investments and services. Notice the sharp rises in disability percentages between age 64 and age 75. About 14 percent of the U.S. population was 65 or older in 2013, and that number is expected to rise to 21 percent by 2050, according to the U.S. Census Bureau. This rise could have significant effects for all Americans in terms of government policies and health care. For example, a large older population—one that tends to vote in larger numbers than younger generations—might impact political debates about Medicare and Social Security. Similarly, older adults consume a disproportionally large share of health care services, and these adults could influence the skills and services, as well as settings, provided by a health care workforce.

These issues provide tremendous opportunities for enterprising journalists to explore stories and issues of great interest to readers and viewers. Journalists should reflect on the generation fault line when writing about disability. By reflecting on fault lines, reporters and editors can better determine the interests, decisions and actions of sources; can provide a way to identify missing cultural voices; can identify additional story angles and perspectives needed for authenticity; and can reframe a story or add complexity.

Journalists also could report on issues such as oppression, discrimination, inequality and poverty while writing about people with disabilities. This focus could lead to the class fault line. People with disabilities do tend to earn less, according to the U.S. Census Bureau. In 2012, the median income for a person with a disability during the previous 12 months was $20,184, which was only 66 percent of the median earnings for those without a disability.[10] Consequently, 23 percent of people with a disability were considered to be below the poverty line, compared to 15 percent for those without a disability.

Further, 30 percent of people who received income-based government assistance had a disability, and 18 percent of those assistance recipients had difficulty walking or climbing stairs. Class, one of the five fault lines, is a combination of one's economic, political, educational and social standing. As journalists educate themselves more about how fault lines such as class intersect with disability, they have the opportunity to better inform the public about the link between disability, earned income and poverty.

BOX 11.3   From the Field: Nick Turkas

Nick Turkas has worked for the Arthritis Foundation for 15 years. He currently serves as a senior vice president of community development, based in Charlotte, NC.

Nick Turkas

Q: *What are some misperceptions or misconceptions about people with arthritis?*

A: Most people have a picture of a person with arthritis as an elderly woman in a rocking chair or old man shuffling behind a walker. While older people most definitely are more likely to live with arthritis, it is far from the whole story. Arthritis is the most common cause of disability in the U.S. Arthritis is an umbrella term used for a group of more than 120 medical conditions, all of which affect one or more joints. The most common forms of arthritis include osteoarthritis, rheumatoid arthritis, gout and osteoporosis. Pain, stiffness, swelling and difficulty moving a joint are common signs and symptoms of arthritis. Arthritis is most common among women and senior citizens. Nonetheless, arthritis is not just an older person's disease. Nearly two thirds of people with arthritis are younger than 65 years old. More than 300,000 children in the U.S. live with arthritis.

Q: *What should journalists do to better understand arthritis—to better report about arthritis and tell the stories of people living with arthritis?*

A: Do what journalists do best. Take time to get to know their subjects and listen to what their experience has been with the diseases. People with chronic conditions will typically tell you about the process of being officially diagnosed, how their life has changed and their response to those changes. The

(Continued)

BOX 11.3 Continued

changes may include periods of frustration and celebration. It's within those periods that great stories can emerge.

For non-profit organizations, it is important to showcase the relationship with its funders and supporters. Investors in a community-based organization often have compelling reasons for that involvement and a vision for a better future.

Q: *What should advertisers and public relations professionals do to feature or showcase people with arthritis without being stereotypical or offensive?*

A: People with arthritis are typically portrayed as severely disabled or superhuman. The truth is that arthritis is a spectrum. In addition, people with arthritis experience flare-ups, which are intense pain and swelling, and remission periods of reduced pain and increased energy. These flares and remissions wax and wane sometimes without known reason.

▶ DISABILITIES IN THE NEWS

There is an intersection between health and disability. Some people are born with a disability. However, health issues, if left unchecked and uncared for, can lead to disability. Other mental and physical disabilities can happen due to occupational hazards, accidents or war. The media recently have focused on four health issues related to disability, each of which we will discuss more below. Each also is related to common issues in all disability stories such as policy, regulation, medical care, accommodations and workplace safety. Journalists easily can obtain this information on government websites such as Disability.gov or NIH.gov, and health groups such as the American Diabetes Association.

When putting information together for your stories, concentrate on a few journalistic tools. First, find the human element in the story (see Ch. 12 for more guidance). The focus structure, which follows one individual as a representative of a larger group, is a useful tool for making complex or abstract stories meaningful to readers. This technique also allows you to put the person first instead of emphasizing the disability. Second, be cautious with language. As the Missouri Group writes in *News Reporting and Writing*, "Words are powerful. When used negatively, they define cultures, create second-class citizens and reveal stereotypical thinking. They also change the way people think about and treat others."[11] It is not about being zealously "politically correct"; instead, it is about having the freedom—and responsibility—to choose precisely the right word. Speaking of word choice, you should define and reword technical terms to make them clearer for readers or viewers. A useful question to ask an expert is "Can you restate that information in terms that would be understandable to a non-expert audience?" Third, add context through the use of historical examples and issues, data and statistics and medical and other academic research. Census.gov has a wealth of statistical information, and your newsroom's clip morgue can provide a treasure trove of material about how an issue has been written about in the past.

Chronic Traumatic Encephalopathy (CTE)

More than 4,500 former professional football players sued the National Football League, claiming that the NFL concealed the link between football and brain damage. CTE is defined by the Centers for Disease Control as a "progressive motor neuron disease characterized by profound weakness, atrophy, spasticity and fasciculation similar to amyotrophic lateral sclerosis (ALS)." Typical signs and symptoms include a decline of recent memory and executive function, and mood and behavioral disturbances—especially depression, impulsivity, aggressiveness, anger, irritability, suicidal behavior and eventual progression to dementia, according to the CDC. Initial signs and symptoms typically do not occur until decades after the trauma was received.

Obesity

Obesity simply means having too much body fat, according to the National Institutes of Health. Researchers conducting the 2009–2010 National Health and Nutrition Examination Survey found that more than 66 percent of adults and 33 percent of children aged 6–19 are considered to be overweight or obese.[12] Being obese increases the risk of type 2 diabetes, heart disease, high blood pressure, stroke, arthritis and cancer.

About 29.1 million Americans, or 9.3 percent of the total population, have diabetes, and the figure continues to rise.[13] Some population groups—African-Americans, Latinos, Native Americans, Asian-Americans, and Pacific Islanders—have a higher risk of developing type 2 diabetes. This increased risk could lead journalists to focus on the race and ethnicity fault line when reporting stories about type 2 diabetes. People over the age of 65 also were more likely to have diabetes. About 11.8 million people over the age of 65 (or 25.9 percent of the subpopulation) have been diagnosed with diabetes.[14] Journalists have the opportunity to focus on the generation fault line when reporting stories about diabetes.

Attention Deficit Hyperactivity Disorder (ADHD)

The main features of ADHD are inattention, hyperactivity and impulsivity lasting more than six months and causing problems at school, at home or in social situations.[15] In 2013, the Centers for Disease Control reported that 6.4 million American schoolchildren between the ages of 4 and 17 had been diagnosed with ADHD. Boys are more likely to be diagnosed than girls. By high school, nearly 1 in 5 boys are diagnosed with ADHD. When reporting about ADHD, especially among school-aged children, journalists may choose to concentrate on the gender fault line.

Casualties of War

As of the time of this writing, 18,675 American military personnel have been wounded in the war in Afghanistan since 2001, and 32,222 were wounded in Iraq between 2003–2011, according to the Congressional Research Service.[16] Injuries could be physical such as amputations or severe burns, or mental such as post-traumatic stress disorder. Advances in medicine enabling doctors and nurses to save lives where wounds would have been fatal in previous wars are one reason for the increase in non-fatal casualties. Journalists covering such stories should provide that necessary context when telling the stories of wounded military personnel. Further, there is an aspect of complexity to these stories because not all injuries are the same, and the way people react and respond to their injuries can be dramatically different.

▶ A NEGATIVE WORD

President Barack Obama signed Rosa's Law on October 5, 2010. In the bill, the people-first terms "individual with an intellectual disability" and "intellectual disability" replaced "mental retardation" and "mentally retarded" in all federal health, education and labor laws and policy. Forty-three states have enacted laws or are taking steps to remove the word "retarded" from their laws. Why? The "R-word," or "retard," is considered the social equivalent of other offensive terms based on race, gender and sexual orientation.[17] Eliminating hateful language is the impetus for the "spread the word to end the word" campaign.

In the United Kingdom, Nicola Clark started the People Not Punchlines campaign to change hate speech law to include people with disabilities. In the U.K., it was illegal to communicate in a manner that was threatening, abusive or insulting, and intended to harass, alarm or distress. However, the law previously did not extend to people with disabilities even though an estimated 90 percent of people with learning disabilities were verbally abused or assaulted because of their disability. Clark started the campaign after realizing that hate speech directed at people with disabilities was becoming common in society and national television.

FOR DISCUSSION

1. What would you do if someone you are interviewing uses the word "retarded" in an interview?
2. What factors would you use to decide whether to include the word in the story or not? Does it matter if the person who used the word has a disability herself/himself? Why or why not?

BOX 11.4   Associated Press Stylebook

DISABILITY AND EXCELLENT JOURNALISM

The Associated Press is a nonprofit media cooperative owned by its member newspapers, radio and television stations, which contribute stories to the news service and use content produced by its staff journalists. The Associated Press Stylebook is almost universally used in newsrooms and classrooms, and, as the AP writes, it is "essential for journalists, students, editors and writers in all professions." What follows is the 2012 entry for "disabled, handicapped, impaired," edited by Darrel Christian, Sally Jacobsen and David Minthorn.

   Disabled, handicapped, impaired: In general, do not describe an individual as disabled or handicapped unless it is clearly pertinent to a story. If a description must be used, try to be specific. *An ad featuring actor Michael J. Fox swaying noticeably from the effects of Parkinson's disease drew nationwide attention.*

Avoid descriptions that connote pity, such as *afflicted with* or *suffers from multiple sclerosis*. Rather, *has multiple sclerosis*.
Some terms include:
Cripple: Often considered offensive when used to describe a person who is lame or disabled.
Disabled: A general term used for a physical or mental disability. Do not use "mentally retarded."
Handicap: This should be avoided in describing a disability.
Blind: Describes a person with complete loss of sight. For others, use terms such as *visually impaired* or *person with low vision*.
Deaf: Describes a person with total hearing loss. For others, use *partial hearing loss* or *partially deaf*. Avoid using *deaf-mute*. Do not use *deaf and dumb*.
Mute: Describes a person who physically cannot speak. Others with speaking difficulties are *speech impaired*.
Wheelchair user: People use wheelchairs for independent mobility. Do not use *confined to a wheelchair*, or *wheelchair-bound*. If a wheelchair is needed, say why.

▶ PEOPLE-FIRST LANGUAGE

Using people-first language is putting the person before his or her disability.[18] Words have meaning "because the terminology reveals the thinking behind them."[19] Some words are hurtful and can set people apart in a negative way. Other words can be respectful, and it is a matter of respect to see a person or community first, to see a person or community before a disability. People should not be defined by their disability; they are people first.

Double Consciousness: Practicing double-consciousness is understanding different cultures from their cultural perspective. By practicing double-consciousness, journalists and strategic communicators will identify why people-first language matters to many and also why mentioning disability only when it is pertinent to the story makes sense.

People-first language puts the person before the disability, and describes what a person has, not who a person is. Are you "myopic" or do you wear glasses? Are you "cancerous" or do you have cancer? Is a person "handicapped/disabled" or does she have a disability?[20]

People with disabilities want to be accepted just like anyone else. The media shape public perceptions and attitudes; therefore, media use of language is important.

▶ DISABILITY AND STRATEGIC COMMUNICATION

Inclusive Advertising: To show people with disabilities as they really are; part of the mainstream, not superhuman or inferior

Inclusive Advertising

Strategic communication professionals must take into account the needs and preferences of people with disabilities. One characteristic of inclusive advertising is that such ads incorporate images of people with disabilities, a change from previous ideals of physically perfect models in ads.[21] Marie Hardin argues that people with disabilities typically ignore advertising because it does not adequately reflect their lives. However, the people she interviewed were aware of positive advertising images of people with disabilities, and they internalized the able-bodied ideal typically found in advertising and other types of media.[22]

In 1984, blue jeans manufacturer Levi Strauss was the first advertiser to use a person with a disability in one of its ads.[23] The ad featured a man in a wheelchair popping a wheelie. McDonald's followed in 1986, featuring one of its employees, who had a disability, in an ad. DuPont aired a commercial in 1987 featuring Bill Demby, a Vietnam veteran shown playing basketball on his two prosthetic legs. Since these advertisers first showcased people with disabilities, the concept of such advertising has become more commonplace in the United States and the United Kingdom. However, while some improvement has occurred in terms of inclusiveness—such as themes of empowerment and disability pride—advertisements also generally stigmatize people with disabilities. Beth Haller and Sue Ralph argue that certain themes found in ads "convey underlying messages that disabled people are broken and in need of repair, are awash in tragedy, or are Supercrips, who are put on pedestals for just living their lives."[24]

There are four major ways advertisers can approach inclusive advertising. Disability-focused general marketing, which is conducted for profit instead of for philanthropy or social responsibility, "utilizes generic media to promote disability-related products or services." Disability-focused narrowcasting is similar to disability-focused general marketing, but messages are directed to "carefully selected subgroups in ways most likely to reach them and influence their purchasing decision." In disability-highlighted marketing, a company will feature disabilities thematically in its advertising, usually by focusing on a consumer or employee with a disability. While disability issues are not directly discussed in such advertising, the message is front and center. Disability-integrated marketing also features people with disabilities, but draws no particular attention to them or the disability.[25]

The Web offers advertisers new opportunities to reach potential consumers who have disabilities. As a group, people with disabilities are more likely than other groups to use the Internet for getting information about products and services, shopping online, getting information about health, making travel plans and arrangements and paying bills. However, a person with a disability, much like the general population, values the Internet, particular websites and Web advertising only if all three clearly make their lives more manageable.[26] The key for strategic communicators, then, is to focus on the product and how it improves a person's life, not on checking a box by including an image of a person with a disability or narrowcasting the message toward the disability itself.

FOR DISCUSSION

1. What images of people with disabilities have you seen in advertising? Describe how the ad fit into one of the four major categories: disability-focused general marketing, disability-focused narrowcasting, disability-highlighted marketing or disability-integrated marketing.
2. How are images similar and different in traditional advertising, Web-based advertising and advertising on social media?

BOX 11.5   From the Field: Tim O'Brien

Tim O'Brien

Tim O'Brien is the head of the Pittsburgh-based public relations firm O'Brien Communications. He previously worked for Tollgrade, Ketchum and Magnus/Catanzano. He is a frequent contributor to the Public Relations Society of America publications *PR Strategist* and *PR Tactics*, where this article originally appeared.

"One of the tenets of professional communication is, 'Know your audience.' With this in mind, the most serious mistake that a communicator can make is to lump all of those with some form of disability into a single 'disability community' heading on an audience matrix.

While the level of sophistication depends on the nature of the communications program, it is always a good practice to treat any general demographic as an umbrella for many subsets within—each with its own mindset and self-interest. Take the time to customize your communications plans to address the differences between these subsets.

Do the necessary research to identify the attitudes of your targeted audiences. You may be surprised at the results and how they vary between demographics within a targeted audience.

That said, the following are some mistakes to avoid:

* Don't assume that people with disabilities do not work. The [American Community Survey] reported that in 2008, about 39 percent or 7.5 million working age adults with some form of disability were employed. And this does not take into account those who are able to work but were unemployed because of the recession.

* Don't assume that all of those with a particular disability share the same attitudes toward the same societal issues. One person with Parkinson's disease may favor embryonic stem cell research funding, while another may strongly disagree for his or her own reasons.

* Don't project your own feelings about particular disabilities on the targeted audience. How we think we would react if we had a certain disability is probably different from how those who actually have a certain disability have responded to their challenges.

(Continued)

BOX 11.5 Continued

---

* Don't dismiss the emerging language of disability as political correctness run amok. The accepted language of disability is called 'people first,' which simply places the emphasis on the individual and not the disability. It provides proper context for all communications. We know it's not acceptable in general conversation to refer to a colleague as 'the fat guy at the corner table,' or the 'old woman in the conference room.' We should know better than to refer to a colleague as 'that wheelchair-bound sales rep,' or to describe the son of a coworker as 'retarded.'
* Don't patronize. It is common, especially in PR circles, to want to recognize individuals for their dedication or hard work. But when we add a layer to this recognition, calling people with disabilities 'courageous' or 'brave' simply for doing their jobs, we could be crossing a line that has an unintended effect on the individual. Often such recognition could be perceived as disingenuous, shallow and without substance.

The best way to communicate to people with disabilities (and every other demographic in society) is to treat them with even-handed respect. Language is important, of course. But perhaps most important: PR professionals must avoid using a 'one size fits all' approach to communicating with this growing group of individuals."[27]

Ads That Work

Strategic communication practitioners can create ads that feature people with disabilities without those ads being offensive to that community. The key is to show people with disabilities as they really are—not superhuman or inferior, but part of the mainstream, part of "real life." Strategic communicators also must realize that there is a wide scope of disabilities, so they should move away from just depicting people who are deaf or people in wheelchairs. Finally, practitioners should remember that ads and stories are visual and present messages, and think critically about the message that the advertisement is sending both visually and textually.

There are plusses and minuses to the use of advertisements featuring people with disabilities. The audience for such ads is twofold: people with disabilities and people without disabilities. The major advantage to these ads is that using people with disabilities meets important social responsibilities and enhances the potential consumer base to include patrons who have disabilities. There also can be a sense of altruism when people with disabilities are used in advertisements. However, strategic communicators must be careful to avoid perpetuating stereotypes. Public relations practitioners also must be cognizant of depicting people with disabilities as part of normal, everyday life.

▶ CHAPTER SUMMARY

In this chapter, you explored the term disability to understand better that there is no one definition of the word. Further, you learned about group complexity. There are many types of disability, and disabilities are individual and differ in the adjustments required by people. The way that media frame disability can have a major influence on how the general public sees and understands people with disabilities. By using people-first language, which does not define a person by his or her disability, journalists can be more respectful to those people with disabilities and more accurate in their stories. Advertisers and public relations practitioners can incorporate inclusive images of people with disabilities to broaden their target audience without being stereotypical or offensive. Finally, you learned ways to include complexity, context, voices and the five fault lines to tell better, broader stories about people with disabilities.

▶ SUGGESTED ACTIVITIES

1. Rewrite the following sentences to include people-first language.

   1) The wheelchair-bound senator was campaigning for reelection.

   2) New Mexico's handicapped turned out for a rally.

   3) Disabled man wins award for volunteerism.

   4) Agency purchases apartment to house the disabled.

   5) Dental program for the mentally retarded faces cuts.

   6) City to add more handicapped parking spaces.

   7) The mayor's son is autistic.

   8) The principal's daughter is a special-education student at his school.

   9) Peter Dinklage is a famous midget actor.

   10) The quadriplegic veteran does not consider herself handicapped.

2. Find an advertisement featuring a person with a disability. Does the advertisement meet the five criteria in the TARES test? Why or why not? If it does not satisfy one of the criteria, what aspect needs to be changed to make the ad more ethical?

TARES test[28]

The original TARES test is a checklist of questions the creators of every persuasive message should ask themselves to determine the ethical worthiness of the message.

T = Truthfulness: Are the claims, both verbal and visual, truthful? If the message communicates only part of the truth (and many ads do), are the omissions deceptive?

A = Authenticity: Would you buy your own reasoning about the uses and quality of the product advertised?

R = Respect: Am I willing to take full, open and personal responsibility for the content of this ad?

E = Equity: Is the recipient of the message on the same level playing field as the ad's creator? Or, to correctly interpret the ad, must that person be abnormally well-informed, unusually bright or quick-witted and completely without prejudice?

S = Socially responsible: If everyone financially able to purchase this product or service did so, would society as a whole be improved, keeping in mind that recreation and self-improvement are worthy societal goals? If there are some groups in society that would benefit from using this product as advertised, are there others that could be significantly harmed by it? Are there ways to protect them?

3. How do journalists and advertisers get to know the stories and buying profiles of places, people and neighborhoods that have gone uncovered, under-covered, underserved and under-researched? They find places to tune in to a community's frequency, a "listening post." Find such a listening post for people with disabilities in your community. While you're there, "listen" with all your senses. Read bulletin boards, pamphlets, leaflets, etc. Sit down and have a conversation about what's going on in the community. Listen carefully to the language people use to describe themselves and what they do. Take your cue from them. Show up with an open mind and be willing to be wrong about a place or person.

4. Read Mike Sager's article "Vetville" (www.esquire.com/news-politics/a10561/marines-veterans-iraq-0811/). Was Sager's piece an example of excellent journalism? Why or why not? How were the five fault lines used in the article? Were there any necessary fault lines missing?

▶ **NOTES**

1 Michael C. Appleby and Barry Hughes, *Animal Welfare* (Wallingford, UK: CAB International, 1997); Marian Dawkins, "From an Animal's Point of View: Motivation, Fitness, and Animal Welfare," *Behavioral and Brain Sciences* 13 (1990): 1–16.

2 Beth A. Haller, "News Coverage of Disability Issues, Final Report for the Centre for an Accessible Society," http://www.accessiblesociety.org/topics/coverage/0799haller.htm

3 Sandra C. Jones and Valerie Harwood, "Representations of Autism in Australian Print Media," *Disability and Society* 24 (2009): 5–18; Gwyn Symonds, "There's No Other Way to Describe It: Images of Disability and Challenging Behaviour on *A Current Affair*," *Australian Journal of Special Education* 30 (2006): 157–170; Paul A. Darke, "The Changing Face of Representations of Disability in the Media," in *Disabling Barriers, Enabling Environments*, ed. John Swain, Sally French, Colin Barnes and Carol Thomas (London: Sage Publications, 2003); Beth A. Haller, "Paternalism and Protest: Coverage of Deaf Persons in the *Washington Post* and *New York Times*," *Mass Communications Review* 20 (1993): 3–4.

4 Darke, "The Changing Face," 100.

5 Laurie Block, "Stereotypes About People with Disabilities," http://disabilitymuseum.org/dhm/edu/essay.html?id=24.

6 John S. Clogston, "Reporter's Attitudes Toward and Newspaper Coverage of Persons with Disabilities" (PhD diss., Michigan State University, 1991); Haller, "Paternalism and Protest."

7 Susan LoTempio, "Enabling Coverage of Disability," http://www.poynter.org/news/mediawire/74930/enabling-coverage-of-disability/.

8 Susan LoTempio, "From Fear to Storytelling: Covering Disability From Outside Your Comfort Zone," http://www.poynter.org/news/mediawire/76405/from-fear-to-storytelling-covering-disability-from-outside-your-comfort-zone/.

9 Alice-Ann Darrow, "Culturally Responsive Teaching: Understanding Disability Culture," *General Music Today* 26 (2013): 32.

10 Disability.gov.

11 Brian Brooks, George Kennedy, Daryl Moen and Don Ranly, *News Reporting and Writing*, 11th ed. (Boston: Bedford/St. Martin's, 2014), 208–209.

12 National Institutes of Health, nih.gov.

13 American Diabetes Association, diabetes.org.

14 Ibid.

15 National Institutes of Health.

16 Federation of American Scientists, fas.org.

17 "Spread the Word to End the Word," www.r-word.org.

18 Kathie Snow, "To Ensure Inclusion, Freedom, and Respect For All, It's Time to Embrace People First Language," disabilityisnatural.com.

19 British Red Cross, "The Social Model of Disability," redcross.org.uk.

20 Snow, "To Ensure Inclusion," 2.

21 Griff Hogan, *The Inclusive Corporation: A Disability Handbook For Business Professionals* (Athens, OH: Swallow Press, 2003).

22 Marie Hardin, "Marketing the Acceptably Athletic Image: Wheelchair Athletes, Sport-Related Advertising and Capitalist Hegemony," *Disability Studies Quarterly* 23 (2003): 108–125.

23 Laura Kaufman, "Companies Boost Number of Deaf Actors Appearing in Commercials," *Los Angeles Times*, December 3, 1999, C1.

24 Beth A. Haller and Sue Ralph, "Are Disability Images in Advertising Becoming Bold and Daring? An Analysis of Prominent Themes in US and UK Campaigns," *Disability Studies Quarterly* 26 (2006): 1.

25 Hogan, "The Inclusive Corporation," 266–267.

26 John Burnett, "Disabled Consumers: The Use of the Internet and Attitudes Toward Web Advertising," *Journal of Advertising Research* 46 (2006): 324–338.

27 Tim O'Brien, "Case Sensitive: Communicating to Audiences with Disabilities," *Public Relations Tactics*, October 2, 2010, http://www.prsa.org/Intelligence/Tactics/Articles/view/8823/1021/Case_sensitive_Communicating_to_audiences_with_dis#.Vf94oZcutsk

28 Sherry Baker and David L. Martinson, "The TARES Test: Five Principles of Ethical Persuasion," *Journal of Mass Media Ethics* 16 (2001): 148–175.

▶ LINKS TO WEB CONTENT

Americans with Disability Act: ada.gov
Disability information for Australia: australia.gov.au/people/people-with-disabilities
Centers for Disease Control: cdc.gov
U.S. Census and American Community Survey: census.gov
Disability information for Ireland: citizensinformation.ie/en/reference/checklists/checklist_disability.html
Disability information for United States: disability.gov
Disability information for England: gov.uk/browse/disabilities
National Institutes of Health: nih.gov
"Not Acceptable R-Word" PSA: r-word.org/r-word-not-acceptable-psa.aspx
Disability information for Scotland: scotland.gov.uk/Topics/People/Equality/disability
Disability information for Canada: servicecanada.gc.ca/eng/lifeevents/disability.shtml

▶ ADDITIONAL READINGS

Baker, Sherry and David L. Martinson. "The TARES Test: Five Principles of Ethical Persuasion." *Journal of Mass Media Ethics* 16 (2001): 148–175.

Christian, Darrel, Sally Jacobsen and David Minthorn, eds. *The Associated Press Stylebook and Briefing on Media Law.* New York: Associated Press, 2012.

D'Agostino, Ryan. "The Drugging of the American Boy." *Esquire*, March 2014.

Fainaru-Wada, Mark and Steve Fainaru. *League of Denial.* New York: Crown Archetype, 2013.

Grandin, Temple. *Thinking in Pictures: My Life with Autism.* New York: Vintage, 2010.

Grandin, Temple and Richard Panek. *The Autistic Brain: Helping Different Kinds of Minds Succeed.* Boston: Mariner Books, 2014.

Haller, Beth A. and Sue Ralph. "Are Disability Images in Advertising Becoming Bold and Daring? An Analysis of Prominent Themes in US and UK Campaigns." *Disability Studies Quarterly* 26 (2006).

Hamby, Chris. "Breathless and Burdened." *The Center for Public Integrity*. publicintegrity.org.

Hardin, Marie. "Marketing the Acceptably Athletic Image: Wheelchair Athletes, Sport-Related Advertising and Capitalist Hegemony." *Disability Studies Quarterly* 23 (2003): 108–125.

Hogan, Griff. *The Inclusive Corporation: A Disability Handbook for Business Professionals*. Athens, OH: Swallow Press, 2003.

Jackson, Nate. *Slow Getting Up: A Story of NFL Survival From the Bottom of the Pile*. New York: HarperCollins, 2013.

Sager, Mike. "Vetville." *Esquire*, July 2011.

12

Rx for Communicating About Health Inequalities

Amanda Hinnant and María E. Len-Ríos

Bronchiectasis. Myocarditis. Cystic fibrosis. Did you trip up pronouncing those words in your head as you were reading? Well, you may have heard these terms thrown around on the popular medical dramas *Grey's Anatomy*, *The Mindy Project* or reruns of *ER*. However, unless you're a specialized medical reporter who works in health or are a strategic communicator with health sector clients, your first reaction is probably to want to look for lighter reading. (The chapter gets much easier—we promise, stick with us!)

Some of you may already know that cystic fibrosis is a disease that results from a build-up of mucus in the lungs. Medical researchers believe it is caused by a genetic mutation most common among people of Scottish and European descent. Like cystic fibrosis, other health issues can affect specific groups of people. While medical researchers make new discoveries every day, one thing we know is that health results differ in populations. These differences can be due to a person's health insurance status, access to high-quality health care and health literacy. But other factors that might not even seem related to health can play a role in inequality, such as different environments, cultural practices and education. Combine these factors with basic genetics and it is hard to figure out what is causing the problem.

According to the Institute of Medicine, health inequalities rob individuals of their quality of life and also cost communities in many ways. For instance, a study of pregnancy data from 2006–2007 in 14 Southern states showed that if pregnancy outcomes could be improved for pregnant African-American women, communities could save $114 to $214 million that might be put toward other community needs.[1] While communication alone cannot solve health inequalities, communication does provide a means for change. Therefore, journalists and communicators play a significant role in identifying the causes of health inequalities, in educating the public and policy makers and in helping individuals and communities find solutions to their problems.

Of course, in order for us to be effective, we ourselves must fully grasp what we are writing about and explain it well to others. So, for those who are wondering (and aspiring journalists should be curious): *Myocarditis* is a weakening of a person's central heart wall caused by a virus. *Bronchiectasis* is damage to airways in a person's lungs caused by an infection that prevents the lungs clearing mucus leading to bacterial infections and organ problems. OK, no more quizzes, for now. . .

▶ DISPARITIES AND HEALTH REPORTING 101

An important first step to writing about health disparities is understanding that health inequalities exist and that they are shaped by many things. (Once you understand that, you'll be ahead of the majority of Americans who don't understand how forces outside a person's control could possibly influence health!)[2] Some people, especially those in positions of class privilege (see Chapter 1), tend to believe that poor health is brought about by bad choices.[3] This perspective is fundamentally flawed because there is a constellation of circumstances that influences our health—whether it's good health or bad health.

The second step to understanding health inequalities is realizing that media can help the public understand health inequalities faced by others.[4]

▶ WHAT ARE HEALTH INEQUALITIES?

Health inequalities, sometimes referred to as health disparities, occur across fault lines. Policymakers, journalists and researchers have often looked at the inequalities among racial and ethnic minorities and the white "majority" as being due to differences in why people get diseases, how often they get diseases, and whether they are more likely to die from diseases. From HIV/AIDS to diabetes to certain types of cancer, African-Americans, Latino Americans, and Native Americans have higher incidences of disease, receive poorer treatments or are often diagnosed at much later stages in a disease's progression than are white Americans. While there are many reasons for these inequalities—differences in genetics, income, culture, education, health insurance status, health literacy, etc.—the fact that these inequalities exist poses a threat to the wellbeing of society. Additionally, women, rural residents, poor people and those with disabilities are also affected by disease and death at uneven rates. For example, women are more likely than men to die from heart disease, and rates of suicide among rural men are higher than among urban men.

Part of the reason for these differences between men and women or rural and urban people is because the vast majority of medical research and clinical trials have used white, middle-class, well-educated men as research subjects.[5] Who gets included in clinical trials is a central problem. For instance, it is only recently (2014) that the National Institutes of Health started requiring medical researchers to include men and women equally in clinical trials. Previously, not only were women and minorities excluded from studies but, when they were included, they were not always treated with respect. That is why there is hesitancy among certain populations, such as African-Americans and Native Americans, to participate in clinical trials. Historically, the U.S. government and certain medical professionals did not treat all people with human dignity (e.g., the U.S. Public Health Service syphilis study at Tuskegee). Rebecca Skloot, in her 2011 book *The Immortal Life of Henrietta Lacks*, documents how, in 1951, researchers at Johns Hopkins University used Mrs. Lacks' cancer cells to develop modern treatments for cancers without her consent or that of the Lacks family. Lacks was a poor African-American woman, and, at that time, it was not the norm to consider her will. Looking beyond clinical trials, there are a great many other considerations to explaining health inequalities.

▶ INFLUENCES ON A PERSON'S HEALTH

The crucial thing to remember is that people who are affected by health inequalities—due to race, ethnicity, gender, geography, sexual orientation, class or ability—are not always responsible for their poor health. In fact, much of the good or bad health that we experience is out of our hands. Our health risks are mostly determined by factors we can't control. For example, a person's risk for getting a sexually transmitted disease is influenced by his or her levels of literacy, poverty and education. Most people don't have a say in whether they can read or have money. See the figure 12.1 to understand how societal/environmental levels are influencing individual health outcomes.

The main point is this: When a story blames a person as responsible for everything that goes wrong with his or her health, readers and viewers are unlikely to understand all of the factors at play. It is easier to blame a person and ask a person to change than it is to change organizations or our culture. Stories, and how well they are told, shape empathy and understanding.[6] In turn, empathy and understanding can influence whether readers support funding, policies and community reforms. For example, when people

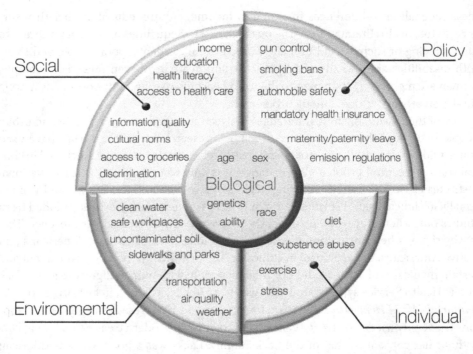

FIGURE 12.1 How societal/environmental levels influence individual health outcomes
Adapted from G. Dahlgren and M. Whitehead, "Policies and Strategies to Promote Social Equity in Health," Stockholm: Institute for Future Studies, 1991. How societal/ environmental levels influence individual health outcomes

read about how food companies use certain food additives, or of how some restaurants might engage in specific food preparation practices that influence obesity rates, people are less likely to place all of the blame on individuals.

From before you were born, several factors helped determine your chances of encountering illness and earlier death in your lifetime. Your mother's medical care while she was pregnant with you, your parents' employment and access to health care, the neighborhood you grew up in, policies in your local schools, etc. all shaped your health, as well as the personal behaviors you've adopted. Although we all start off in life as babies, newborns born to poor parents are less likely to have mothers who were able to breastfeed them, give them healthy foods, provide quality childcare, live in safe environments for exercise and play or reside in areas with excellent schools. (If you were lucky enough to have all these things—great! As a society, we should hope everyone does.) Generally, people who have a lower social status are more at risk for diseases and disabilities.[7] And did you know that people of color generally receive worse treatment in health-care settings? The graphic in this chapter shows how all of these details influence decisions you currently make.

▶ WHAT IS HEALTH JOURNALISM?

Health journalism includes stories, news and advice about issues of personal and pub-lic health that appear across all media platforms. Health stories are some of the most popular stories that run in consumer media, and health journalists cater to readers or viewers with little or no medical knowledge. Journalists alert their audiences to poten-tial personal health issues, medical developments and new research, as well as coverage about insurance, health facilities and types of care. Doctors and nurses routinely deal with patients' questions and attitudes that are shaped by the health stories they read in media. Policymakers also learn about health news via journalistic outlets, which can influence how lawmakers develop and make policies that affect you and me. Hot-button policy issues, such as whether abortion should be banned after 20 weeks of pregnancy or whether organizations can opt out of providing health insurance coverage for contraception—whether or not their objections are based on religious affiliation—are issues that have relevance for our entire population.[8]

Most health journalists have not practiced medicine, but they commonly translate complex medical information to make it understandable to average readers.

▶ WHAT IS HEALTH PROMOTION?

There are many opportunities to work in health promotion. Strategic communicators can work for private companies (e.g., Kraft Foods, The Coca-Cola Co., McDonald's Corp., hospitals, insurance companies), policy institutes (e.g., Aspen Institute, Cato Institute), think tanks and local, state or federal governments. Sometimes it's not easy to see the work of strategic communication professionals until something goes wrong. For instance, in October 2014, when Texas Health Presbyterian Hospital in Dallas faced criticism for its treatment of its employees and Ebola patient Thomas Eric Duncan, the hospital hired the public relations agency Burson-Marsteller to help the hospital with its media relations and image repair.

While strategic communicators who do health promotion may work in many con-texts, they share common goals and know-how, and use similar techniques. They understand public opinion and risk communication; they build strategies for influenc-ing health knowledge, information, and behaviors and they engage in campaigns to change health environments.

Let's look at an example. Research shows that most Americans consume too much salt and that salt is linked to high blood pressure, which is bad for your heart and can ultimately lead to stroke (rupture or blockage of a blood vessel). Strategic communica-tors for health advocates can focus on changing the food environments in restaurants to address high blood pressure. One strategy has been to inform people about how much salt goes into their food, so they can make better choices. Evaluation of this strategy shows that some people, when told the amount of salt that goes into their food, will make better health decisions, but others do not. For instance, one evaluation of a nutritional menu-labeling program in Philadelphia showed that menu labeling primarily benefits the choices of the more highly educated and well-to-do consumers.[9] Why doesn't menu-labeling work for everyone? Some researchers say that restaurants don't promote healthful appetizers or entrées as much as they do unhealthful items. Others say people don't go out to eat to eat healthy food. Of course, item price, taste and appearance make a difference, too! What is crucial for you to understand is that these findings underscore the complexity of health and why single efforts and research studies are rarely final. (If you decide to take a snack break at this point in the chapter, we recommend celery with peanut butter, an apple or perhaps some cheese.)

▶ IMPROVING NEWS COVERAGE AND COMMUNICATION ABOUT HEALTH DISPARITIES

Now we're getting to the bare bones. When you're putting information together to write stories or communicate about health issues, our research[10] has shown that journalists rank these story elements, in order of importance, as helpful: (1) voices of medical experts, (2) definitions/rewording of technical terms/conversational tone, (3) data and statistics, (4) a narrative element/real-person story, (5) mobilizing information/contact information, (6) photos/infographics/illustrations, (7) added context and (8) metaphors/analogies/anecdotes.

When you work with each of these elements, remember how context, complexity, voices, authenticity and proportionality can each shape the strength of your message. While a message might feel right to you because it comes from your worldview and your experiences, stop and ask yourself: Does this message have context so that people who are from outside of this situation can understand it? Does it have complexity in the types of people it is representing? Does it have a multitude of voices? Do those voices have authenticity to make them real and believable to your audience? Is the tone in the message proportional to the potential health risk? Running through those questions and being honest with yourself about the answers can strengthen your message.

1. *Medical experts* are researchers, doctors who see patients, directors of medical associations, and the list goes on. Whenever possible, look for a diversity of voices, including female and male experts, doctors and specialists who work in different communities with people of varying ages, doctors of different races and ethnicities and, if appropriate for the outlet, search for sources from outside your ZIP code. Medical experts can be invaluable because they (a) have knowledge from their experience with the topic, (b) explain medical information to patients and other people regularly and (c) their credentials lend credibility to your message.

That said, not all medical experts provide good, story-size quotes. It never hurts to directly communicate your needs, "Hi Dr. Perotti, I'm writing a story about suicide prevention and how friends and family can help loved ones who have talked about suicide. Can you explain it to me as if you were telling a 16-year-old?" As the storyteller, take charge and ensure that your source is providing information your reader can use. Also, make sure *you* understand the information, or you're not going to be good at explaining it to your audience. Always check back with your source to make sure you've understood and communicated the information correctly *before* anyone else sees it.

2. We can improve our health stories if we ensure that we *define technical terms* for our readers. For instance, we cannot assume our readers know what human chorionic gonadotropin is (tip: it's the hormone that pregnancy tests measure), or that hypertension is the same thing as high blood pressure. It is good to avoid medical jargon and unfamiliar acronyms, too (e.g., capital letters that represent a series of words: BMI = body mass index). Including jargon can lead readers to feel left out, believing that the conversation is reserved solely for health professionals.

3. *Using data and statistics* can be tricky, and, to use them correctly, we need to know what they mean. What is problematic with using health risk statistics is that, while accurate, they do tend to identify groups that are winners and losers.

Data from the American Heart Association and American Stroke Association 2014 Fact Sheet shows us that our chances of having high blood pressure increases as we age (i.e., older artery walls get weaker with use). Further, its data show that on average there are 18.8 deaths per 100,000 people attributable to high blood pressure. But if we look at it by racial category, the death rate for black males is 50.2 per 100,000, and it is 37.1 per 100,000 for black females.

Note that these health risk data simply represent averages. They don't help us understand why this trend exists in individuals. As communicators we need to understand what leads to this inequality. In the past, communicators might perceive the cause of inequality as primarily influenced by an individual's behavior. While a person's behavior can certainly lead to different outcomes, the more we learn from science, the more we understand that genetics, life stress, income, quality of health care, education level, perceptions of fatalism and doctor–patient interactions, individually or in combination, contribute to an individual's health outcomes. As a strategic communicator, journalist or storyteller, you will communicate better if you remember the complexity involved in health issues and understand and explain the *why* behind statistics and health information.

When we write stories about these statistics, we must be careful about the perception and effect these statistics have on the reader. It almost sounds like political horserace coverage. Who's ahead in the polls? Is it "my people"? Once a white student told me he was upset when, discussing the terms majority and minority, I pointed out that whites are no longer a racial majority in many U.S. cities. I was simply stating a fact. It is a fact.

However, it bothered the student, and he couldn't tell me why, except it felt offensive. No one likes to feel like they are being diminished—even if that's *not* the intent—and even though it does not really diminish any one person in a real way. The thing is, you can't tell people how to feel. And people don't want to feel like they're losing. So what do you do when you still need to accurately report on the facts? You need to provide context, offer voices and perspectives and, when possible, provide mobilizing information (read on for more on this).

4. In health stories, we, as communicators, like to include the voices of *real people*—the narrative or human element. As our research points out,[11] narratives draw reader interest and put a human face on a health problem. There are problems with this though, and you need to consider proportionality—one person's experience may not represent the "common experience" and may contradict peer-reviewed medical data (research conducted by medical experts that has been examined by other medical experts and determined to meet quality standards). For example, if you write about an individual's negative experience with the HPV (human papillomavirus) vaccine, and research shows that a few people have had an adverse effect from the vaccine, this is misleading since most people do not have adverse effects. It is unethical and can persuade readers to skip the vaccine (which can leave unvaccinated individuals open to becoming infected with life-threatening forms of oral or cervical cancer). It can also affect policy, as legislators might believe the cherry-picked individual anecdote and stop covering the cost of the vaccines for teenagers. The take-home point is, be very careful with real-people stories because they are persuasive and have the power to be sensationalist. Adding context to a personal story is a good way to be responsible.

Let's look at another example of how one person's story may be perceived as representing that of a group. Writing a story about U.S. health inequalities among Native Americans and the general U.S. population requires the audience to know that if a Native American belongs to a tribe and lives on a reservation, she may get her health care from the Indian Health Service. (You will want to research the Indian Health Service.) However, the vast majority of Native Americans do not live on reservations and may have other health care challenges. Moreover, Native Americans show up so little in the news, readers may not realize that there more than 500 Native American tribes. Comparing the culture and experience of someone living on the Cheyenne River Sioux reservation in South Dakota to someone living at the Tohono O'odham Nation in Arizona would be like comparing someone who lived in Canada to someone living in Belize. The context, complexity and proportionality that go with the personal examples need explanation.

In 1997, Anne Fadiman wrote an excellent journalistic book (we recommend it): *The Spirit Catches You and You Fall Down*, about how a Hmong family in California interacted with the U.S. health care system. Her book points out the cultural chasms between the ways medicine is practiced in the U.S. and how that can interact with people's cultural and religious beliefs. This book excerpt shows how cultural differences can lead to poorer health outcomes:

> When doctors conferred with a Hmong family, it was tempting to address the reassuringly Americanized teenaged girl who wore lipstick and spoke English rather than the old man who squatted silently in the corner. Yet failing to work within the traditional Hmong hierarchy, in which males ranked higher than females and old people higher than young ones, not only insulted the entire family but also yielded confused results, since the crucial questions had not been directed toward those who had the power to make decisions.[12]

While Anne Fadiman had 341 pages to examine the cultural interplay among U.S. doctors and one family, and you may not have that much story space, you should be aware of how culture affects the individuals you highlight in your stories. Fadiman's award-winning book was originally planned as a three-part article in the *New Yorker*, so you never know where a good story will take you.

5. While some journalists believe that giving people information to act on, i.e. *mobilizing information*, crosses an ethical line from providing information to inciting action, health stories often offer some form of "how to." This could include instructing readers how to find more information, whom to consult for help ("call your doctor") or what to do to change a health behavior ("tips and advice"). If a story you write has bad advice, however, then you are partly responsible for what comes of it, so you can see why some journalists avoid it.

The best bet for giving responsible mobilizing information is to provide your audience with credible, well-researched sources for more information. There are new health discoveries all the time, so something that seems like good advice today ("drink 64 ounces of water!") could become tomorrow's bloodletting by leeches. Giving advice, especially to a mass audience of people with diverse backgrounds and medical histories, is difficult and potentially dangerous. Providing information so readers can go to credible, free health clinics or visit government websites—or suggesting questions for readers to ask their health professional—are probably safer options.

6. Images and graphics are possibly the most powerful tools communicators have to communicate important details of their story. This is why journalists should consider the role *photos, illustrations and infographics* can play in the story from its inception. Photos can also instantly communicate details about a person's race, gender, age, socio-economic status and able-bodiedness. For as much as we know about how important images are, there are as many questions about why some images trigger certain reactions from viewers, and journalists should consider the possible effects visuals have

and how well they may contribute or detract from your story. The Rudd Center for Food Policy and Obesity found that images of obese people can further stigmatize people who are overweight.[13] How you choose visuals to communicate can have consequences.

One familiar example of a health-based infographic is the food pyramid, which was designed to teach people healthy eating habits. In 2011, the government replaced the food pyramid with an infographic of a dinner plate identifying portion sizes for grains, protein, vegetables, etc. The food plate is intended to give people an idea of what to put on their plates, whereas the food pyramid was confusing and not as easy to apply to everyday life.

7. *Adding context* to a story is one way for writers to let audiences in on how to determine how reliable the information is. For example, if you explain that a research study was conducted on 30 rats instead of 30,000 human participants, then your reader has a better shot at evaluating the quality of the study.

Although it might seem perfectly logical to cover health inequalities to give context, a focus on how certain groups are doing worse than other groups along fault lines can have surprising consequences on the audience. For example, one study[14] found that reading stories focusing on how poorly African-Americans are doing with regard to colorectal cancer diagnosis and survival rates—as opposed to stories about how African-Americans have made progress against the disease—caused black adults to be less likely to get screened for cancer. In other words, bad news can cultivate bad health behaviors—perhaps with audience members thinking that any change is pointless given the tide working against them.

By the same token, if journalists do not cover health inequalities (out of concern for audience members in the affected group), this could be considered untruthful and could possibly affect policy decisions. For example, if a governor reads that health inequalities across racial groups is not a problem in her state, she might be less likely to prioritize funding for health among disenfranchised people. The same goes for citizens. If the public isn't properly informed about health inequalities, it could affect the way people vote and their support for policies and politicians.

What to do? When relaying this type of information, it could be helpful to think about whom your audience is and to whom you are writing. If you are a journalist and the information is relayed to African-Americans, you can ensure that while the statistics may sound discouraging, you can also include mobilizing information and identify steps that can be made to improve the numbers. As strategic communicators, we have specialized media channels and can send policy makers and decision-makers specific policy issue briefs, or send mobilizing messages specifically to ethnic media.

8. Medicine is a technical field with many subspecialties. Just as you wouldn't expect everyone to understand concepts and processes from aerospace engineering, neither should you expect that with the field of medicine. This is where *metaphors and*

analogies can really help people grasp how to understand something. For example, fever is to disease as firefighters are to a fire—fever is the response to the disease, not the disease itself. Doctors use metaphors all of the time to communicate with patients. Some metaphors become so commonplace that they lose meaning. Can you think of a cancer patient without war metaphors springing to mind, such as: warrior, battling or fighting cancer and in the end surviving or succumbing? Metaphors, while useful, are not *always* helpful.

One risk of using metaphors is that they can oversimplify a complex problem. Also, metaphors are culturally dependent. For example, in the previous example, for some audiences the idea of having the firefighter respond (as a fever responds to a disease) could be unduly alarming. A metaphor that makes sense to you might not resonate for someone with a different background.

BOX 12.1   From the Field: Health Inequality in an International Context

Dawn Fallik (Missouri School of Journalism, MA, 1999) is an award-winning medical and science reporter specializing in database analysis. She worked for the Associated Press and the *Philadelphia Inquirer* as a staff writer before joining the University of Delaware faculty in 2007. She was a visiting professor at the University of Kansas and also freelances for *Al-Jazeera America*, the *Wall Street Journal* and the *New Republic*.

Dawn Fallik

MY EXPERIENCE IN POST-TSUNAMI INDIA

In India, medical scrubs are often hung out to dry in the sun, dust is everywhere and surgeons operate in flip-flops.

When the Indian Ocean tsunami hit the day after Christmas, I was a medical reporter at the *Philadelphia Inquirer*. Millions were affected and I knew we'd be sending someone to cover the tragedy and its aftermath.

(Continued)

BOX 12.1 Continued

I teamed up with two local doctors who were heading back to India to help where they could. Dr. Manju Balasubramanian, a pathologist, and her husband, Dr. E. "Bala" Balasubramanian, an orthopedic surgeon, were from Chennai and they still had their license to practice in India.

I followed them for almost a month, starting up north at a charity hospital, and then down to Chennai and then Nagapattinam, where the tsunami had slammed into fishing villages.

For the most part, we were too late. The bodies of the dead had been burned and most of those left needed mental, not medical, assistance. At one clinic, the most common ailment was nightmares.

As we traveled farther south into the tsunami zone and into rural clinics, the Balas felt helpless and frustrated. An orthopedic surgeon can't do much to help a family whose child wakes up screaming at night. Despite millions of dollars in giving, I didn't see a single U.S. aid group anywhere.

Traveling through India's medical system was a world away from the U.S. system. There were no HIPAA (i.e., patient privacy protection) forms here. I was allowed into surgery without question. I came along with the doctor's visits. The very concept of privacy wasn't even brought up with patients or with doctors, unless the U.S. doctors I was with mentioned it.

In Philadelphia, I often had to fight hospitals to get any sort of access—even a simple story about a new hospital food system required a week of wrangling to get a patient to talk about their roast beef dinner (true story).

That expectation of privacy—that your health records will remain between you and your medical team—exists across the board in the U.S. It exists because of federal law, whether the patient is at a rural health clinic in Georgia or in Beyoncé's birthing suite in New York.

There was none of that in India.

And maybe it's good for reporters to have to fight to see what's happening in the medical world.

Don't let the fight get in the way of reporting on conditions in the medical world, whether it's checking out emergency room crowds or not taking a "no" for electronic records that should be public.

If a person is in a medical situation where their dignity or rights are compromised, remember to extend the same kind of respect to them as you would expect to have yourself. Be honest about what you're looking for, and tell them why sharing their story—with integrity and compassion, not exploitation—could help other people in the same situation.

▶ SPECIAL CONSIDERATIONS WHEN REPORTING ON THE CAUSES OF HEALTH DISPARITIES

Techniques

It is difficult to understand, much less explain, how various issues outside of a person's control can affect their health. These issues are called "social determinants of health," but some audience members would consider this jargon. The Robert Wood Johnson (RWJ) Foundation released a helpful report about how to talk about these issues.[15] For example, the Foundation provides statements like "All Americans should have the opportunity to make the choices that allow them to live a long, healthy life, regardless of their income, education or ethnic background," or "Health starts—long before illness—in our homes, schools and jobs." Not only do these statements focus on the solution, they reflect values that are common in American society.

Another great tip from the RWJ Foundation is to redefine "them" as "us." This can be accomplished in a number of ways. Instead of "impoverished people" try "Americans who are struggling to get by." Instead of "the elderly," say "our aging parents and grandparents." Instead of "the uninsured," say "people who can't afford to see a doctor when they are sick." Instead of "low-income workers," say "people who work for a living and can't pay the rent." There are many ways to help people understand that more opportunities for better health across the population improves society and the country's ability to be a global leader in public health.

How to Be Responsible

It is essential to cover causes of health inequalities that are beyond an individual's control. This is true even in cases when we commonly blame a person for his or her own "bad" behavior (think drug addiction).

Avoid defining a person by his or her health condition. For example, instead of describing someone as *an epileptic*, or *a morbidly obese man*, or *a schizophrenic woman*, or *an alcoholic*, go with "a person with epilepsy/morbid obesity/schizophrenia/alcoholism." This helps your audience understand that there is an actual person behind the illness.

Also, don't exaggerate the likelihood that your audience is going to encounter this health problem. A clickbait headline like "You'll Never Believe How This Mom-of-Three Got Brain Cancer" makes the reader feel an elevated risk of developing cancer, which is irresponsible journalism. The best strategy is to give examples of people's stories to represent actual risk, including examples of people who do not have sensational stories. Speaking of sensationalism. . .

Gary Schwitzer's blog healthnewsreviews.org lists seven words health journalists should *never use.* They include cure, miracle, breakthrough, promising, dramatic, hope and victim. Many of these words are problematic because they mislead, manipulate the emotions of the reader or try to increase the sense of scientific certainty about a health finding.

Regarding suicide and mental illnesses,[16] there are many ways to reduce stigma and to avoid sensationalism. For example, some stories about mental illness focus on how people with mental illness are a menace to society and dangerous to those around them. If you are confronting a story like that, ask whether mental illness history is relevant to the story. Most of the time we don't know whether a person's history with mental illness has anything to do with the reported violence, but so many are eager to look for solutions and something to blame. With suicide reporting, the stakes are even higher because research has shown news coverage on suicide can lead to a copycat effect. Do not show pictures of grieving family members or describe suicide as a result of a single incident. Both of these can romanticize suicide and mislead people about the long and painful battle that the person who died from suicide faced. If possible, do not report the method of suicide or use the word "suicide" in the headline. Finally, this is a place where mobilizing information (see section 5) is crucial—a phone number for a suicide prevention or crisis intervention line could save the life of someone reading your work.

 BOX 12.2   From the Field: Q&A with Patricia Thomas

Patricia Thomas Knight, Chair in Health and Medical Journalism, Grady College, University of Georgia

Q: *In your experience, what do students find the most challenging in writing about health inequalities?*

A: Students who have grown up in the middle class are often uncomfortable interviewing people who are going through a bad time or who are living in poverty. Faced with people who don't have enough to eat, who live in substandard housing or who have serious health problems but can't obtain needed care or treatments, some young reporters are too flustered to engage. They worry

(Continued)

BOX 12.2 Continued

about sounding condescending. Or their impulse to fix things supersedes their desire to learn more about the situation.

At the same time, there may be students in our journalism classes who grew up in poverty and who are the first in their families to make it to college. And these students often remain silent when classmates voice their discomfort.

Q: *How can students prepare to meet those challenges?*

A: Before students do their first interviews for my health journalism courses, we view the first episode of the TV series *Unnatural Causes*, the segment called "Is inequality making us sick?" It summarizes decades of research on how structural and social factors, as well as individual choices, shape health status and outcomes. It also shows how different the U.S. is from other industrialized nations, because we are the only one without universal health care. Discussion of these issues, using the TV show as a jumping off point, helps put all students on a similar footing, regardless of personal history. I also introduce students to news and feature stories that incorporate information from the Dartmouth Atlas, a database showing dramatic regional variations in Medicare spending. The point is to equip them with two big ideas: First, you can't write about health without writing about wealth. Second, where you live may determine the amount and quality of care you receive.

I hope this conceptual grounding will help them do better interviews. I'm big on the Golden Rule. Treat people with respect. Don't undermine their dignity. Know that the reporter's most important tools are curiosity and empathy. The latter does not mean trying to save people; it does mean being able to see the world through their eyes.

Q: *What do you do if you feel the person you're going to interview may be unreceptive or even hostile to your questions?*

A: If you need to ask a question so confrontational that you're afraid the source may stop talking and throw you off his/her property, distance yourself from it. "I hate to ask this, but some people (or the district attorney or the NAACP) say that you knew the working conditions were dangerous but you did nothing (or falsified your results or charged people a fortune for snake oil)." Framing the question so that it seems to originate with someone not in the room can be very helpful. When talking to families living in dire straits, reporters can use a similar strategy: "I'll bet most of my readers have no idea

(Continued)

BOX 12.2 Continued

> how to keep children safe in such a situation: can you help me explain this so they'll understand?" I'm a big believer in open-ended questions like "Where do you turn for help when you (or your child) are sick or hurt?" The ability to wait for answers is key.

► CONSIDERATIONS FOR TAILORING A HEALTH CAMPAIGN

Just as do journalists, strategic communicators can use many writing techniques for explaining health information. What students need to know is, how do I put together a health communication campaign? As other classes will also teach you, strategic communication campaigns contain research, the setting of goals and objectives, development of strategy, and evaluation.

We begin with *research*. In public relations firms and advertising agencies, you may get your research from the research department, your account planners or your client. If you work in a company or organization, you may have to generate your own research. As you know, you can't communicate about electronic health records, Ebola or high blood pressure unless you have a thorough understanding of the issue yourself. This is how a journalist's job and that of a strategic communicator are similar. You have to study up: read past news stories on the topic, visit nonprofit association "fact sheet" sections, search PubMed.gov for the latest research articles or scour the Institute of Medicine's website for reports about the current medical consensus on the topic.

Remember, our research already has shown us that black Americans have greater death rates from high blood pressure than the general population. Based on what you have learned, you must shape your communication *goals* and *objectives*. Your goal may be to reduce health inequalities related to deaths attributed to high blood pressure. Further, your objective might be stated as "To reduce the disparity in death rates attributable to high blood pressure by 10% (*measureable outcome*) among black males (*audience*) in the South (*specific location/media market*) in the next two years (*time frame*)." Now you've got an informed direction—a specific task to complete.

Next, you must determine your *strategy*. Who is your *audience*? You may say, "Duh," the audience has been identified, and we want to talk with black males, probably older than 50. Not so fast. Yes, this group is a priority public, but to reach this group you may have to communicate with other people. Scientific studies[17] show that low-income African-Americans with poor adherence to blood pressure medicine (i.e., taking it as prescribed) perceive that their physicians do not communicate well with them. This may suggest that medical students and physicians practicing in clinics that serve low-income patients in the South should be a primary audience. You may want physicians to talk to their patients about high blood pressure in new ways, identify cases where patients are not managing their blood pressures and help physicians provide patients a plan and dispel their concerns about medications. Thus, your strategy may be to improve physician-patient communication. Of course, this isn't the only strategy you might choose.

After you've decided who the audience is, you have to help plan the *messages*. With regard to the physicians, you will need to think about how you can convince physicians to fit this communication into their already busy schedules. Then you have to plan for the *key messages* that should be included in physician communication to patients. Research can help explain patient attitudes and inform your message. What messages will be effective in changing audience opinions and behaviors?

Next, you must decide how you will convey or *execute* the messages. Will physicians hand patients a checklist card to keep in their wallets? Is it better that you create an app for the patient's smartphone? How will you reach men in the community with high blood pressure? Again, research must be used to inform you of where you can best reach your audience.

The final step in any strategic communication campaign is to *evaluate* whether you have met your goals and objectives. As the original objective you've set for your campaign is based on change within two years, you will want to build in benchmarks along the way to determine whether the disparities in death rates are reduced.

The case study Box 12.3 here explains how FleishmanHillard reached Iowa teens, a demographic requiring specialized information, with information about teen sexual health.

 BOX 12.3   Campaign Focus: Talking Sex Together (TxT)

As a strategic communication professional, one career choice is to specialize in health communication. FleishmanHillard (FH) is a leading communications agency, headquartered in St. Louis, which works for a variety of clients and offers client service in the health care practice area. In 2008, its Kansas City office was hired by the Iowa Department of Human Services and Eyes Open Iowa, a non-profit organization, committed to improving teen sexual health. The group's communication goal was to increase pregnancy prevention awareness among Iowa teens, ages

(Continued)

BOX 12.3 Continued

12–19. As teens spend an average of 70 minutes daily texting on their cell phones, FH helped develop an edgy campaign—Talking Sex Together (TxT)—to answer teen questions about sex and pregnancy. FH and its partners were determined to surpass the traditional "Birds and Bees" discussions by creating a campaign that uses social networks, online channels and text messaging to answer the questions teens have on their minds. Preventing unintended pregnancies has positive benefits for young people. Teens who have unplanned pregnancies in high school are less likely than other teens to graduate. Not graduating from high school can negatively affect the ability to get a good job, and that can affect one's future earnings.

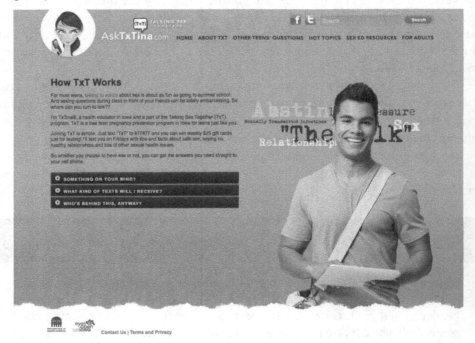

FIGURE 12.4 The Txt website.
Courtesy of Eyes Wide Open Iowa and FleishmanHillard

The campaign has evolved over the years, but essentially invites teens to opt-in to receive weekly text messages about safer sex and abstinence and have the

(Continued)

BOX 12.3 Continued

option of participating in a live text message hotline twice a month. The weekly text messages include facts, quizzes and polls with incentives to win cash prizes to encourage participation. For example, "When used correctly, the pill is 99% effective? A. True, B. False. What do U think? Txt 4 UR chance to win $25!" In addition, during the two-hour hotline, participants can text questions to a trained sexual-health educator and receive real-time responses. This unique text messaging strategy allows Eyes Open Iowa to deliver sensitive sexual health messages to teens via a channel they trust, in an anonymous, confidential and safe environment.

Also, Eyes Open Iowa grantees help in promoting the program locally, gaining support from high schools and organizations for the campaign and an incentive program. Radio public service announcements (PSA), a Facebook page and campaign materials help keep the campaign fresh in teen's minds. While teen pregnancy rates have been declining nationally, teen pregnancy rates in Iowa are greater among African-American and Hispanic teens. Campaign materials were developed to specifically reach these teens and their parents through culturally relevant means.

 BOX 12.4   From the Field: Q&A with Mary Heinrich

Q: *What aspect of the TxT campaign are you most proud of?*

A: It's a pretty novel and cutting-edge campaign. We were able to successfully pull off providing teens access to quality sexual health information in an anonymous way. We used channels that young people know and trust. Each year we have increased the reach of the campaign. Initially, in the first year, we were reaching 1,000 teens and it has now increased to more than 4,200 teens. We also implemented a hotline every other Friday, which receives about 100 calls each session.

Q: *Was the campaign group concerned that some teens may not have access to the program because of the cost of text messages?*

A: When we first began the campaign, we did a lot of research, and initially we decided to send one text per week. We found that teens in low-income households were more likely to have a phone with texting capabilities than they were a computer. Today, many plans now offer much better text

(Continued)

BOX 12.4   Continued

Mary Heinrich, senior vice president, FleishmanHillard, Kansas City

rates, and the number of teens that have and are engaged with using their phones has increased dramatically. Now text messaging has proven to be a low-cost way to reach teens.

Q: *Are there any special considerations you must take into account in reaching diverse audiences?*

A: When conducting campaigns, a basic strategy is to go where the audience is. You would have to do an audit and see what the community resources are and where information access-points are located. If you're trying to reach African-American audiences in urban core areas, sometimes a TV commercial isn't the way to go. You may find going into churches to be more effective. If you want to reach audiences in rural areas, radio and movie theater ads may be the way to go.

Q: *If you choose to use text messaging in a campaign, do you need to know the technology?*

A: As a communicator the most important thing is to craft the message. For the TxT campaign it was about conveying sexual health messages in a way that was teen friendly and would resonate with their experiences. You'll have a coder in the IT department 99 percent of the time who manages and loads all the messages you create.

Q: *Why did you choose to go into health communication?*

A: I started out as a pre-med major and I became interested because I saw that there was so much misinformation out there. As a communicator, I really enjoy distilling health information into lay terms so it's easier for people to understand. I am motivated to make a difference by using public relations to impact people's health behaviors in a positive way—it can make a difference.

▶ **CHAPTER SUMMARY**

In this chapter, you have learned that there are many factors that contribute to health inequalities, and that many of these factors are out of an individual's control. By understanding the complexity that underlies health stories (and we didn't even touch on the intricacies of health insurance, the Indian Health Service or Veteran's Affairs

Administration), you are in a good position to identify the context and voices you will need to tell good stories. Although we have given you a checklist of factors that can help you communicate more effectively with readers and target audiences, perhaps the most critical elements you need for excellent communication are inquisitiveness and the ability to identify with the situations of others who may not be like you. Everyone benefits from good health. Good health is a common desire.

▶ LITERACY AND NUMERACY QUIZ

True or false:

1. People who have low health-literacy have a low IQ. (*False, health literacy can affect people who are highly intelligent.*)

2. People can be low health-literate in one area of medicine and high health-literate in another area. (*True, someone can know a lot about diabetes but may know nothing about skin diseases or heart disease.*)

3. If you have a 1 in 80 risk for getting a disease, you have more of a chance than if your risk is 1 in 40. (*False, but many people with low health literacy see the higher number (80) and connect it with greater risk.*)

4. Health literacy includes the ability to understand numbers AND the ability to make decisions on health information. (*True*)

▶ SUGGESTED ACTIVITIES

1. *Langston gets embarrassed when he can't breathe. When his mom has to pull out the breathing machine from under the bleachers at little league, and everyone stops to watch, Langston, is mortified. On days when the smog is especially bad in Dallas, this 8-year-old skips games, since he can't breathe at home anyway. Of course, not being able to breathe is not as bad as going to the emergency room—and dealing with the bills that follow. Medications, hospital bills and stress seem to pile up on this African-American working-class family, but Langston is not alone. African-American children are more likely to get asthma.*

   Take the case described above—it seems like the writer hit on lots of important details, but there are landmines lurking. Is there enough room to provide background and context of asthma? Will the story discourage African-Americans from seeking asthma treatment? Can readers of the story understand how there are many factors that influence this boy's health? What do you need to know to approach this topic well?

2. Domestic abuse is a public health issue. Proportionally, Native American women are more likely to be victims of domestic abuse. What information do you need to know to be able to write an accurate story about this issue? How will you narrow your story and provide context?

3. Look up the following medical article at your library. H. K. Seligman and D. Schillinger, "Hunger and Socioeconomic Disparities in Chronic Disease," *The New England Journal of Medicine* 363, no. 1 (2010): 6–9. Read the short article. What did the authors say was a cause of obesity? What type of story could you write about this?

▶ NOTES

1 Shun Zhang et al., "Racial Disparities in Economic and Clinical Outcomes of Pregnancy among Medicaid Recipients," *Maternal and Child Health Journal* 17, no. 8 (2013): 1518–25, doi: 10.1007/s10995–012–1162–0; Carter M. Owen, Ellen H. Goldstein, Janine A. Clayton and James H. Segars, "Racial and Ethnic Health Disparities in Reproductive Medicine: An Evidence-Based Overview," *Semin Reprod Med* 31, no. 5 (2013): 317–24, doi: 10.1055/s-0033–1348889.

2 J. K. Benz, O. Espinosa, V. Welsh and A. Fontes, "Awareness of Racial and Ethnic Health Disparities has Improved Only Modestly Over a Decade," *Health Affairs* 30, no. 10 (2011): 1860–1867.

3 R. Davidson, J. Kitzinger and K. Hunt, "The Wealthy get Healthy, the Poor get Poorly? Lay Perceptions of Health Inequalities," *Social Science & Medicine* 62, no. 9 (2006): 2171–2182; S. A. Robert and B. C. Booske, "US Opinions on Health Determinants and Social Policy as Health Policy," *American Journal of Public Health* 101, no. 9 (2011): 1655–1663.

4 Cabral A. Bigman, Social Comparison Framing in Health News and its Effect on Perceptions of Group Risk. *Health Communication* 29, no. 3 (2013): 1–14.

5 S. E. Geller, A. Koch, B. Pellettieri and M. Carnes, "Inclusion, Analysis, and Reporting of Sex and Race/Ethnicity in Clinical Trials: Have We Made Progress?" *J Womens Health (Larchmt)* 20, no. 3 (2011): 315–320.

6 N. Kristof, "Where's the empathy?" *The New York Times*, January 24, 2015.

7 N. E. Adler et al., "Reaching for a Healthier Life," The John D. and Catherine T. MacArthur Foundation Research Network on Socioeconomic Status and Health, San Francisco, CA, 2007.

8 N. Martin, "7 Reproductive Rights Issues to Watch in 2015," *ProPublica*, February 4, 2015, Http://www.propublica.org/article/7-reproductive-rights-issues-to-watch-in-2015#.

9 Amy H. Auchincloss et al., "Customer Responses to Mandatory Menu Labeling at Full-Service Restaurants," *American Journal of Preventive Medicine* 45, no. 6 (2013): 710–19, doi: http://dx.doi.org/10.1016/j.amepre.2013.07.014.

10 Amanda Hinnant and María E. Len-Ríos, "Tacit Understandings of Health Literacy: Interview and Survey Research with Health Journalists," *Science Communication* 31, no. 1 (2009): 84–115.

11 Amanda Hinnant, María E. Len-Ríos and Rachel Young, "Journalistic Use of Exemplar to Humanize Health News," *Journalism Studies* 14, no. 4 (2013): 539–54, doi: 10.1080/1461670X.2012.721633.

12 Anne Fadiman, The Spirit Catches You and You Fall Down: A Hmong Child, Her American Doctors and the Collision of Two Cultures. New York: Farrar, Straus, and Giroux, 1998.

13 C. A. Heuer, K. J. McClure and R. M. Puhl, "Obesity Stigma in Online News: A Visual Content Analysis," *Health Communication* 16 (2011): 976–987.

14 Robert A. Nicholson et al., "Unintended Effects of Emphasizing Disparities in Cancer Communication to African-Americans," *Cancer Epidemiology, Biomarkers & Prevention* 17, no. 11 (2008): 2946–53.

15 "A New Way to Talk about the Social Determinants of Health," Robert Wood Johnson Foundation, 2010, http://www.rwjf.org/content/dam/farm/reports/reports/2010/rwjf63023.

16 http://depts.washington.edu/mhreport/index.php.

17 A. Schoenthaler et al., "Provider Communication Affects Medication Adherence in Hypertensive African Americans," *Patient Education and Counseling* 75, no. 2 (2009): 185–191, doi: http://dx.doi.org/10.1016/j.pec.2008.09.018.

▶ ADDITIONAL READINGS

Berzon, Alexandra. "Pace Is New Peril: Amid Pressure to Finish Massive Projects, 9 Men Have Died in 16 Months." *Las Vegas Sun*, March 30, 2008. http://lasvegassun.com/news/2008/mar/30/construction-deaths/.

Bornstein, David. "Protecting Children from Toxic Stress." *The New York Times*, November 3, 2013.

Caburnay, Charlene A., Matthew W. Kreuter, Glen T. Cameron, Douglas A. Luke, Elisia Cohen, Lillie Mcdaniels, Monica Wohlberg and Paul Atkins. "Black Newspapers as a Tool for Cancer Education in African American Communities." *Ethnicity & Disease* 18, no. 4 (2008): 488–95.

Cohen, Elisia L., Charlene A. Caburnay, María E. Len-Ríos, Timothy J. Poor, Glen T. Cameron, Douglas A. Luke, Barbara Powe, Jon Stemmle and Matthew W. Kreuter. "Engaging Ethnic Media to Expand the Reach and Effectiveness of Communication Strategies to Reduce Health Disparities." *Health Communication* 25, no. 6/7 (2010): 569–71. doi: 10.1080/10410236.2010.496717.

Grady, Denise. "Cancer Patients, Lost in a Maze of Uneven Care." *The New York Times*, July 29, 2007. http://www.nytimes.com/2007/07/29/health/29Cancer.html?pagewanted=all.

Hinnant, Amanda, Hyun Jee Oh, Charlene A. Caburnay and Matthew W. Kreuter. "What Makes African American Health Disparities Newsworthy? An Experiment Among Journalists About Story Framing." *Health Education Research* 26, no. 6 (2011): 937–47. doi: 10.1093/her/cyr086.

Institute of Medicine. "Report Brief: U.S. Health in International Perspective: Shorter Lives, Poorer Health." Washington, DC: National Academy of Sciences, 2013.

Institute of Medicine. *Unequal Treatment: Confronting Racial and Ethnic Disparities in Health.* Washington, DC: National Academies Press, 2003.

Hurd, Michael D., Paco Martorell, Adeline Delavande, Kathleen J. Mullen and Kenneth M. Langa. "Monetary Costs of Dementia in the United States." *New England Journal of Medicine* 368, no. 14 (2013): 1326–34. doi: doi:10.1056/NEJMsa1204629.

Kim, Yong-Chan, Meghan B. Moran, Holley A. Wilkin and Sandra J. Ball-Rokeach. "Integrated Connection to Neighborhood Storytelling Network, Education, and Chronic Disease Knowledge among African Americans and Latinos in Los Angeles." *Journal of Health Communication* 16, no. 4 (2011): 393–415. doi: 10.1080/10810730.2010.546483.

Kreuter, Matthew W., Karen Steger-May, Sonal Bobra, Angela Booker, Cheryl L. Holt, Susan N. Lukwago and Celette Sugg Skinner. "Sociocultural Characteristics and Responses to Cancer Education Materials among African American Women." *Cancer Control* 10, no. 5 (2003): 69–80.

Len-Rios, M.E. "The Potential for Communication Scholars to Set Priorities that Curb Health Disparities." *Howard Journal of Communications* 23, no. 2 (2012): 111–18. doi: 10.1080/10646175.2012.667732.

Len-Ríos, María E. "Communication Strategies for Reducing Racial and Cultural Disparities." In *Health Communication in the New Media Landscape*, ed. J. C. Parker and E. Thorson, 41–58. New York: Springer Publishing Company, 2008.

Lundell, Helen, Jeff Niederdeppe and Christopher Clarke. "Public Views About Health Causation, Attributions of Responsibility, and Inequality." *Journal of Health Communication* 18, no. 9 (2013): 1116–30. doi: 10.1080/10810730.2013.768724.

Sullivan, John, Susan Snyder, Kristen A. Graham and Dylan Purcell. "Climate of Violence Stifles City Schools." *Philadelphia Inquirer*, March 27, 2011. http://www.philly.com/philly/news/special_packages/inquirer/school-violence/20110324_SVPart1.html.

Thayer, Zaneta M. and Christopher W. Kuzawa. "Biological Memories of Past Environments: Epigenetic Pathways to Health Disparities." *Epigenetics* 6, no. 7 (2011): 798–803. doi: 10.4161/epi.6.7.16222.

Tough, Paul. "The Poverty Clinic: Can a Stressful Childhood Make You a Sick Adult?" *New Yorker*, March 21, 2011.

Unnatural Causes Documentary. http://www.unnaturalcauses.org/about_the_series.php.

Viswanath, Kasisomayajula and Leland K. Ackerson. "Race, Ethnicity, Language, Social Class, and Health Communication Inequalities: A Nationally-Representative Cross-Sectional Study." *PLoS ONE* 6, no. 1 (2011): 1–8. doi: 10.1371/journal.pone.0014550.

13

Talkin' 'bout My Generation: Understanding Generational Differences

Teri Finneman

Imagine a conversation between Rosa Parks and Tupac. Or how about between Dr. Spock and Beavis and Butthead? Weird, isn't it?

Yet every day, people from the generations who grew up with these icons gather at work to collaborate and communicate toward one goal.

Or at least they try to.

For the first time in the history of the U.S. work force, four generations are working together—and colliding—in the workplace, said Joan Engeseth, manager of corporate training at Noridian in Fargo, ND.

And whether they're veterans, baby boomers, Gen X'ers or Gen Y'ers may make a difference in how they communicate, receive feedback and view authority, she said.

> **LEARNING OBJECTIVES**
>
> By the end of this chapter, students should be able to:
>
> • explain the meaning of "generational differences."
>
> • classify the generations based on their characteristics.
>
> • critique generational stereotypes.
>
> • recognize how generational differences impact journalism.
>
> • apply knowledge about generational differences.

This story from the July 9, 2006, edition of *The Forum of Fargo-Moorhead* [1] illustrates the increasing media attention and public interest in recent years toward understanding and explaining generational differences. As Engeseth points out, the United States is in a unique period of increased age diversity in the workforce. This topic rose in popularity in the mid-2000s when the early members of Generation Y began graduating from college and finding full-time jobs. At the same time, members of the older generations are living longer and are in better health than their predecessors. Therefore, many are choosing to remain working and to stay active well past their 60s. This increased interaction among the generations has attracted attention from researchers, businesses and journalists. As a result, generational differences are an important fault line for you to consider in your work since, as we will discuss throughout this chapter, your age and your experiences growing up also play an important role in how you perceive the world.

You likely have already heard of baby boomers and Generation Y, the generations that tend to get the most publicity. However, are you familiar with the characteristics of the generations? Do you even know who Dr. Spock was? If not, this is a generational difference as members of the older generations would know that Dr. Spock wrote a book about raising children in 1946 that became one of the most popular books in U.S. history. This chapter will help you understand what it means to say someone belongs to a particular generation, as well as explain why an understanding of generational differences is beneficial for you as a future journalist or strategic communicator. This chapter focuses on characteristics of generational differences within the U.S., but keep in mind that there are also generational differences in other countries if you end up pursuing international work.

▶ WHAT IS A GENERATION?

Before we discuss generational differences, it's important to understand what "generation" means. Research on this topic goes back to at least the 1920s and sociologist Karl Mannheim. He viewed a generation as a cohort of people who share "a common location in the social and historical process," which results in this cohort being exposed to "a specific range of potential experiences, predisposing them for a certain characteristic mode of thought and experience."[2] In other words, belonging to a generation means you and others in your age range grew up with similar experiences and events that impacted your perception of the world. Burstein (2013) refers to the "key time in our lives, just when we were in transition and trying to establish our identities."[3] This tends to occur at age 17 but can range between the early teen years to age 25.[4] These are key years for forming generational identity. Mannheim believed that these early impressions "tend to coalesce into a natural view of the world. All later experiences then tend to receive their meaning from this original set."[5] Indeed, collective memory research has found Americans frequently refer back to memories from their teens or early 20s when asked to remember important national or world events.[6]

To put this more simply, we have all heard stories about a grandma who grew up during the Great Depression and who—even 50 years later—refused to put money in the bank and kept it under her mattress instead. This is considered a generational characteristic. Different experiences and events such as these help explain how "each generation has adopted its own personality."[7] We will further explore these personalities shortly.

Because generational categories tend to span between 15 and 20 years (for example, the baby boomers are defined as people born between 1946 and 1964), some people born toward the end of a generation may identify more with the next generation. Others may say they have characteristics of both. These people are referred to as *cuspers* since they are "born on the cusp between two generations."[8] Therefore, there can be blurring lines of generational identity. Mannheim also cautioned against too broad of an interpretation of a generation. For example, teenagers in the United States in 1962 likely would have found little in common with teenagers in North Korea in 1962, even though they grew up during the same time period. Even within the United States, people from different classes, regions, races and genders may have some variation in generational influences. Mannheim noted there needs to be "participation in the common destiny,"[9] or some sharing of common experiences for generational identity to form. Therefore, generational identity is about more than birth years. A generation is also defined by "common tastes [and] attitudes," as well as "news events, music, national catastrophes, heroes and heroic efforts."[10] You will find specific examples of these in the upcoming explanations of each generation.

First, however, it's important to note that researchers such as Zemke, Raines and Filipczak (2000) acknowledge generational characteristics contain stereotypes. Therefore, they emphasize the importance of getting to know individuals, just as you will hear from your professors. However, Zemke, Raines and Filipczak also believe that "knowing generational information is also tremendously valuable; it often explains the baffling and confusing differences behind our unspoken assumptions underneath our attitudes."[11] In other words, the stereotypes at least provide a starting point for further discussion.

Let's now explore the characteristics of each generation and hear what journalists and strategic communicators from around the country have to say about them. Keep in mind the precise birth years defining a generation vary depending upon whom you ask. For this chapter, we used data and statistics from the Pew Research Center. We also provide a generation guide created by *The Forum of Fargo-Moorhead*. This graphic was created in 2006 when members of Generation Y were between ages 6 and 25, but the characteristics outlined for each of the generations still apply. We will discuss later in this chapter that there is disagreement on when Generation Y ends and Generation Z begins.

Traditionalist 61+ years old 1900-1945	Baby Boomers 60-42 years old 1946-1964	Generation Xers 41-26 years old 1965-1980	Gen Y 25-6 years old 1981-2000
Experiences: -Great Depression -Pearl Harbor -WWII -D-Day -FDR dies **People:** -Joe DiMaggio -Joe McCarthy -Bob Hope -FDR **Generational Personality:** -Loyal -Formal -Cooperative -Respect rules -Duty before pleasure -Patriotic -Leaders lead and troops follow **Population today:** ND:19% MN: 16% **Mayo Clinic tips for getting along with traditionalist co-workers:** -Offer them job security -Value their experience -Appreciate their dedication	**Experiences:** -U.S. sends ground troops to Vietnam -Martin Luther King Jr. and Robert Kennedy assassinated -Woodstock **People:** -Martin Luther King Jr. -John F. Kennedy -Captian Kangaroo -The Beatles **Generational Personality:** -Highly cooperative -Optimistic -Idealistic -Started the workaholic trend -Personal growth and gratification -Challenge authority **Population today:** ND: 28% MN: 29% **Mayo Clinic tips for getting along with baby boomer co-workers:** -Show respect -Choose face-to-face conversations -Give them your full attention	**Experiences:** -Roe vs. Wade -John Lennon shot and killed -Space Shuttle Challenger disaster -Fall of the Berlin Wall **People:** -Michael Jordan -Bill Gates -O.J. Simpson -Princess Diana **Generational Personality:** -Skeptical -Independent and self-reliant -Entrepreneurial thinkers -Challenge command -Disagree with "pay your dues" mentality -View lifetime careers with the same employer as unrealistic **Population today:** ND: 18% MN: 20% **Mayo Clinic tips for getting along with Generation X co-workers:** -Get to the point -Don't micromanage them -Lighten up and remind yourself it's OK for work to be fun.	**Experiences:** -Oklahoma City bombing -Clinton/Lewinsky scandal -Columbine High School shooting -Sept. 11 terrorist attacks **People:** -Britney Spears -Tupac Shakur -Barney -Tiger Woods **Generational Personality:** -Realistic -Practical -Well educated -Prefer coaching management style -Technology-savvy -Civic minded -Contributor **Population today:** ND: 29% MN: 29% **Mayo Clinic tips for getting along with Gen Y co-workers:** -Challenge them -Ask their opinion -Provide timely feedback
Motto: "Save for a rainy day."	Motto: "Me generation"	Motto: "Be like Mike"	Motto: "Take the ball and run with it."

Source: Eide Bailly   The Forum

* The state population percentages for each generation are estimates due to how population by age is grouped by the Census. Minnesota information is provided by the State Demographic Center and is based on 2002 projections of the 2005 state population. North Dakota information is provided by the State Data Center and is based on 2002 projections of the 2005 state population.

FIGURE 13.1 Generational Differences.
This graphic originally appeared in *The Forum of Fargo-Moorhead*, July 9, 2006.

Definition: Generational identity is based upon the belief that people form many of their views about the world during their impressionable teenage and early adult years. Therefore, people within the same age range tend to have similar attitudes and behaviors that are related to the major news events, music, fads, trends, heroes, celebrities and economic situation that they experienced while growing up.

▶ THE TRADITIONALISTS

Born: Before 1945
Age in 2014: 69 to 86
Share of adult population: 12 percent
Share non-Hispanic white: 79 percent

The Traditionalist generation is known by several names, including the Veterans, the Greatest Generation, the G.I. Generation and the Silent Generation. For the sake of simplicity, we refer to them as Traditionalists.

As the generational chart notes, this generation is influenced by the Great Depression and World War II. In the early 1930s, Bing Crosby was singing "Brother, Can You Spare a Dime?"—a telling sign of the tough economic times. One woman still vividly remembered 40 years later what it was like to grow up during the war years, noting "the lines you had to go through to get your sugar and coffee and gas stamps."[12] As a result, the Traditionalists are known for being money conscious even decades later since "between two world wars and the Great Depression, this generation had plenty of opportunities to learn to do without. The need to 'save for a rainy day' was tangible."[13] Comedian Bob Hope, baseball player Joe DiMaggio, aviator Charles Lindbergh and radio journalist Edward Murrow were among the influential public figures during this time.[14] However, perhaps the biggest hero was Franklin Roosevelt, who spent 12 years as president and guided the nation through the Depression and World War II. Each generation has key "I remember where I was when . . ." moments. For this generation, those days are when Pearl Harbor was attacked and when Roosevelt died.

This generation was significantly influenced by the military since more than 50 percent of Traditionalist men are veterans.[15] Therefore, Traditionalists are known for their loyalty, hard work, patriotism, respect for authority and "immense amount of faith in institutions from the church to the government to the military."[16] In other words, they believe "leaders need to lead and troops need to follow,"[17] an ideal that guided them to win a war, beat a depression and improve the nation through public works programs. Steinhorn (2006) further explains:

This was a generation that sacrificed their blood, their lives and their futures to defend our country against implacable enemies of freedom. They suffered through the Great Depression without ever losing faith in the promise of America.[18]

Perhaps due to all that they went through, the Traditionalists tend to be "past-oriented and history absorbed."[19] They want to be valued for their experiences and knowledge. At the same time, this generation has faced criticism from future generations for fighting against discrimination and the Nazis abroad but "doing little to oppose racism, sexism and injustice at home."[20]

Former Missouri newspaper owner Jim Sterling is among the members of the Traditionalist generation who believe younger generations don't take into account historical context as much as they should. They judge older generations based on today's standards rather than taking time to understand what life was like when other generations were growing up, he said. "Our fathers and mothers and older family members did lots of things wrong by today's standards, but they were considered OK at the time," he said. Therefore, it's important for journalists to understand the history behind a particular generation or an issue, rather than simply passing judgment, in order to provide more accurate context in their reports.

Traditionalist Carol Loomis, a senior editor at *Fortune* magazine, also said context is important in journalism in order to reach across generations. "The relatively narrow experiences of the different generations leave them oblivious to what other generations take for granted," she said. "So, if a writer hopes to reach a wide audience, he or she had better be aware of what requires special explanation. Only with that kind of care will a story be understood across generations." In other words, don't assume other generations know what Snapchat is any more than you know what Medicare is. Context and explanation in journalism and communication matter.

FOR DISCUSSION

1. As you continue reading the chapter, think about the people you know who belong to each of the generations. Do they fit the stereotypes being discussed or not?
2. Do you think it's worthwhile for you as a future journalist or strategic communicator to learn about the generational stereotypes?

▶ THE BABY BOOMERS

Born: 1946 to 1964
Age in 2014: 50 to 68
Share of adult population: 32 percent
Share non-Hispanic white: 72 percent

If you talk to the baby boomers, they will likely tell you that they should be called the greatest generation. They have spent their entire lives being told they were special. (As has Generation Y, which we will get to later.) Due to the tremendous size and influence of this generation, it's important to understand the boomers.

Following World War II, the United States experienced a baby boom as soldiers returned home after the long war and wanted to regain stability and normalcy through family. The resulting explosion in birth rates meant that "children were, for the first time in history, in the spotlight, representing as they did to veterans the symbols and fruit of their victories and the hopes for the future they fought to preserve."[21] At the same time, "the booming postwar economy gave the United States of the late 1940s, the 1950s and the 1960s a sense that anything was possible."[22] This is the generation that grew up with Martin Luther King Jr. telling them to have a dream and John F. Kennedy challenging them to "Ask not what your country can do for you. Ask what you can do for your country." Add in the United States sending a man to the moon, and there seemed to be no stopping the innovation. This is the generation that fought for civil rights and women's rights while also protesting the Vietnam War and getting groovy at Woodstock. Besides King Jr. and Kennedy, Elvis Presley, Rosa Parks, the Beatles, the Partridge Family, Beaver Cleaver and Captain Kangaroo were notable figures for this generation.[23]

One cannot talk about the baby boomers without talking about television, a medium that transformed the country. Boomers grew up watching history happen in their living rooms in contrast to their parents who came of age in the golden era of radio. Boomers turned on their TVs and saw images that disturbed them, such as "black Americans beaten by police and mauled by attack dogs simply for seeking the same rights as all Americans."[24] They would later watch footage of the Vietnam War. Realizing the country "was not living up to its ideals" proved to be a "motivating force behind boomer activism in the '60s."[25] Therefore, boomers grew up challenging authority, a characteristic in stark contrast to their parents' generation, which was also appalled by the gyrating hips of Elvis and their children's free-love hippie culture that defied moral values.

Because boomers were so different from their parents, they bonded as a group and started the slogan "don't trust anyone over 30."[26] With 76 million members, boomers learned early how to cooperate with others. At the same time, they are competitive due to the fact there are so many of them. Boomers developed the workaholic trend as they worried about losing their jobs to another boomer. You have likely heard the phrase "keeping up with the Joneses." Many of the consumer-oriented boomers felt they had to buy possessions to maintain the same status level as their neighbors.

Glorified as youth, it's not surprising that baby boomers today are "having trouble getting their minds around the idea that they aren't young anymore . . . it's a bummer."[27] By 2030, 1 in 5 Americans will be 65 years or older due in large part to the baby boomers.[28] But if boomers have anything to say about it, they will "never, never grow up [or] grow old" and "intend to be fit, healthy, active, self-indulgent older people."[29] As a result, strategic communication professionals should avoid stressing that a product is geared toward seniors or "older folks" when targeting boomers, said Becky Gillan, senior vice president for AARP's Research Center. "Boomers are ageless, idealistic mold breakers and routinely say 'old age' is 15 years older than they currently are when asked what 'old age' is in surveys," Gillan said. "Marketers need to stress the value and benefits of their products to boomers. Age-defying makeup from L'Oreal comes to mind with the actress Diane Keaton."

Anyone interested in strategic communication should pay special attention to the baby boom generation and stop focusing on only the 18 to 49 demographic, Gillan said. "Why are boomers no longer pursued by many mainstream marketers when the other generations are smaller in size and/or have less buying power?" Gillan said. "There is a certain irony here. The reason the 18–49 demographic became *the* desired target was to reach baby boomers as they bought their way through each decade." AARP tries to demonstrate to advertisers why the 50-and-older market is attractive, pointing to its $2.7 trillion in annual spending, she said. The AARP Research Center frequently researches generational differences by conducting surveys, focus groups, in-depth interviews and ethnography, Gillan said.

Baby boomer newspaper editor Dennis Ellsworth also said print journalists need to understand the differences among the generations to correctly target an audience. Although legacy media try to attract a young audience, the primary readership and viewership skews older, he said. Therefore, the media need to balance coverage to interest different demographics. In-depth stories about later-in-life health care, retirement and financial security resonate with baby boomers and Traditionalists, he said. Journalists may also want to consider a senior living section in print or a noontime news segment on TV that targets this audience, Ellsworth said. Ellsworth, who has spent nearly 30 years as an editor in Wichita, Kansas, west Texas and northwest Missouri, recalled a five-week fellowship at Duke University where he studied the aging population of America and the implications for newspapers. "It was eye-opening to learn more about aging adults," said Ellsworth, who is now executive editor of the *St. Joseph News-Press*, Missouri. "The one takeaway I always will remember is that everyone ages differently, and it is harshly wrong to stereotype everyone as the same, and especially to think of aging as simply being a decline in capabilities and health."

As far as generational differences within the newsroom, Ellsworth said he's noticed different approaches to work among his younger and more experienced employees. The younger journalists tend to put on headphones and tune out the world while working, he said. Reporter/photographer teams from different generations also have differing approaches to sources, Ellsworth said. Senior journalists tend to want to get to know a source personally and spend more time with them while gathering information, whereas younger journalists are in a hurry, he said. "I would guess over time, though, that each generation benefits from being around the other," Ellsworth said.

Former magazine editor Julia Kagan has also observed differences in generationally diverse newsrooms. The baby boomer's background includes working as an editor at *McCall's, Working Woman, Psychology Today, Fitness, Consumer Reports* and *Ladies' Home Journal*. Kagan has noticed that she prefers to speak to employees on the phone or in person, while younger workers prefer electronic messaging to communicate. "I realized the world of the telephone that was so comfortable for me may not be as comfortable to a younger generation," she said. Kagan has also noticed the influence of being a baby boomer in other ways. As a young adult during the second wave of feminism, Kagan said she and her female colleagues felt like their accomplishments had a larger meaning as they proved that working women could succeed. Still, baby boomer women in newsrooms also faced male chauvinism as they sought to reframe roles for women in journalism, she said. "Certainly being part of that generation had a huge influence on me and probably still does," Kagan said.

Although Kagan warns against putting too much emphasis on the stereotypes of each generation, she said it's important to learn about the influences that shape people's lives. "Almost everything that happens has some kind of context: social, historical, demographic. Things don't happen in a vacuum," said Kagan, who now works for the financial website Investopedia. "Certainly it's important to understand where people are coming from when you're talking to them, when you're reporting on them, when you're trying to understand why they did what they did."

FOR DISCUSSION

1. What do you think about the emphasis on creating products and advertisements that make baby boomers feel young?
2. Should companies invest time and money in "age-defying" products like Botox and Viagra?

 BOX 13.1   Are Generational Differences a Myth?

In her 2007 book, *Retiring the Generation Gap*, Jennifer Deal downplays the emphasis on generational differences. "The so-called generation gap is, in large part, the result of miscommunication and misunderstanding, fueled by common insecurities and the desire for clout—which includes control, power, authority and position," she wrote.[30] Deal argues that conflicts in the workplace are more so generated by one group that expects another to follow its rules, particularly the older workers who believe its preferred practices should be followed by younger co-workers. In the United States, the cultural norm is to grant authority to those who are older, not younger, and conflict arises when this dynamic is challenged, she said. In other words, conflict stems from "the natural desire of older people to maintain their clout and the desire for younger people to increase their clout," she said.[31]

Deal discusses a number of the characteristics that have been used to define generational differences and argues the claims don't have merit. For example, she notes older generations complain that younger generations lack values. However, research has found all generations share similar values even though how they

(Continued)

BOX 13.1 Continued

express those values may differ, Deal said. Similarly, all generations want respect but define it in different ways, she said. Deal also addresses the stereotypes that older generations were more loyal to their employers and that the youngest generation places a higher value on workplace coaching. Research has found the older generations weren't more loyal when they were the same age as the younger generations and that workers in every generation want coaching, she said. She argues that there are more differences within members of each generation than there are between generations.

Deal thinks it's time for the concept of the "generation gap" to be retired and advises employers not to worry about it. "You don't have to worry about learning a new set of whims when the next generation comes along," she wrote. "People from different generations are largely alike in what they think, believe and want from their work life."[32]

Talk about it: *What do you think of Deal's argument? Are generational differences a myth? Are people within the Traditionalist Generation, baby boom, Generation X and Generation Y more similar than different? Should journalists still report on generational differences?*

▶ GENERATION X

Born: 1965 to 1980
Age in 2014: 34 to 49
Share of adult population: 27 percent
Share non-Hispanic white: 61 percent

Trying to explain Generation X can be difficult as this generation does not want to be labeled, and, in contrast to the boomers, is a "deeply segmented, fragmented cohort."[33] How did this happen? Well, once again, we look to history and to the influence of the prior generation.

Gen X has been referred to as the "latchkey" generation and is considered "the most attention deprived, neglected group of kids in a long time."[34] Not only were they raised by workaholic parents, but many were children of divorce who bounced back and forth between their parents.[35] Combine those factors with the advances in women's rights that prompted more women to go to work rather than be stay-at-home mothers. As a result, many Gen Xers spent much of their childhood on their own. This created their self-reliance and independence, yet also "feelings of abandonment . . . They wanted more attention from their parents."[36] Generation X turned to their friends for a sense of family and belonging.[37] Think of the TV sitcom "Friends" or the movie "The Breakfast Club," both of which were popular in Gen X culture. Generation X also grew up in the "leviathan shadow of the boomers," which created "a sense of apartness."[38] Xers have since observed that the baby boomers and Generation Y are "siphoning up all of [the] mass media oxygen . . . somebody seems to have forgotten Generation X," wrote author Jeff Gordinier in his book "X Saves the World: How Generation X Got the Shaft but Can Still Keep Everything from Sucking."[39]

Referred to as a "defiant demographic,"[40] Generation X's skepticism and cynicism was also influenced by world events. This is the generation that grew up with the Cold War, the contentious Vietnam War, Watergate, President Richard Nixon's resignation and the 1970s energy crisis. In other words, "Generation X watched as America seemed to fail militarily, politically, diplomatically and economically."[41] Unlike their idealistic boomer parents, Xers had to "learn to survive in a world where everything was not going to be all right . . . where the American Dream looked like a running joke."[42]

As a result, this is a generation with strikingly different heroes than the political and military heroes of prior generations. Michael Jordan, Michael Jackson, Madonna, Kurt Cobain, Andrew McCarthy, Emilio Estevez and Molly Ringwald were popular figures for Generation X.[43] As for other cultural factors, the generation of 46 million saw the rise of cable and satellite TV, 24-hour news, VCRs, video games, microwaves and personal computers, while facing frequent warnings about drunk drivers, AIDS, child molesters and crack cocaine.[44]

Xers have been stereotyped as being a "slacker, lazy, grungy, unmotivated" generation.[45] However, they are an "extremely resourceful and independent generation"[46] that wants more work/life balance: "they work to live, not live to work."[47] Forum News Service director Mary Jo Hotzler thinks newsrooms are starting to focus more on culture, balance and happiness of employees now that Generation X is moving into leadership positions. "I think we are doing a decent job today of being aware of generational differences in the newsroom, and we are starting to adapt," said Hotzler, a Gen Xer based in Fargo, ND. "I'm not sure we're looking ahead far enough, though, to the next generation of employees and what that will mean for us. It would be great if we could be more proactive rather than reactive to the generational shifts."

Gen Xer Derrick Hinds, a former radio and TV news director, said he's found the different generations can work well together when they take time to understand the perspective of their colleagues. Younger reporters can improve their newsgathering and reporting by learning from their older colleagues, and older members of the newsroom can learn new ways to tell stories from their younger counterparts, he said. "It doesn't mean that younger reporters need to follow outmoded rules or that older reporters need to try too hard to be 'hip,' but it does mean being in an ongoing state of learning,"

Hinds said. "If all generations take a moment to think about how we got from where we were to where we are, and don't shy away from learning new skills, we can all benefit."

Gen Xer Lisa Griffin, a senior communications consultant and owner of a media management company, said her generation falls between the "old school" baby boomer approach to technology and journalism and the tech-savvy millennials, leaving Generation X juggling both approaches. From a public relations perspective, being knowledgeable about both styles is beneficial for serving older and younger clients, she said. While helping baby boomers in Congress improve their social media and online presence, she noticed a generational difference when one wanted a text-heavy website to provide the public with a lot of information. She wanted the site to be more accessible and readable for younger generations. Griffin advises the younger generations to do their homework to be successful with older clients. "Millennials can do this work if they understand the mentality of baby boomers and the technology that audience uses compared to their own," Griffin said.

 BOX 13.2   From the Field: Q&A with Mary Jo Hotzler

GENERATION X: PRINT AND DIGITAL NEWS

Mary Jo Hotzler, Vice President of Content at Forum Communications Co.

As director of a news service that gathers content from 35 newspapers in four states, Mary Jo Hotzler knows the importance of reaching a broad audience. The Fargo, ND,-based executive for Forum Communications is a believer of generational differences and said her Generation X upbringing influences her as both an employee and as a manager.

Below, Hotzler explains why being cognizant of generational differences is important to the future of journalism.

Q. *Why is it important for the media to be aware overall of generational differences?*

A. We are trying to reach a more diverse audience of readers today. We need to be aware of generational differences because that's all part of knowing our

(Continued)

BOX 13.2 Continued

audience and, in turn, making good decisions about what kinds of stories we cover and how we play them.

If we know we have both baby boomer readers and Gen Y readers and we understand what makes both groups tick, we will plan our product accordingly. Hopefully that makes us better and more successful. It's always important to know your audience, whether you are a newspaper editor or a TV news director.

Q. *What kinds of generational difference issues do you see within your newsroom?*

A. I think more and more we are starting to see Generation X rise up the ranks into many of the leadership positions in the newsrooms. That's beginning to change the dynamic of the workplace, and we find ourselves really placing a high value on culture, balance and overall happiness of employees.

Generation Y employees do want and need more feedback and direct interaction with their supervisors, and that's not a bad thing when we are seeking to create an open, positive workplace. They also are more likely to take advantage of new technology (cell phones, video cameras, etc.) to do their work. That also is a good thing, though I will say that I once had an interaction with a young reporter who wasn't familiar with the concept of an actual phone book to look up a source's contact information. That was interesting!

You also see generational differences in small ways in the newsroom—for example, in what employees wear to work. On any given day you will certainly find a Generation Y employee wearing a nice pair of jeans to work and thinking nothing of it.

You don't see the baby boomers or even all of the Generation X folks following in those footsteps. They still are more likely to stick to more traditional work attire, but to varying degrees.

Q. *How do you think being a member of Generation X influences who you are?*

A. It influences what I value as an employee—balance, flexibility, an inspiring and harmonic work environment—and in how I manage, for example allowing an employee to work from home if circumstances call for that. I love my job and want to work hard while I am at the office. But when the day is done, I want to leave my work behind and go enjoy my family.

BOX 13.3   Generational Differences Fast Facts

Racially diverse—Millennials are the most racially diverse generation in American history, a trend driven by the large wave of Hispanic and Asian immigrants coming to the U.S. during the past half century. Some 43 percent of millennial adults are non-white.

Financial disparity—Millennials are the first in the modern era to have higher levels of student loan debt, poverty and unemployment, and lower levels of wealth and personal income than their two immediate predecessor generations (Gen Xers and boomers) had at the same stage of their life cycles. The Great Recession is one factor in this disparity as older members of Generation Y struggled to find jobs and parents of younger members may have had greater difficulty supporting the cost of their children's college education. In addition, the cost of attending college has nearly tripled since 1980, which includes adjusting for inflation.

Marriage views—Just 26 percent of millennials are married. When they were the age that millennials are now, 36 percent of Generation X, 48 percent of baby boomers and 65 percent of the members of the Silent Generation were married.

Religious differences—58 percent of millennials are "absolutely certain" that God exists compared to 69 percent of Generation X, 73 percent of baby boomers and 74 percent of the Silent Generation.

Sources: 2014 Pew Research Center data, 2013 Current Population Survey and Taylor 2014.[48]

▶ GENERATION Y

Born: 1981 to ? (Still debated)
Age of adults in 2014: 18 to 33
Share of adult population: 27 percent
Share non-Hispanic white: 57 percent

As you likely have noticed by now, the generational identity of parents has a significant impact on their children's generation. This certainly rings true for members of Generation Y, also called the millennials, who were raised by parents determined to be more involved in their children's lives than their parents were in theirs. Therefore, Generation Y grew up with "helicopter parents" and became "the great oversupervised generation."[49] Bruce Tulgan, author of "Not Everyone Gets a Trophy: How to Manage Generation Y," explains:

> Making children feel great about themselves and building up their self-esteem became the dominant theme in parenting, teaching and counseling. Throughout their childhood, Gen Yers were told over and over, "Whatever you think, say or do, that's okay" . . . As children, most Gen Yers simply showed up and participated—and actually did get a trophy.[50]

Generation Y has developed a reputation of being high maintenance. However, this is a generation that grew up being friends with their parents, being connected to the Internet and being told their opinion mattered. Therefore, they expect to be involved in decision-making, expect fast results and expect to be valued for their contributions. However, as the most-educated generation that grew up with so many opportunities, Gen Yers also tend to feel tremendous pressure to excel in life. Although this drives them to work hard, a number of them experience a "quarter-life crisis" around age 25 when they feel they have not lived up to societal expectations for them.[51] It doesn't help that many Gen Yers are saddled with student debt since so many went to college and experienced tuition hikes. Not to mention many graduated from college during the Great Recession and struggled to find jobs, resulting in a number of them needing to move back home with their parents.[52] As a result, Gen Y is "having trouble finding the road map to adulthood" and is "the first generation in American history in danger of having a lower standard of living than the one their parents enjoyed."[53]

From a cultural perspective, the 80 million Gen Yers grew up with Britney Spears, Tiger Woods, Tupac, N'Sync and Barney the dinosaur as icons, while watching "Dawson's Creek," "Beverly Hills 90210," "The Real World" and "Saved by the Bell." Despite accusations that they are "lazy, entitled, narcissists,"[54] Gen Yers tend to be civic minded, perhaps due to all of the volunteer work they did and clubs they belonged to in high school to have a competitive college application. Gen Yers are also known for being realistic, practical, collaborative, tech-savvy and global.[55] The diversity of this generation is also notable, with 40 percent of its members being nonwhite.[56] This is a generation that experienced the Oklahoma City bombing, Columbine and 9/11 during their impressionable years. School shootings and concerns about global terrorism have been issues for much of their lives.

A fifth generation, Generation Z, is growing up now. However, researchers still disagree on when Generation Y ends and Generation Z begins. Some have said 2000; others point to the mid-1990s. Although it's too soon to define Gen Z, certainly technology, the Great Recession, the election of the first black president and the generation's diverse racial makeup are early clues to this generation's developing identity.

Tayler Overschmidt, a Generation Y producer for a CBS affiliate in North Carolina, thinks a generationally diverse newsroom is an asset. "People from every age group in my newsroom help each other look at things and ideas in ways that we might not have otherwise," she said. There are struggles between the more tech-savvy Generation Y and the older generations still learning new technology, she said. Those with more experience also sometimes forget that the younger employees are still learning what the more seasoned staff learned years ago. Yet the benefits of working together far outweigh the problems, Overschmidt said. "As long as we're open to admitting when we don't know something and are willing to incorporate ideas from all generations, our product will be better off than if we're working in a more homogenous environment," she said.

From a photography perspective, Madeline Beyer said she's noticed generational differences on both sides of the camera. The Missouri-based owner of Madexposure Photography said older generations want a physical product that they can pass down to their children. Meanwhile, younger generations prefer digital files and place a higher importance on photos for social media.

"Millennials want what they want, and they want to do it now. Every photo and thought has to be shared immediately and phrases like "pics or it didn't happen" and "YOLO" (you only live once) dictate how we function," she said. "I think millennials are constantly plugged in, which is both a blessing and a curse. We have access to more information and the ability to learn more than ever, but are experiencing less tangible experiences." As Beyer points out, there are concerns about what millennials are missing out on when they're checking their phones.

Gen Yer Ladan Nikravan has also reflected on generational differences. Nikravan, a Chicago-based senior editor for MediaTec Publishing, manages an "Ask a Gen Y" blog and a video channel for *Chief Learning Officer* magazine that debunk myths about and discuss generational issues in the workplace. It's important to distinguish generational traits from life stages and from changes in society, she said. For example, the desire for a more flexible work environment is part of a changing society as opposed to being strictly a characteristic of Generation Y, she said. Likewise, the claim that Generation Y is entitled and immature is associated with the life stage of its members and is not a generational trait, she said. Boomers and Traditionalists experienced the same accusations when they were young adults, she said.

Generational differences can be a strong angle in stories about trends and history, Nikravan said. Still, she cautions against placing too much emphasis on them. "It's part of a person's identity and could be telling of a number of things, but like any other diversity element, it shouldn't necessarily dominate the conversation," Nikravan said. "It's important to know what generation a source or subject of a story is from; it could say a lot, but it doesn't say everything."

BOX 13.4   From the Field: Q&A with Lyndsey Slawkowski

GENERATION Y: PUBLIC RELATIONS

Lyndsey Slawkowski knows growing up as a millennial influences her approach to work. The Chicago-based account executive for Zeno Group said she is very aware of the social ramifications associated with making a wrong move, as well as the significance of a brand's digital presence for maintaining a company's reputation. Her firm specializes in consumer, health, technology and corporate communications, all supported by planning, digital engagement and media.

Lyndsey Slawkowski, account executive for Zeno Group

Here, Slawkowski shares her thoughts on why generational differences (and similarities) matter for future journalists.

Q. *How aware are you of generational differences when creating your campaigns?*

A. We're always thinking about the specific target audience, so we're extremely aware if that is dependent on a specific generation. During the idea generation stage, we think about where we reach these people and what is most relevant to them.

Often times, it goes much further than just generation but to specific subsets such as moms, teen drivers, boomers at risk for a specific health issue, etc. Choosing the right communication channels has a huge impact on the delivery of the message.

Q. *How important is it for future PR/ad practitioners to be aware of generational differences?*

A. It's extremely important, but the reason why is somewhat two-fold. If you're targeting a specific generation, then you need to know what that generation stands for, what resonates with them and how they are getting their news. Are they reading newspapers? Or scanning mobile apps or social networks? As a PR practitioner, it's then your job to find a way to get relevant messaging in those spaces.

But I think you also need to be aware of generational *similarities*. Where is the middle ground that brings consumers of different generations together, and how does your brand fit into that? Some of the best campaigns build

(Continued)

BOX 13.4 Continued

strong relationships with their target generation without alienating any of the others.

Q. *How do you keep informed about generational differences?*

A. Keeping a pulse on the news—scanning newspapers, online outlets and Twitter periodically throughout the day. Whenever my team sees a study that reveals something new about a specific generation, we file it away in our resources folder so that we have an arsenal of secondary research whenever we're looking to target a specific population.

Zeno Group also has a great planning team that not only shares its own research with our entire network, but also provides access to resources and research databases so that we're as informed as we can possibly be before generating campaign tactics.

Q. *Talk more about how you apply what you know about generational differences within your work.*

A. As a communications professional, I always find it important to not only think about what messages you're sending, but also *how* you're sending them. All generations might not respond as effectively to specific tactics. Millennials tend to be earlier adopters of new technology, so communicating through social media networks, mobile apps, etc. becomes more important.

That being said, I think many people assume that just because someone comes from an older generation, they aren't as tech-savvy. You still need to do your research and find out how people want to be communicated with.

FOR DISCUSSION

1. There are differing views among generational differences researchers as to when Generation Y ends and Generation Z begins. What do you think? What characteristics, heroes and events would you include in a definition of Generation?

▶ GENERATIONAL DIFFERENCES AND YOU

So why are generational differences of interest to you as future journalists and communicators? Hopefully this chapter provided you with a lot to consider and provided you with necessary context to not only understand the other generations but to better understand your own. This will benefit you not only as you create your own excellent journalism but also as you go into the workforce and must collaborate and communicate with co-workers of diverse ages.

How generational differences will impact the future of the media is still an open question. Right now, the differing media habits of the generations mean media outlets need to offer something for everyone, said Hinds, the communications, marketing and digital media manager for the Radio Television Digital News Association (referred to as RTDNA) in Washington, DC. Baby boomers and Traditionalists are more apt to read the morning newspaper in print and to watch the evening news on their favorite network, he said. Meanwhile, the younger generations want instant news on their computers, tablets and smartphones and are less concerned about which information source provides them news. "Quality, trusted journalism still matters, but with each new generation of journalists coming up, come new challenges to getting that message out and standing out from the noise," Hinds said.

A recent study illustrates the media may have more challenges ahead. On an average day, Traditionalists spend 84 minutes consuming news compared to 77 minutes by boomers, 66 minutes by Generation X and 46 minutes by Generation Y.[57] Some of this can be explained by life cycle. For example, older adults are more established in their community and therefore are more likely to want to be informed of news. However, Taylor said the differences in numbers go beyond life cycle. Overall, Generation Y is consuming less news than the older generations did when they were the same age. As Taylor explains:

> Low level of news consumption among the younger generations is likely the result of a variety of factors—such as having more activities and [entertainment options] that compete with the news or fewer compelling major historical events during childhood and adolescence . . . Older people simply enjoy the news more than the young do.[58]

As new journalists, you will play a critical role in shaping the direction of the media. Therefore, awareness of the generational differences fault line will become increasingly necessary to not only ensure that future generations value and consume journalism, but to secure our own future as an industry.

▶ CHAPTER SUMMARY

The topic of generational differences has garnered increasing attention in recent years due to the uniqueness of having four generations in the workforce. Therefore, it is an important fault line to remember in your work.

Generations are categorized by birth years and generally span 15 to 20 years. However, generational identity is more so defined by the major news events, public figures and cultural trends that influence people who grew up within the same time period. The four main generations are:

1. the Traditionalists, who were born during World War II or earlier

2. the baby boomers, who were born between 1946 and 1964

3. Generation X, who were born between 1965 and 1980

4. Generation Y, who were born after 1980.

A fifth, Generation Z, is growing up now and is still in the process of being defined. Generational differences are important for you to understand since you will work with people of varying ages, and your journalism will need to try to capture an increasingly diverse audience.

▶ SUGGESTED ACTIVITIES

1. AARP criticized the media's heavy focus on the 18 to 49 demographic, which leaves out the influential baby boom generation that was once advertisers' primary target. Spend an evening analyzing TV commercials on different channels. Take notes on the products and whom you think are the intended targets. Which generation is targeted the most on each channel? Which is targeted the least? Why do you think that is? Do ads targeted at baby boomers appeal to being youthful and idealistic as AARP advises? Share your findings with the class.

2. Interview international students at your school to find out what they consider to be generational differences. How are generational differences defined in other countries?

3. There are a number of story ideas that have a generational angle. For example, some Generation Y members have had a quarter-life crisis, which is unique to their generation. In addition, assisted-living facilities have undergone major changes in recent years to meet the demands of aging boomers who want to spend their later years in a more youthful environment, not an institutional-type nursing home. Break into groups and create a list of story ideas that you think would be relevant to each of the generations.

4. Analyze the stories in your local newspaper or on your local TV station for a week. Take note of every story included and then, for each one, determine which generation(s) would be most interested in that content. At the end of the week, study your notes and create a report outlining which generations are best served by the local media and which aren't. In the report, include your recommendations for how the outlet could improve and why it is important that they make changes. If you believe the outlet did a good job, explain why.

▶ NOTES

1 Teri Finneman, "Talking 'Bout My Generation," *The Forum of Fargo-Moorhead*, July 9, 2006, A1, A8.
2 Karl Mannheim, *Essays on the Sociology of Knowledge* (London: Routledge and Kegan Paul, 1952), 291.
3 David Burstein, *Fast Future: How the Millennial Generation is Shaping Our World* (Boston: Beacon Press, 2013), 35.
4 Howard Schuman and Jacqueline Scott, "Generations and Collective Memories," *American Sociological Review* 54, no. 3 (June 1989): 359–381.
5 Mannheim, *Essays*, 298.
6 Schuman and Scott, "Generations," 377.
7 Lynne Lancaster and David Stillman, *When Generations Collide* (New York: HarperBusiness, 2002), 32.
8 Ibid, 32.
9 Mannheim, *Essays*, 303.
10 Ron Zemke, Claire Raines and Bob Filipczak, *Generations at Work: Managing the Clash of Veterans, Boomers, Xers, and Nexters in Your Workplace* (New York: Amacom, 2000), 16–17.
11 Ibid, 14.
12 Schuman and Scott, "Generations," 373.
13 Lancaster and Stillman, *Generations Collide*, 18–19.
14 Ibid.
15 Ibid.
16 Ibid, 19.
17 Ibid, 20.
18 Leonard Steinhorn, *The Greater Generation: In Defense of the Baby Boom Legacy* (New York: St. Martin's Press, 2006), 1.
19 Zemke, Raines and Filipczak, *Generations at Work*, 37.
20 Burstein, *Fast Future*, xxi.
21 Zemke, Raines and Filipczak, *Generations at Work*, 66.
22 Lancaster and Stillman, *Generations Collide*, 21.
23 Ibid.

24 Steinhorn, *Greater Generation*, 72.

25 Ibid, 73.

26 Zemke, Raines and Filipczak, *Generations at Work*, 20.

27 Paul Taylor and the Pew Research Center, *The Next America: Boomers, Millennials, and the Looming Generational Showdown* (New York: BBS Public Affairs, 2014), 25–26.

28 Ibid.

29 Zemke, Raines and Filipczak, *Generations at Work*, 69, 88.

30 Jennifer Deal, *Retiring the Generation Gap: How Employees Young and Old Can Find Common Ground* (San Francisco, CA: Jossey-Bass, 2007), 1.

31 Ibid, 13.

32 Ibid, 213.

33 Zemke, Raines and Filipczak, *Generations at Work*, 21.

34 Ibid, 98.

35 Lancaster and Stillman, *Generations Collide*, 25.

36 Zemke, Raines and Filipczak, *Generations at Work*, 98.

37 Ibid.

38 Jeff Gordinier, *X Saves the World: How Generation X Got the Shaft but Can Still Keep Everything from Sucking* (New York: Viking, 2008), xxi.

39 Ibid, xix.

40 Ibid, xxi.

41 Zemke, Raines and Filipczak, *Generations at Work*, 96.

42 Ibid, 96.

43 Lancaster and Stillman, *Generations Collide*, 24; Gordinier, *X Saves the World* xix, xxi.

44 Lancaster and Stillman, *Generations Collide* 24–25.

45 Ibid, 42.

46 Ibid, 26.

47 Zemke, Raines and Filipczak, *Generations at Work*, 21.

48 "Millennials in Adulthood," Pew Research Center, www.pewsocialtrends.org/files/2014/03/2014–03–07_generations-report-version-for-web.pdf, 5–9; Taylor and Pew, *The Next America*.

49 Bruce Tulgan, *Not Everyone Gets a Trophy: How to Manage Generation Y* (San Francisco, CA: Jossey-Bass, 2009), 7.

50 Ibid, 7–8.

51 Christine Hassler, *20 Something, 20 Everything: A Quarter-life Woman's Guide to Balance and Direction* (Novato, CA: New World Library, 2005).

52 Taylor and Pew, *The Next America*.

53 Ibid, vii, 26.

54 Ibid, 27.

55 Lancaster and Stillman, *Generations Collide*, 27, 30.

56 Taylor and Pew, *The Next America*, 29.

57 Ibid.

58 Ibid, 44.

▶ ADDITIONAL READINGS

American Press Institute. "How Millennials Get News: Inside the Habits of America's First Digital Generation." Last modified March 16, 2015. www.americanpressinstitute.org/publications/reports/survey-research/millennials-news/.

Fried, Linda P. "Making Aging Positive." *The Atlantic*, June 1, 2014. www.theatlantic.com/health/archive/2014/06/valuing-the-elderly-improving-public-health/371245/.

Voorveld, Hilde A.M. and Margot Van Der Goot. "Age Differences in Media Multitasking: A Diary Study." *Journal of Broadcasting & Electronic Media* 57 (2013): 392–408. doi: 10.1080/08838151.2013.816709.

14

Race and Gender in Sports

Cynthia M. Frisby

The fact that sports are a major part of American culture is supported by the hundreds of thousands of fans that get caught up in events like the "Super Bowl," the "World Series," "March Madness" and the "World Cup." An examination of the amount of resources and media time spent on sports-related events also points to the social significance of sports. However, it was not too long ago that athletes of color and women were not allowed to contribute or participate in this important product of our American culture. For decades, athletes of color were prohibited from participating in the professional sports leagues of white America. And, before the 1972 inception of Title IX, only 32,000 females participated in collegiate athletics.[1] Since then, the popularity of women's athletics has been on the rise.[2]

Breaking the color and gender barriers in sports has not, however, broken down the stereotypes and the exclusion of women and athletes of color in sports media. Research shows that obstacles still appear to preclude journalists from including athletes of color and female athletes proportionally in stories and headlines in national sports media.[3] In spite of the all-pervasive nature of sports in our culture, major sports

LEARNING OBJECTIVES

After completing this chapter, students should be able to:

- demonstrate a balanced awareness of the issues and debates involving African-American athletes, women and sports.

- think critically about sports and how they are portrayed in American culture.

- recognize the impact of societal norms, the lack of (but improving) athletic opportunities and resources for women and persons of color.

- understand why gender and racial equality in sports journalism is important and needed.

media seem to ignore the significance, contribution of and importance of inclusion of women and athletes of color.

▶ AFRICAN-AMERICAN MALE ATHLETES

The roles that media and society play in shaping individual attitudes and beliefs about male athletes have been of great importance to many scholars.[4] In fact, Whisenant and Pedersen (2004) assert that media's "words and images have a major impact on societal processes and institutions . . . the influence of the media is projected not only by what is being said, but also what is not being reported through the absence of coverage."[5] According to media scholar Fujioka (2005), "negative minority images have been prevalent in the mainstream media."[6] As a result, the negative portrayals of African-Americans have led many white viewers of sports to perceive African-Americans in a more negative context.[7] News media, research suggests, tend to cover stories that perpetuate stereotypes of the black male.[8]

According to Fujioka, news media do not generally publish stories about an African-American male athlete who is a positive role model, or one who also gives back to his community, or has never been to jail. There has been a small amount of recent research that examines sports media differences in coverage of black and white male athletes. However, research has focused on broadcast news and tends to show that the stereotypes are mostly the same—that is, white athletes are depicted as being more dedicated and mentally skilled, while black athletes tend to be depicted as being gifted more in terms of athletic abilities.[9]

Research provides three dominant media images of black males: criminals, athletes and entertainers. Research by Entman and Gross also found that black male athletes and black entertainers often receive more publicity for alleged crimes than they do for positive contributions.[10] My own analysis of news stories reveals that white male athletes are given both more media attention (i.e., space in stories) and more front-page newspaper story space than are black male athletes. This finding supports earlier research conducted by Billings, Halone, and Denham. My content analysis further shows that coverage of athletes is not equal either quantitatively or qualitatively, with disproportionate coverage involving black male athletes found in news stories that involved instances of crime, domestic/sexual violence, moral failure and/or the athlete's reputed "natural" skills and abilities.[11]

▶ STEREOTYPICAL COVERAGE OF ATHLETES OF COLOR IN THE MEDIA

Participation in contemporary sports by African-Americans (just as by women) has risen. Even though African-American men may have achieved equality in terms of playing for intercollegiate and professional teams, they continue to remain subject to differential treatment by media that cover these sports.[12] Sports commentators have been found to describe African-American athletes in terms of their physical power or physique, using descriptors that seem, on the surface, to be complimentary.[13] But as Rada and Wulfemeyer explain, these "so-called" athletic compliments actually reinforce racial biases and stereotypes in that the "compliments" differ from descriptors applied and used by sports commentators to describe Caucasian athletes. According to Rada and Wulfemeyer, African-American athletes receive a greater number of negative comments than do Caucasian athletes related to comments of on-field intelligence. Since black men show up in the media in limited roles—as athletes as one of those roles—limiting how they are portrayed is problematic. According to Wenner,

> This is troubling because the focus on the sports star role limits both blacks and whites in their thinking. Confronted by media to focus on black men as athletes, we miss out on seeing the diversity of everyday successes by African-American men.[14]

The aspirations of young black men to play professional sports are shaped largely, though not entirely, by television and other media. Thus, it is extremely important for sports reporters and journalists to highlight other aspects of black male athletes beyond illegal criminal activity and/or athletic prowess. Studies of black male athletes have also demonstrated a recurrent media stereotype wherein the black athlete is characterized through an emphasis on "natural athleticism"—a description consistent with racist theories that "propose that blacks possess physiological characteristics that contribute to superior speed, reflexes and jumping ability."[15] These depictions contrast with media accounts of the white athlete, who is more often said to be "smart" and "hard working."[16]

More reporting must be done on young adolescent black boys and men, who simultaneously perform well in classrooms and on the field or court. For example, media content could focus on positive stories involving former black male student-athletes who attended college, achieved academic and athletic success, were engaged campus leaders within and beyond athletics, graduated in four to six year, and took divergent post-college pathways, meaning that some enrolled in graduate school, some began full-time jobs in their fields of study and others embarked on professional sports careers. Such positive stories would not only advance a more complete understanding and realistic depiction of this population, but also might possibly preclude the perpetuation of negative stereotypes of black male athletes.

In short, sports media must stop the irresponsible, biased, stereotypic journalistic practices that continually yield one-sided portrayals of black male athletes.

▶ STEREOTYPICAL COVERAGE OF MALE ATHLETES IN THE MEDIA

The media does not always present a fair and pleasant picture of male athletes. Researchers have analyzed the televised coverage found to be watched most by young audiences. Messner, Dunbar and Gunt (2000) studied an extensive list of organizations, including the commercials, pre-game, halftime and post-game shows, ranging from SportsCenter on ESPN to professional wrestling on TNT Night Nitro. Both quantitative and qualitative data revealed that televised sports and their accompanying advertisements present boys with a narrow scope of what is masculine, known as the Televised Sports Manhood Formula.[17]

The 10 distinct themes comprising the Televised Sports Manhood Formula[18] are: 1) white males are the voices of authority, 2) sports is a man's world, 3) men are foregrounded in commercials, 4) women are sexy props or prizes for men's successful sport performances or consumption choices, 5) whites are foregrounded in commercials, 6) aggressive players get the prize. 7) nice guys finish last, 8) boys will be (violent) boys, 9) give up your body for the team and 10) sports is war! Young boys are presented with these views of what manhood means and are rarely exposed to women and sport. Alternative views that might be suggested are portrayals of males able to feel a range of emotions, including fear, hurt, confusion or despair. It seems that media messages suggest that men who happen to express any of these emotions are unmanly. Other alternative representations could encourage men to emphasize teamwork, demonstrate love in a nonsexual way, model good friendships and compassion and present ways that conflict can be resolved without violence.

So, while receiving more coverage, males are also subjected to stereotypes and "norms" that restrict who they are and how they should behave. Boys are taught to be aggressive, not passive, and sport commercials are designed to get at male insecurities, getting them to buy products making them the "ideal man."[19] This aggressive stereotype can lead to many problems. Men who remove themselves from a game due to injuries are looked upon as weak and questions are raised about their manhood.[20] Thus, the man who does not fit the stereotype tends to be made fun of.

The message for boys is that a real man is "strong, tough, aggressive, and above all else, is a winner in what is still a Man's World."[21] It is necessary to note that, in terms of sports journalism, most play-by-play commentators, sports writers and announcers are white males.[22] In general, women and black males rarely appeared as the main commentators for sporting events, according to Messner et al. (2000). When scholars of gender and sport note that "men make sports, and sports make men,"[23] they refer to the role of sport in constructing the dominant perspective of what it means to be a man.

▶ RESEARCH ON SEXUALIZATION OF WOMEN IN SPORTS

The passage of Title IX in 1972 called for male and female athletes in collegiate sports to have equal access to equipment and practice facilities, media representation, coaches of the same quality and scholarship money proportional to participation.[24] Since then, women's participation in sports has reached unprecedented highs.[25] Nevertheless, research shows that media coverage of female athletes still lags behind that of male athletes.[26] Additionally, the quality or ways in which journalists cover men's and women's sports is inequitable.[27] In addition to an absence of coverage, the way women are shown in sports media tends to treat their bodies more as sex objects rather than as powerful and agile athletes.

For example, in the 1999 women's soccer World Cup when Brandi Chastain won the final round for the USA by scoring on a penalty shot—a defining moment in women's soccer—*Sports Illustrated* chose to put on its cover a photo of Chastain removing her jersey in celebration and showing her sports bra. At the time, the fact of a female removing her shirt became the topic of conversation, and not the team's athletic achievements. Ultimately, it is believed that media hype surrounding her removal of the jersey set sexual overtones that ultimately may have distracted readers from what might have been revered as the women's soccer team's greatest triumph—winning the world cup.

In sport media, women athletes are frequently portrayed in non-athlete roles.[28] For example, in a content analysis of *Sports Illustrated* (SI) and now-defunct *Sports Illustrated for Women* (SIW) from 1997–1999, Fink and Kensicki found that the majority of the photographs in SI were of female athletes in non-sport settings such as at home with their family (55 percent compared to 23 percent of similar photographs of male athletes), about a third depicted female athletes performing a sport (34 percent compared to 66 percent of similar photographs of male athletes) and 5 percent of photographs were considered pornographic or sexually suggestive (compared to 0 percent of such photographs of male athletes). SIW depicted more images of female athletes performing a sport (56 percent), but 24 percent of images showed female athletes in non-sport settings and 2 percent were pornographic or sexually suggestive. Of particular note, this study was conducted after the highly publicized success of U.S. women athletes in the 1996 Atlanta Olympics, yet female athletes were still presented in sexualized and non-sport roles.

The way sports media have tended to visually represent women is just one way that journalists signal to audiences that women athletes should not be taken seriously. When the media comment on women's sports, female athletes may well be referred to (depending on the sport) in either a sexual manner or a brutish, demeaning manner. For example, during a women's road race, commentators continually referred to the competitors as "girls," despite the fact that the top finishers for the U.S. were Shelley Olds, 32, Evelyn Stevens, 28, and Kristin Armstrong, 27. That adult women, at the top of their profession, with full lives and countless accomplishments continue to be referred to as "girls" is a perfect example of the demeaning commentary some journalists use referring to women. Another example of the sexual manner in which media comment on female athletes, one of the most talked about of issues, was whether the women's Olympic beach volleyball competitors would be allowed to wear bikinis. The problem lies in the fact that these incredible female athletes worked hard for their accomplishments, yet media coverage became nearly all about the bikinis. For example, NBC's New York affiliate ran the headline "Olympic Beach Volleyball: Great Bodies, Bikinis and More." Perhaps a better headline might have read "World-class Volleyball Athletes Represent U.S. in Olympic Games."

The media praises men for athletic ability in sports, but too often praises women only for their physical attractiveness. A perfect example of this can be found in *Sports Illustrated*. Long established as the premier magazine for sports, SI is also famous for its use of women portrayed as sexual objects (see swimsuit edition).

In sport media, the pattern of disproportionate and skewed portrayals is especially problematic for female athletes of color.[29] In a study of SI magazine covers, researchers found that African-American women were placed on only 5 of 1,835 covers between 1954 and 1987; overall, women landed on only 6 percent of covers during this time period.[30] Feature articles about African-American women were also rare.[31] Media coverage of other ethnic groups is similarly sparse. It can be argued that women of color and many other women are marginalized by dominant ideals and standards of what it means to be female in our culture that favor a heterosexual, white ideal body over other bodies. The white female ideal body has been described as being thin and conventionally beautiful.[32] In contrast, men who display dominant ideals and standards of masculinity have been known to be Caucasian, tough, dominant and professional.[33]

FOR DISCUSSION

1. Do female athletes have to objectify themselves to sell magazines? Why or why not?
2. Do male athletes objectify themselves in female media to sell products?
3. Do you think women are depicted more in sexual ways than are male athletes? Why or why not?

BOX 14.1   From the Field: Dr. Michael Messner

Dr. Michael Messner
Professor of Sociology and Gender Studies
Dornsife Director of Faculty Development
University of Southern California

There are three ways in which I have studied what sports media ignores, what it covers and how it covers it.

First, I have conducted a longitudinal content and textual analysis of gender in televised news and highlights programs. Started in 1989–90

Michael Messner

with Margaret Carlisle Duncan and continuing in recent years with Cheryl Cooky, we have examined both the quantity and quality of coverage of men's and women's sports, replicating this study every five years. Second, I am interested in how the sports media handles a particular story, especially a "scandal." In a 1993 analysis of a drugs and wife-abuse story about boxer Sugar Ray Leonard, William Solomon and I developed an approach for examining how journalists deploy news frames that illuminate certain aspects of a story, while obscuring others.

In addition to these sorts of "content" studies, scholars and students of sports media should turn their attention to the "production" side of sports media, with an eye to understanding how the dearth of women sports reporters and commentators impacts what we hear and see. We also need more "reception studies" that probe how audiences interpret, for instance, the common race and gender frames deployed in sports media.

▶ EXCLUSION AND TRIVIALIZATION OF FEMALE ATHLETES

Two major themes are associated with female athletes in sports coverage: exclusion and trivialization. Exclusion happens when sports media fail to cover women's sports. Furthermore, when sports journalists do cover women's sports, they often trivialize female athletes by comparing their abilities to men, minimizing their accomplishments, highlighting their personal lives over their athletic feats or describing them as sex objects. So there's always a 'but' to their athleticism, as if it's a secondary attribute. They're women athletes, but. . .

There are consequences to making attractiveness a key factor in sports coverage of women. For instance, older, or less stereotypically "attractive" female athletes tend to receive little media attention at all. Dedication to sports must be moderated by demure and ladylike character traits, or she is seen as manly, overaggressive, unattractive or "butch." Examples of this sexist media coverage include stories about women of color like Venus and Serena Williams. Sports journalists have described the Williams sisters as "savage" along with a range of other animalistic adjectives. Often sports journalists describe their bodies as manly and overweight—this probably because, as discussed earlier, the Williams sisters do not meet the Eurocentric beauty ideals our culture has for what it means to be feminine AND attractive. The Caucasian woman athlete as preferred by sports media is often an attractive, highly feminized young woman who happens to have a talent for her sport.

The stereotyping of sport as "masculine" or "feminine" affects both male and female participation and can be difficult to overcome. Men may be branded as "effeminate" if they abstain from sporting activities, and women are often encouraged to participate in the more feminine, "more appropriate sports" such as gymnastics and ice-skating, sports where traits and behaviors perceived as "female" are exhibited. These sports, it can be speculated, demonstrate the more accepted norms of behavior that our society comes to accept: we expect women to be "ladylike." We reject sports and behaviors that have women exhibiting traditional male characteristics, especially those sports that involve contact (such as football, basketball, rugby) and/or the more "painful" sports (like boxing, wrestling, etc.). When women and girls engage in such sports, they are often described negatively, such as being "unattractive," "masculine" or "unfeminine." In a society where women play rugby, box at the Olympics and play football, sport in our culture still retains many of its traditions, gender disparities and inequalities. In the article, "Is Sport Sexist? Six Sports where Men and Women are Still Set Apart," reporter Aimee Lewis examines these six sports and she examines why those distinctions continue (go to http://www.bbc.com/sport/0/golf/29242699).

There has been an increase in the coverage of female athletes. An extensive boost in terms of sports participation has also been identified among female athletes. Despite increased opportunities for female athletes, media coverage of them still lags significantly behind that of male athletes. The quality of that coverage is sorely lacking. Depictions that lower the status of women or girls and ultimately cause them to be viewed as inanimate objects, void of emotion, feelings, intelligence and valued only for their sexual accessibility to men is known as *sexual objectification*, and the media targets male viewers with this sexualization of female athletes. But through objectifying women, the media ultimately fail to engage men in women's sports.[34]

Through commentaries and broadcasts, sport media use phrases like "in other news" to reinforce "already-existing negative attitudes or ambivalences about women's sports and women athletes."[35] Thus, through the use of objectification strategies, sports media distract men from the real essence of women's athletics. Furthermore, by focusing solely on a female athletes' sex appeal and demeaning her athletic accomplishments, sports media effectively perpetuate stereotypes of what it means to be female, attractive and perhaps athletic. Thus, it can be argued that because of media portrayals of female athletes, male viewers may be unintentionally led to feel uninspired to attend women's sporting events and competitions. Even though the sports media may target its sexual objectification of female athletes toward men (i.e., *Sports Illustrated* swimsuit edition), they may actually be reinforcing harmful stereotypes and, at the same time, failing to encourage men into becoming dedicated female sports fans. To explain this in more detail, we explore the theory that provides a framework for understanding sexual objectification.

▶ OBJECTIFICATION THEORY

Objectification theory[36] assumes that women's primary value is seen as coming from their bodies and their physical appearance. Extending this argument to compare some images of female athletes to women in music videos, previous content analyses suggest that women are valued for their ability to use their bodies to be sexually alluring.[37] For example, Sommers-Flanagan et al. found that female characters in music videos were more likely than male characters were to exhibit behaviors meant to elicit sexual arousal, e.g., lip licking, stroking one's body, pelvic thrusting. Also, Seidman found that female characters in music videos were more likely than male characters were to wear sexually provocative attire.

First, an obvious way in which sexual objectification can be conveyed is through body exposure, as in the case of a person who is not wearing much clothing.[38] In essence, the way we define the concept of objectification reflects the amount of skin revealed by the female artists or athletes. Take for instance, women's beach volleyball. This sport has been known for being objectified for its "sexiness" and its "uniforms." Examples of sexual objectification can be found in the numerous close-up shots of a female athlete bending over ready to serve. Another example is the 2012 GoDaddy commercial featuring Danica Patrick, a respected female athlete who has succeeded in a predominantly male sport. The commercial had the accomplished athlete in a skimpy dress and employed close-up shots that encourage the sexual objectification of her body. This type of portrayal clearly distracts from her athletic accomplishments. Indeed, Fredrickson and Roberts specifically mention that sexual objectification entails the representation of a woman as a "collection of body parts,"[39] which might be contrasted with a visual portrayal of a woman as a total person. Thus, one indicator of sexual objectification is the extent to which athletes are segmented into different body parts (i.e., cleavage/chest, butt, legs, stomach, etc.).

Research has proffered many explanations for why female athletes are objectified in the media. First, it is hypothesized that this objectification in the media is an attempt to limit female power, thereby reinforcing cultural ideals that sport is a masculine activity.[40] In a masculine society like in the United States, masculine beliefs often give privilege to males. The mass media and sports are linked as two of the most prominent social institutions in our culture, and within that relationship, the relationship between athletics and masculinity has made gender a very pertinent issue. Sports media then may possibly encourage this masculine value as one of importance simply because of their extensive coverage of male-dominated sporting events. This media coverage may then strengthen the idea that female athletes are in many ways considered inferior. In other words, extensive coverage of male-dominated sports like football and basketball may lead people to believe that female athletes have no place in sports—ultimately supporting notions of male power and control. This serves as one reason why sports media tend to underrepresent, stereotype, trivialize, marginalize and sexualize female athletes in their coverage; it is simply a way in which the idea of what is masculine and what is feminine is maintained.

Some might argue that female athletes may allow themselves to be objectified or sexualized and do not understand this part of the debate. It can be argued that females who allow themselves to be sexualized in the media or who choose to be represented in this manner may do so because of the pressure to be attractive and/or feminine. That is, female athletes may be under pressure to engage in behaviors that show that they are both attractive and heterosexual. Because of such pressure, not just from society, but from the mass media to uphold masculine ideals, those female athletes participating in aggressive, more masculine sports, such as basketball, soccer and softball—sports which are viewed in society as being less feminine—may especially feel this pressure to allow themselves to be portrayed in a sexual manner in the media so as to avoid being labeled as lesbian, thereby potentially maximizing their social and career status.[41]

 BOX 14.2   From the Academy: Dr. Kathleen McElroy

Kathleen McElroy, Assistant Professor
Oklahoma State School of Media and Strategic Communications
Sports journalists have to be mindful of this country's historical treatment of women and people of color. Phrases, perspectives and analysis that continue to frame

(Continued)

BOX 14.2 Continued

female athletes and athletes of color as "The Other" perpetuate myths that go beyond sports.

The best sports journalists approach race with two widely different but complementary perspectives: women and people of color have not had the same political and cultural advantages of white men, and that this is a white patriarchal society that often fails to acknowledge how its benefits are mainly heaped on its dominant group. That the WNBA and NBA have a majority of African-American athletes does not "even" any scores.

Kathleen McElroy

On the other hand, don't pretend to be colorblind—people can't be. When people say they are being colorblind, two negatives happen: they are ignoring the benefits of white privilege, or they are treating whiteness as the preferred default. Women and athletes of color deserve to be treated with athletic and cultural respect. To perpetuate that Magic Johnson was more gifted than Larry Bird, who "worked harder" to achieve his greatness is to disrespect the preternatural talent and determination of both athletes.

Aspiring sports journalists should consider:

- softball is not weaker than baseball—it's just different. Same with women's golf, tennis, etc.

- women's basketball, or Ivy League men's basketball, isn't more cerebral just because it's played under the basket.

- why do football players have to attend college before turning pro, while tennis players don't?

- if college athletes are getting a "free ride," then why do they have to practice, travel, play a dangerous sport AND show up to class? I don't recall physics students on scholarship having to work as hard.

Sports journalists have to be mindful that calling black athletes "studs" and "freaks" is more damaging than other silly sports clichés—it's feeding into stereotypes that disregard blacks as equal human beings.

▶ GENDER APPROPRIATE SPORTS

Research shows that female athletes competing in traditionally "gender-appropriate" individual sports, such as swimming, diving, gymnastics and tennis, which represent a narrow, culturally stereotyped view of female athleticism, receive more electronic and print media coverage than female athletes competing in the traditionally "gender-inappropriate" team sports such as field hockey, soft-ball and rugby.[42] In the video "Media Coverage and Female Athletes," an Emmy Award–winning documentary presents evidence-based research that shows that although 40 percent of all sports participants are female, women's sports receive only 4 percent of all sports media coverage. The documentary also shows that female athletes are much more likely than male athletes to be portrayed in sexually provocative poses (go to http://www.cehd.umn.edu/tuckercenter/multimedia/mediacoverage.html).

Many researchers have found that female athletes competing in sports deemed as "sex-appropriate," such as gymnastics or figure-skating, get much better coverage in terms of length and number of features than do those who participate in sports such as body building or wrestling.[43]

According to a story found in the *Bleacher Report*, the reason for the gender dispar-ity in sports is because consumer interest drives content, and the consumer interest is not there for women's sports. For some consumers, it is perceived that women's sports aren't at the same level or quality of men's sports and that is what makes it less enter-taining, less fascinating and less worthy of watching.[44]

The highest growth sports among women, however, are team sports such as soccer, and the most frequently found college varsity sports for women include basketball, vol-leyball, softball, tennis, track and swimming—none of which are aesthetically oriented, "feminine" sports[45] but are (with the exception of tennis) sports in which women's performances are generally marginalized by the sports/media complex.[46] One recent example is the scant coverage of the U.S. women's soccer team in the 2007 World Cup competition.[47]

FOR DISCUSSION

1. What are the strategic communication implications? If you are promoting female athletes and doing their PR, what should you consider for photo shoots or when they are featured in the press?

BOX 14.3   Implications for Media Relations and
                                Sports Managers

- **Commit to using non-sexist language.** A great reference for sports journalists, sports promoters and strategic communications practitioners is a position paper titled "Images and Words in Women's Sports," published by the Women's Sports Foundation.[48] This reference should be used by every sports information director, communications officer and sports writer who is committed to non-sexist communications and writing. If it is true that media are disrespectful to female athletes, this resource provides specific guidelines that can reduce conflicts and mistakes that could cause significant public relations liabilities.

- **Contract negotiations.** Exposure of ALL men's and women's sports programs in broadcast television (TV, cable and satellite) should be a goal, even if the carrier or third-party broker is only interested in the most popular sport program. TV coverage of events represents free advertising for a university and its athletics programs. When so-called "minor" sports are covered, this promotion is an investment in developing the value of other sports in the athletics department portfolio.

- **Sports shows.** Encourage sports journalists, coaches and others to "share the wealth" in who gets to be commented on regularly, being sure to include women's sports.

- **Advertisements and other publications.** Strategic communication professionals must be aware of their own possible biases and pay careful attention to photos and words in all mediated messages and visual communications. Sexist language, objectification and stereotyping is seldom intentional and is more a reflection of culturally ingrained habits. Therefore, strategic communication professionals interested in sports media must be aware of their biases. Make sure they are not getting in the way of your visual communication, advertisements and language/words used in your press releases.

- **Conduct strategic research to cultivate public interest.** The issue of increased exposure for women's sports is often misunderstood (i.e.

(Continued)

BOX 14.3 Continued

"women sports is not as entertaining, physical, will not sell tickets, etc.). This is an optimal time for athletic directors, sports editors and reporters to engage in strategic research with the target audience and viewers. Do you have evidence to support the idea that consumers lack interest in women's sports? Keep in mind that research shows that what gets into a newspaper has little to do with "public interest" and is more about what interests the sports editor.

- **Educate athletes/conduct media literacy training.** All athletes should be able to engage in critical thinking when confronted with images and messages in media. This means that male and female athletes should be educated about media with regard to sexist language and proper professional dress.

- **Create public interest stories.** All print and electronic media are interested in public interest stories. Strategic communication directors in sports media should write feature stories and disseminate these stories about the lives and positive successes that many women and athletes of color are engaged in.

▶ EQUITABLE COVERAGE OF RACE AND GENDER IN SPORTS MEDIA

In their research, Hardin, Shen and Yu argue that the framing of sports is so firmly entrenched as a male domain in U.S. culture that the acceptance of such has largely become taken-for-granted.[49] So, how do we achieve equitable coverage? Equitable sports media coverage can be defined in several ways. One is by understanding that equity is not an equal number of articles and photographs of male and female athletes. Rather, equity can be achieved by simply portraying female athletes as powerful and talented just as men are.[50] Equitable sports coverage could also be taken to mean equal coverage in news media given to all types of sports. For instance, females participating in sports deemed by society as masculine (e.g., rugby, basketball, soccer) should be covered at the same level as sports considered feminine (e.g., golf, tennis, swimming).[51]

FOR DISCUSSION

What does equality in sport coverage mean to you?

▶ CHAPTER SUMMARY

Acknowledgement that there is a problem with sports media is the first step sports communication professionals can take to overcome faulty images of and disparities among athletes and athletic coverage. Media scholars, editors, journalists, strategic communications practitioners and others interested in this topic must advocate for a change in the content of media, especially media targeted at adolescent boys and girls. It is worth mentioning that, in terms of equity in coverage, and positive portrayals of female athletes, some media are trying to get it right. Take for example, *ESPN Magazine*'s "Body Issue."[52] The "Body Issue" online magazine features nude female AND male athletes. The magazine also depicts women athletes of all body types (including Paralympians). What is most significant about this magazine and the images portrayed is that the athletes are shown in generally active, gender-neutral poses. The magazine praises women athletes for their athleticism, not their attractiveness. It also emphasizes the hard work and dedication that athletes devote to staying fit and toned.

Nike's "Voices" ad, released in recognition of the 40th anniversary of Title IX, is yet another example of how strategic communication practitioners are using their skills to create positive portrayals of female athletes. In the ad, women Olympians, including Lisa Leslie, Marlen Esparza and Joan Benoit-Samuelson, discuss their individual experiences with gender-based discrimination alongside a diverse range of little girls who should never have to face the same type of gender-based discrimination.

The responsibility of creating equality in media coverage for athletes of color and female athletes lies with sportscasters, sportswriters, players and fans across all races. We must begin talking intelligently about race, gender, racism, media, sports and athleticism. As the saying goes, "practice makes perfect." So too will practice make perfect regarding media and sports—the more practice everyone involved has at meaningfully talking about gender, race and stereotyping within sports media, the more equity in sports coverage will improve.

FOR DISCUSSION

1. How do you think the media portray athletes in general? Male athletes? Female athletes? Are portrayals positive? Negative? Neutral/objective? Explain.

2. Do you think that elite female athletes receive more or less coverage than their male counterparts? Why or why not? What about major international sporting events such as the Olympic Games? What do you think about the coverage in these instances?

3. If sports journalism attracted more female journalists, would that facilitate a more equitable and balanced coverage? Why or why not?

▶ SUGGESTED ACTIVITIES

1. Can you make a list of female athletes who have been portrayed in media in their uniform and described using similar attributes that are used to describe male athletes?

2. Flip through the pages of a magazine targeted to women. Compare it to a magazine targeted to men. Is there a difference in how the women are portrayed in the publications? Replicate this process using sports magazines this time. Is there much difference in how female athletes are portrayed in the publications? Now replicate the above using printed news stories. Are the stories similar? How are female athletes portrayed? How are male athletes portrayed? How are black male athletes portrayed?

3. Who are the most influential and celebrated athletes in sports media today? What cues can you find in the media that make them important? What cues or ideas are found in the stories that support the idea that this is a celebrated athlete?

4. Do a comparison of sports websites like espn.go.com and si.com. Analyze the landing/home pages. How are these sports sites using words, images and photographs of athletes to reach and appeal to the reader?

5. Compare and contrast the way female athletes are presented in a variety of media. How do the portrayals vary? Do you see different manifestations or versions of the differences in attributes and stereotypes? What similarities do you see in how athletes are portrayed? How are male athletes portrayed?

▶ NOTES

1 Cole, C. L., (2000), "Testing for Sex or Drugs," *Journal of Sport and Social Issues*, 24, no. 4: 331–333.

2 Grau, Stacy Landreth, Georgina Roselli, and Charles R. Taylor. "Where's Tamika Catchings? A Content Analysis of Female Athlete Endorsers in Magazine Advertisements," Journal of Current Issues and Research in Advertising 29, no. 1 (2007), 55–65; "Title IX Legal Manual," U.S. Department of Justice, 2013, http://www.justice.gov/crt/about/cor/coord/titlevi.php.

3 Elizabeth A. Daniels, "Athlete or Sex Symbol: What Girls Think of Media Representations of Women Athletes," paper presented at the Biennial Society for Research on Adolescence meeting, Chicago, IL, March 2008;. Margaret C. Duncan, "Sports Photographs and Sexual Difference: Images of Women and Men in the 1984 and 1988 Olympic Games," *Sociology of Sport Journal* 7, no. 1 (March 1990); Marie Hardin, Susan Lynn and Kristie Walsdorf, "Challenge and Conformity on "Contested Terrain": Images of Women in Four Women's Sport/Fitness Magazines," *Sex Roles* 53, no. 1 (2005): 105–117; Mary Jo Kane, "Media Coverage of the Post Title IX Athlete," *Duke Journal of Gender Law and Policy* 3 (1996), http://web/

lexis-nexis.com/universe/printdoc; Nathalie Koivula, "Gender Stereotyping in Televised Media Sport Coverage," *Sex Roles: A Journal of Research* 33 (October 1999): 543–557, http:// findarticles.com/p/articles/mim2294/is1999Oct/ai59426460; Virginia M. Leath and Angela Lumpkin, "An Analysis of Sportswomen on the Covers and in the Feature Articles of *Women's Sports and Fitness* magazine, 1975–1989," *Journal of Sport and Social Issues* 16 (1992): 121–126; Angela Lumpkin and Linda D. Williams, "An Analysis of *Sports Illustrated* Feature Articles, 1954–1987," *Sociology of Sport Journal* 8 (1991): 16–32; M. A. Messner, *Taking the Field: Women, Men, and Sports* (Minneapolis, MN: University of Minnesota Press, 2002); P. M. Pedersen and W. A. Whisenant, "Examining Stereotypical Written and Photographic Reporting on the Sports Page: An Analysis of Newspaper Coverage of Interscholastic Athletics," *Women in Sport and Physical Activity Journal* 12 (2003): 67–86; E. Primm, R. R. Preuhs, and J. D. Hewitt, "The More Things Change the More They Stay the Same: Race on the Cover of Sports Illustrated," *The Journal of American Culture* 30, no. 2 (2007): 239–250.

4 W. A. Whisenant and P. M. Pedersen, "The Influence of Managerial Activities on the Success of Intercollegiate Athletic Directors," *American Business Review* 22 (2004): 21–26.

5 Ibid., 55.

6 Yuki Fujioka, "Emotional Television Viewing and Minority Audience: How Mexican Americans Process and Evaluate TV News about In-Group Members," *Communication Research* 32 (2005): 451.

7 James Rada, "Color Blind-Sided: Racial Bias in Network Television's Coverage of Professional Football Games," *The Howard Journal of Communications* 7 (1996): 231–23.

8 Ibid.; Fujioka, "Emotional Television Viewing. . ."

9 T. Bruce, "Marking the Boundaries of the "Normal" in Televised Sports: The Play-by-Play of Race," *Media, Culture, and Society* 26, no. 6 (2004): 861–879; B. E. Denham, A. C. Billings and K. K. Halone, "Differential Accounts of Race in Broadcast Commentary of the 2000 NCAA Men's and Women's Final Four Basketball Tournaments," *Sociology of Sport Journal* 19, no. 3 (2002): 315–332; Rada, "Color Blind-Sided"; R. E. Rainville and E. McCormick, "Extent of Covert Racial Prejudice in Pro Football Announcers' Speech," *Journalism Quarterly* 54 (2007): 20–26.

10 Robert Entman, Young Men of Color in the Media: Images and Impacts. Washington, DC: Joint Center for Political and Economic Studies, 2006; Robert M Entman and Andrew Rojecki The Black image in the White mind: Media and race in America. Chicago, IL, US: University of Chicago Press, 2001; Robert M. Entman & Kimberly A. Gross, Race to Judgment: Stereotyping Media and Criminal Defendants, *71 Law and Contemporary Problems* 93-133 (Fall 2008) Available at: http://scholarship.law.duke.edu/lcp/vol71/iss4/6.

11 Frisby 2015a and b

12 James A. Rada and K. Tim Wulfemeyer, "Color Coded: Racial Descriptors in Television Coverage of Intercollegiate Sports," *Journal of Broadcasting and Electronic Media* 49, no. 1 (March 2005): 65–85.

13 See Ibid.

14 Lawrence A. Wenner, "The Good, the Bad, and the Ugly: Race, Sport, and the Public Eye. Brains versus Brawn 50," *Journal of Sport and Social Issues* 19, no. 2 (1995): 228. J. A. Rada and K. T. Wulfemeyer (2005, March). Color coded: Racial descriptors in television coverage of intercollegiate sports. Journal of Broadcasting and Electronic Media, 49(1), 65–85.

Retrieved December 6, 2007, from HYPERLINK "http://find.galegroup.com/ips/%20start. do?prodId=IPS" http://find.galegroup.com/ips/ start.do?prodId=IPS

15 Carlston, Donald E., An environmental explanation for race differences in basketball performance. In Richard Lapchick (Ed.), *Fractured focus: Sport as a reflection of society* (pp. 87–110) Toronto, ON: Lexington Books, 1986.

16 Jay J. Coakley, *Sport in Society: Issues and Controversies* (St. Louis, MO: Times Mirror/ Mosby College Publishing, 1990); Staples, Robert, and Terry Jones. "Culture, Ideology and Black Television Images." *The Black Scholar* 16, no. 3 (1985/05/01 1985): 10–20.

17 M. A. Messner, M. Dunbar and D. Hunt, "The Televised Sports Manhood Formula," *Journal of Sport and Social Issues* 24 (2000): 380–394.

18 Ibid.

19 Ibid.

20 Ibid.

21 Ibid.

22 Ibid.; D. Sabo, S. C. Jansen, D. Tate, M. C. Duncan and S. Leggett, "Televising International Sport: Race, Ethnicity, and Nationalistic Bias," *Journal of Sport & Social Issues* 20, no. 1 (1996): 7–21.

23 S. Birrell and D. Richter, "Is a Diamond Forever? Feminist Transformations of Sport," in *Women, Sport, and Culture*, ed. Susan Birrell and Cheryl L. Cole, 221–248 (Champaign, IL: Human Kinetics, 1994), 226.

24 Huffman, Suzanne, C. A. Tuggle, and Dana Scott Rosengard. "How Campus Media Cover Sports: The Gender-Equity Issue, One Generation Later." *Mass Communication and Society* 7, no. 4 (2004): 475–89.

25 Acosta, R. Vivian, and Linda Jean Carpenter. "Women in Intercollegiate Sport: A Longitudinal, National Study Thirty One Year Update 1977–2008." 2008.

26 Duncan, Margaret Carlisle, Michael A. Messner, and S. Solomon William. "Coverage of Women's Sports in Four Daily Newspapers." Los Angeles: Amateur Athletic Foundation, 1991. Janet S. Fink and Linda J. Kensicki, "An Imperceptible Difference: Visual and Textual Constructions of Femininity in *Sports Illustrated* and *Sports Illustrated for Women*," *Mass Communication & Society* 5 (2002): 317–339; C. A. Tuggle and A. Owen, "A descriptive analysis of NBC's coverage of the Centennial Olympics. The "Games of the woman?" *Journal or Sport and Social Issues* 23, no. 2 (1999): 171–182.

27 Michael A. Messner, Margaret C. Duncan and Cheryl Cooky, "Silence, Sports Bras, and Wrestling Porn," *Journal of Sport & Social Issues* 27 (2003): 38–51.

28 Elizabeth A. Daniels and Nicole M. LaVoi, "Athletics as Solution and Problem: Sports Participation for Girls and the Sexualization of Women Athletes," in *The Sexualization of Girls and Girlhood*, ed. Eileen L. Zurbriggen and Tomi-Ann Roberts (Oxford University Press, forthcoming).

29 Kane, "Media Coverage. . ."

30 Lumpkin and Williams, "An Analysis of . . ."

31 Ibid., Leath and Lumpkin, "An Analysis of . . ."

32 J. R. Aulette and J. Wittner, *Gendered Worlds* (New York: Oxford University Press, 2009).

33 Ibid.

34 M. A. Messner, M. C. Duncan and K. Jensen, "Separating the Men from the Girls: The Gendered Language of Televised Sports," *Gender and Society* 7 (1993): 121–137.

35 Ibid., 129.

36 B. L. Fredrickson and T-A Roberts, "Objectification Theory: Toward an Understanding of Women's Lived Experiences and Mental Health Risks," *Psychology of Women Quarterly* 21 (1997): 173–206.

37 J. L. Andsager and K. Roe, "Country Music Video in Country's Year of the Woman," *Journal of Communication* 49 (1999): 69–82; Seidman, 1992; R. C. Vincent, "Clio's Consciousness Raised? Portrayal of Women in Rock Videos, Reexamined," *Journalism Quarterly* 66 (1989): 155–160.

38 Aubrey, Jennifer Stevens, Jayne R. Henson, K. Megan Hopper, and Siobhan E. Smith. "A Picture Is Worth Twenty Words (About the Self): Testing the Priming Influence of Visual Sexual Objectification on Women's Self-Objectification." *Communication Research Reports* 26, no. 4 (2009): 271–84.

39 Fredrickson & Roberts, "Objectification Theory. . .", 174.

40 Pederson, 2002

41 Harrison & Fredrickson, 2003

42 Pirinen, 1997; Tuggle & Owen, 1999; J. Vincent, C. Imwold, J. T. Johnson and D. Massey, "Newspaper Coverage of Female Athletes Competing in Selected Sports in the 1996 Centennial Olympic Games: The More Things Change the More They Stay the Same," *Women in Sport and Physical Activity Journal* 12 (2003): 1–21.

43 Patricia Clasen, "The Female Athlete: Dualisms and Paradox in Practice," *Women & Language* 24, no. 2 (2001): 36–42; R. Jones, A. J. Murrell and J. Jackson, "Pretty Versus Powerful in the Sports Pages," *Journal of Sport and Social Issues* 23 (1999): 183–192; M. B. Salwen and N. Wood, "Depictions of Female Athletes on *Sports Illustrated* Covers, 1957–1989," *Journal of Sport Behavior* 17, no. 2 (1994): 98.

44 See *Bleacher Report*, http://bleacherreport.com/articles/2148497-examining-the-growth-and-popularity-of-womens-mixed-martial-arts.

45 Acosta, R. Vivian, and Linda Jean Carpenter. "Women in Intercollegiate Sport: A Longitudinal, National Study- Twenty Seven Year Update." Brooklyn, N.Y.: Brooklyn College, 2004.

46 Pedersen, 2002; Pedersen & Guerin, 2007; Vincent et al., "Newspaper Coverage. . ."

47 George Vescey "Admirable Spirit, but Rules Are Rules," Published: January 10, 2008, New York Times.

48 "Images and Words in Women's Sports," Women's Sports Foundation, http://www.womens sportsfoundation.org/home/advocate/foundation-positions/media-issues/images_and_words.

49 Marie Hardin, Fuyuan Shen and NanYu, "Sex-Typing of Sports: The Influence of Gender, Participation, and Media on Visual Priming Responses," paper presented at the annual meeting of the Association for Education in Journalism and Mass Communication, Marriott Downtown, Chicago, IL, August 6, 2008, http://citation.allacademic.com/meta/p271441_index.html.

50 See Fink and Kensicki, "An Imperceptible Difference. . ."

51 Kane, "Media Coverage. . ."

52 "Body Issue," ESPN, http://espn.go.com/espn/bodyissue.

▶ **ADDITIONAL READINGS**

Vivian Acosta and Linda Jean Carpenter. Women in intercollegiate sport: A longitudinal, national study- twenty seven year update. Unpublished manuscript. Brooklyn College, Brooklyn, NY, 2004.

Antunovic, Dunja and Marie Hardin. "Women Bloggers: Identity and the Conceptualization of Sports." *New Media & Society* 15, no. 8 (2013): 1374–92. doi: 10.1177/1461444812472323.

Mark Aubry, Robert C. Cantu, Jiri Dvoøák, Toni Graf-Baumann, Keith Johnston, James Kelly J, Mark Lovell, Paul McCrory , William Meeuwisse, Paul Schamasch. (2009) Summary and agreement statement of the first International Conference on Concussion in Sport, Vienna 2001. British Journal of Sports Medicine, 36(1):6–10.

Brennan, Christine. "Jets Deserve Penalty in Sainz Case." *USA Today*, September 16, 2010.

Brown, Kenon A., Andrew C. Billings, Dana Mastro and Natalie Brown-Devlin. "Changing the Image Repair Equation: Impact of Race and Gender on Sport-Related Transgressions." *Journalism & Mass Communication Quarterly* 92, no. 2 (2015): 487–506. doi: 10.1177/1077699015574484.

Andrea N. Eagleman & Paul M. Pedersen. Female athletes in (and out of) print. Women's Sports Foundation, 2007.

Fox, Ashley. "Ashley Fox: Professionalism Is the Priority for Women Covering Sports." *Philadelphia Inquirer*, September 16, 2010, D03.

Frederick, Evan L., Lauren M. Burch, Jimmy Sanderson and Marion E. Hambrick. "To Invest in the Invisible: A Case Study of Manti Te'o's Image Repair Strategies During the Katie Couric Interview." *Public Relations Review* 40, no. 5 (2014): 780–88. doi: http://dx.doi.org/10.1016/j.pubrev.2014.05.003.

Grau, Stacy Landreth, Georgina Roselli and Charles R. Taylor. "Where's Tamika Catchings? A Content Analysis of Female Athlete Endorsers in Magazine Advertisements." *Journal of Current Issues & Research in Advertising (CTC Press)* 29, no. 1 (2007): 55–65.

Hardin, Marie, Julie E. Dodd and Kimberly Lauffer. "Passing It On: The Reinforcement of Male Hegemony in Sports Journalism Textbooks." *Mass Communication & Society* 9, no. 4 (2006): 429–46. doi: 10.1207/s15327825mcs0904_3.

Hardin, Marie and Stacie Shain. "Strength in Numbers? The Experiences and Attitudes of Women in Sports Media Careers." *Journalism & Mass Communication Quarterly* 82, no. 4 (2005): 804–19.

Hardin, Marie and Stacie Shain. "'Feeling Much Smaller Than You Know You Are': The Fragmented Professional Identity of Female Sports Journalists." *Critical Studies in Media Communication* 23, no. 4 (2006): 322–38. doi: 10.1080/07393180600933147.

Harrison, Kristen & Barbara L. Fredrickson. Women's sports media, self-objectification and mental health in Black and White adolescent females. Journal of Communication, no. 53 (2003), 216–232.

Hong, Seoyeon and María E. Len-Ríos. "Does Race Matter? Implicit and Explicit Measures of the Effect of the PR Spokesman's Race on Evaluations of Spokesman Source Credibility and Perceptions of a PR Crisis' Severity." *Journal of Public Relations Research* 27, no. 1 (2015): 63–80. doi: 10.1080/1062726X.2014.929502.

Messner, Michael A. *Taking the Field: Women, Men, and Sports*. Minneapolis, MN: University of Minnesota Press, 2003.

Messner, Michael A. and Donald F. Sabo. *Sex, Violence & Power in Sports: Rethinking Masculinity*. Freedom, CA: Crossing Press, 1994.

Northup, Temple and Francesca Dillman Carpentier. "Michael Jordan, Michael Vick, or Michael Who?: Activating Stereotypes in a Complex Media Environment." *Howard Journal of Communications* 26, no. 2 (2015): 132–52. doi: 10.1080/10646175.2015.1011354.

Painter, Chad and Patrick Ferrucci. "Unprofessional, Ineffective, and Weak: A Textual Analysis of the Portrayal of Female Journalists on Sports Night." *Journal of Mass Media Ethics* 27, no. 4 (2012): 248–62. doi: 10.1080/08900523.2012.746107.

Paul M. Pedersen. Examining equity in newspaper photographs: A content analysis of the print media photographic coverage of interscholastic athletics. International Review for the Sociology of Sport, 37(3-4) (2002), 303–318.

Riitta M. Pirinen "The construction of women's positions in sport: a textual analysis of articles on female athletes in Finnish women's magazines." Sociology Of Sport Journal 14, no. 3 (1997): 290–301

Rada, James A. "Color Blind-Sided: Racial Bias in Network Television's Coverage of Professional Football Games." *Howard Journal of Communications* 7, no. 3 (1996): 231–39.

Steven A. Seidman (1992). An investigation of sex-role stereotyping in music videos. Journal of Broadcasting & Electronic Media, 36, 209–216.

Tuggle, C. A., and A. Owen. "A descriptive analysis of NBC's coverage of the Centennial Olympics. The "Games of the woman"?." Journal Of Sport And Social Issues 23, no. 2 (1999): 171–182.

George Vescey. "Admirable Spirit, but Rules Are Rules," Published: January 10, 2008, New York Times, 2007.

Williams, L. D. "Sportswomen in Black and White: Sports History from an Afro-American Perspective." In *Women, Media and Sport*, ed. P. J. Creedon, 45–66. Thousand Oaks, CA: Sage, 1994.

References

"Report of the APA task force on the sexualization of girls," Task Force on the Sexualization of Girls, American Psychological Association, 2007, www.apa.org/pi/wpo/sexualization.html.

Baker, C.N. (2005). Images of Women's Sexuality in Advertisements: A Content Analysis of Black- and White-Oriented Women's and Men's Magazines. Sex Roles, 52, 13–27.

Banet-Weiser, S. (1999). Hoop Dreams: Professional Basketball and the Politics of Race and Gender. Journal of Sport & Social Issues, 23, 403–420.

Benedict, J. & Klein, A. (2013). Arrest and Conviction Rates for Athletes Accused of Sexual Assault, Sociology of Sport Journal, vol. 14(1), pps. 169–175.

Billings, A.C., & Eastman, S.T. (2003). Framing identities: Gender ethnic, and national parity in network announcing of the 2002 Winter Olympics. Journal of Communication, 53(4), 369–386.

Billings, A.C., Halone, K.K., & Denham, B.E. (2002). "Man, that was a pretty shot": An analysis of gendered broadcast commentary surrounding the 2000 Men's and Women's NCAA Final Four Basketball Championships. Mass Communication & Society, 5(3), 295–315.

"Children and Sport Media," Amateur Athletic Foundation of Los Angeles and ESPN, 2001.

Daniels, E.A. (2012). Sexy versus strong: What girls and women think of female athletes. Journal of Applied Developmental Psychology, 33(2), 79–90.

Daniels, E.A. (2009). Sex objects, athletes, and sexy athletes: How media representations of women athletes can impact adolescent girls and young women. Journal of Research on Adolescence, 24, 399–422.

Duncan, M.C. & Messner, M.A. (1998) The media image of sport and gender. pp. 170–185 in Lawrence A. Wenner, Ed. *MediaSport*. New York: Routledge.

Eastman, S.T. & Billings, A.C. (2001). Biased voices of sports: racial and gender stereotyping in college basketball announcing. *The Howard Journal of Communications, 12*, 183–201.

Frisby, C.M. (2015a). "Delay of Game: A Content Analysis of Coverage of Black Male Athletes by Magazines and News Websites 2002–2012," A paper accepted and presented to the International Communication Association conference held in San Juan, Puerto Rico, May 2015.

Frisby, C.M. (2015b). "Sidelined: Racial and Gender Biases on the Covers of Popular Sports Magazines," A paper submitted to the Association for Education in Journalism and Mass Communication conference held in San Francisco, CA, August 2015.

Harrison, L., Jr. (1995). African-Americans: Race as a self-schema affecting sport and physical activity choices. Quest, 47, 7–18.

Harrison, L., Jr. (2001). Understanding the influence of stereotypes: Implications for the African-American in sport and physical activity. Quest, 53, 97–114.

Harrison, L., Jr., Azzarito, L., & Burden, J., Jr. (2004). Perceptions of athletic superiority: A view from the other side. Race, Ethnicity and Education, 7, 149–166.

Harrison, L., Jr., & Belcher, D. (2006). Race and ethnicity in physical education, In D. Kirk, D. Macdonald, and M. O'Sullivan (Eds.), The handbook of physical education (pp.740–751). Thousand Oaks, CA: Sage.

Harrison, L., Jr., Harrison, C.K., & Moore, L.N. (2002). African-American racial identity and sport. Sport, Education and Society, 7, 121–133.

Harrison, L., Jr., Lee, A., & Belcher, D. (1999). Self-schemata for specific sports and physical activities: The influence of race and gender. Journal of Sport and Social Issues, 23, 287–307.

Jones, R., Murrell, A.J., & Jackson, J. (1990). Pretty versus powerful in the sports pages: Print media coverage of U.S. Women's Olympic Gold Medal winning teams. Journal of Sport and Social Issues, 23 (20, 182–192.

Kane, M.J., & LaVoi, N.M. (Eds.). (2007). The 2007 Tucker Center Research Report, developing physically active girls: An evidence-based multidisciplinary approach. University of Minnesota, Minneapolis, MN: Tucker Center for Research on Girls & Women in Sport.

Kennedy, C. (2010). A new frontier for women's sports (beyond Title IX). Gender Issues, 27, 78–90. doi: 10.1007/s12147–010–9091-y

Krane,V., Choi, P.Y.L., Baird, S.M., Aimar, C.M., & Kauer, K.J. (2004). Living the paradox: Female athletes negotiate femininity and muscularity. Sex Roles, 50, 315–329.

Magazine Publishers of America. (2004a). Teen market profile. Retrieved April 23, 2007, from www.magazine.org/content/files/teenprofile04.pdf.

Magazine Publishers of America. (2004b). Average circulation for top 100 ABC magazines. Retrieved July 10, 2014, from http://www.magazine.org/CONSUMER_MARKETING/CIRC_TRENDS/11186.aspx.

Magazine Publishers of America. (2006). Fact sheet average circulation. Retrieved October 1, 2014, from http://www.magazine.org/Circulation/circulation_trends_and_magazine_hand-book/.

Phillip, S.F. (1998). Race and gender differences in adolescent peer group approval of leisure activities: The Decline in Baseball Participation Amongst African-American Youth. *Journal of Leisure Research*, 30(2), 214–232.

Phillip, S.F. (1999). Are we welcome? African-American racial acceptance in leisure activities and the importance given to children's leisure. *Journal of Leisure Research*, 31(4), 385–403.

Primm, E., Dubois, S., & Regoli, J.D. (2007). Every Picture Tells a Story: Racial Representation on *Sports Illustrated* Covers" *The Journal of American Culture*, 30(2), 239–250.

"Report of the APA task force on the sexualization of girls," Task Force on the Sexualization of Girls, American Psychological Association, 2007, www.apa.org/pi/wpo/sexualization.html.

Shugart, H.A. (2003). She shoots, she scores: Mediated construction of contemporary female athletes in coverage of the 1999 U.S. women's soccer team. Western Journal of Communication, 67(1), 1.

Schultz, J. (2005). Reading the catsuit: Serena Williams and the production of blackness at the 2002 U.S. Open. Journal of Sport & Social Issues, 29, 338–357.

Sexton, P.C. (1969). The feminized male: Classrooms, White collars & the decline of manliness. New York: Random House.

Shugart, H.A. (2003). She shoots, she scores: Mediated constructions of contemporary female athletes in coverage of the 1999 US women's soccer team. Western Journal of Communication, 67, 1–31.

Slater, A., & Tiggemann, M. (2010). Gender differences in adolescent sport participation, teasing, self- objectification and body image concerns. Journal of Adolescence, 34(3), 455–463.

Steinfeldt, J.A., Zakrajsek, R.A., Bodey, K.J., Middendorf, K.G., & Martin, S.B. (2012). Role of uniforms in the body image of female college volleyball players. *The Counseling Psychologist*, 4(5), 791–806.

Smolak, L., Murnen, S.K., & Ruble, A.E. (2000). Female athletes and eating problems: A meta-analysis. International Journal of Eating Disorders, 27, 371–380.

Sommers-Flanagan, R., Sommers-Flanagan, J., & Davis, B. (1993). What's happening on music television? A gender role content analysis. *Sex Roles*, 28, 745–753.

Stone, J., Perry, Z.W., Darley, J.M. (1997). "White Men Can't Jump": Evidence for the Perceptual Confirmation of Racial Stereotypes Following a Basketball Game. *Basic and Applied Social Psychology*, 79(3), 291–306

Urquhart, J., & Crossman, J. (1999). The Globe and Mail Coverage of the Winter Olympic Games: A Cold Place for Women Athletes. Journal of Sport & Social Issues, 23, 193–202.

15

Next: Where Do We Go from Here?

María E. Len-Ríos[1] and Earnest L. Perry[2]

We thought about titling this chapter "Conclusion" or "Summary," but in reality, there is not a conclusion—there must be a continuation (Applause here!). Moreover, what we would like to do, at this point, is share with you our observations from more than a decade of working with and teaching the topic of cross-cultural journalism and strategic communication. These are questions below are ones we frequently hear from students and others. Our answers are based on our experience, research and knowledge, gained over time, in addition to insights from professionals with whom we've interacted over the years.

So, grab a cup of Joe or tea, take a deep breath and settle in . . . we will try to make this as succinct and direct as possible.

Q1: **Isn't this diversity stuff just political correctness B.S.?** *(Whoa!)*

A1: We decided to start off with a softball question, right? To answer this, we should agree on what we mean by "political correctness." If political correctness means saying what people want to hear so we won't "get in trouble," which is the way we commonly see it defined, then we're not on the same page. That "placating" type of conversation could well be defined as B.S. because that would not be authentic or true. That's like being in a bad romantic relationship where there are conversations on the surface, but both partners are suffering on the inside **because there is nothing real there**. They're just going through the motions. Therefore, we are not encouraging saying what people want to hear so that everyone is comfortable. That leads to a false sense of security and everyone is really just unhappy.

Real conversations, we admit, can sometimes be intimidating and uncomfortable. In Chapter 12's pull-out box, Pat Thomas addresses what you can do when conversations become uncomfortable. "Framing the question so that it seems to originate with someone not in the room can be very helpful." Try not to make the conversation personal—you're discussing ideas, not attempting to criticize a person's sense of self. So, you can see that we do not believe that what we are advocating is political correctness as we see it commonly defined because that does not lead to *authentic conversations*. Authentic conversations are those when you are able to show enough respect for how others feel or think, and they for you as well, so that you can discuss each other's ideas even when they may come from another place. You have to leave your comfort zone.

Of course, you have to consider the context. We don't often start conversations leading off with differences. We don't walk up to people we don't know and say, "You look like you don't take care of yourself." You have to establish a mutually respectful relationship, and then set ground rules for difficult conversations. If I'm going to tell you how I feel, will you withhold judgment and listen to what I have to say and try to understand my perspective? Can we agree that we might not agree, but this is an important story to tell or conversation to have? Can I write a story about someone I don't like and still convey the story with empathy and compassion? The thing is, if you're worried about saying something wrong—not being "politically correct"—then you're using your brainpower on that nagging worry in the back of your mind. That's a waste of brainpower.

Q2:   <u>**So, I'm**</u> _____ (**insert word:** privileged/white/male/hetero/able-bodied/healthy/Christian/beautiful/rich/of a high social-class/not a felon)—<u>**this book makes me feel guilty**</u>. *(Whoa! Whoa! Some of you may wonder, but this is a common response to the course.)*

A2:   We definitely don't want to make students feel guilty for having privilege. That's not something you can control. We cannot tell you how to feel, because you feel what you feel and we cannot deny that or tell you not to feel it. What we do know (and we're guessing you know this too) is that guilt is not a very productive feeling. Guilt is only useful if it causes you to realize that your privilege is not a result of anything intrinsically more valuable about you than someone born with less privilege. In other words, those with less privilege didn't necessarily do anything "bad" or "worse" to be where they are in life—they started off at a different place in life with different resources and opportunities. And we're only speaking from our experience, but guilt often makes us uncomfortable and not willing to engage. So feel your guilt, embrace your guilt and then throw it away. Say this out loud (no, we're not joking), **"Hello guilt, you are not helping me. I am going to say 'Goodbye to you.'"** (We suggest that you say this to the tune of "Goodbye to You" by The Veronicas or the Patti Smith version—you've likely heard this song before. Look for it on YouTube.)

We all have to try to understand other people's experiences and withhold judgment. (No, it's not always easy, and you won't get it right all the time.) Privilege isn't necessarily positive or negative—it just is. Our realization that it exists and that it influences our chances in life is what matters. As a communicator, understanding this can help you add humanity and humility to the work that you do.

Q3: **I'm tired of "representing" and talking about race—are things _ever_ going to change?**

A3: Students who are not white often tell us they're one of several students of color in the class and are tired of talking about race and listening to white students' perspectives. They don't want to hear about how talking about race makes white students feel guilty. They want change now. We (the professors/authors) are not being strong enough advocates. We need revolutionary change. Other students of color don't want attention drawn to their difference. They're tired of students and professors singling them out and having to "represent" the minority opinion. Being someone's "black," "Latino," "Asian," "fill-in-the-blank" friend. (This may sound weird to you as you read this, but believe us: we have heard this from our students over the last 10-plus years.) It's not easy to wonder if people are reacting to you because of your race or because it's something that you said.

Students who are not white think about race almost every day if not daily. Here is some of that stream of consciousness: when you're shopping at the grocery store (I'm in my sweats, will they think I'm shoplifting?); walking down a dark street (will other people cross over to the other side of the street?); going through airport security (will I get stopped because I'm wearing a headscarf?); going to a Chinese restaurant (are they going to look at me funny because I asked for a fork and look Asian?); using the bathroom at the Miami airport (will people think I'm a drug mule?); talking with an accent (yes, I'm American!) etc. If these examples make no sense to you, consider that you're not aware of what it's like to live these experiences and consider what it's like to live with these thoughts ALL the time. Whew! It is tiring. Research shows there is a mental burden to living as a minority in the United States. Consider having all these thoughts weighing on your mind all the time, then consider whether we live in an equal society. So that is where the anger comes from sometimes. Will things change? It takes a village. When people don't have to worry about difference, then we will be there.

Q4: **I'm white and I'm tired of talking about race. Can you make it stop?**

A4: We get it. Our response is that it depends on where this question is coming from. If it's the guilt thing, reread the previous paragraphs. If it's because it's too heavy to have this burden of thought on your mind and you find that it is just emotionally exhausting, we truly sympathize. It is heavy. It is an emotional burden if you care. However, we would point you to the previous paragraph. People of color have to think about race/ethnicity their entire lives. There may be those times when they don't think about it for hours, maybe even days, but that usually doesn't last very long. It's just like mom and dad said—life is not fair. We understand your complaint as so many of our students tell us they feel like they are made out to be "the bad guys." We've told you that that is not our intention. We need you to be part of the conversation. As Keith Woods points out in Chapter 2, you have to stay in the room for the conversation to happen.

Q5: <u>**Why should I care about communicating across fault lines**</u> (race/ethnicity, generation/age, socioeconomic status/class, gender/sexual orientation, geography and religion)?

A5: Most of you already know this, yet we still get asked the question. Simply—it's a requirement of our profession in the 21st century. The authors of Chapters 3 and 8 clearly demonstrate that to communicate well to publics in the U.S. and internationally, communication professionals need to engage with groups of people that may have concerns, experiences, values and beliefs that are somewhat different from their own. That's it.

Q6: **How can I possibly think about all of these things when I'm working on deadlines?**

A6: It's not easy. Don't give up. You will learn through trial and error. Remember what Jacqui Banaszynski said—don't quit until you get good. It is hard to keep all of the things we present in this book in mind when you're crunched, sources don't call you back, your photographer returns with pictures that don't represent the community, the expert you want is out of the country doing a talk, the word count was changed, the client has a new idea, you have a new baby at home (congratulations!) or you're going through a bad break-up (we certainly hope not, but—be strong!). The thing is, life happens. Do your best and don't forget that what you do matters—strive to do your best at all times. Be the difference; make the difference.

Q7: **I'm so scared of making a mistake that I don't want to even enter conversations about diversity.**

A7: Everyone has some fear of saying the wrong thing. Just like most people are scared of giving public speeches (even those with lots of experience). There are conversations we in communications dread having. In our professions, we have to have difficult conversations when it doesn't have to do with diversity, so we should have even more practice at this. For instance, reporters who cover homicide, write health stories or write obituaries; ad agencies that have to tell their client their ideas are trite, offensive and juvenile; PR strategists that tell clients they can't lie or cover up the truth. Living life is about difficult conversations.

We all do or say the wrong thing from time to time. (If you haven't, then you're better than we are.) If you do or say something wrong, or something that others perceive as wrong, forgive yourself, clarify and correct your words or actions if possible, learn from your error and move on with the commitment to do better. Medical doctors, a profession to which journalism is sometimes compared, must do this all the time. Learning from your errors is called *experience*.

In Chapter 2, Keith Woods talks about how conversations, if honest, can make a difference, and that journalists have a key role in making sure people's voices are heard. Advertisers can do this as well. Dove's Campaign for Real Beauty has expanded our conversation on pressures put on girls to be a certain way. From a public relations perspective, Walmart's Women's Economic Empowerment initiative raises policy issues of inequality and gender participation in the workforce. Failing to enter into real conversations deprives you and us (your readers or target audience) of an authentic experience.

Q8. **Won't good diversity in coverage just happen naturally? I mean, why should I make an effort?**

A8: We know this is a genuine assumption and is asked with good intentions. But let us ask you this: Will you stay fit and healthy if you never exercise? Will you stay fit if you don't make a conscious effort to eat healthfully? You know that things start to decline when we don't pay attention. Imagine if you ate every snack you were offered, sampled all the desserts in the dining hall buffet, went to all the campus free-pizza events (how many free pizzas are you offered in college?) and sat at your desk all day. Will you have a great relationship with your partner if you never make an effort? We're quite sure you know that the answer to these scenarios would be "no." You will not be fit, healthy or in good relationships if you don't make an effort. So, no. Diversity coverage just doesn't "naturally happen." You have to make an effort.

Q9: Is excellent journalism achievable?

A9: Yes. There are many examples offered in this text (definitely check out Jacqui Banaszynski's "AIDS in the Heartland" series and the recommended readings). It's not for the lazy though. And, if you've read this far in the book, you are definitely not lazy. You can do it.

Q10: What is the first small thing that I can do to make a difference in how I do my job?

A10: Look and listen. Find ways that you can incorporate excellence into everything you do.

Q11: When I become a manager, what can I do to encourage better cross-cultural communication?

A11: We suggest that you buy a copy of our book for all your staff! Just kidding (well, sort of. . .). The best thing you can do is to be the example. Be the leader that other people will want to emulate. Incorporate excellence in what you do. Listen to your employees and help them understand *why* it's important.

Here are a couple things to remember:

- **It's not about you.** Surprise! You've probably heard from marketers that it's all about you . . . and you are special, but it's not *ALL* about you. A lot of people go into journalism, advertising and public relations because they want to see their name in lights. Fame. A Pulitzer. A Super Bowl ad. A presidential election campaign. While it's true that people in our profession definitely do accomplish those things, a lot of times we see students and professionals get caught up in "their story," "their ad" or "their campaign." It's not "your" story alone—it's the story of the people, places and things that have lent you their stories. It's not your ad. It belongs to the company or organization that hired you to work on it, and your piece was just one part of a bunch of other people who worked to make it happen. Similarly, a campaign? The candidate had something to do with it, as well as the hopes and dreams of many people who voted. Remember, journalism, advertising and public relations are service professions—and you get very little of it done solo.

- **Leave your pride at the door.** Be open to what you don't know. We know that our book is not the definitive book on communicating across cultures and subcultures. Every piece of advice, example and insight we offer is not going to work in all situations. We hope we will hear from you to help us make this a better book. Everyone makes mistakes—it's going to happen. Learn from them, get feedback and try to do better next time.

- **Pause before you react.** Sometimes people will say something you don't agree with. Sometimes you feel it is offensive. Just like you shouldn't send an email when you're angry, drive angry or make important decisions when you're angry, pause before you react to someone who has said or written something you don't agree with. Ask and listen first. Was what they meant what you heard? If so, examine your reaction. What made you angry? It is usually because you feel that someone has injured something important to you (like your ego or identity). Try to understand the other person's opinion. You control your response.

- **Enjoy being a part of your profession.** Communication professions are so rewarding. Enjoy being the person who gets to write the story about

FIGURE 15.1 Dr. Earnest L. Perry and Dr. María E. Len-Ríos in the Frank Lee Martin Journalism Library at the Missouri School of Journalism.

the first baby born in the new year. Wow, you got to watch life happen! What an honor. Be glad that you can write a good story about crime that informs the community on what to do to be safe. You got the client to accept your creatives' concepts for the Super Bowl and sales are up 140 percent. Fantastic! Your anti-domestic violence campaign reached more than 2,000 women whose lives are forever changed. Good on you. Enjoy those moments because not all moments will be like that. Take the victories and know that you played a part. Remember them especially when things aren't going right. They will be right again. Just listen. Be authentic. Strive for excellence.

▶ NOTES

1 Associate professor, Department of Advertising and Public Relations, Grady College of Journalism and Mass Communication, University of Georgia
2 Associate professor, Journalism Studies, Missouri School of Journalism, University of Missouri

About the Cover Design

Kara Wexler:

My initial cover design intended to capture the wide array of labels we use to characterize people's identities, which has become increasingly profuse as new descriptions enter our cultural vocabulary. As journalists and strategic communicators, it's imperative to recognize the subtle, yet powerful impact our word choices can have in our storytelling. Each individual has the potential to be labeled with dozens of terms, and journalists have the unique opportunity to help frame society's perspective and minimize bias through their communications. With vivid descriptions crafted carefully and respectfully, our stories will not only demonstrate tolerance, but celebrate diversity among all people.

María E. Len-Ríos and Earnest L. Perry:

We believe Kara Wexler's initial design incorporated the complexity of what it means to discuss diversity. Labels can be self-prescribed, imposed and contested. People that are thought to belong to the same "groups" do not agree on labels for their groups. Humans don't like to be "put in a box." Yet, the reality is that people are uneasy if they cannot define someone's identity. Words make our ideas and thoughts concrete. The cover symbolizes the fact that journalists and strategic communicators, who are arbiters of societal conversations, should be aware of the power of words and how words might strike reactions from people in different ways. Our professions require us to use language purposefully: our choice of words can shape national dialogue and policy.

Contributors

Saleem E. Alhabash possesses a joint appointment as an assistant professor in the Department of Advertising and Public Relations, as well as the Department of Media and Information at Michigan State University. Dr. Alhabash studies media effects with a particular emphasis on investigating how social media and new technologies can be used in intercultural and cross-cultural settings. He teaches courses in media psychology, new media and public relations management, as well as cross-cultural journalism.

Jacqui Banaszynski worked in newspapers for 30 years, and now teaches students and professionals around the world. She holds a Knight Chair Professorship at the Missouri School of Journalism and is a faculty fellow at the Poynter Institute. While at the *St. Paul (Minn.) Pioneer Press*, her series "AIDS in the Heartland" won the 1988 Pulitzer Prize in feature writing. In 1986, her eyewitness account of the African famine was a finalist for the Pulitzer Prize in international reporting. Projects she has edited have won national awards for business, investigative, social issues, environmental, sports and human interest reporting.

Jean Marie Brown is an instructor in the School of Journalism in the Bob Schieffer College of Communication at Texas Christian University in Fort Worth, Texas. She worked in newsrooms for more 20 years. One of her early assignments was an award-winning report on the effects of racial segregation in Lake and Porter counties in northwest Indiana. She has taught Fault Lines for the Maynard Institute for Journalism Education for more than a decade. She has a master's degree in journalism from TCU and earned her bachelor's degree from Northwestern University's Medill School of Journalism. Prior to teaching at TCU, she worked for Knight-Ridder and later, McClatchy, newspapers.

Carie Cunningham is a student in the Media and Information Studies Ph.D. program at Michigan State University. She is a former television news producer for the NBC affiliates in Reno, Nevada, and Detroit, Michigan. She currently studies visual attention and cognitive processing.

Teri Finneman is an instructor in the Journalism and Mass Communication department at South Dakota State University. She previously taught cross-cultural journalism and news writing at the Missouri School of Journalism. Dr. Finneman primarily studies news coverage of first ladies and women politicians, though she also conducts research related to media ethics, media history and oral history. Her book, *Politics, Power, and the Press: The Historical Path to an American Woman President*, is scheduled to be released in 2016. Twitter: @finnemte. Instagram: journoprofteri.

Cynthia M. Frisby, an associate professor of Strategic Communication at the University of Missouri School of Journalism, is a nationally recognized authority on media portrayals of minorities, women and teens. She received her Ph.D. in mass communication research from the University of Florida in 1997. She studies the effects of media messages and the role they play in creating or maintaining stereotypes and biases. She is co-editor of the book *Journalism Across Cultures* and lead author of the book, *How You See Me, How You Don't: Essays on the Representations and Portrayals of Minorities in Media*. Dr. Frisby teaches courses in sports and entertainment promotion, strategic communication campaigns, and cross-cultural journalism. In 2002 she won the William T. Kemper Teaching Fellowship, a top university-wide teaching honor.

Melita M. Garza, an award-winning journalist with more than 20 years professional experience in national and international media, joined Texas Christian University's Schieffer College in 2012 after earning her Ph.D. at the University of North Carolina at Chapel Hill. Dr. Garza is a 20th-century journalism historian whose research focuses on English- and Spanish-language news and the social construction of reality. Her other research interests include business and economics reporting, the media and civil rights, literary journalism and digital media.

Marina A. Hendricks is a doctoral student at the Missouri School of Journalism. Her research focuses on student journalists, youth journalism and social media use by journalists of all ages. Previously, she was director of communications at the Newspaper Association of America. She also served as founding editor of the FlipSide program for teen journalists at *The Charleston Gazette* in West Virginia.

Gary R. Hicks is a professor in the Department of Mass Communications at Southern Illinois University Edwardsville. Dr. Hicks studies the relationship between media and marginalized people, particularly how they are represented in news and entertainment media. He teaches courses in media law, media ethics and cultural studies.

Amanda Hinnant is an associate professor at the University of Missouri School of Journalism. Her research interests include health journalism, health disparities, feminist theory, sociology of news and climate change communication. Dr. Hinnant has recently focused on how journalists communicate social and environmental determinants of health and how audience members interpret and are influenced by those concepts. She is a magazine faculty member and teaches qualitative methods, magazine scholarship, journalism and democracy and magazine writing.

Beverly Horvit is an assistant professor of Journalism Studies at the University of Missouri School of Journalism and teaches courses in news writing and international journalism. She worked previously as a journalist in Texas. Dr. Horvit's research examines how news organizations produce international news and frame news events important to foreign policy. Dr. Horvit's award-winning research has appeared in the *International Journal of Press/Politics, International Communication Gazette* and *Newspaper Research Journal.*

Debra L. Mason is a veteran scholar on media, religion and culture. She also directs the Center on Religion and the Professions, an interdisciplinary center at the Missouri School of Journalism that works to improve the understanding of diverse faiths. She researches the cross-section of media, religion and culture, and directs a professional association of religion news specialists.

Yulia Medvedeva is a doctoral candidate at the University of Missouri School of Journalism. Her research focuses on the tailoring of health-related news for minority populations and on immigrants' learning from English-language news. Her teaching areas include cross-cultural journalism and news reporting and writing.

Chad Painter is an assistant professor of Communication at Eastern New Mexico University, where he teaches media ethics, media law, theory, methods and news reporting. Dr. Painter studies media ethics with emphases on diversity studies, the alternative press and the depiction of journalists in popular culture. He has eight years of professional experience as a reporter, editor, and public relations practitioner for print and online publications.

Jason Rosenbaum dove head first into the world of politics, policy and even rock 'n' roll music since entering the enticing world of professional journalism in the mid-2000s. After writing for a number of print publications, Rosenbaum transitioned into broadcast journalism and is now a political reporter for St. Louis Public Radio. He won a number of awards for his work covering the Ferguson unrest in 2014, including a regional Edward R. Murrow Award and two Missouri Broadcasters Association Awards. Before joining St. Louis Public Radio in December 2013, Rosenbaum spent more than four years covering Missouri politics and legislation from the State Capitol in Jefferson City.

Ryan J. Thomas is an assistant professor of Journalism Studies at the Missouri School of Journalism, where he teaches courses in media ethics, qualitative research methods and cross-cultural journalism. His research concerns how journalists articulate their roles and responsibilities in a democracy, the ethics of journalism at a time of technological change and financial uncertainty, and the representation of marginalized groups (e.g., labor unions, immigrants) in journalism.

Yong Volz is an associate professor of Journalism Studies at the Missouri School of Journalism. Her research centers on journalists and their place in history. One stream of her research focuses on women journalists and their professional aspirations, career paths and historical roles. Dr. Volz is the project leader of the Herstory: Journalism and Women Symposium (JAWS) Oral History Project, which documents the rich and varied experiences of women who made inroads into the traditionally male-dominated field of journalism (see http://www.herstory.rjionline.org).

Keith M. Woods is vice-president of Diversity in News & Operations at NPR. He leads diversity strategy for the network and works with public radio stations across the country to bring the fullest range of voices and stories to all platforms in public media. Formerly, he was dean of Faculty at the Poynter Institute, one of the world's leading training centers for professional journalists.

Index

Note: Italicized page numbers indicate a figure on the corresponding page. Page numbers in bold indicate a table on the corresponding page.